PARADOXES OF POLITICAL ETHICS

JOHN M. PARRISH

Loyola Marymount University

CAMBRIDGE UNIVERSITY PRESS

CAMBRIDGE UNIVERSITY PRESS
Cambridge, New York, Melbourne, Madrid, Cape Town, Singapore, São Paulo

Cambridge University Press
The Edinburgh Building, Cambridge CB2 8RU, UK

Published in the United States of America by Cambridge University Press, New York

www.cambridge.org
Information on this title: www.cambridge.org/9780521873550

First published 2007

Printed in the United Kingdom at the University Press, Cambridge

A catalogue record for this publication is available from the British Library

ISBN 978-0-521-87355-0 hardback

For my parents
John W. Parrish and
Mary Kay Parrish
and in memory of
Gary Phelps

Contents

Preface

During my second year of graduate school, one of my advisers asked me, a little exasperatedly: "But do you see dirty hands *everywhere?*" I realized that the answer I wanted to give was an enthusiastic *"yes"* – but that it would require a great deal more thought and work to begin to show that there was something to justify this urge. This book records the results of the thought and the work. The reader will have to judge whether it has been enough.

I owe much to many. My thanks must begin with Richard Tuck, in whose company this whole endeavor began. Richard was the principal supervisor of my graduate work and in particular of the doctoral dissertation from which this book emerged. Throughout the long process, Richard urged me to sharpen my focus without narrowing my view; to dare to pursue major figures and large, complex themes; to treat my own encounter with primary sources as primary in the scholarly process; and to trust my own capacity to be *gripped* as an accurate barometer of broad intellectual interest. Each chapter of this book bears the mark of Richard's wide learning, incisive intelligence, good humor, and friendship – as do I.

Let me next thank those individuals who read part or all of the manuscript of this book in its various stages of drafting and disarray, enabling those readers who came after to be spared some of its worst obscurities, infelicities, and mistakes. In addition to Richard, four other persons read and commented on this book in its entirety during the years it was a doctoral dissertation: Christopher Brooke, Pratap Bhanu Mehta, Dennis F. Thompson, and Alex Tuckness. Together they contributed more than anyone else to shaping the resulting book. More recently, Paulann Canty, Kenneth Chatlos, and several anonymous reviewers were kind enough to read the full manuscript and provide valuable thoughts about it.

Many other individuals read one or more separate chapters of the manuscript and provided comments that have been collectively indispensable. They include: Arash Abizadeh, Jonathan Allen, Arthur Applbaum, Deborah Baumgold, Nicholas Constas, Michaele Ferguson, Bryan

Garsten, Justin Hardin, Clarissa Hayward, Kinch Hoekstra, Istvan Hont, Jill Horwitz, Alan Jacobs, Aaron James, Madeline Kochen, Dale Kuehne, Wayne LeCheminant, Harvey Mansfield, Bryan McGraw, Tamara Metz, Russell Muirhead, Michael Neblo, Andy Sabl, Michael Sandel, Allan Silverman, David Siu, Travis Smith, and Alexander Wendt. I have learned much from all of them. It is customary to say that any remaining mistakes are my fault alone: but that seems a bit out of keeping with a book whose central theme is collective responsibility (as well as more than a bit obvious). Anyway: blame whom you like, but certainly start with me.

Several worthy institutions supported my work financially. The most significant have been: the Mustard Seed Foundation; the Government Department at Harvard University; the Center for Ethics and the Professions at Harvard; Harvard's Packard Fellowship; the Ohio State University; and Loyola Marymount University. Thanks in particular to the staffs of the various libraries at Cambridge University, Harvard University, and the Ohio State University for their help. I must also acknowledge the excellent research assistance I received from the following persons: Richard Arnold, Zac Cogley, Melissa Daugherty, John Hickey, Ben Jones, Ryan Peterson, and Yusuf Sarfati. Commissioning Editor Hilary Gaskin and Production Editor Elizabeth Davey at Cambridge University Press shepherded the manuscript from draft to publication. Richard Arnold and Melissa Daugherty doublechecked the book's numerous references. Joanne Hill copy-edited the text with great care. Melissa Daugherty and Ryan Peterson helped extensively in compiling the index.

Most of Chapter 2 appeared first as "Two Cities and Two Loves: Imitation in Augustine's Moral Psychology and Political Theory," *History of Political Thought* 26 (2005), 209–235, and is reprinted here with the kind permission of the publisher, Imprint Academic.

Any scholarly book has in back of it a set of intellectual and personal struggles that motivate and fuel one's study – and those who share one's struggles make their own special contribution to the product of one's labors. In this respect I must thank many of the persons mentioned above, plus: Jason Burnett, David Campbell, Derek Cowan, Jared Denslow, Eric Dickson, Kyla Ebels Duggan, Antje Ellerman, Joan Ford, Todd Hulin, Macartan Humphreys, Kathryn Linehan, Allison MacLaren, Robin Parrish McAlister, Bryan McGraw, Karyn Johnson Pace, Michael Pace, Ben Read, Michael Sandel, Todd Shepherd, Kevin Stenzel, Annie Stilz, Charley Turner, Larry Walker, Scott Wasson, Stephanie Wasson, Nicholas Wolterstorff, and Iris Marion Young. Alan Jacobs deserves special mention here. During the years I wrote this book, no one talked with me more extensively about these matters than he – and no one helped more.

My struggles with dirty hands first took sharp focus in a cramped college newspaper office at William Jewell College; those experiences were the first (and roughest) draft of this book. During that period, I learned from and alongside: Elspeth Grindstaff, Lois Anne Harris, Gordon Kingsley, Bob McGill, Mike Mirakian, Brandi Rathbun, Jim Tanner, and Stacy Williams. The most valuable lessons I learned about ethics and public responsibility during those years were from Gary Phelps, to whose memory this book is in part dedicated.

Lynn Mitchell-Parrish has shared life with me during the years between the dissertation's first draft and the book's appearance in print. Thanks mainly to her love and friendship, those years have been my happiest yet. Readers who enjoy the book owe much to Lynn for enduring my alternating bouts of uncertainty, pedantry, avoidance, and despair while I was writing it – and for giving me a life better than the book to come home to.

To my parents I (and this book) owe most of all. From them I learned to do practically everything I have done in these pages: it is they who taught me to read, to think, to play, to worry, to search, to question, and to persist. I dedicate this work to them, as a small token of recognition for all the work they did for me.

Introduction

Do you think you can govern innocently?   Jean-Paul Sartre, *Dirty Hands*

Politics, people say, is a dirty business. "All kings is mostly rapscallions," Huckleberry Finn observed, and Huck's characterization still seems to apply to most of those bureaucrats, glad-handers, and occasional statesmen who rise as best they can to what was once the business of kings. Our sense that politics is "dirty" appears well grounded. Popular cynicism about politics is at a peak, especially in the United States, and not without reason. In recent decades we have witnessed some truly astonishing acts of brutality, intemperance, dishonesty, and selfishness among our national leaders and public officials. Compared with the relative infrequency with which we glimpse true political decency (much less heroism) in public life, it is hard to avoid perceiving politics as a place where one is lucky indeed not to pick up some of the taint and odor that go with the territory of unsavory work.

Our perception of politics as a dirty business, however, is not merely a product of recent events. It also reflects something deeper and more permanent in our understanding of the relationship between ethics and politics. Across the centuries we find an enduring and surprisingly resilient belief that, of all the scenes of human life, perhaps the hardest in which to play one's role with true moral dignity is the sphere of public action. Of course moral action is difficult in general; that fact is as old as the idea of morality itself. There are a variety of reasons why human beings find it difficult to be moral: one may not know what action is morally best and, even when one does know, one may lack the power or the will to do what one ought. But there is also another, more intriguing set of cases: those where there seems to be *no* right thing to do, where anything one might do seems to be wrong in some important respect.

This last set of situations is, roughly speaking, what philosophers refer to as *moral dilemmas*: ethical conflicts in which, in order to do the right thing, one has to do the wrong thing; in which in order to be or do good, one

I

must also be or do evil. Among those who have practiced the trade of politics or reflected on the character of public life, it has long been a truism that significant moral dilemmas arise more frequently within the political arena than they do anywhere else. Power seems to invite its practitioners to do what would be unthinkable to them in ordinary life: indeed, it often seems to insist that doing the unthinkable has, because of their public responsibility, become not merely their prerogative but their duty.

In contemporary moral philosophy and political theory, this particular kind of publicly driven moral dilemma has gone by the name of the problem of "dirty hands" in public life. Michael Walzer proposed the term in an influential article, drawing on the title of Jean-Paul Sartre's drama of moral dilemmas in revolutionary politics.[1] But the image this metaphor evokes is more ancient, recalling a time when the ideas of morality and cleanliness, as well as immorality and uncleanliness, remained closely linked. Sometimes the hands are bloody, as in Pilate's washing his hands of the decision to crucify a Nazarene troublemaker, or Lady Macbeth's obsessive scrubbing away of a long-since-vanished stain. But murder is not the only crime that has sometimes seemed necessary to political actors: it often seems also that one must lie, betray, compromise, abandon, mislead, manipulate, coerce, or otherwise act in ways that, were one not to claim one's political responsibilities as an excuse, would seem thoroughly vicious and corrupt.

This book examines the problem of dirty hands: the claim made by political actors that genuine moral dilemmas arise with special frequency and potency in public life. More specifically, it offers an analytical history of philosophical reflection on this problem from antiquity to the Enlightenment – a history of the different ways in which the problem came to be formulated and understood, and of the different answers that have been offered to address the various moral worries it raised. In addition to describing the various versions of the problem at each stage, the book also shows how various responses to dirty hands – including Augustine's interiorized ethics, Hobbes's sovereign state, and Adam Smith's commercial market – came to occupy crucial positions in the development of the Western moral and political tradition.

DIRTY HANDS AS A PHILOSOPHICAL PROBLEM

How do the hard facts of political responsibility shape and constrain the demands of ethical life? That question lies at the heart of what political

[1] Michael Walzer, "Political Action: The Problem of Dirty Hands," *Philosophy and Public Affairs* 2 (1973): 160–180.

theorists call the problem of "dirty hands" in public life. Those who exercise political power feel they must act in ways that would otherwise be considered immoral: indeed, they feel that frequently it would be immoral of them *not* to perform or condone such acts as killing, lying, or betraying.

The question of dirty hands as it has been treated in contemporary philosophical reflection has focused principally on the implications of the possibility of moral dilemmas for the coherence of the most prominent ethical frameworks on offer. Though the urgency of the problem has always been felt most vividly at the level of applied ethics, by far the greatest part of the work to resolve the problem has been done at the level of ethical theory. The experienced phenomenon itself is generally accepted without argument: there are, even critics concede, at least *apparent* moral dilemmas, and they do seem to arise in political or social life more frequently than anywhere else. But from this shared starting point, assessments diverge dramatically. Some prefer to characterize these ethical challenges as genuine moral dilemmas, while others claim to show on the basis of arguments drawn from ethical theory that it is impossible by definition for such a thing as a moral dilemma to exist.[2] In these scenarios, the debates usually focus not on what constitutes the public good, but on whether it is possible to achieve what is manifestly for the public good without compromising unacceptably on grounds of moral principle.

In his seminal article on dirty hands, Michael Walzer offers two examples that help to illustrate the problem's intuitively compelling character. The more dramatic example – especially so in light of recent events – is that of a public leader who must decide whether or not to authorize torture in order to extract information about a terrorist plot to bomb innocent civilians.[3] The other, less dramatic but perhaps more realistic and familiar, example concerns a candidate for public office who can only win election

---

[2] Important proponents of the first view have included Thomas Nagel, "War and Massacre," *Philosophy and Public Affairs* 1 (1972): 123–144, and "Ruthlessness in Public Life," in *Mortal Thoughts* (Cambridge University Press, 1979), and Bernard Williams, "Ethical Consistency," in Christopher Gowans, ed., *Moral Dilemmas* (Oxford University Press, 1987), and "Conflicts of Values," in Williams's *Moral Luck* (Cambridge University Press, 1982), respectively. Proponents of the opposite view include R. M. Hare, Alan Donagan (see their selections in Gowans, *Moral Dilemmas*) and, in a more qualified way, Arthur Applbaum, *Ethics for Adversaries* (Princeton University Press, 1999).

[3] For a sense of the range of contemporary views on this problem, compare Alan Dershowitz, *Why Terrorism Works* (Yale University Press, 2002); the various contributions to Sanford Levinson, ed., *Torture: A Collection* (Oxford University Press, 2004); Charles Krauthammer, "The Truth about Torture," *Weekly Standard* (Dec. 5, 2005); and Andrew Sullivan, "The Abolition of Torture," *New Republic* (Dec. 19, 2005).

by making a shady deal with a campaign donor regarding a public construction project. In both these cases, Walzer contends, the public responsibility held by the leader in question (to protect her citizens, or pursue her policy goals) conflicts irresolvably with some principle that ought to bind every moral agent (to maintain one's integrity in the face of potential corruption, for example, or not to use cruelty and torture as a means).

Such situations, according to Walzer, constitute *moral dilemmas*: that is, they are cases in which there is nothing one can do that will not qualify as morally wrong in some relevant respect, where one is literally damned if one does and damned if one doesn't. Many other contemporary theorists have endorsed the possibility of moral dilemmas, even those such as Thomas Nagel who believe in a demanding set of objective moral obligations. "Given the limitations on human action," Nagel has argued, "it is naïve to suppose that there is a solution to every moral problem with which the world can face us"; instead, we must expect that "the world can present us with situations in which there is no honorable or moral course for a man to take, no course free of guilt and responsibility for evil."[4] In such situations, wrongdoing in some form proves ultimately to be inescapable.

Facing a moral dilemma does not of course mean that we cannot make a choice between alternatives: indeed, Walzer seems to think that in certain cases the right and necessary thing for the politician to do is to abandon his scruples and commit torture in order to save his citizens' lives, or to compromise his personal integrity in order to keep faith with his followers and their policy objectives. But there is an important difference, Walzer thinks, between there being a reason to make the choice and the choice being fully *justified* from a moral point of view. In the case of a genuine moral dilemma, this kind of full justification is always lacking. Instead, even after the choice is made we find there is a kind of moral residue: something is left over to stain or tarnish what would otherwise be a praiseworthy accomplishment.[5] Such moral conflicts, Bernard Williams says, are "neither systematically avoidable, nor soluble without remainder."[6]

There are of course those who deny that such things as moral dilemmas exist at all. Among contemporary philosophers, most such denials fall into one of two categories: one variety of response is grounded in *utilitarian* moral theory, while another variety draws on some version of *deontological*

---

[4] Nagel, "War and Massacre."
[5] On this point see in particular Williams, "Ethical Consistency," as well as Williams's further reflections in his "Conflicts of Values."
[6] Williams, "Ethical Consistency."

ethics.[7] Utilitarianism holds that the full explanation of the rightness or wrongness of an action or policy depends exclusively on the consequences for human happiness which that action tends to produce. "Actions," argued utilitarianism's most widely read apologist, John Stuart Mill, "are right in proportion as they tend to promote happiness, wrong as they tend to produce the reverse of happiness," where happiness is defined as the maximization of pleasure coupled with the minimization of pain.[8]

The utilitarian typically responds to suggestions of dirty hands by accepting that certain apparent evils must in fact be done in order to achieve maximum social utility, while in turn denying that such a decision really constitutes a genuine moral dilemma. Mill isolates this issue as the key criticism the utilitarian doctrine must refute in the final chapter of his essay *Utilitarianism*. Questions of justice or moral rightness in a non-utilitarian sense sometimes appear to conflict with the priorities of utility, Mill argues, because we have wisely taken such questions of justice off the table in terms of our ordinary moral calculations.[9] But ultimately our notions of justice and moral rightness are grounded in utility alone; indeed, it is the criterion of utility that gives us our only criterion for deciding which of several apparently "morally right" considerations has priority in an instance of apparent conflict.[10]

Thus, for the utilitarian, though a situation may sometimes *feel* like a moral dilemma, there cannot be such a thing as a moral dilemma properly understood.[11] Because good consequences constitute the sum and substance of the moral universe, there simply cannot, if the consequences are good enough, be any moral residue left to clean up. Mill acknowledges that of course values can *conflict*: but it is intolerable (so it seems to Mill) that they should not ultimately be resolvable.[12] If so, then there must be some

---

[7] The earliest contemporary treatments of the issue, such as Walzer's, tend to use the term "absolutist"; I substitute the somewhat less polemical "deontological," since it is essentially deontological views broadly defined which these writers had in mind.

[8] John Stuart Mill, *Utilitarianism*, ch. 1, in Mill, *On Liberty and Other Essays*, ed. John Gray (Oxford University Press, 1991), p. 137.

[9] In this respect Mill's version of utilitarianism bears a resemblance to the "rule-utilitarianism" developed more fully by his twentieth-century utilitarian successors. For an example of this approach as applied to the problem of dirty hands, see R. B. Brandt, "Utilitarianism and the rules of war," *Philosophy and Public Affairs* 1 (Winter 1972): 145–165.

[10] Mill, *Utilitarianism*, ch. 5, esp. at pp. 194–196.

[11] One representative utilitarian arguing in this vein chooses precisely these words as his title: see Kai Nielsen, "There is no dilemma of dirty hands," in Paul Rynard and David P. Shugarman, eds., *Cruelty and Deception: The Controversy over Dirty Hands in Public Life* (Broadview/Pluto, 2000). Another influential argument addressed to the broader issue of value conflicts is R. M. Hare, "Moral conflicts," in Gowans, *Moral Dilemmas*.

[12] See further John Stuart Mill, *A System of Logic*, bk. 6, ch. 12, section 7 (Longmans, Green, 1911).

single standard (lest there be conflicts in infinite regress) by which to adjudicate conflicts of value: and because of its demonstrably universal appeal as a good, utility is the only plausible candidate on offer.

If utilitarianism can be successfully defended as an ethical theory, its promise to resolve value conflicts would be of great significance for the problem of dirty hands. This is especially so because – as nearly all writers on this topic seem to agree – considerations of utility seem to have a *special* moral importance to the choices of political actors and institutions. Indeed, the most attractive versions of utilitarianism view the theory as primarily addressing itself to questions of public policy with broad impact, and not as a handy moral abacus for the street-level practitioner.[13] Our intuitions about the moral importance of utility in public life run very strong. Thinkers as varied as Thomas Nagel, Michael Walzer, and Bernard Williams, despite their abhorrence for utilitarianism as a widely applied ethical dictum, are prepared to acknowledge that at least sometimes utilitarian considerations weigh so heavily in a moral dilemma that they must hold sway.

But there are significant problems with the utilitarian view that make it an unsatisfactory way of resolving dirty hands dilemmas. One common objection is the problem of how the utilitarian can be certain he can judge with such precision what is good and best for us all, when so few of us can judge well at all what is good for our mere selves.[14] Another view doubts that utility is itself a single, homogenous value; instead, it has often been interpreted even by sympathetic writers as a composite of different hetero-geneous values (in which case it can hardly serve as the ultimate arbiter of value conflict its admirers wish to make it).[15] Yet another critique doubts that morality works in such a way that its ends can be traded off directly against all other moral costs, so as to justify and even require the sacrifice of anything of lesser consequence that stands in its way.[16] In general, skeptics of utilitarian moral theory maintain that to characterize good consequences

---

[13] This is a fact of historical significance – Bentham's great exposition of his theory was after all entitled *An Introduction to the Principles of Morals and Legislation* – as well as of analytical relevance – helping to alleviate many (though not all) of the intuitive problems the theory raises at the level of individual application. See Robert Goodin, *Utilitarianism as a Public Philosophy* (Cambridge University Press, 1995), esp. chs. 1 and 4.

[14] For a more comprehensive review of the standard objections to utilitarianism, see Sterling Harwood, "Eleven Objections to Utilitarianism," collected in Louis Pojman, ed., *Moral Philosophy: A Reader*, 3rd edn (Hackett, 2003).

[15] See Amartya Sen, "Plural utility," *Proceedings of the Aristotelian Society*, 1980–1981.

[16] See the elegant discussion of Bernard Williams, "A critique of consequentialism," in J. J. C. Smart and Bernard Williams, *Utilitarianism: For and Against* (Cambridge University Press, 1983).

as the sole criterion by which to judge the rightness of action is to truncate drastically the full range and depth of human moral experience.

An alternative philosophical approach is that of the *deontologist* (also frequently called an *absolutist* by those who have written on dirty hands). The most famous philosophical exponent of such a view is Immanuel Kant, who inaugurated the influential tradition holding that only those actions done from a motive of moral duty can be considered truly valuable from a moral point of view. We know an action is morally worthy, Kant says, "*not from the purpose* which is to be attained by it, but from the maxim [or principle] by which it is determined"; it follows that the morality of action "does not depend on the realization of the object of the action, but merely on the *principle of volition* by which the action has taken place, without regard to any object of desire."[17] This does not mean that deontologists believe consequences to be of no importance: on the contrary, they properly occupy a good deal of our attention as we try to choose what is prudentially the best course of action. But, for these philosophers, we pursue good consequences *solely* within a framework marked out by the bounds of moral permissibility. No amount of social benefit can justify overstepping these bounds of our duty and integrity; no amount of suffering can compel us to respond in a way that contravenes the strict commands of our moral nature.

Though there are myriad variations, the most familiar deontological response to the problem of dirty hands is to urge the strict priority of questions of the right over questions of the good.[18] This tends to convey the impression – reinforced by the label "absolutist" – that the deontological response to the problem of dirty hands is to urge that moral actors must not get their hands dirty, period. There is a significant element of truth to this characterization of the deontological view, perhaps best depicted by Kant's (in)famous discussion of the problem of the murderer at the door. Kant considers a case (made vivid for contemporary readers by stories of Nazis searching for Jews) of a person of known murderous intent who comes to the door of a house asking its owner if the murderer's intended victim is inside (which she is). Kant believes every agent has an absolute duty to tell the truth – in a way this is the firmest moral requirement in Kant's

---

[17] Immanuel Kant, "Groundwork of the Metaphysics of Morals," in Allen Wood, ed., *Basic Writings of Kant* (Modern Library, 2001), p. 158.

[18] On the priority of the right to the good, see the discussions in John Rawls, *A Theory of Justice* (Harvard University Press, 1971), esp. pp. 130–136 and 446–452; Michael Sandel, *Liberalism and the Limits of Justice* (Cambridge University Press, 1982); John Rawls, *Political Liberalism* (Columbia University Press, 1993), Lecture v; and Charles Larmore, *The Morals of Modernity* (Cambridge University Press, 1996), ch. 1.

system – yet it seems virtually certain that to answer the murderer truth-fully in this instance will lead to the death of the homeowner's guest.

Is the case of the murderer at the door a moral dilemma? Not for Kant: for him a real conflict of moral duties is "inconceivable" because the very notion of a moral duty entails "the objective practical necessity" of the act in question.[19] It is possible, Kant thinks, to have a conflict of the various *grounds* of our moral duties – that is, moral *rules* can conflict, though not the duties they prescribe in particular cases – and this is what gives rise to the illusion of moral dilemmas. So in the case of the murderer at the door, there are two sources of practical reasons that might in principle have moral claims on us: under certain circumstances, our beneficence might be the ground of a duty to protect a fellow human being from danger, while our integrity might be the ground of a duty to speak the truth when questioned. But when two different grounds of obligation conflict, Kant believes, the stronger ground takes precedence – in the case of the murderer at the door, the absolute obligation to tell the truth – and that obligation constitutes our real moral duty.[20] Any apparent duty connected with the weaker ground of obligation is therefore *not* really obligatory; and, since that action is incompatible with our real duty, it is in fact *contrary* to our duty.[21]

The objections to a strictly interpreted deontological ethic are obvious and familiar. At a practical level, the refusal to get one's hands dirty is unhelpful in the project of building a politics in the real world. The deontological absolutist cannot hold firm to her position unless she is willing to let the heavens fall if necessary rather than surrender her principles. There is also a certain callousness to her refusal – seen in the ruthlessness required to let the world go to hell in order to preserve her own integrity – that intuitively renders her position not just politically but also morally unten-able. To refuse to get one's hands dirty on grounds of absolute principle is to abandon the central place that the notion of *responsibility* for others must invariably hold at the heart of our moral conceptions.

---

[19] Immanuel Kant, *The Metaphysics of Morals*, ed. Mary Gregor (Cambridge University Press, 1996), "Introduction," section 3, pp. 16–17. The implied comparison is with deductive reasoning: as in logic, so also in morality "two rules opposed to each other cannot be necessary at the same time." Since Kant grounds morality firmly in the faculty of practical reason, he cannot acknowledge the possibility of a contradiction of imperatives within the system.

[20] Kant's reason for resolving the conflict this way is hard to grasp and certainly runs counter to the intuitions of many contemporary readers. For a helpful treatment of the problem, see Roger J. Sullivan, *Immanuel Kant's Moral Theory* (Cambridge University Press, 1989), pp. 170–177.

[21] For a contemporary adaptation of Kant's view that retains much of his uncompromising stand on issues of moral conflict, see Alan Donagan, "Consistency in Rationalist Moral Systems," in Gowans, *Moral Dilemmas*, esp. at pp. 287–288, as well as Alan Donagan, *The Theory of Morality* (University of Chicago Press, 1977), ch. 6.

Not all deontological thinkers take such an unyielding position on such questions. While not accepting the consequentialist view that utility is the source of all value, some deontologists nevertheless concede that considerations of consequence may serve to modify substantially the application of an absolute deontological stricture. In Thomas Nagel's qualified defense of deontological absolutism, for example, he acknowledges that, under rare conditions in which utilitarian considerations are "overpoweringly weighty and extremely certain," it may well prove "impossible to adhere to an absolutist position."[22] Charles Fried, likewise, outlines a deontological theory that has as its central concept the tenet that "there are some things which a moral man will not do, no matter what."[23] But Fried also allows that, in certain extreme cases (such as where "killing an innocent person may save a whole nation"), "the catastrophic may cause the absoluteness of right and wrong to yield" and that indeed "it seems fanatical to maintain the absoluteness of the judgment, to do right even if the heavens will in fact fall."[24] And similarly, Kantian philosopher Christine Korsgaard offers a complex rationale for extending the bounds of the morally permissible beyond what Kant himself envisioned, in cases where it is necessary to find consequentially effective ways of responding to the evil behavior of others.[25]

These modifications of the deontological position make it cohere more easily with our moral intuitions and give deontological strictures a greater emotional plausibility. But at the same time, these gains are bought at the risk of losing at least some – and potentially much – of the clarity and certainty that are among the deontological ethic's most potent appeals. Framed in this way, both the utilitarian and the Kantian responses to the dirty hands problem re-enact the enduring struggle and intractable misunderstandings between consequentialism and deontology more generally. Neither response seems satisfying; neither response seems fully capable of accounting for the powerful intuitive claims invoked by the rival point of view.

Some critics of both perspectives, often called *value pluralists*, have rejected both utilitarianism and deontology as providing final and universally

---

[22] Nagel, "War and Massacre," p. 126.
[23] Charles Fried, *Right and Wrong* (Harvard University Press, 1978), ch. 1, p. 7.   [24] Ibid., p. 10.
[25] Christine Korsgaard, *Creating the Kingdom of Ends* (Cambridge University Press, 1996), ch. 5. Korsgaard's response is the subtlest of these revisions of deontology, retaining intact a modified invocation of the categorical imperative (reframed as a version of Kant's third formulation of the categorical imperative as the pursuit of a "kingdom of ends"). See also Korsgaard's related discussion in "Taking the Law into our Own Hands: Kant on the Right to Revolution," in Andrews Reath, Barbara Herman, and Christine Korsgaard, eds., *Reclaiming the History of Ethics: Essays for John Rawls* (Cambridge University Press, 2004).

persuasive answers to moral questions. These theorists argue instead that there are different *spheres* of value between which serious and sometimes incommensurable conflicts of value are possible.[26] One of the most influential modern articulations of this idea is to be found in the thought of Max Weber, whose understanding of the moral world rests on the premise that "the various value spheres of the world stand in irreconcilable tension to one another."[27] Truth, beauty, moral goodness, utility, fairness, integrity: these and other values bear some relation to one another, certainly, but they cannot be cashed out, Weber believes, into a single common currency of evaluation, as Mill had believed was true of utility, nor can any such standard be given comprehensive priority over rival claimants, as Kant had thought true of the superior standard of duty.

Value pluralism does not commit its proponents to a robust relativism: the view does not imply there is *no* rhyme or reason to human systems of value, and thus no meaning, no real value, to be found in human existence. On the contrary, the value pluralist is perhaps inclined to think there is too *much* value in the moral world, rather than too little. Instead, value pluralism commits its subscribers to a deep skepticism about the claim of human wisdom to be capable of attaining a systematic knowledge about values, and about the existence of any standard or algorithm that yields correct ethical answers to those who perform their calculations correctly.[28] It argues instead for deep, ineliminable moral complexity, while at the

---

[26] The literature on value pluralism is voluminous; but the most influential pieces on the subject can be found in the essays by Thomas Nagel and Bernard Williams previously cited, plus: Isaiah Berlin, "Two Concepts of Liberty," in *The Proper Study of Mankind* (Farrar, Straus, and Giroux, 1997); William Galston, *The Practice of Liberal Pluralism* (Cambridge University Press, 2005), esp. chs. 2 and 5–6; John Gray, *Isaiah Berlin* (Princeton University Press, 1996), ch. 2; Thomas Nagel, "The fragmentation of value," in Gowans, *Moral Dilemmas*; Joseph Raz, *The Practice of Value* (Clarendon Press/Oxford University Press, 2003); John Skorupski, *Ethical Explorations* (Oxford University Press, 2000), ch. 4; Michael Stocker, *Plural and Conflicting Values* (Clarendon Press/Oxford University Press, 1990); and Charles Taylor, *Sources of the Self* (Harvard University Press, 1989), esp. chs. 4 and 25. On the crucially related issue of incommensurability, see in addition to the above Elizabeth Anderson, *Value in Ethics and Economics* (Harvard University Press, 1995); Ruth Chang, ed., *Incommensurability, Incomparability, and Practical Reason* (Harvard University Press, 1998); Alasdair MacIntyre, *After Virtue*, 2nd edn (Notre Dame University Press, 1984); Joseph Raz, *The Morality of Freedom* (Clarendon Press/Oxford University Press, 1986); and Michael Walzer, *Spheres of Justice* (Basic Books, 1983).

[27] Max Weber, "Science as a Vocation," in H. H. Gerth and C. Wright Mills, eds., *From Max Weber: Essays in Sociology* (Oxford University Press, 1946), p. 147.

[28] Consider Alasdair MacIntyre's account of Sophocles' moral realist version of value pluralism (with which MacIntyre himself clearly has some sympathies): "There *is* an objective moral order, but our perceptions of it are such that we cannot bring rival moral truths into complete harmony with each other . . ." MacIntyre, *After Virtue*, p. 143.

same time taking this complexity as a profound motivation for moral choice, not an excuse for avoiding it.[29]

It is this view of a plural moral universe that underlies Weber's famous exposition of the problem of dirty hands in his essay "Politics as a Vocation." In that essay, Weber sets an absolutist "ethic of ultimate ends" in irreconcilable opposition to a more consequentialist "ethic of responsibility," and urges that no fully satisfactory accord can be found between them – only an existential choice grounded in nothing firmer than faith and will. "No ethics in the world," Weber argues,

can dodge the fact that in numerous instances the attainment of "good" ends is bound to the fact that one must be willing to pay the price of using morally dubious means or at least dangerous ones – and facing the possibility or even the probability of evil ramifications. From no ethics in the world can it be concluded when and to what extent the ethically good purpose "justifies" the ethically dangerous means and ramifications.[30]

Thus, for the value pluralist, the end does not "justify the means"; but neither does it decisively justify *not* employing the means. Instead, such moral dilemmas constitute "a confrontation of ultimate conceptions of life, between which in the end a *choice* must be made."[31] Though Weber in the end endorses, or at least expresses admiration for the politician who chooses, the ethic of responsibility, he acknowledges that this comes at a profound, irreparable moral cost to the agent for whom an ethic of ultimate ends retains its own independent authority.

The idea of value pluralism thus carries vital consequences for the problem of dirty hands. Indeed, in a way one needs to subscribe to some form of value pluralism in order to get the most serious versions of the dirty hands problem off the ground: for without the irreconcilable clash of values to which pluralist theories point, it is difficult to motivate the truly tragic and paradoxical dimensions of the problem. Yet value pluralism remains an under-defined – at times even vague – metaphor for making sense of moral complexity in a multi-faceted world. Arrived at by a kind of process of elimination, value pluralism may feel intuitively persuasive.[32] Yet as a

[29] There are of course views that combine value pluralism and relativism. Its most profound exponents, however, from Weber to Berlin to the contemporary theorists Nagel and Raz, have all been moral realists rather than relativists.

[30] Max Weber, "Politics as a Vocation," in Gerth and Mills, *From Max Weber*, p. 121.

[31] Weber, "Science as a Vocation," p. 501.

[32] The roots of value pluralism as a contemporary moral theory can be traced in part to the intuitionism of such twentieth-century ethicists as F. H. Bradley and W. D. Ross. For the treatment of the problem of moral dilemmas in these moral theories, see the selections from Bradley and Ross collected in Gowans, ed., *Moral Dilemmas*.

comprehensive theory of ethics, value pluralism appears ill equipped to offer us direct guidance: we know too little about how the various values relate; in which spheres of life one value might possess greater power or import than another; where our understandings of the various values come from, and how precisely they have got their hooks into us.

One aim of this book, then, is to offer a preliminary contribution to the conceptual archaeology of value pluralism, at least in one of its important aspects.[33] This may mean that readers already committed to a moral theory that excludes the possibility of value pluralism will to that extent find the book's argument less compelling (though hopefully there will be something of interest to them in the historical account itself). But if there is some degree of truth to value pluralism, then we must expect conflicts of values like dirty hands to go on and on, because they are motivated by a fundamental incommensurability among our most deeply felt human demands, and by a moral schizophrenia that seems increasingly to characterize our late modern condition.

DIRTY HANDS AS A POLITICAL PROBLEM

The contemporary mode of dealing with the problem of dirty hands among moral and political theorists has tended to obscure a number of suggestive lines of inquiry. The text that follows focuses on two such lines of inquiry. First, contemporary theorists have been so quick to assume that the definitive answer to the problem must hinge on the philosophical coherence of the notion of an iron-clad moral dilemma that they have tended to underrate the significance of a fact about which there is no disagreement: namely, that things that *look like* moral dilemmas arise all the time in politics and similar contexts. And, second, this way of looking at the problem of dirty hands suggests that it may have a very different (and much older) heritage than utilitarian and deontological ethics, one that employs different moral vocabularies capable of helping us to analyze the problem afresh. The problem of dirty hands will remain, inescapably, a *philosophical* problem; but to grapple fully with the problem in all its complexity, we need to reconceive it as also in part a *political* problem and a *historical* problem.

So instead of trying to settle right out of the gate the theoretical question of whether there are or can be genuine moral dilemmas, this book takes an

---

[33] The most substantial (self-conscious) contribution to the conceptual archaeology of value pluralism so far is Charles Taylor's rich *Sources of the Self: The Making of the Modern Identity*.

alternative and more inductive starting point. It observes that moral dilemmas seem to arise more frequently in *politics* than anywhere else: and, beginning with that premise, it investigates what features of politics have historically been recognized as giving rise to such moral dilemmas.[34] If we bracket for the moment any theoretical resolution of these issues, we can instead approach the problem of dirty hands as a *political* phenomenon, asking ourselves what it is about politics that seems to make it the uniquely inviting site of humanity's most troubling moral conundrums. In the course of trying to answer this question, we can hope to uncover important truths about both the nature of politics and the place of humanity's moral nature within it.

So what is it about politics that tends to engender the distinctive moral risks encountered by those who lead in public life? There are a variety of factors that doubtless contribute to produce the effect. First, the political state acts with a monopoly on the legitimate use of violence and coercive means.[35] States must command, and must compel those who disobey their commands to comply, by force if necessary. Perhaps there are domestic alternatives to that violence – recalcitrant citizens can be jailed, coerced, or persuaded without needing to be physically injured or killed. But at the boundaries of its domestic authority, where its self-defense or vital interests may be at stake, a state must ultimately be prepared to back its commands with decisive and even lethal force. The power to use such means may always tempt, and will frequently corrupt, those who hold it: even the pure of heart will find in such means a potential source of moral peril.

Another quality of political life that makes morality hard to observe within its confines is the frequent presence of ruthless and unscrupulous competitors.[36] In some circumstances one may be able to take the high ground and decline to fight fire with fire, but at the end of the day given the stakes one must fight fire with *something*. Thus strategic questions about suitable responses to the vicious or at least ungenerous behavior of others also sharply limits the range of effective actions available to the serious politician in many situations.

[34] This aspect of the problem has not of course been completely ignored; Walzer's seminal article, for one, offers some speculations about what drives the problem politically. But it is certainly fair to say that it has not been at all the major focus of most inquiries about dirty hands by contemporary moral philosophers or political theorists.

[35] The point is made most famously by Weber in "Politics as a Vocation," p. 119.

[36] Machiavelli, *The Prince*, trans. and ed. Harvey Mansfield, 2nd edn (University of Chicago Press, 1998), ch. 15, pp. 60–61, is the most famous expression of this particular worry.

A third feature of political life that makes morality difficult to practice within it is the special status held (in contemporary democratic politics at least) by the claims of universalism, neutrality, and the objective point of view. This aspiration to an impartial "view from nowhere" tends to rule out the consideration of particularities which in other circumstances would correctly influence our moral judgment; and this in turn may make the practice of certain moral virtues, such as generosity and mercy, difficult or impossible to practice in public life.[37]

Finally, and probably most importantly, the experience of dirty hands is common in politics simply because of the high consequential stakes for which the state is accountable, and the corresponding special force which the claim of necessity carries in the public sphere. For although violence, strategic interaction, and impartiality may frequently find their way into dirty hands situations, they are contingently rather than necessarily related to the phenomenon as a whole. In politics, claims of large-scale social benefits seem to possess a peculiar moral importance: in no other scene of human life is it the case that the well-being of so many can be shaped so profoundly by the decisions of so few. It is unsurprising, then, that those who get their hands dirty frequently appeal to consequences as a way of justifying their actions: they often claim personal responsibility for those consequences by pointing to their status as the representatives or caretakers of others.

But it is also true – a truth that will be a key theme of this book – that, in politics, moral responsibility for great ends is typically diffused through complex and ambiguous relations of human agency, which tend to disrupt our ordinary ethical mechanisms for relating consequences to the choices that produce them. Thus there are intricate issues of agency surrounding political action which also have to be untangled in order to analyze dirty hands situations. One important issue for the analysis of moral responsibility in politics is the idea of *roles* and the obligations and permissions associated with them.[38] That roles make a difference in ethics is a generally acknowledged feature of common-sense morality: notice, for

---

[37] Thomas Nagel, *The View From Nowhere* (Oxford University Press, 1986) and *Equality and Partiality* (Oxford University Press, 1991), explores this general area and its implications for moral and liberal political theory. On the disqualification of certain virtues, see for example Ross Harrison's suggestive essay "The equality of mercy," in Hyman Gross and Ross Harrison, eds., *Jurisprudence: Cambridge Essays* (Clarendon Press, 1992).

[38] The most comprehensive treatment of the issue of role morality is by Arthur Applbaum, *Ethics for Adversaries*. Other important treatments of the issue can be found in Michael Hardimon, "Role Obligations," *Journal of Philosophy* 91 (1994): 333–363, and David Luban, *Lawyers and Justice* (Princeton University Press, 1988), chs. 6–7.

example, the way that praise (or blame) can be waved off with the observation "It's my job." Typically politicians claim their actions are authorized by others; they always (when they are being morally serious) claim their wrongdoing benefits others, and that this fact makes a moral difference. Thus the most important role to which political leaders typically appeal for moral excuse is their status as representatives of the public will and as providers of the public good.

Isolating these dimensions discloses how intimately citizen needs and preferences are implicated in the concept of dirty hands. And this in turn suggests that, in approaching the problem, we need to ask not only what it is to have dirty hands, but also precisely whose hands we think are dirty. The standard model of the dirty hands problem is what we might call the "heroic" or "aristocratic" model. Machiavelli's theory is the classic articulation of this version of dirty hands. On this account, the problem of dirty hands is one that confronts a lone heroic political actor, who faces an inescapable moral dilemma in which he is asked to sacrifice his own moral purity on behalf of the public good.

This is an important model for understanding dirty hands, but it is not necessarily the only one. Another important version suggests that there might be "democratic" dirty hands: that is, that in political structures in which the powers and responsibilities of governing reside in many hands instead of just a few, the moral dilemmas associated with the lonely heroic transgressor prince of Machiavelli's imagination might equally confront ordinary men and women in their everyday lives.[39] We are not accustomed to thinking of the democratic populace at large as potentially affected by the dirty hands dilemma. In fact, most explorations of democratic dirty hands have tended to focus on the question of whether dirty-handed actions are compatible with the principles of democracy, not whether democracies could themselves be implicated in dirty hands situations.[40] Yet these questions are of crucial importance both in thinking about how to evaluate the actions of political leaders in moments of moral crisis, and even more importantly in thinking about what features of political and social life tend to give rise to those crises in the first place.

[39] This idea is first introduced in the contemporary literature by Dennis Thompson in *Political Ethics and Public Office* (Harvard University Press, 1987), ch. 1. One of the few pieces to pursue Thompson's suggestion is David Shugarman, "Democratic Dirty Hands?," in Rynard and Shugarman, *Cruelty and Deception*.

[40] An intriguing exception is Judith Shklar, *Ordinary Vices* (Harvard University Press, 1984), particularly at pp. 243–246. There are also interesting though briefer treatments of this theme in Ronald Beiner, "Missionaries and Mercenaries" (in Rynard and Shugarman, *Cruelty and Deception*) and Stocker, *Plural and Conflicting Values*.

There are two questions here that it is helpful to separate. One is the idea that there is a democratic *justification* for dirty hands. This is the notion that certain evils may be justifiable if they are done on behalf of the people at large. Such a conception typically invokes the value of the people's welfare as a justification for evil actions, but at the same time claims to shield the people from the full weight of moral responsibility for those evils done in their name. As Dennis Thompson points out, however, what the heroic conception of dirty hands overlooks "is that the bad the official does he does not only for us, but with our consent – not only in our name, but on our principles."[41] In some cases of course it may be worse to do the action than to have it done for you; yet in other cases it may conceivably be even worse to authorize evil than to do evil. In any event, it remains impossible to distinguish the responsibilities of leaders from those of their charges quite so neatly as proponents of the heroic model might like.

This line of reasoning suggests the second idea we should consider, which is that dirty hands may have, in addition to a democratic justification, a democratic *agency* as well. This is a topic which the literature on dirty hands has barely explored, but which is a vital background assumption of the narrative pursued in these pages. For if we turn to the pre-modern and early modern vocabularies in which this problem was discussed in the centuries before modern ethics assumed its present structure, we find that the problem of dirty hands may potentially touch a much wider range of cases than is typically understood to be the case. The heroic conception of moral agency conceals the fact that, in a society with relatively open institutions of power, such as the democratic state and the commercial market, no one is truly insulated from the performance of those necessary evils which contribute to the common good. On this view, the people at large may turn out to be not just beneficiaries of necessary evils, but in many cases the very agents who carry out those evils – though often in the less conspicuous fashion captured so well in Judith Shklar's notion of the "ordinary vices" that help to sustain liberal society.[42]

Thus, an important part of the argument of this book will be the claim that many of our most familiar modern moral conceptions and political institutions tend to conceal this everyday dimension of dirty hands, as well as the potential moral complicity of citizens in the wrongs their representatives do. In particular, the three distinctive conceptions on which the history that follows focuses – Augustine's interiorized ethics, Hobbes's impersonal nation-states, and Smith's invisibly guided markets – all help

---

[41] Thompson, *Political Ethics and Public Office*, ch. 1, p. 18.   [42] Shklar, *Ordinary Vices*.

to conceal how many of the necessary evils of social life draw their ultimate justification from the needs and preferences of the people at large. In a way, the moral of the book is that this is not entirely an accident. For one of its central arguments is that the success of these conceptions in concealing the democratic dimensions of dirty hands has been one of the reasons, historically, why those conceptions came to be accepted in place of rival theoretical accounts.

DIRTY HANDS AS A HISTORICAL PROBLEM

If the problem of dirty hands needs to be reconceived as a *political* problem, it also needs to be reconceived as a *historical* problem – that is, as a problem with a real history. How then should we approach the problem historically? One way would be to trace the ways in which the debate between utilitarians on the one hand and deontologists influenced by Kant on the other has played itself out from the late eighteenth century to the present. Such a study would perhaps describe how the current disagreement arose, and where the theories of one or both sides of the dispute have gone astray. While such a study would undoubtedly be useful, it is not the project undertaken in this book.

Instead, the present work turns to an older tradition of moral reflection on this topic, and traces its development up to the moment just before utilitarianism on the one hand and Kantian deontology on the other became the obvious and mutually exclusive choices for explaining ethical phenomena.[43] For long before contemporary philosophers had carved the moral world up into rival utilitarian and deontological possibilities, there was an awareness among those who reflected on politics of something that bears at least a strong family resemblance to the problem of dirty hands, something that for that reason they *couldn't* have understood as a conflict of Kantian and utilitarian imperatives.

There are of course a variety of responses one could have toward this fact about the problem's history. One possibility is to believe that the underlying rational dynamic of the problem has always really consisted of a conflict between utilitarian and deontological considerations, and that those who dwelt on this conflict simply lacked the appropriate conceptual frameworks for capturing what actually troubled them. But an alternate

---

[43] On the emergence of these two traditions as well as, in some ways, the falsity of the choice it proposes, see the magisterial *The Invention of Autonomy* by J. B. Schneewind (Cambridge University Press, 1997).

possibility – the one pursued in the pages that follow – is that the problem itself has a real history: that is, that rather than making sense only within a constant and determinate analytical framework, the problem itself may have changed over time. If so, then we might be able to investigate, not the problem of dirty hands *per se*, but rather a succession of dirty hands problems, each of which could tell us something important about the people and the conceptual frameworks that find the problem, or don't find the problem, troubling. Such a history could hope to generate new insights into the underexplained contemporary notions of moral conflict and moral pluralism through a conceptual archaeology of the underlying philosophical issues.

That possibility, in turn, raises two questions to consider. First, if there was a pre-modern version of the problem of dirty hands different from the one that confronts us today, what did the pre-modern version look like? And, second, if there was a pre-modern version of the problem, where did it go? What happened to *that* problem to make it no longer appear problematic in the same way?

Perhaps the first important thing to observe about the pre-modern version of the dirty hands problem is that it was framed in significantly different terms from the contemporary account. From antiquity to the late Enlightenment, those who addressed this issue saw it not as a conflict between utilitarian and deontological imperatives, but rather between the requirements of the public benefit on the one hand and the requirements of moral *virtue* on the other. This is the mode in which Machiavelli, for example, frames the problem: the actions necessary to produce sufficient utility for the community's good life cannot be consistently produced merely by the conventionally virtuous actions of conventionally virtuous politicians. Instead, what is necessary for politics to be done well requires, eventually but inevitably, the abandonment of conventional moral virtue by its political leaders.

In contemporary moral philosophy there has been a resurgence of interest in the concept of virtue, and "virtue ethics" has become a growth industry within the field.[44] But the debate over the problem of dirty hands has largely taken shape outside that resurgence, such that the insights of the virtue orientation have not been prevalent in contemporary treatments of

---

[44] The most influential statement of the virtue model is perhaps that of Alasdair MacIntyre in *After Virtue*. Of significance also for the dirty hands problem in particular is Philippa Foot, "Utilitarianism and the Virtues," in Samuel Scheffler, ed., *Consequentialism and Its Critics* (Oxford University Press, 1988).

the problem.[45] This is regrettable, since (as this book's narrative will show) there is a rich tradition in Western thought that approaches the problem of dirty hands from a virtue-oriented perspective, one which might offer a fresh outlook on this enduring puzzle. While this book does not undertake a full-scale analytical application of virtue ethics to the problem of dirty hands, it lays a historical foundation for such analysis by re-conceptualizing the problem (as ancient and early modern thinkers virtually always did) as a conflict between a virtue-centered ethic and an ethic of public responsibility. This matters not just for historical reasons, but also because it captures an important truth obscured by the contemporary account. That truth is that much (though of course not all) of what intuitively troubles us most about the problem of dirty hands is not just that it seems to require morally bad *actions* to be done, but also that it seems to pose an ongoing threat to the moral *character* of those who must do them.[46]

Attention to the different moral vocabularies employed by pre-modern and early modern authors will help to give our inquiry greater precision as well as access to the rather different imaginative resources of their age. Such care in approaching the thought of historical figures – seeking to elicit from them not answers to questions they did not themselves ask, but rather the answers *and* questions which in fact they did – has been a hallmark of recent scholarship in the history of political thought, in a way that has much improved the overall quality of work in the field.[47] Some indeed might carry a concern for context to the point of questioning whether a wide-ranging inquiry of the kind undertaken in this book is even coherent; they might very reasonably wonder whether there is any sense in which authors from Plato to Augustine to Machiavelli to Adam Smith might be said to be addressing the *same* problem at all. Mistakenly seeking to find pre-modern answers to a thoroughly modern question, such critics might worry, must doom such a project to anachronism and conceptual confusion.

The dangers envisioned by such critics are real, but they need not inhibit an inquiry such as this provided we approach the problem with the proper care. For with regard to this issue at least, there are analytical similarities between the problems of political ethics these authors wrestle with which

---

[45] One thought-provoking exception is MacIntyre, *After Virtue*, esp. ch. 11.

[46] One of the few contemporary articles to focus on this aspect of the problem is Bernard Williams, "Politics and Moral Character," in *Moral Luck*.

[47] The most influential proponents of this approach have been Quentin Skinner and John Pocock. Among many writings, see in particular Skinner, *Visions of Politics*, vol. 1 (Cambridge University Press, 2002) and Pocock, *Politics, Language, and Time* (University of Chicago Press, 1989).

are just as important as the various differences between them. The problems these thinkers confront are not identical, but there is a striking family resemblance between them that is itself both a puzzle to be explained and a diagnostic indication that bears on our treatment of the problem itself.[48] This book therefore aims to exemplify an approach to the history of political theory which remains sensitive to the historical contexts of its subjects, while at the same time, by means of a careful and precise translation of their various concerns, bringing thinkers from widely disparate contexts into philosophical dialogue with one another and with the present.

A history of the problem of "dirty hands," therefore, cannot be a history of the attempts of different philosophers and political thinkers to offer their answers to the historically constant analytical problem we today designate by that odd hygienic metaphor. It must instead constitute a history of *different* formulations of that problem, accompanied at each stage by different strategies designed to cope with their own particular formulations. As the book's subtitle suggests, the story is one in which different versions of what we today call the dirty hands problem emerge at particular moments as problematic in a vividly felt sense, and are grappled with by leading thinkers of that age. But it is at the same time the story of the attempted (and sometimes apparently successful) resolution, and often also the receding from view, of those various formulations of the problem.

The following narrative traces how three distinct versions of the problem of dirty hands emerged in antiquity, the Renaissance, and modernity, as well as how key political theorists in each period developed three influential "solutions" to the moral quandaries the problem presented. Thus the book shows how, in late antiquity, Augustine responded to anxieties about the irreconcilability of both classical and Christian morality to political life by developing an interiorized moral psychology and an account of the moral opacity of the social world. In early modernity, Thomas Hobbes helped to develop a theory of the impersonal sovereign state that defused the unease of Renaissance thinkers regarding the moral culpability of both rulers and ordinary citizens. And in the Enlightenment, Adam Smith responded to the "private vices, public benefits" arguments of Pierre Nicole and Bernard Mandeville with his enduring apology for the moral advantages of the modern commercial market.

---

[48] In introducing the metaphor of "family resemblances," I allude to the usage of that phrase by Ludwig Wittgenstein in his *Philosophical Investigations*, trans. G. E. M. Anscombe, 3rd edn (Prentice-Hall, 1958).

The book as a whole traces the development of a set of complex philosophical strategies for coping with the problem of dirty hands – and indeed, its central concern is less with tracing the different versions of the *problem* of dirty hands than with the story of the most influential *solutions* to the problem that have been offered. (This focus is one reason why I do not discuss the early modern "reason of state" tradition, except in passing – because while these arguments were influential in disseminating the idea of dirty hands, especially at the level of practical politics, the philosophical quality of that tradition's *solution* to the problem does not compare in sophistication or in lasting influence to the solutions of Augustine, Hobbes, and Adam Smith that I trace here.)[49] By means of these strategies, in the process of creating and justifying some of the fundamental political concepts of modernity such as the sovereign state and the commercial market, worries about the dirty hands problem came to be calmed and, by many, forgotten. Yet this serenity may well be illusory, and if so it is also for that reason even more dangerous.

Part I of the book explores the earliest emergence of the major elements of the problem of dirty hands in ancient classical and Christian thought. Chapter 1 considers some of the most influential ways in which the moral problems associated with political action were treated in ancient philosophy and religion. It begins with a consideration of ancient debates about the relative merits of the active and the contemplative life, contrasting the withdrawal from politics advocated by Plato and the other philosophical schools with the endorsement of political engagement advanced by Cicero and the rhetorical schools. It then surveys ancient treatments of potential value conflicts by both philosophers and rhetoricians, culminating in Cicero's treatise *On Duties*, which investigates potential conflicts between utility and moral rightness. The chapter then turns to explain and critique Cicero's proffered solution to this problem, by considering first his skeptical distinction between apparent and real value conflicts and then his assertion of the preeminent status which public moral claims have over their private counterparts. Finally, the chapter contrasts Cicero's theory of political responsibility with early Christian responses to Roman politics

---

[49] Another reason for focusing on writers outside the "reason of state" tradition is the substantial achievement of recent scholarship in increasing our knowledge of that tradition. The classic work is Friedrich Meinecke, *Machiavellism: The Doctrine of Raison d'Etat and Its Place in Modern History*, new edn (Transaction, 1997). Other influential works include Nannerl Keohane, *Philosophy and the State in France* (Princeton University Press, 1980), Richard Tuck, *Philosophy and Government 1572–1651* (Cambridge University Press, 1993) and *The Rights of War and Peace* (Oxford University Press, 1999), Maurizio Viroli, *From Politics to Reason of State*, new edn (Cambridge University Press, 2005), and Harro Höpfl, *Jesuit Political Thought* (Cambridge University Press, 2004).

and culture, focusing on Lactantius's *Divine Institutes*. This analysis identifies a deep and seemingly irreconcilable tension between Roman and Christian perspectives on public life, particularly with respect to the early Christians' pacifism, commitment to equality, and prioritization of moral and religious over political claims.

Chapter 2 shows how these potential moral conflicts received an ingenious, but also fundamentally unstable, resolution in the moral and political theory of St. Augustine. The chapter begins with Augustine's conception of the fundamentally *imitative* relationship that human pride bears to charity, producing good effects from unworthy motives. This conclusion leads Augustine to posit that crucial features of human moral life are profoundly opaque to external observation, and in response to interiorize his account of moral action and evaluation more profoundly than any previous moral thinker had attempted. The chapter then considers the corresponding imitative relationship between the worldly city of human politics and the higher universe of moral priorities envisioned in Augustine's heavenly city. It shows that the fundamental ambiguity of moral judgment implied by these imitative relationships comprises the basis of Augustine's distinctive ethics of political action, which excuses necessary evils committed by well-intentioned political actors. For Augustine, political action and judgment are unavoidably necessary, but they must also take place within conditions of moral opacity and can therefore be excused when their apparent evils are a result of acting within those limits.

Part II examines the resurgence of concern with these paradoxes of political ethics in the middle and late Renaissance, and then examines the distinctive solution to the problem of dirty hands offered by Thomas Hobbes in the form of the modern state. In Chapter 3 we begin to observe the unraveling of Augustine's solution, and the consequent re-emergence of widespread concern with the problem of dirty hands. The chapter focuses chiefly on Machiavelli and on Thomas More's *Utopia*. In Machiavelli we find the classic account of what we might call the "aristocratic" response to the problem. By urging his political leaders to abandon the project of reconciling the classical Roman ethic of political responsibility with Christian ethical teachings, he offers those leaders a free moral hand to meet the demands of political necessity. At the same time, his theory of leadership provides ordinary citizens with a degree of insulation from the moral dangers of politics (dangers in part created by the moral failings of their own civic corruption). And, further, he offers a deeper implicit challenge to the traditional modes of ethical evaluation by signaling his admiration for the prince's choice.

More's *Utopia* frames the problem less radically, but ultimately with greater sophistication about the problem's fundamental roots. In Book I of *Utopia* we find a powerful statement of the tension between the requirements of political responsibility on the one hand and the uncompromising demands of Christian morality on the other. Book II, which describes the imaginary society of Utopia, appears to dissolve the tensions between these two moral worlds. Yet More insists that Utopia is literally "nowhere," drawing our attention to the fact that these tensions are "nowhere" resolved, and thus to the continuing (and disturbing) relevance of this problem to those influenced by both classical and Christian values. In the process, More argues that the morally corrupting dimension of politics originates in the pride-driven desires and practices of the people at large. Thus *Utopia* produces the first complex analysis of a "democratic" understanding of dirty hands.

Chapter 4 shows how Thomas Hobbes provides the first quintessentially modern response to the problem of dirty hands, by suggesting that citizens can find absolution from the moral difficulties involved in exercising political authority in the representative devices of the modern state. The Hobbesian state, the chapter suggests, uses a combination of democratic justification and aristocratic agency to take the sting out of the democratic dimension of dirty hands. Hobbes's theory thus attempts to eliminate the psychological conflict between political necessity and Christian conscience for ordinary citizens. At the same time, however, the Hobbesian state morally justifies those representatives who perform the necessary acts on their behalf. But this commits Hobbes to an argument that ultimately rests on an implausible – or at least unflattering – appeal to a brutal state of nature to justify the extensive moral permissions the state claims to exercise on behalf of its citizens. Thus the dominant theory of the modern state, the chapter argues, is founded on a kind of shell game of moral responsibility, one that obscures the ongoing implication of citizens in the vast moral permissions to which the Hobbesian sovereign lays claim.[50]

Part III shows how a new version of the dirty hands problem, one which potentially held even deeper implications for the ethics of everyday life, emerged in late seventeenth-century neo-Augustinian theology and in eighteenth-century moral philosophy and political economy. Chapter 5

---

[50] For those unfamiliar with the term, a "shell game" is a classic confidence trick (similar to the "three-card trick") in which an object is placed under one of three shells which are then rapidly shuffled in a manner designed to confuse the observer's eye. The combination of complexity, rapid movement, and sleight of hand together make it extremely difficult for observers to keep track of where the object is located at any given moment in the trick.

picks up where Chapter 2 left off, by describing modern attempts to revive and extend Augustine's moral theory, first by Pierre Nicole and other French Jansenists in the late seventeenth century, and later by Bernard Mandeville and the early tradition of political economy. The chapter traces Nicole's argument (adapted from Augustine) that self-love, while entirely vicious from an ultimate point of view, was nevertheless capable of producing *all* the beneficial social effects that would be achieved by perfect charity. The chapter then shows how Mandeville redeploys this Augustinian moral tradition in a new and controversial way. Mandeville argues in the form of his famous "paradox" that private vices frequently produce public benefits, drawing attention in the process to the disturbing conflicts between traditional Christian moral thinking and the realities of the emerging commercial world. By arguing successfully, even if "paradoxically," that public utility might be irreducibly entangled with personal vice, Mandeville promoted a kind of popularized Machiavellism suited to broader questions of everyday morality. In Mandeville's theory, the privilege and duty of performing necessary evils, previously reserved to great leaders in extraordinary situations, were now offered to ordinary citizens in their routine commercial transactions. But it turns out that this commercialized Machiavellism itself involves a subtle reassertion of the Machiavellian prerogative by a nation's political leadership. For on Mandeville's theory, the state must now take responsibility for trying to promote and cultivate among its citizens those vicious appetites without which the public benefits necessary to a commercial society could never be achieved.

Hobbes provided the first great solution to the problem of dirty hands, in the form of the modern state; Chapter 6 shows how Smith helped to justify a second and less obvious solution to the problem in the form of the modern commercial market. It shows that, contrary to Smith's attempts to distance himself from Mandeville, his argument in *The Theory of Moral Sentiments* and in the *Wealth of Nations* can be seen as in many ways a modified restatement of Mandeville's "private vices, public benefits" argument. Instead of contradicting the dynamics of Mandeville's framework, Smith instead challenges Mandeville's account of what counts as vice, in particular by rehabilitating self-love (*contra* Augustine) as a moral motivation. It is this anti-Augustinian moral psychology, coupled with Smith's qualified acceptance of the "private vices, public benefits" argument, that lies at the heart of Smith's familiar arguments about the unintended beneficial effects of self-love in the *Wealth of Nations*. Thus the commercialization of dirty hands begun by Mandeville receives its definitive modern moral justification (or at least excuse) in the form of Smith's theory of the invisible hand guiding the modern global market.

This is not to claim that the modern state and the modern commercial market developed *as institutions* to cope with the dirty hands problem. Even if institutions that large were amenable to conscious social choice, nowhere near the relevant number of people have ever taken these kinds of problems seriously enough to effect that kind of response. Instead, the kind of influence contemplated here is more modest, though still significant. The claim is that one of the reasons our distinctive modern understandings of the state and the market were able to win out against rival accounts was the fact that these understandings seem to provide adequate answers to the versions of the problem of dirty hands they confronted. In other words, one advantage which the concepts of the state and the market had as legitimating structures in the culture in which they emerged was that they constituted a way of providing public benefits without (apparently) morally endangering those individuals who did the providing; and one of the reasons why these institutions succeeded in winning legitimation was that they performed this function well.[51] Whether they really *do* provide adequate answers to the problem of dirty hands will be drawn into question in the course of the following pages; but the plausibility of their *claim* to answer it was and is one of the chief features of their attraction to those who subscribe to them. Showing that they do perform this function well, or at least appear to do so, will be the burden of the text that follows.

---

[51] For examples of what I have in mind here, see Skinner, *Visions of Politics*, vol. 1, chs. 8–9.

PART I

The pre-modern origins of dirty hands

CHAPTER I

For the sake of the city

... but when his turn comes, he drudges in politics and rules for the city's sake, not as though he were doing a thing that is fine, but one that is necessary.   Plato, *Republic* 521ab

What gives the problem of dirty hands its intuitive power? Certainly one important reason the problem so forcefully grips us resides in the great moral weight we assign to claims of public *responsibility*. The idea that political leaders may have special moral permissions not afforded to ordinary citizens rests at least in large part on the fact that the goods of the public are placed in their care. It is right, we think, for political leaders to feel they are not *morally* entitled to forego or sacrifice the goods of those for whose welfare they bear responsibility, as perhaps they could if only their own personal welfare were at stake.

In investigating the historical roots of this problem, then, we can begin with the following question: where does this idea of differential ethical requirements for public and private responsibilities originate? Where in our shared intellectual past do we find the beginnings of the intuition that it is permissible to do on behalf of others what it is not permissible to do on our own behalf?

The roots of this issue stretch back to the foundations of the Western tradition. In Plato's *Republic*, we find Plato's alter ego Socrates proposing a set of moral permissions reserved specially for political leaders; we also find him expressing concern about what these permissions implied for the project of a rational and ethical politics more generally. Among Plato's successors, perhaps the most important engagements with this problem took place within the prominent debate in ancient philosophy and literature over the relative merits of the active life of public duty versus the contemplative life of philosophical and private virtue. Of related importance are the intimations of the problem among both ancient philosophers and ancient rhetoricians as they debated the possibility of multiple competing, and seemingly incompatible, sources of moral value in human experience. We find the classic ancient response to these tensions in Cicero's treatise *On Duties*, which (as we will see) argues influentially, but ultimately untenably, that there can be no genuine conflict whatsoever between competing moral spheres.

In proposing this resolution, however, Cicero complicates and deepens the problem by arguing that the source of all special moral permissions is to be found in the needs of the public sphere, and that its claims are a sufficient basis for overriding all but the firmest of ethical requirements. While largely consistent with the moral principles common to ancient philosophy, this move of Cicero's captures quite well the apparently irreconcilable differences that emerged between ancient and specifically Roman political morality, on the one hand, and the ethical principles at the heart of the Christian religion, on the other. For it was impossible for the early Christians to acquiesce in the potentially idolatrous claims of moral priority made by Cicero on behalf of the public sphere, especially when the purposes of that sphere seemed to call forth the violence, pride, greed and ruthlessness against which the new Christian ethic had defined itself. Thus, in the process of identifying and (ostensibly) resolving this early version of the problem of dirty hands on ancient terms, Cicero and the Roman moral tradition highlighted precisely those features of their political ethic that would be hardest to reconcile with the rival Christian moral tradition just beginning to emerge.

PLATO AND POLITICAL ACTION

[The city's guards must be] gentle in their dealings with their own people, and fierce in their dealings with the enemy ... If someone is deficient in these qualities, he cannot possibly be a good guard ...[1]

Plato's *Republic* is the first great masterwork of moral and political theory in the Western tradition; and so it is unsurprising to find in the *Republic* a compelling analysis of the special ethical problems associated with political leadership. Such problems seem to have played a prominent role in Plato's own biography. Many of the ancient traditions about Plato's own life held that Plato himself undertook to offer political advice to a real-life monarch, Dionysius of Syracuse – though with disappointing results. Whether or not this foray of Plato's into practical politics truly occurred (and there are reasons to be skeptical of this traditional story), another

---

[1] Plato, *Republic* 375 ce. I employ the translation of Tom Griffith, ed. G. R. F. Ferrari (Cambridge University Press, 2000). Throughout I substitute the more literal term "guard" for the more traditional translation "guardian."

event unquestionably took place that forcefully brings these problems to the foreground of any account of Plato's life: the death by execution of Plato's mentor Socrates. In the *Republic* and other dialogues, Plato revived Socrates as a literary character and philosophical spokesman; and throughout those writings, the fact that Socrates had been put to death by Plato's fellow Athenians – in part because of Socrates' unconventional approach to ethics and its unsettling political implications – is never far from Plato's mind.

In any event, by the time Plato undertook his dialogue *The Republic*, perhaps his most systematic exploration of the relation between politics and individual ethics, these questions have taken center stage. In the *Republic* we find an extended consideration of the claim – presumably long incubated in political practice but never thoroughly explored in theory – that the responsibilities held by political leaders permit them to act in ways that would otherwise be ruled out by the strictures of moral theory. These special moral permissions are held by that class of citizens Plato designates as "guardians" (or more properly "guards"): those chosen to serve as the soldiers and leaders of the Kallipolis (the "Republic" of the popular but inaccurate translation of the dialogue's title).

Perhaps the most famous example of the special moral permissions afforded to Plato's guards is to be found in the policy of the "noble lie." In the regime of the Republic, ordinary citizens are strictly forbidden to be untruthful in any way. But Plato acknowledges that under certain circumstances it may be appropriate for the guards, if anyone, "to lie for the benefit of the city."[2] Lying is such a significant matter, Plato elaborates, that it must "be entrusted to specialists," that is, to the political leaders.[3] The city's leaders employ this permission most extensively in their deception about the origins of the city, in which Plato's guards seek to indoctrinate their citizens into adequate fellow-feeling and respect for the guards' rule by spinning an implausible tale about the mixture of metals into human souls through an alleged process of subterranean smelting which originally forged human beings.

But this deception about the city's origins is by no means the only one that Plato's guards undertake. The *Republic*'s elaborate regime of eugenic planning, designed to produce genetically superior children in future

---

[2] *Republic* 389c. For a helpful account of this passage and an important context for interpreting it, see Jane S. Zembarty, "Plato's *Republic* and Greek Morality on Lying," *Journal of the History of Philosophy* 26 (1988): 517–545.

[3] *Republic* 389bc.

generations, relies on extensive (and surely sometimes transparent) deceptions facilitating each necessary step of courtship, mating, and child rearing in the guards' social plan. In addition, Plato's remark that the guards may be permitted to lie "in response to the actions of either enemies or citizens" suggests a wider range of potential deceptive tactics than might appear to be included at first glance.

Nor is lying the only form of moral permission to which the guards in the *Republic* are able to lay special claim. As noted before, the guards serve as the military wing of the Kallipolis, and as such they must engage in fighting and sometimes killing other people, on occasion including their fellow Greeks. Yet this places the guards in the position of having to undertake tasks that at least on the surface might not appear to be the worthiest pursuits of a virtuous nature by Plato's own standards.[4] Plato himself draws attention to this conflict in a paradox framed by Socrates about the contradictory elements that must compose the character of the guards. What is fundamental to the guards' character, Socrates asserts, is that they must be "gentle in their dealings with their own people, and fierce in their dealings with the enemy."[5] Yet there is a kind of paradox here: it is not easy, Socrates tells us, to find "a disposition which is both gentle and full of spirit, for by the nature of things a gentle disposition is the opposite of spirit." At the same time politics requires the resolution of just this paradox, since "if someone is deficient in these qualities, he cannot possibly be a good guard."[6]

At first, these apparently contradictory requirements about the character of the guards looks profoundly worrying to Socrates, seeming to carry the implication that "a good guard is an impossibility."[7] But there is indeed a parallel resolution of this paradox in nature, Socrates tells us, though it is a strange one: we find the same characteristic of being at once gentle and fierce among dogs. So although Plato will later tell us that the rulers must be philosophers, that is, wise and virtuous men and women, he begins by characterizing them instead as resembling in their disposition the dumb, loyal shepherd's companion, the guard dog.[8] Such dogs, Socrates explains,

---

[4] *Republic* 335ae; cf. *Crito* in J. M. Cooper, ed., *Plato: Complete Works* (Hackett, 1997), pp. 42–43, hereafter cited as *P:CW*.

[5] *Republic* 375c.

[6] *Republic* 375ce. The paradox is one that is especially vivid given the unity of function in political action required by the "one man, one job" principle (discussed further below).

[7] *Republic* 375cd.

[8] Plato's description of the guards as "philosophical" is an odd choice as it seems to conflate two senses of the term "knowledge" which Plato himself surely would have wanted to distinguish. Socrates states that the dogs are philosophical in that they "love what they know," being kind even to an abusive

are naturally disposed "to be as gentle as possible to those they know and recognize, and the exact opposite to those they don't know."[9] Like the dogs they resemble, the guards in Plato's *Republic* care for and watch over their flock; like these dogs, too, their role asks them to command and guide the sheep, but for the purpose of the sheep's own good rather than their own.

There is also an oddity to Plato's use of the metaphor of the guard dog which casts further light on the unusual role that the guards are asked to play in the Kallipolis. Though the dogs (and guards) are supposed to be gentle with their familiars, they are also supposed to be "fierce" with their enemies. Since the guards are to be both the ruling class domestically and the soldier class externally, we can infer that Plato means the guards will be kind to their citizens and "fierce" toward their neighbors. And since they are soldiers, their ferocity must play out in their prosecution of necessary wars. Yet in both *Republic* Book I and elsewhere,[10] Socrates adopts the position that the truly philosophical person will never harm others, since harm makes people worse, and the virtuous person will never contribute to the diminishing of virtue in the world. How then can it be the part of the philosophers to have a "fierce" character and be prepared to do harm to others, when according to Socrates it is not the part of philosophers or virtuous people to do harm to anyone?[11] Once again it seems that, in order to exercise their responsibilities in caring for the citizens, Plato needs to claim for the guards special moral permissions that are at odds with the theory of virtue he might promote in other circumstances.

Why does Plato believe that the guards (and the guards alone) have this special set of moral permissions? To answer that question fully, it is necessary to consider the role the guards play in the larger conceptual system that Plato's *Republic* imagines. To begin with, the role of the guards emerges by deduction from Plato's articulation of the "one man, one job" principle: Socrates' inference from the interdependence of human beings and the consequent need for a division of labor that the best society would most perfectly embody the principle of specialization (the principle that

---

owner because they "know" him. But this sense of "knowledge" as "familiarity" is surely far too shallow to be the kind of "knowledge" Plato thinks the true philosopher will love: one can be comfortable with the familiar without being the least bit "knowledgeable" of it in the philosophical sense, whereas one can also surely be more truly "knowledgeable" in being critical of an abusive master than in being uncritically devoted and obedient to him.

[9] *Republic* 375c.

[10] In *Crito*, pp. 42–43; cf. *Republic* 335ae.

[11] This might have something to do with the issue of differential treatment of Greeks vs. barbarians discussed later in the work (*Republic* 470de). But even if this provided an adequate answer to the moral question (which it doesn't), it seems unlikely that as a practical political matter they will be able to limit their "harming" to just Greeks.

turns out later to be the very foundation of what Socrates will say "justice" really is). Since for each social function there must be some class of persons best suited for it, it follows that, if a city is to be well guarded, there must be some class of citizens best suited to the function of guarding – in the sense of both bearing arms externally and keeping peace and order internally. At first Plato's description of the guards' duties – that they will be not only warriors but also *rulers* – seems to defy the logic of the "one man, one job" principle, since the principle seems to require two different classes to perform what are after all at least analytically distinguishable functions. Later this apparent paradox is resolved by the clarification of the distinction between the rulers and the auxiliaries: so that the class of rulers is chosen from the eldest and best of the larger class of warriors with philosophical training.

Plato's belief that the guards' special role of public leadership requires them to contravene the rules of morality prescribed for ordinary citizens helps to explain the extraordinary requirements of education and character that he places on the office of guard. But it also helps to explain Plato's advocacy of retreat from public service amidst the conditions prevailing in the actual political world. This attitude is a feature of Plato's thought from his earliest writings. One of the most notable of its earliest appearances comes in the *Apology*, when Socrates tells his accusers why he has never led an overtly political life. He cites two sorts of dangers, those to a wise man's character as well as to his life. First, Socrates says he believes it would have been wrong for him to have engaged actively in political affairs: Socrates reminds his listeners that he has always claimed to be led by a sign from God that prevents him from doing what is morally wrong, and this sign, he further claims, forbade him to enter a life of direct political involvement. Additionally, Socrates cites the practical dangers that would inevitably have followed on his attempt to assume a position of political leadership in Athens due to his uncompromising commitment to pursuing the Good. "If I had long ago attempted to take part in politics, I should have died long ago," Socrates tells his accusers, because "a man who really fights for justice must lead a private, not a public, life if he is to survive for even a short time."[12]

The dangers that politics holds for the good man remain at the center of Plato's concerns in his later writings. Throughout the *Republic*, Plato dwells on the problem that, in the world as we know it, good individuals will find the sphere of politics inhospitable and unsatisfying and will seek

---

[12] Plato, *Apology*, p. 29 (*P:CW*).

to evade positions of political responsibility. Politics in his day, Plato believed, was in bad shape: there was no city-state and no people worthy of a philosopher's attention, because all of them failed to make use of what philosophers had to offer, and in some cases (such as Socrates') even threatened or destroyed those who tried to intervene. In addition to this risk to their personal safety, there were the further risks that their advice might never be listened to, and that in the process the good person's character might become corrupted. So the philosopher, predictably, will retreat from politics on Plato's account, like a person who knows better than to risk going out in a storm.[13]

At the same time, however, Plato believed that politics *needs* philosophical knowledge for guidance, because Plato held that philosophical knowledge really was relevant to political problems, if only the people affected could better understand *how*. In Plato's most famous metaphor, the world of politics as we know it is likened to a dark cave lit by flickering torchlight, in which only the philosopher has ever seen the outside world in its full illumination and clarity, and therefore possesses the exclusive ability to distinguish mere appearance from reality on all the practical questions confronting those in darkness. This is why Plato insists at such length that the philosophers must be *compelled* to rule. They must be forced to go down again into the cave among the prisoners (which temporarily makes it harder for them to see the real truth) in order to take care of their fellow human beings who are lost without their enlightened guidance.[14] Of course, given their personal preferences, the philosophers would choose the life of contemplative clarity and self-sufficiency to the dim conflicts of political activity. But, Plato tells us, "when their turn comes, then for the benefit of the city each group must endure the trials of politics and be rulers, not as if they were doing a thing that is fine, but one that is necessary."[15] Thus, paradoxically, for Plato not only must the philosophers be forced to rule, but their rule will only be valuable if they are philosophical enough to prefer not to rule. This is a further refutation of Book I's figure of Thrasymachus: to rule really is *not* in the good man's interest, and only someone wise enough to understand this truth can in fact be trusted to rule in such a manner that he pursues, not his own advantage, but the advantage of those he rules.

---

[13] *Republic* 496de.
[14] On this issue, see further in particular Allan Silverman, "Ascent and Descent: The Philosopher's Regret," *Social Philosophy and Policy* 24 (2007): 40–69.
[15] *Republic* 540b. Here I substitute in part the translation of Allan Bloom, *The Republic*, 2nd edn (Basic Books, 1968), p. 219.

The special moral responsibilities – and permissions – which the guards exercise in Plato's *Republic* are among the most important reasons why Plato insists in such great detail on the extraordinary educational regimen – and the accompanying surveillance – of the Kallipolis's regime. At every stage, Plato says, the guards must be tested to show their exclusive devotion to the city and its flourishing. Those from the soldier class who actually rise to the position of ruler, after all the trials and tests of the guards' education and observation, will be those of them who are most "utterly determined to do what is in the city's interests."[16]

Moreover, Plato makes clear, what is best for the city is defined not by the simple and austere needs of the true philosopher, but rather by the more extensive conventional desires of ordinary citizens. In the dialogue's introductory passages, Socrates and his interlocutors specifically choose *not* to define their task in terms of what is needed to maintain a life satisfying the mere subsistence needs of a Diogenes, for example. Glaucon and Adeimantus win over Socrates, who teasingly urges on them a regime characterized by such "relishes" as salt, olives, cheese and boiled vegetables, with figs and beans for dessert, persuading him to abandon this "city of pigs" for a "luxurious city." To include in the city such conventionally valued goods as couches and other furniture, clothes and shoes, painting and jewelry, a different set of values must be invoked and a different set of institutions must likewise be implemented.[17]

In particular, it is the introduction of luxury that ensures that political leaders will have to become instruments of violence, as it becomes increasingly likely that the city will come into armed conflict with other city-states. Under a luxurious regime, Socrates reasons, the city's land holdings will not be large enough to produce the goods necessary to satisfy its expanded appetites: so the city will be forced to appropriate its neighbors' land, as other (luxurious) cities will be forced to do the same in turn to them.[18] As both the warriors and the political leaders of the city, the guards will find themselves forced to play the role of providers for appetites that exceed the merely necessary and aim at unlimited acquisition. It is this above all else that accounts for the origin of war, in Plato's view.

---

[16] *Republic* 412e.

[17] *Republic* 372a–373d. Socrates makes clear that in his opinion the "true city" is the "healthy" if austere city of his first draft version of the Republic, instead of the "swollen and inflamed city" implied by the demand that citizens should have elaborate "relishes." Nevertheless, Socrates concedes, there is some value in conducting the other inquiry, as we can "perhaps" observe the origin of justice there as well (*Republic* 372e–373a). See further Myles Burnyeat, "Culture and Society in Plato's Republic," *Tanner Lectures on Human Values* (University of Utah Press, 1980–), vol. 18.

[18] *Republic* 373de.

This is intrinsic to the nature of the relationship between wealth and virtue, which on Plato's account are ultimately incompatible. Though Plato does not go on to say that the same process applies to the public leader in the luxurious city, he would be hard pressed to explain the difference in situation. For ultimately in the luxurious city political leaders must be procurers of what satisfies even excessive appetites: and so, just as the successful businessman invariably finds the value of morally dubious methods in procuring his own good, so too the guards of the luxurious city seem constrained to be just this kind of businessmen on behalf of the city, providential figures who cannot allow themselves to forego pursuits that might profit the community in their charge. Yet there are limits to this demand as well. In his later dialogue *The Laws*, Plato explains:

> The aim of the statesman who knows what he's about is not in fact the one which most people say the good legislator should have. They'd say that if he knows what he's doing the laws should make the state as huge as and rich as possible; he should give the citizens gold mines and silver mines, and enable them to control as many people as possible by land and sea. And they'd add, too, that to be a satisfactory legislator he must want to see the state as good and as happy as possible. But some of these demands are practical politics, and some are not, and the legislator will confine himself to what can be done, without bothering his head with wishful thinking about impossibilities.[19]

The limits to this providential role of the guards thus appear to be practical rather than moral in nature. They should not aim at *impracticable* acquisition: but they must certainly engage in fighting and killing, in appropriating land that already belongs to their neighbors, and in a variety of other morally exceptional actions, in order to secure the good (very broadly understood) of their inhabitants.

To ensure their capacity for discharging these obligations of their office, the city must shape the guards in such a way that they may share an exclusive devotion to the common good. This is the principal reason why the guards hold both their property and their families in common. By means of these unusual institutions, Plato's regime seeks to eliminate any private interest or attachment that might prevent its guards from choosing on each occasion "what seems best for the city." At the heart of the rationale for these peculiar institutions is the lingering memory of the dispute between Socrates and Thrasymachus in Book I over the question of *whose* good it is the proper role of the rulers to seek – their own good, as Thrasymachus held, or the good of their people, as Socrates contends. In

<hr>

[19] Plato, *Laws* 742–743, trans. Trevor J. Saunders (Penguin, 1972).

defending his view that the proper role of the rulers is to seek the welfare of their people rather than their own good, Socrates constantly has in view Thrasymachus's contention that the nature of ruling is to seek one's own good through using the people for one's own purposes, rather than to seek primarily what is good for them. If the purpose of the guards – like good guard dogs – is to ensure the good of the sheep, but if their role requires them to have power over the sheep to command, what is to ensure that the guards do not themselves become the greatest threat to the sheep?

For Plato, the only answer is that we must rely on the guards' *nature*, which in turn relies on shaping their education so as to produce a responsible rather than a self-seeking personality. So the guards' everyday institutions of communal property and communal family life, as well as the strictures of their odd education, all aim at eliminating any function or purpose from the guards' lives that might rival their exclusive devotion to the people's good. In this light, we can recall that the conceptual origin of the "one man, one job" principle in Plato's argument occurs not in Book II, where the various functions to be performed in the city are defined, but rather in the distinction Socrates draws in Book I between the various social roles (and their accompanying purposes) which may be assigned to persons (in particular to shepherds) in economic life. Socrates' claim is that we must distinguish between the shepherd *qua* shepherd, in his basic function, and the rival role of "money-maker" which the shepherd is obliged to play in economic life, which gives him different (and possibly conflicting) imperatives from those of his basic function. This is thus the moral as well as the practical significance of the "one man, one job" principle. The function of the guards is so important, Plato wants to contend, that no rival role or responsibility can be allowed to interfere with its performance. Thus, whenever the guards privately "possess their own land, houses, and money," Plato tells us, "they will have become householders and farmers instead of guards," and instead of being "the allies of the other citizens," they will instead become "hostile masters."[20] To truly *be* guards, they have to eliminate all competing roles and become exclusively identified with the role of procurer of the public good.

This authenticity of identity and purpose is at the heart of Plato's conception of what makes both a good ruler and a good human being: indeed, it is the philosopher's special preparation to be authentic across both these roles that makes him uniquely suited to take up the role of guard. It is the need for such authenticity between appearance and reality

---

[20] *Republic* 417ab.

that leads Plato to frame the entire inquiry in terms of a search for authentic virtue as opposed to mere appearance, which we find in the moral quandary presented by the example of the invisibility-granting ring belonging to the mythical figure of Gyges. In the story Plato tells, Gyges has the ability to do what he will without anyone else's knowledge, and therefore also without any threat of punishment or other personal consequences. Possessing such a power, Plato has Socrates' interlocutors suggest, there is seemingly no reason why anyone would continue to be just.[21] It is against this standard that Plato proposes to test the claims of his moral theory. The *reality* of moral goodness must be firmly separated from the *appearance* of moral goodness: the good man must be made to seem unjust in others' eyes, and so be stripped of "everything but justice" in order to test whether he truly prefers the reality of justice to its appearance.[22]

The rigorous educational and surveillance institutions which the Republic employs to test the virtue of its aspiring guards aim at isolating this characteristic of moral authenticity which alone can justify entrusting them with the care of the Kallipolis – and with the discretion to decide when it may be necessary for them to supersede the morality it prescribes to ordinary citizens. Yet Plato also remains aware that, under the political and cultural institutions we encounter in the real world, most people will be unable to pass this test, and that therefore the task of attempting to rule is one that is perilous to the real, and the aspiring, philosopher. In saying this, Plato never suggests that there is something intrinsically *wrong* with the actions the true philosopher must undertake in the process of ruling when the occasion requires: his knowledge of the Good will enable him to discriminate between what is really wrong and what is only apparently or conventionally so. But the philosopher who engages in politics in the real world nevertheless runs two sorts of risk: first a risk to his personal safety, since his advice will be received ungraciously in most political circumstances, and may ultimately threaten his life; and, second, a risk that his character may be diminished by encountering those non-philosophical "goods" which constantly present themselves to those in positions of power.

But this conflict within Plato's thought, while introducing some important elements of the problem of dirty hands, has not yet generated that problem's core characteristic: a genuine conflict between real moral duties

---

[21] *Republic* 359d–360c. On this see further Terence Irwin, *Plato's Ethics* (Oxford University Press, 1995), ch. 12.
[22] *Republic* 361bd.

and real public necessities. Certainly Plato *wants* to deny the existence of dirty hands, and frames his argument so that for the most part the choices faced by his Kallipolis's guards do not constitute authentic moral dilemmas. Yet even here Plato has difficulty preventing elements of a dirty hands framework from emerging through the cracks – evidence, perhaps, that Plato's rigorous value monism cannot account for the plurality of genuine moral values at stake in the world he envisions. Moreover, if the shadow of dirty hands can fall across the path of even Plato's political leaders – philosopher-kings possessing scientific knowledge of the good – how much more treacherous is the problem facing the wise man in ordinary non-ideal political circumstances? For, in the real political world, not only are there moral as well as purely self-interested costs to governing but, Plato believes, those costs are clearly so extensive as to make assuming the burdens of political leadership insupportable.

ETHICS AND THE *VITA ACTIVA*

But if that republic which we dream of can nowhere be found, then leisure begins to be a necessity for all of us, because the one thing that might have been preferred to leisure nowhere exists.[23]

Plato's view of the moral and practical dangers of active participation in public life was shared to some degree by all the prominent philosophical traditions of antiquity. Aristotle and his followers, for example, while not endorsing Plato's account, agreed with him that the life of contemplation was in principle the highest attainable by man and therefore was usually to be preferred.[24] Similarly, Epicurus and his followers held that the life of contemplation was unquestionably the most pleasurable, and that the wise man should therefore shun the active life unless something compelled him to participate.[25]

Alone among the ancient philosophical schools, it was the Stoics who defended the life of active participation. Zeno, the founder of Stoicism, maintained that the wise man would participate in public life "unless something prevents him," and generations of Stoic devotees followed

---

[23] Seneca, *De otio*, in Seneca, *Moral Essays*, vol. III, trans. John W. Basore, Loeb Classical Library (Harvard University Press, 1932), p. 200.

[24] Aristotle, *Nicomachean Ethics* I.5; X.7–8; *Politics* VII.2; VII.13. *Complete Works of Aristotle*, ed. Jonathan Barnes (Princeton University Press, 1984).

[25] Diogenes Laertius, "Life of Epicurus," in *Lives of Eminent Philosophers*, vol. II, trans. R. D. Hicks, Loeb Classical Library (Harvard University Press, 1925), p. 446.

Zeno in his limited endorsement of the active life.[26] (This feature of
Stoicism contributed greatly to its favor among Roman politicians such
as Cicero.) But even this vague warmth toward the life of public activity
remained shrouded in ambiguity and eventually provoked internal dissent
within Stoicism, as we can see most evidently in Seneca's treatise *On
Leisure*.[27] In that work, Seneca argues ingeniously from Stoic premises
that, contrary to Zeno's opinion, the wise man would in this world
invariably find himself forced to retreat from public affairs (as indeed
Seneca himself had done).[28] Accepting Zeno's premise that the wise man
will engage in public affairs "unless something prevents him," Seneca goes
on to assert that something will *always* prevent him: for "if the state is too
corrupt to be helped, if it is wholly dominated by evils, then the wise man
will not struggle to no purpose, nor spend himself where nothing is to be
gained."[29]

The life of leisure and philosophical contemplation, on Seneca's view,
can at least be of service to the Stoic *cosmopolis*, the larger commonwealth
constituted by the human race, by advancing the frontiers of knowledge
and understanding. But this is not so, Seneca believes, with regard to the
republics to which we find ourselves attached by mere accident of birth, the
vulgar city-states with which we have to contend in reality. Among such
cities, Seneca contends, there is not "a single one which could tolerate the
wise man, or which the wise man could tolerate."[30] Therefore there is,
according to Seneca, no city where it is genuinely possible for the wise man
to contribute to the public benefit by his political action. On the contrary,
Zeno's condition that the wise man will participate "unless something
prevents him" is a condition that can never truly be fulfilled. Seneca goes
on to draw the appropriate conclusion: "But if that republic which we
dream of can nowhere be found," he tells us, "then leisure begins to be a
necessity for all of us, because the one thing that might have been preferred
to leisure nowhere exists."[31] Thus the Stoic injunction to participate in

---

[26] Diogenes Laertius, "Life of Zeno," in *Lives of Eminent Philosophers*, vol. II, trans. R. D. Hicks, Loeb
Classical Library (Harvard University Press, 1925), p. 224.
[27] Only a portion of this treatise has survived from antiquity. Seneca's readers would have understood
his argument to constitute a self-conscious adaptation of traditional Stoic premises to reach a
surprising conclusion, at odds with the traditional Stoic orthodoxy on the subject.
[28] Seneca retired from the tyrant Nero's service in 62 A.D., followed three years later by his suicide
(prompted by Nero's suggestion).
[29] Seneca, *De otio*, p. 186.   [30] Ibid., p. 200.
[31] Ibid. A similar conclusion is reached in Plato's *Republic* 592ac. On the difficulties of interpreting this
passage, see among many relevant works Allan Bloom's "Interpretive Essay," in Bloom's edition of
The Republic of Plato; and Bernard Williams, "The Analogy of City and Soul in Plato's *Republic*," in

public affairs turns out to be grounded on a utopian aspiration for a non-existent politics in which painful truths and the costly measures of real reform are welcomed rather than resisted.

There was, then, no clear consensus among the schools of ancient philosophy regarding the relative merits of the active versus the contemplative life. But to the extent that ancient philosophy as a whole tended to exhibit a general inclination on the question, that tendency was decidedly against the life of public action; and at least one of the major reasons for this was the potential moral and personal peril which the political arena was thought likely to present for those who acted in it.

If one wishes to hear a spirited ancient defense of public activity against contemplative leisure, therefore, one needs to turn from the schools of the philosophers to that other great locus of ancient moral and political thought, the public forums and law courts that were home to the classical rhetoricians. There we find a broad and firm consensus in *favor* of the life of public activity, grounded in claims not only of personal achievement and glory but also of the benefits to one's fellow citizens derived from a life devoted to public service.

This dispute between the philosophers and the rhetoricians over the relative merits of the active and contemplative lives became (like so many questions of enduring philosophical interest) something of a commonplace in speculative writing and conversation in the ancient world; indeed, it came to be one of the standard exercises that students of both philosophy and rhetoric were expected to discuss in their training. Although there was no shortage of proponents and critics of political activity among the ancient Greeks, the topic came to possess a special significance in the Roman world, where the political and especially military achievements of both individuals and families carried such exceptional importance. To a great extent, in the ancient Greek city-states and even more so in republican Rome, a man was nothing if he was not a soldier or a citizen pursuing fame and glory in the service of his country's greatness.

So just as the rhetoricians came to be more firmly committed than any previous group of thinkers to the defense of political activity, so too the Romans came to bear an equally firm commitment to the active political life as a cultural norm. It is therefore not surprising to find that it is among

E. N. Lee, A. P. D. Mourelatos and R. M. Rorty, eds., *Exegesis and Argument*, *Phronesis* supplementary vol. 1 (1973): 196–206. On the possible connection of this passage to More's *Utopia*, see John M. Parrish, "A New Source for More's 'Utopia'," *Historical Journal* 40 (1997): 493–498.

the rhetorical schools and amidst the Roman people that we find the most sustained effort to discredit the notion that political activity necessarily carried with it serious and ineliminable moral risks – and that we find articulated as well, for the purpose of debunking such claims, the most perspicuous and detailed statement yet to emerge of exactly what was supposed to be at moral risk.

What emerged from these expositions, the most famous of which is probably Cicero's *De Officiis* (or *On Duties*, discussed in greater detail in the following section), was the notion that the supposed moral dangers of politics were intimately bound up with a persistent problem treated in rhetorical theory, namely the idea that there were different spheres of moral appeal with different dimensions of value appropriate to each. Politics, according to this way of thinking, happened to be an area with a built-in dynamic of apparent conflict between the different dimensions of value. To frame the issue as the rhetoricians did: what makes political life appear to be the locus of so much moral conflict is the fact that in politics an additional dimension of moral value weighs far more heavily and urgently than it does in the private lives of individuals, and this dimension was what the rhetoricians called *utilitas*, that is, "benefit" or "expediency." In private life, these theorists claimed, the individual could in a situation of moral conflict choose to focus solely on pursuing *honestas*, that is, what is "honorable" or "morally right," whereas in political life leaders must also consider the impact of the benefits, or costs, of their choices for all those citizens and families in their care.

This framework of moral evaluation emerged above all in the ancient rhetoricians' comments about the special importance that certain values held in certain kinds of debates or arguments. According to most of the ancient rhetorical textbooks, there were three genres of rhetoric: first, *deliberative* rhetoric, speeches endorsing or opposing particular policies in a democratic general assembly or aristocratic council; second, *forensic* rhetoric, speeches made in prosecuting or defending a person or cause in the law courts; and finally, *epideitic* rhetoric, speeches made in praise of a person's life or character, for example in a funeral eulogy. Each of these genres had its own peculiar good on which it naturally focused. For our purposes, we may for convenience's sake collapse the last two categories into a single frame of analysis, as Cicero himself essentially does when treating the problem in *On Duties*. The genre of deliberative rhetoric, set in the public assembly, had as its special good the consideration of advantage or utility: appeals to expediency properly had greatest weight in the councils of state, where the actions and policies of the city were debated to great consequence. The other genres of rhetoric, the forensic rhetoric of the law courts and the epedeitic rhetoric of personal eulogy, focused on evaluating the actions and character of individuals. As such, these genres had as their own peculiar good not the advantage of a city as a whole, but rather the considerations of *honorableness* and *justice*: the moral goodness of a person's character, and the moral rightness of judging him in a particular way.[32]

If possible, the textbooks taught, rhetoricians should always try to arrange their arguments so as to contend that *both* advantage on the one hand, and honorableness or justice on the other, converged in endorsing their chosen cause. So, for example, in the first scene of Thucydides' great *History of the Peloponnesian War* we find the Corinthians contending both that the Athenians have *wronged* the Peloponnesians and that they pose an imminent *threat* to the balance of power.[33] But the rhetoricians also realized that it might not always be possible to arrange a compelling argument in such a way as to appeal to both values with equal plausibility: and in such circumstances, the rhetoricians urged, the speaker must concentrate specifically on that set of values that were the peculiar good of the forum in which they were arguing. Thus, later in Thucydides' *History*, in the famous dialogue at the court of Melos, the Athenians explicitly frame their argument to the Melian council solely in terms of the advantage of the city, abandoning any pretence of a claim that honorableness or justice were also on their side.[34]

The idea that advantage lay in some sense at the foundation of all moral questions was something of an ancient commonplace. Even a thinker such as Plato, who at first glance might appear hostile to such a view, carefully sets up the problem investigated in *The Republic* so that its resolution maintains that justice itself ultimately *is* some kind of advantage (a belief it shares even with the discarded view of the shamed interlocutor Thrasymachus). Among the rhetoricians themselves, the moral authority of advantage was taken for granted even more directly. Thus, in his exposition of the concept, Cicero tells us that the pursuit of utility, or that which is conducive to comfort and happiness in life, is a natural and even necessary component of political life. Indeed, Cicero goes on to claim that we are

[32] Again, because of the gendered character of such societies, the subjects of such speeches would almost invariably have been male.
[33] Thucydides, *History of the Peloponnesian War*, ed. T. E. Wick (Random House, 1982), p. 39.
[34] Ibid., pp. 350–351. The Melians in reply make the interesting move of accepting the terms of discussion, then arguing that it is to the *advantage* of the Athenians in the long run to have norms of honorableness or justice to which to appeal (an argument which fails however to move the Athenians themselves).

"irresistibly drawn toward" advantage, and that each person will of necessity "exert himself to the utmost to secure it."[35]

But justice and especially the closely related quality of honorableness or moral rightness would also have held a special importance in ancient culture because of its connection with the two great ancient values of virtue and glory. On Cicero's account, honorableness was grounded firmly in the virtues: what was honorable was ultimately what conduced to Plato's four cardinal virtues of wisdom, courage, moderation, and most importantly justice. In addition, the concept of honorableness was, as its translation suggests, closely linked with the concept of glory: what was honorable was, if not what actually *received* glory and renown, then at the very least what was *worthy* of glory and renown, what would receive such praise if all the relevant moral facts were known to good and impartial judges.

Because of this feature of the framework of their craft, the rhetoricians found themselves almost of necessity adopting a moral view somewhat akin to what contemporary ethical theorists would refer to as value pluralism (though that was not of course the terminology that the rhetoricians themselves used). As Max Weber was later to observe (employing yet another conceptual vocabulary), the idea of a plurality of values was easier to accept in a polytheistic culture whose religions featured a plurality of gods, each of whom represented, ostensibly, different and sometimes competing moral and cultural concerns.[36]

This worldview, however, was yet another point at which the rhetoricians found themselves sharply at odds with the prevailing wisdom within the schools of ancient philosophy. For within those schools all the major figures (with the sole exception of Aristotle) were united in their belief that there was only *one* good – though they were *not* agreed in any sense on what that one good actually was. The classic exposition of a system of value monism is that of Plato. We have seen that Plato exhibits an unusual degree of anxiety about internal conflict in both the city and the soul, an anxiety that leads him to adopt unusually strenuous measures designed to promote unity and to eliminate private and divisive institutions. It is from this anxiety of Plato's that the doctrine of the *divided self* finds its most influential point of entry in Western thought; and that concept, as we will see further in the chapters that follow, would come to hold sway over

[35] Cicero, *De Officiis* (hereafter *DO*), ed. and trans. Walter Miller, Loeb Classical Library (Harvard University Press, 1913), III.101, p. 378.
[36] Max Weber, "Science as a Vocation," in H. H. Gerth and C. Wright Mills, eds., *From Max Weber: Essays in Sociology* (Oxford University Press, 1946), pp. 148–149.

the most influential theories of human psychology from that point on, from St. Augustine through Dr. Freud through to contemporary philosophy's interest in the idea of value pluralism.[37] Yet Plato introduces the divided self not to recommend value pluralism as such; rather, he sees the moral division within the city and the soul as a problem to be overcome. For Plato, the divided character of the soul represents a disorder that needs to be eliminated, a mutinous self-aggrandizement of the lesser parts of the soul (such as the appetites) that threatens the rightful authority and rule of the greater faculties of the soul (in particular its reason). Thus Plato posits one Good that is the source of all value and meaning in the world, just as the sun is the fundamental source that both nurtures and illuminates the life of our physical existence.

Plato's classical value monism was an extreme version of the position. But the other ancient philosophical schools, while disagreeing about what the good was, nevertheless agreed that the good must be unitary, that there must be *one* good: some single standard by which all other good things must be measured and with respect to which all the other apparent goodnesses in the world were ultimately grounded. The Epicureans, for example, notoriously held that the only true good was pleasure (and the absence of pain). The Stoics, likewise, held that the only true good was virtue. Aristotle alone among the ancient theorists suggested that values might be plural, though his was by today's standards quite a soft version of value pluralism: he held that goods were plural and incommensurable, though not ultimately *incomparable*,[38] and that consequently real conflicts of value could arise which could be practically resolved though not theoretically eliminated.

Ancient philosophy, then, committed to the view that the source of moral value was ultimately unitary, tended to dismiss any genuine possibility of an ultimate conflict between incommensurable values. Instead, that problem found its most thorough and searching treatment in Cicero's celebrated treatise *On Duties*, perhaps the most widely read and influential textbook of moral philosophy for more than a thousand years to come.[39]

[37] On this theme in Augustine, see especially E. J. Hundert, "Augustine and the Sources of the Divided Self," *Political Theory* 20 (1992): 86–104; more generally, see also Charles Taylor, *Sources of the Self* (Harvard University Press, 1989) esp. Part One and Conclusion, and Michael Walzer, *Thick and Thin*, ch. 5. (Notre Dame University Press, 1994).

[38] On this distinction see Ruth Chang, "Introduction" to Ruth Chang, ed., *Incommensurability, Incomparability, and Practical Reason* (Harvard University Press, 1998).

[39] On the influence of Cicero's work, see especially (among many sources) Quentin Skinner, *The Foundations of Modern Political Thought*, vol. 1 (Cambridge University Press, 1978) and Richard Tuck, "Humanism and Political Thought," in Anthony Goodman and Angus MacKay, eds., *The Impact of Humanism on Western Europe* (Longman, 1990).

Although Cicero takes the possibility of conflicting values more seriously than any of his philosophical predecessors, in the end he too argues that what is truly expedient can never ultimately conflict with what is truly morally right. Yet despite his own certitude, Cicero's treatment of the issue exposes deeper fault lines of value conflict than he was willing to acknowledge, in a way that, while ostensibly solving the ethical problems surrounding political action, in fact makes it even more apparent how difficult they are to resolve.

CICERO'S POLITICAL THOUGHT

There are some acts either so repulsive or so wicked, that a wise man will not commit them even to save his country ... [But] it turns out conveniently that the occasion cannot arise when it could be to the state's interest to have the wise man do any of those things ... [40]

Few societies have ever ingrained into their culture more thoroughly than the Romans the notion that political service and leadership were of key moral significance. And perhaps no Roman defended that notion more aggressively and influentially than Marcus Tullius Cicero. A leading Roman orator and legal advocate, Cicero's moment of glory came during his year-long service as consul, when (as he never tired of reminding his readers) his actions helped avert an attempted coup led by the conspirator Catiline. Cicero's actions in the case of Catiline – which included the extra-legal executions of several key conspirators – left his subsequent public career a bit besmirched and subject to continuing legal jeopardy. Yet even in his subsequent career (mainly literary in nature) Cicero relished the memory of his momentous public actions in office. As one of the most earnest advocates of the life of public action as opposed to philosophical withdrawal, it makes sense that Cicero focused much of his attention on questions of political ethics. In particular, Cicero made it one of his central aims to disarm the idea that there could possibly be a genuine conflict between moral rightness on the one hand and expediency on the other. Such a concern would naturally have been a priority for an advocate of public activity addressing an ancient and particularly a Roman audience. For within the Roman system of values the possibility of such a conflict, if allowed, would be a potential cause of serious moral and political instability.

No ancient work displays the distinctive moral values that animated Roman public life more vividly than Cicero's treatise *On Duties*. First

[40] *DO* 1.159, p. 162.

among these values, we find an unrivaled desire for political and military *glory* and an unrivaled ferocity in its pursuit. Cicero observes that practically all Romans pursue difficult and dangerous work in their public careers with the expectation that they will eventually have glory as a reward for their achievements.[41] The historian Sallust, similarly, had attributed the great achievements of the Roman republic to the strength of "the desire for glory that had possessed men's hearts."[42] For Sallust, the Roman people's "lust for glory" was "insatiable," and that desire drove them on to greater deeds of military courage and daring in order to win what they counted as "true wealth": namely reputation and nobility in the eyes of their fellow citizens.[43] Consequently, for the *vir virtutis*, that manly and virtuous ideal of Roman achievement, nothing could be more costly than the loss of one's honorableness,[44] since this was to cut at the very heart of one's worthiness of glory and respect.

Equally central to the Roman value system was the preeminence of one's loyalties to one's republic above all other commitments, even the central and extensive commitment owed to one's family. The *vir virtutis* of Roman life was expected to put his city above all rivals. In a remark that would sum up for later generations Cicero's striking claims about the moral supremacy of the republic, Cicero asserts that for every citizen the republic "ought to be the dearest thing in the world."[45] Even the contemplative man of leisure, Cicero expects, would unquestionably cast aside all his private pursuits if his country were seriously threatened and he could save it.[46]

If one wished to promote and glorify the life of political activity, therefore, no challenge could be more potent than the suggestion that there could possibly (much less inevitably) be irresolvable conflicts between what the utility of the city required on the one hand and what individual honorableness or moral rightness might demand on the other. For, given

---

[41] *DO* 1.65, p. 66. Cicero's full views on the subject of glory, set forth in his *De Gloria*, are now lost.

[42] Sallust, *The Jugurthine War and the Conspiracy of Catiline* (Penguin, 1963), p. 179.

[43] Ibid., p. 180. This desire for glory, Sallust acknowledges, could go to morally deleterious extremes, but even such ambition was "a fault which after all comes nearer to being a virtue" (p. 182). What really set the Romans downhill, according to Sallust, was when their lust for honor became replaced by a lust for wealth. See pp. 181–183.

[44] I will use the terms "honorableness" and "moral rightness" interchangeably as translations of *honestas* and its variants (following the practice of many translators). It is important to recognize, however, that the "moral" in "moral rightness" invokes not the technical philosophical sense that term carries especially among contemporary post-Kantian ethicists, but rather the looser sense which the term carries in popular culture.

[45] "Debet esse carissima" (*DO* III.95, p. 372). This remark of Cicero's is made a central focus of attention in Richard Tuck's article "Humanism and Political Thought."

[46] *DO* 1.154, p. 158.

his preeminent loyalties to the welfare of the Roman republic, the political actor, as public servant, knew his duties required him to pursue the public interest, or what was publicly expedient. But if this duty could regularly be expected to tarnish his most treasured moral commodity, his honorableness – the indispensable precondition for the glory he sought through political activity in the first place – the *vir virtutis* could hardly be blamed if he chose to avoid such conflicts by steering clear altogether of the morally treacherous domain of public life.

So throughout his treatise *On Duties* Cicero repeatedly attacks the "pernicious" idea that the honorable and the beneficial could ever genuinely conflict, offering in the process perhaps the most extensive ancient analysis of the phenomenon of plural and conflicting values. Indeed, he maintains, it is immoral even to suggest that the value of moral rightness can be compared with that of utility.[47] It is of course possible to have conflicts *within* these frameworks, Cicero acknowledges: for example, of two morally right actions, one may be morally better, and of two expedient acts, one may be more expedient than the other.[48] These conflicts we can resolve merely by exercising comparative judgment. But he insists that no comparison *across* these spheres of value are possible, for roughly the classic Stoic reason that the claims of what is morally right always trump those of expediency. "If anything is morally right," Cicero explains, "it is expedient, and if anything is not morally right, it is not expedient."[49] Yet the reverse is not true for Cicero: what is expedient is *not* necessarily morally right. So, at least on the face of things, Cicero thinks what is morally right always trumps what is expedient, and questions of what is expedient only arise once one has already settled whether the action in question is morally right.[50]

But Cicero's treatment of this issue runs considerably deeper than his surface pronouncement of the impossibility of a conflict between the honorable and the beneficial. For despite Cicero's repeated avowals that no conflict is possible, the ghost of the suggestion that there might be such a conflict continues to loom over Cicero's moral and political theory,

---

[47] *DO* II.9, p. 176; *DO* III.17–18, pp. 284–286.   [48] *DO* I.152. pp. 154–156.

[49] *DO* III.11, pp. 278–280. He acknowledges that if one held a different standard of value, for example the Epicurean standard of pleasure and the absence of pain, and as a consequence believed that "virtue is worth cultivating only because it is productive of advantage," then one might well believe "that expediency sometimes clashes with moral rectitude" (*DO* III.12–13, p. 280).

[50] This makes Cicero's view, on this dimension at least, similar to Kantian and neo-Kantian moral theories that prioritize "the right" over "the good," and set questions of right as a threshold condition for evaluating questions of utility. See further John Rawls, *A Theory of Justice* (Harvard University Press, 1971); Michael Sandel, *Liberalism and the Limits of Justice* (Cambridge University Press, 1983).

sustained in particular by his vividly rendered depiction of the feeling of *apparent* conflicts between these two spheres of value. "When expediency seems to be pulling one way," Cicero tells us, "moral right seems to be calling back in the opposite direction," with the result that "the mind is distracted in its inquiry and brings to it the irresolution that is born of deliberation."[51] Nor is this feeling entirely baseless, according to Cicero: it is instead a consequence of the disturbing ambiguity introduced by Cicero's assertion that the claims of moral rightness and of expediency may not always be what they appear to be at first glance.

Cicero's suggestion that what *appears* to be a moral conflict might not be in fact a genuine moral conflict would prove to be a profoundly influential move in the development of the story we are pursuing. This was a natural move for Cicero to make, since he had identified himself especially with the philosophical tradition of skepticism, even more than with the teachings of the Stoics (with respect to which he has been perhaps more familiarly recognized). Ancient skepticism had maintained that what was crucial to moral life was to prevent ourselves from being swept up in our passions, and therefore also in those beliefs that gave our passions their warrant and import.[52] Instead, the skeptics held, the wise man would learn to withhold his assent from those beliefs that tended to sweep him up in unwarranted passions and commitments, and instead reserve his mental and spiritual energies for those few beliefs and principles without which he could not get along practically in the world.

Cicero's association with this school of thought stemmed partly from its natural affinity with the ancient theory and practice of rhetoric, which also held that nothing in life was indubitable and that with respect to virtually any question there were two sides to be fairly argued. In particular, the schools of ancient rhetoric preached that analysis of any problem required close attention to context: often it was possible to argue that an ordinarily accepted principle did not apply in the context of altered circumstances. Among the rhetoricians' favorite ways of expressing this was by employing the metaphor of the stage: the actions of a person playing a role, in the midst of a drama neither scripted nor produced by their own choice, were not the same actions, and should not be judged in the same way, as they might be in a different, non-theatrical context.[53]

---

[51] *DO* 1.9, p. 10.

[52] Here I follow a line of argument developed most familiarly by Martha Nussbaum, *The Therapy of Desire* (Princeton University Press, 1996).

[53] The metaphor was used not only by the rhetoricians but also by a variety of ancient philosophical schools, notably the Stoics (and in particular Epictetus). See A. A. Long, *Epictetus* (Clarendon Press, 2002), p. 243.

The position Cicero takes on the question of *apparent* conflicts of moral value in *On Duties* shows his reliance on the traditions of both ancient rhetoric and philosophical skepticism. On Cicero's analysis, there are two distinct ways in which this problem of deceptive appearances might play itself out. The first is that what appears to be morally wrong but expedient might turn out not to be expedient after all. Sometimes, Cicero claims, what is morally wrong tries to masquerade as what is expedient in order to win approval; indeed, he asserts (in language reminiscent of contemporary discussions of dirty hands dilemmas), in certain cases "expediency is so presented as to make it appear not only morally right to do what seems expedient, but even morally wrong not to do it."[54] In claiming this, Cicero draws on an observation developed within the moral tradition of the schools of rhetoric: namely that there were particular virtues that bore a resemblance to, and could even be described as "neighbors" of, particular vices.[55] So, for example, the vice of foolhardiness closely resembled, and thus might easily be mistaken for, the virtue of courage; the virtue of generosity closely resembled, and might easily be mistaken for, the actions of the spendthrift. Practitioners of ancient rhetoric relied on this "neighboring" proximity of evaluative terms as one of the crucial weapons in their arsenal, since it was through this mechanism that they were frequently able to redescribe, and thus re-evaluate, those actions or policies that it fell to them to declaim or defend. This blurry feature of the moral landscape (on the rhetoricians' view) helped make it possible to mistake a mere appearance of expediency for what was truly expedient; and, accordingly, it also became possible to create the (false) appearance of a conflict between what was expedient and what was morally right.

Cicero offers as an example the murder by Romulus the founder of Rome of his brother Remus. Romulus, Cicero tells us, under a "specious appearance of expediency," decided "that it was more expedient for him to reign alone than to share the throne with another," thus prompting him to commit the horrific crime of fratricide in the (mistaken) pursuit of his own (apparent) expediency.[56] Cicero also considers the case of the merchant who must choose whether to conceal information in a commercial transaction that might benefit those with whom he is trading, such as failing to disclose the faults of a house for sale, or even selling famine victims food at

---

[54] *DO* III.56, p. 324.
[55] On this see further Quentin Skinner, *Reason and Rhetoric in the Philosophy of Hobbes* (Cambridge University Press, 1997), pp. 153–161.
[56] *DO* III.41, p. 308.

exorbitant prices while concealing the fact that a cargo of grain will shortly arrive in the port. In these cases Cicero concludes that the sellers are morally required to reveal the truth to their customers, and that the appearance of expediency from such shady business practices is merely illusory. There is nothing dishonest about "merely holding one's peace," Cicero claims, but a moral line is crossed when for one's own profit one tries "to keep others from finding out something that you know, when it is for their interest to know it."[57]

We must be extremely careful in the face of such "deceptive" appearances, Cicero tells us, because of the devastating potential consequences for the character of the person who allows himself to be misled by them. For someone who believes that moral rightness and expediency can truly conflict and that he may have to choose between them, Cicero believes,

> will be capable of any sort of dishonesty, any sort of crime. For if he reasons, "That is, to be sure, the right course, but this course brings advantage," he will not hesitate in his mistaken judgment to divorce two conceptions that Nature has made one; and that spirit opens the door to all sorts of dishonesty, wrongdoing, and crime.[58]

Cicero's stern condemnation of such reasoning, however, rests on arguments that are not entirely convincing. He recognizes the force of Plato's argument about the Ring of Gyges and seems committed to finding a rationale for the true inexpediency of vice which would satisfy that rigorous standard.[59] Like Plato, Cicero wants to offer a prudential, even self-interested, argument for the ultimate value of honesty, qualified (again as in Plato's argument) by the larger-view consideration that dishonesty is somehow damaging to one's most precious possession, one's character. Yet, unlike Plato, Cicero, ever conscious of the public eye, cannot quite refrain from casting the prudential considerations he offers in terms of the effect of dishonesty on one's reputation. For example, Cicero asserts that a man who concealed information in a business transaction would be "no candid or sincere or straightforward or upright or honest man, but rather one who is shifty, sly, artful, shrewd, underhand, cunning, one grown old in fraud or subtlety."[60] Yet he immediately goes on to appeal not to the intrinsic demerits of such character traits but rather to their costs to one's reputation, asking: "is it not inexpedient to subject oneself to all these terms of reproach and many more beside?"[61] Thus Cicero's argument that moral

---

[57] *DO* III.57, pp. 324–326.   [58] *DO* III.75, pp. 344–346.
[59] *DO* III.37–39, pp. 304–308; cf. *DO* III.76–78, pp. 346–350.   [60] *DO* III.57, p. 326.   [61] Ibid.

rightness can never conflict with expediency seems, at least in the instances covered by this rationale, to rely upon considerations of reputation ultimately grounded in prudential considerations rather than the intrinsic value of moral rightness itself.

But the second and even more important variation for our purposes is the reverse of the situation just discussed: namely, the possibility that what appears to be expedient but morally wrong might turn out after all not to be *really* morally wrong.[62] On its face, this might appear to be simply the mirror image of the claim we have just considered: namely, that what is morally wrong but expedient could turn out to be not really expedient. But in fact this seemingly parallel move transports Cicero's argument to a new plane entirely. To begin with, the significance of Cicero's argument, as we observed earlier, was always heavily weighted toward the priority of what is morally right over what is expedient: if something is expedient, it could still be morally wrong, but if something is morally wrong, it could never really be expedient. Thus, to claim that something morally wrong might appear (falsely) to be expedient is merely to reiterate the central premise of Cicero's treatment of this issue. But to claim that what is expedient but apparently morally wrong might not be *really* morally wrong is to open a major loophole in the theory, one wide enough to accommodate a much broader range of conduct than might otherwise have been contemplated.

In addition, there is another and equally significant reason why this second move of Cicero's goes beyond mere parallel argument into new theoretical territory. When Cicero discusses the possibility that what is morally wrong might sometimes be mistaken for what is expedient, he seems to allow that any number of contingent factors might lead to such cases of mistaken identity: there are as many possible misidentifications of what is truly expedient as there are reasons that something could *be* expedient. But in the case of Cicero's second reason, we find a new and different reasoning at work. For Cicero's contention is that there is a *single* reason why something that appears to be morally wrong might turn out not to be actually morally wrong: and this reason is the fact that there might be a *political* justification for the action, or at least a justification grounded at some level in the responsibility that citizens have for the welfare of their fellows.

We can see that this is at the basis of Cicero's logic first by means of the examples he employs in illustrating this claim. Cicero first considers the classic case of the madman's sword, familiar to readers of Book I of Plato's

---

[62] *DO* III.19, p. 286.

Republic. If a friend loans you his sword, which you promise to return, and subsequently madness overtakes him, ought you to observe your promise? Cicero (like Plato) answers that you should not, because your responsibility for your friend's safety and welfare – and for the safety and welfare of others he might harm – obviates or at least outweighs the duty created by the promise. A similar logic applies to Cicero's reference to a tyrannicide who betrays and murders the tyrant even though they are the closest of friends.[63] Sometimes in promise-keeping as in other areas of moral action, Cicero concludes, we will find it "right and proper . . . to evade and not to observe what truth and honor would usually demand"; and when such occasions arise we find that "those duties which seem most becoming" to the good man "undergo a change and take on a contrary aspect."[64]

This kind of appeal to public responsibility stands at the basis of every instance in which Cicero suggests that what is apparently morally wrong may not in fact be morally wrong: and at its root seems to lie the belief that the preeminent claims of the public sphere can actually make what would ordinarily be morally wrong count instead as morally right. Extending the example of the madman's sword, Cicero frames the problem in terms of a stark dilemma of public priorities opposing private morality:

Suppose that a man who has entrusted money to you proposes to make war upon your common country, should you restore the trust? I believe you should not; for you would be acting against the state, which ought to be the dearest thing in the world to you.[65]

Why should this be so? In Cicero's theory, the basis of the moral preeminence exercised by political claims is to be found in the extensive moral duties stemming from our natural *sociability* as human beings. According to Cicero, individuals are inclined by nature to associate with their fellow human beings, and this sociability precedes and is the cause of their mutual interdependence, rather than its effect. "As swarms of bees do not gather for the sake of making honeycomb but make the honeycomb because they are gregarious by nature," Cicero explains, "so human beings – and to a much higher degree – exercise their skill together in action and thought because they are naturally gregarious."[66] There are of course limits to this natural sociability. It is also natural, Cicero believes, that we weigh our own concerns more heavily than those of others and tend to give

---

[63] Ibid. This is likely a reference to Marcus Brutus's recent role in the assassination of his friend Julius Caesar.

[64] *DO* I.31, p. 30.   [65] *DO* III.95, pp. 370–372.   [66] *DO* I.157, p. 160.

ourselves preferential treatment in most cases.[67] And this is as it should be: "we are not required to sacrifice our own interests and surrender to others what we need for ourselves"; instead "each one should consider his own interests, as far as he may without injury to his neighbour's."[68] Nevertheless, we must restrain this self-preference whenever it would tend to lead us into dishonorable or dishonest conduct. "For a man to take something from his neighbour and to profit by his neighbour's loss," Cicero asserts,

is more contrary to Nature than is death or poverty or pain or anything else that can affect either our person or our property. For, in the first place, injustice is fatal to social life and fellowship between man and man. For, if we are so disposed that each, to gain some personal profit, will defraud or injure his neighbour, then those bonds of human society which are most in accord with Nature's laws, must of necessity be broken.[69]

Thus for Cicero it is fundamental to our humanity, and consequently also to our status as moral agents, that we allow ourselves to be guided by our human sociability and its two fundamental principles (drawn in part from the Stoics and later echoed through centuries of natural law tradition): "first, that no harm be done to anyone," and "second, that the common interests be conserved."[70] In following these general principles rigorously, Cicero claims we will find that they are sometimes "modified under changing circumstances," and when this occurs "moral duty also undergoes a change, and it does not always remain the same."[71] For example, a good person will ordinarily accord the claims of property great respect,[72] and consequently will not steal for his own benefit even from a person he judges to be "perfectly useless."[73] But even such an ordinarily contemptible act, Cicero believes, might be permissible if the motivation for the theft is not selfish gain but rather the public good. For example, if the good person in question is a philosopher who steals bread to

---

[67] *DO* I.30, p. 30; *DO* III.22, pp. 288–290.   [68] *DO* III.42, p. 310.
[69] *DO* III.21–22, p. 288.   [70] *DO* I.31, pp. 30–32.   [71] Ibid.
[72] *DO* II.73–78, pp. 248–254. On this subject see further Julia Annas, "Cicero on Stoic Moral Philosophy and Private Property," in Miriam Griffin and Jonathan Barnes, eds., *Philosophia Togata* (Oxford University Press, 1989), as well as Neal Wood, *Cicero's Social and Political Thought* (University of California Press, 1988), ch. 6. In our societies, of course, where advocacy of property rights typically goes together with championing commercial society, it would be easy to interpret Cicero as being merely concerned with promoting commercial interests at the expense of rival values. But in Roman society, the principal virtue of owning property from a political point of view was that it freed you up to perform public service, since you were not bound to follow your own affairs at the expense of the public affairs. (And indeed Cicero explicitly takes this position, arguing that those professions which required people to work for a living were unsuitable to the kind of life he idealized, a life of public action.)
[73] *DO* III.29, p. 296.

survive so that he might be able, "by remaining alive, to render signal service to the state and to human society – if from that motive one should take something from another, it would not be a matter for censure."[74] Cicero's one caveat is that such a person must "beware that self-esteem and self-love do not find in such a transfer of possessions a pretext for wrongdoing."[75]

Each of Cicero's illustrations of how an apparently dishonorable action might actually prove honorable in specific circumstances finds its ultimate justification in the preeminent moral claims of the republic over its citizens. For example, in the classic case of the sinking ship with no lifeboat, two wise men who have only one plank to bear one of them to safety will conclude that they must decide between them which one's life "is more valuable either for his own sake or for that of his country," and then agree to distribute the lone plank accordingly.[76] Similarly, Cicero considers a case where a son discovers that his father means to commit some crime. Should the son turn the father in, betraying his family, or shield him, thus betraying his country? Cicero, recognizing the powerful claims of family loyalty in the Roman system of honor, acknowledges that, so long as the son can prevent the crime from occurring, he should avoid turning his father in – though even this turns out to have a political justification, in that it is in the country's interest to have sons who are fiercely loyal to their fathers. But when pressed Cicero is perfectly prepared to acknowledge that "if things point toward the destruction of the state, he will sacrifice his father to the safety of his country."[77] Thus, throughout this set of cases Cicero tries to preserve as much authority as he can for the intuitions of conventional morality while at the same time arguing that a rationale of public utility can in the final analysis be an absolute trump over competing moral considerations.

Perhaps the oddest illustration can be found in Cicero's remarks on the case of the dance-contingent inheritance. Suppose, Cicero suggests, that a benefactor offers to leave someone 100 million sesterces in his will provided the prospective heir promises

to dance publicly in broad daylight in the forum; and suppose that the wise man has given his promise to do so, because the rich man would not leave him his fortune on any other condition; should he keep his promise or not? I wish he had made no such promise; that, I think, would have been in keeping with his dignity. But, seeing that he has made it, it will be morally better for him, if he believes it

---

[74] *DO* III.30, p. 296.   [75] *DO* III.31, p. 296.   [76] *DO* III.90, p. 364.   [77] Ibid., pp. 364–366.

morally wrong to dance in the forum, to break his promise and refuse to accept his inheritance rather than to keep his promise and accept it . . .[78]

Thus far Cicero has cast the situation as a conflict among two ostensibly dishonorable courses of action: and the *less* dishonorable, he has concluded – in a stunning contrast with modern moral intuitions – is to break one's vow rather than submit to the great indignity of dancing in the forum. But no sooner has Cicero settled this apparent conflict on the grounds of the greater degree of honorableness of one of the heir's choices than he proceeds to open a backdoor by which to admit an even *stronger* claim on behalf of the public utility. Thus, having established that the dishonorableness of dancing in the forum is sufficiently morally powerful to override the obligation to keep a promise, Cicero immediately goes on to establish that this dishonorableness *cannot* rival the moral claims asserted by the needs of the public realm. So the heir should break his vow and refuse to dance in the forum "unless perhaps," Cicero proceeds to argue, "he contributes the money to the state to meet some grave crisis."[79] In that sort of case, Cicero goes on to assert, "to promote thereby the interests of one's country, it would not be morally wrong even to dance, if you please, in the forum."[80]

So, as we have seen, for Cicero our moral principles, including our honorableness, are ultimately founded upon our sociability, and conse-quently they can be trumped by sociable motives (provided only that we are suitably impartial about their application). Cicero does gesture toward a limit to this priority of the public utility over private honorableness. In Book I, Cicero tells us that "there are some acts either so repulsive or so wicked, that a wise man will not commit them even to save his country."[81] Such outrages, Cicero claims, "the wise man . . . will not think of doing . . . for the sake of his country; no more will his country consent to have it done for her."[82] But Cicero very shortly lets himself off the hook with respect to even these limits, by letting us know that such a conflict is ultimately impossible: it turns out "conveniently," Cicero asserts with unintentional irony, "that the occasion cannot arise when it could be to the state's interest to have the wise man do any of those things."[83] It is this confidence that the republic's necessities will never require any of its citizens to undertake anything truly (rather than apparently) dishonorable, coupled with his willingness to adjust his moral yardstick whenever the public utility is the motive of action, that Cicero offers as the ultimate justification of his claim that the honorable and the

---

[78] *DO* III.93, p. 368. [79] Ibid. [80] Ibid., pp. 368–370.
[81] *DO* I.159, p. 162. [82] Ibid. [83] Ibid.

useful can never conflict. If the public interest *does* conflict with private honorableness, then we move the goal posts accordingly.

It is for this reason also that Cicero can call without embarrassment for the good man to leap into the fray of the active life in pursuit of the public good, for "in no other way can a government be administered or greatness of spirit be made manifest."[84] This was a difficult enough argument for Cicero to sustain even within his own conveniently arranged moral and political framework: but its underlying rationale was to infect Western philosophy with an even greater degree of instability when it came to be juxtaposed against an almost directly opposite value system, that promoted by the early (pre-Augustinian) Christians of the first centuries A.D.

THE EARLY CHRISTIAN POLITICAL ETHIC

*When it comes to taking a stand for the faith, there is no room for the plea of necessity.
You can be under no necessity to sin if you have made up your mind that the one
necessity is not to sin.*[85]

The political ethic of early Christianity was inhospitable in a variety of significant ways to the moral priorities of Cicero and his fellow Romans. The thought of the early Christians was diverse; but we can generalize to an extent about the moral and political preoccupations of the early movement. One such generalization concerns their attitude toward the Roman world in which they found themselves situated. While it is possible to overstate the hostility of Constantinian-age Christians to Rome, it is clear that the early Christian thinkers reflexively tended to set themselves in self-conscious opposition to the priorities and values of Roman politics and culture.[86] Central to their opposition to Rome was their absolute rejection of the claim, most famously articulated by Cicero but pervasive throughout Roman political thought, that the welfare of the Roman republic was the touchstone for all moral standards of public and private life.

This reflexive opposition to Roman values was hardly a contingent reaction. Rather, it showed the extent to which those values central to the identity of the early Christian movement were seen to be fundamentally

---

[84] *DO* 1.72, p. 74.

[85] Tertullian, "The Military Chaplet," in Oliver O'Donovan and Joan Lockwood O'Donovan, eds., *From Irenaeus to Grotius: A Sourcebook in Christian Political Thought, 100–1625* (Eerdmans, 1999), pp. 27–28.

[86] On the dangers of overstating this opposition, see for example Oliver Nicholson, "*Civitas Quae Adhuc Sustentat Omnia*: Lactantius and the City of Rome," in William E. Klingshirn and Mark Vessey, eds., *The Limits of Ancient Christianity: Essays on Late Antique Thought and Culture in Honor of R. A. Markus* (University of Michigan Press, 1999).

at odds with the values that had led Rome to its empire and glory. One of the central factors in this opposition was the early Christians' preoccupation (derived in large part from Christianity's foundations in Judaism) with personal moral purity. Despite a key strain of Jesus's own teachings that aggressively questioned the relation of the purity ethic to the new moral order he claimed to herald, a concern with keeping oneself uncontaminated by impure elements remained a central theme of early Christian discourse. So when, for example, the early Christians sought to depict the trial and sentencing of the innocent Jesus at the hands of the Roman governor Pontius Pilate, they represented Pilate as literally seeking to wash his hands of the blood guilt of Jesus's death (betraying a concern for purity perhaps more Hebrew than Roman in its choice of motifs).

What Jesus's teaching on the subject did change was the principal (though by no means the only) relevant locus of purity concerns among the early Christians. Following Jesus's sayings (as described in the Sermon on the Mount and other Gospel texts), the early Christians emphasized especially the importance of *internal* as well as physical purity before God.[87] It was crucial not only to have clean hands, they agreed, but a clean heart as well, to satisfy God's creative purpose for his people. The issue area in which this theme most obviously dominated early Christian discourse was in the controversies surrounding idolatry and the religious pluralism of ancient societies. Among the many birth pangs that accompanied the introduction of Gentiles into the early Church (discussed at length, for example, in St. Paul's epistles) was the question of how to associate with Gentiles without becoming defiled by the impurities of their lifestyle, including their consumption of meats and other foods offered as sacrifices to false gods and idols.

But the purity ethic also figured quite importantly in the early Church's discourse about war and peace. Ancient Christians, far more than their medieval or modern counterparts, insisted that an ethic of peace was central to the commitments that distinguished their faith from other forms of ancient religion.[88] And when the early churches came to discuss the inevitable questions of conscience associated with their pacifist ethic, they typically chose to frame the issues at stake in terms of how to keep themselves pure from the defilement caused by violence and bloodshed.

Perhaps the most revealing statement of these attitudes is the early Church father Tertullian's commentary on the issue of whether

---

[87] I do not suggest that this view originated with Jesus, only that Jesus's endorsement of it explains its importance to the early Christian movement.
[88] L. J. Swift, *The Early Fathers on War and Military Service* (Michael Glazier, 1983).

membership in the Christian Church is compatible with service in the Roman military. Yielding no ground, Tertullian asserts that the Christian ethic requires a rule of personal conduct utterly at odds with the contemporary practices of military servants of the Roman state. He asks rhetorically:

> Shall a Christian be free to walk around in a sword, when the Lord has said that whoever takes the sword shall perish by the sword? Shall a son of peace, who would not even go to law, be embroiled in battle? Shall he administer chains and imprisonment and torture and punishment, though he will not even take vengeance for wrongs done himself? ... You can see at a glance how many further offenses are attributable to the one decisive step of assuming military duties.[89]

In addition to this concern about the threat which a life of military service posed to one's personal moral purity, however, there was an even more fundamental objection to the military life which led the early Christians to avoid it – and this objection had implications not just for the military life, but more generally for any kind of involvement in the public sphere of the Roman world. What disqualified Christians from political involvement more than anything else, authors like Tertullian contended, was precisely the feature of Roman political culture that Cicero had stressed so centrally, namely the expansive and even holistic claims of loyalty that the Roman state laid on its citizens. Tertullian finds this holism fundamentally incompatible with the life-consuming moral claims of the Christian gospel as these early Christians understood it. "Can we believe," he asks, that "we may take a human pledge (*sacramentum*) on top of a divine one? May one who owns Christ as master answer to another master, renouncing father and mother and nearest relations, whom the law bids us honor and, after God, love, to whom the Gospel, too, accords comparable honor, giving precedence to Christ alone?"[90] Instead, Tertullian flatly denies that a Christian may voluntarily assume the responsibility of a soldier while being true to his Christian commitments to God and to God's peace.[91] Directly contradicting Cicero's claim that

---

[89] Tertullian, "The Military Chaplet," p. 27.   [90] Ibid.

[91] Ibid. Tertullian is willing to make a limited exception to this blanket claim for those whose conversion occurs after they have already undertaken the responsibilities of military service. For such people, however, it will almost certainly still be best to leave military service as soon as possible, "once faith has been born and sealed in baptism." Interestingly, it seems to have been a common practice among the early Christians for those who must assume political or military responsibility to postpone baptism until after they had left military service, so that their baptismal vows would not be tainted by the risk of sin that inevitably accompanied these public duties. Henry Chadwick, *The Early Church* (Penguin, 1967), p. 127. I am grateful to Byron Karathanos for bringing this fact to my attention.

"the republic ought to be the dearest thing in the world to us," Tertullian instead insists that "nothing is more foreign to us than the state (*res publica*)." Instead, echoing the cosmopolitan doctrine of the Stoics, he insists that for Christians there is only "one state we know, of which we are all citizens – the universe."[92]

So, starkly at odds with the Roman ethic endorsing the life of public activity and glorifying those who made sacrifices on behalf of the public sphere, the doctrine taught by Tertullian and other early Christians was that it was best to avoid or abandon military and political responsibilities rather than risk being tainted by the uncleanliness of political activity. If one acquires or retains such responsibilities, Tertullian argues, one will almost certainly be forced to "practice constant equivocation" in order to "avoid committing some act against God," or else ultimately "suffer for God" which is "just what the faith of a civilian can lead to."[93] What Tertullian wants to challenge most strongly is the belief of those who might be tempted to run these moral risks that one's military duties might somehow constitute "an excuse for one's crimes or an insurance against martyrdom."[94] For the sincere Christian, our public duties as the world understands them provide one with neither.

When it comes to taking a stand for the faith, there is no room for the plea of necessity. You can be under no necessity to sin if you have made up your mind that the one necessity is not to sin. True, one may be driven by necessity to offer sacrifice or deny Christ outright under threat of torture or punishment. Yet our teaching makes no concessions even to that necessity, since there is a greater necessity than avoiding suffering and discharging duties, which is to shun denial and accomplish one's martyrdom ... It is precisely to avoid occasions of sin that we should keep clear of official responsibilities; or else, accepting martyrdom, we should break with our responsibilities for ever.[95]

In addition to these issues of conflict between the early Christian purity ethic and the Roman ethic of political responsibility, there was another important conflict between the early Christian Church and the dominant values of Roman life regarding the dignity, worth, and equality of individual human beings. As we have seen, the moral and political culture of the ancient world, and especially ancient Rome, put special emphasis on worldly greatness, glory, and wealth in identifying the values of a flourishing life, and assumed that a great deal of inequality between persons – including

[92] Tertullian, "Apology," in O'Donovan and O'Donovan, *From Irenaeus to Grotius*, p. 26.
[93] Tertullian, "The Military Chaplet," p. 27.   [94] Ibid.   [95] Ibid., pp. 27–28.

the radical inequalities inherent in the institution of slavery – was a necessary feature of the good community. The early Christians, in striking
contrast, committed themselves at least in principle to the equal treatment
of all, regardless of their relative degree of wealth or poverty, their social
class, their status as a slave or a free person, or even to a remarkable degree
their gender.[96] Even among those Christians of the Constantinian age like
Lactantius who tended to be more accommodating in their rhetoric to the
Roman order than the Christians of previous generations, we find a striking
conflict with ancient and particularly Roman values.

As a matter of individual conduct, the most important implications of the
new ethic of equality concerned the duties of Christians toward the poor and
weak within the community. For Lactantius, human beings were sociable by
nature, and this divinely ordained sociability underlay our duty to aid the
oppressed and feed the destitute.[97] God's original and perfect design for
humanity was to give the earth "in common to all" in order that "that which
was produced for all might not be wanting to any."[98] But in the ancient
world precisely the opposite occurred, according to Lactantius: those who
possessed more than they needed not only refused to share with those who
lacked, but used their power to seize the remaining property of the needy.[99]
This led to the value systems of ancient societies resting on a condition of
"proud and swollen inequality," one in which the rich "made themselves
higher than other men, by a retinue of attendants, and by the sword, and by
the brilliancy of their garments."[100] Thus these early Christian writers taught
that living in accordance with equity understood as equality was fundamental to their religious ethic; and so consequently the early Christians aimed at

[96] Of course, their practices in this regard tend to be impressive only by comparison with the even
harsher gender differentiations imposed by their contemporaries.

[97] Lactantius, *Divine Institutes* (hereafter *DI*) VI.c, trans. William Fletcher, *The Works of Lactantius*,
vol. I (Edinburgh, 1871), p. 375. This sociability, Lactantius acknowledges, is also in its nature
interdependent and implicitly reciprocal, "a mutual sharing of kind offices" consisting in "affording
help, that we may be able to receive it." Yet this idea of reciprocity must not be permitted to justify
us in refusing to give help unless reciprocity is assured. The epitome of injustice, Lactantius claims,
is where one measures "the offices of piety and humanity by utility," meaning particularly the
practice encouraged by Roman culture and by Cicero in particular of bestowing generosity only on
"suitable" persons (meaning "those who are able to restore and give back the favor.") On the
contrary, Lactantius insists, the true Christian ethic teaches that it is not "suitable" but rather "as
much as possible . . . unsuitable objects," on which we should bestow our generosity "without the
hope of any return" (*DI* VI.x–xi, pp. 377–379).

[98] *DI* V.v, p. 303. This same principle of equality is according to Lactantius the ultimate justification
behind Christian pacifist attitudes as well. Since we are all brothers and sisters, it follows that it is
"bestial savagery" for us "to hurt, despoil, torture, kill, eliminate a human being, contrary to the law
of humanity and every religious principle." Lactantius, *Divine Institutes*, in O'Donovan and
O'Donovan, *From Irenaeus to Grotius*, p. 54.

[99] *DI* V.vi, p. 305.   [100] Ibid.

overturning this Roman value system of individual glory and pride by means of practices designed to promote true equality.

The early Christians also believed that their egalitarian ethic had significant implications for social reform which again set them at odds with the political values and practices of most of the ancient world. In conceiving of these political implications of their religious beliefs, the early Christians exhibited an astonishing optimism about the possibilities for bringing about egalitarian reforms in human societies.[101] John Chrysostom, for example, argued that, if Christians were actually to sell all their possessions and put them into a common store, the resulting collection would be more than sufficient to feed 50,000 people each day, since (as he claims can be observed in the monasteries) no great sum of food is required to feed a multitude "if the food were provided in bulk and they ate together."[102] Both as a matter of right and as a pragmatic matter, they believed, the unity found in community has vast powers to alleviate need. Those doubtful of such methods can be easily answered:

So what happens when the money runs out? Do you think it *could* run out? . . . Would we not make a heaven on earth? . . . Just do as I say, and we will get things right stage by stage. And if God gives us life, I am confident we shall bring ourselves before long to such a level of social order (*politeia*).[103]

Lactantius exhibits a similar confidence about the social improvements that must follow in a society in which citizens showed both the piety and equity that constituted true justice. In a world of true religious devotion, Lactantius held, there would be no "dissensions and wars," no "frauds and plunderings," no need of "prisons, of the swords of rulers, or the terror of punishments." In particular, it would be impossible in a world of the devout for there to be any plotting or conspiracy, since all would know that God "sees through secret crimes, and even the very thoughts themselves."[104]

---

[101] For a criticism of this optimism in Lactantius, see Charles Norris Cochrane, *Christianity and Classical Culture* (Oxford University Press, 1944), pp. 196–197.

[102] John Chrysostom, 11th Homily, s. 3, in O'Donovan and O'Donovan, *From Irenaeus to Grotius*, p. 100.

[103] Ibid.

[104] *DI* v.viii, p. 309. On this claim as a departure from Roman thinking about *pietas*, see further Cochrane, *Christianity and Classical Culture*, p. 193. In this quotation we can see some indication, amply confirmed elsewhere in Lactantius's writings, that the opacity of the moral universe already canvassed by Plato and the skeptical tradition (including Cicero and the rhetoricians) was shared and furthered by at least some of the early Christians, including Lactantius. There are some situations – such as the shipwreck episode from Cicero – that do have the appearance of moral

The common view of these early Christian writers, then, was that the possession of riches constituted a grave moral danger to the human soul and implied the ever-present threat of sin. In a world of desperate human need, the early Christians held the decision to possess wealth to be intrinsically immoral. John Chrysostom believes that it is "simply not possible" for anyone who possesses wealth amidst need to be morally good: for since a person "is good when he distributes his wealth," it follows that "when he no longer has it, he is good, when he gives it to others, he is good; but while he still has it, he cannot be good."[105]

In addition to this claim of intrinsic moral wrongness, however, the early Christians also held that the acquisition of riches inevitably threatened their possessors with the corruption of their characters, since it is hard to acquire great wealth "without committing every kind of evil."[106] Additionally, once riches are acquired there is equal moral peril in maintaining one's wealth, a fact that makes the sin of avarice especially deadly. In the case of bodily sins such as lust or gluttony, eventually limits are reached: "satiety arouses a certain feeling of repugnance" even among those who are enamored of a certain pleasure when they have overindulged too much. But avarice, "since it is insatiable," has the opposite dynamic: "the more it increases the more completely they love it, and, as it grows old with them, so it grows in strength also."[107]

The moral dangers of wealth are further compounded by the fact that, according to these early Christian thinkers, there is an inseverable

dilemmas due to this problem of moral opacity, caused by God's desire to conceal virtue and justice under the appearance of folly (*DI* v.xviii, pp. 319–320, 330; v.xix, p. 336). He also argues that virtue needs vice as a means of being discerned and tested; that God likewise included evil in his providential plan as a means of bringing about good; and that evils have what power they possess precisely because of their nearness to, and resemblance to, related goods; all themes that were important foundations for Augustine's theological innovations (*DI* v.vii, p. 307; v.xviii, p. 330; v.xix, p. 336).

[105] John Chrysostom, 12th Homily on 1 Timothy, in O' Donovan and O'Donovan, *From Irenaeus to Grotius*, p. 103.
[106] "On Riches" (anonymous Pelagian writer), 17.1, in B. R. Rees, ed., *The Letters of Pelagius and His Followers* (Boydell, 1991), p. 199.
[107] "On Riches" 1.3, p. 175. The early Christians never tire of repeating the theme of the self-reinforcing qualities of the vice of greed. "Greed is inflamed, not assuaged, by gain," Ambrose of Milan tells us; "the more you possess, the more you demand, and however much you acquire you go on needing more." The author of "On Riches" likewise compares greed to "a fire that derives its kindling from the materials provided by worldly things"; as fuel added to a fire makes it "grow into an immense blaze," so also to "add to avarice what is not its own" is to lead it to develop "an even greater fire of greed for more." To have what is sufficient for the needs of nature is good, but it is not good enough to satisfy the demands of avarice: "for nothing can ever be sufficient for avarice, even if it possessed the whole world, so extravagant are its demands, and covetousness increases as the substance on which it feeds spreads by contagion." Ambrose of Milan, "Story of Naboth," s. 4, in O'Donovan and O'Donovan, *From Irenaeus to Grotius*, p. 76; "On Riches" 5.2, pp. 175–178.

connection between riches and the vice of pride. Wealthy men inevitably become proud and arrogant, the author of "On Riches" writes, and any person who obtains wealth necessarily in the process becomes "puffed up with haughtiness, swollen with pride, inflamed with anger, and goaded into madness as his riches increase."[108] This association of riches with pride, furthermore, inevitably spreads to corrupt not just those who possess wealth but all who share a society with them. All inhabitants of wealthy societies, and not just wealth's possessors, learn to "glory in pride, in riches, in splendid clothing, in agreeable food, in the nobility of this world, in the transitory praises of men";[109] we all tend to give preference to the rich and powerful, no matter how wicked they may be, over poor people no matter how virtuous and holy, in precise contradiction to the proper set of Christian values.

Thus, from a certain perspective, these early Christians suggest, it is not *wealth* at all but rather the *pride* it gives rise to and nourishes that is the true basis of the evils associated with contemporary society. Thus Ambrose of Milan accuses the rich of caring about wealth only as the basis for a favorable comparison with others:

Your desires have no pretext of utility; you simply want to drive other people off! You are more interested in despoiling the poor than in enriching yourselves. You consider it an affront if a poor man owns anything worth a rich man's getting hold of. A credit on another's balance you count as a loss on your own.[110]

The early Christians even begin to move in the direction of defining the morally troubling feature of inequality *as* its contribution to pride and other internal states of mind, rather than being morally problematic in its own right (a move which, as we will see, St. Augustine was later to complete). Lactantius, for example, asserts that what is ultimately wrong with inequality is less the actual distributive condition it represents than the kinds of attitude or mental intention that are required to permit it. Thus he says:

For justice is not expressed in outward conditions, nor even in the conditions of the human body, but operates wholly upon the human mind. So making men equal is not a matter of abolishing marriage and private property, but of abolishing ambition, pride, and self-importance, of making those self-confident wielders of power realize that they are the equals of beggars. Take from the rich

---

[108] "On Riches" 17.4, p. 200.   [109] "On Riches" 14.2, p. 196.
[110] Ambrose of Milan, "Story of Naboth," p. 77, s. 11.

their insolence and injustice, and the difference between the rich and the poor will cease to matter, since they will think of themselves as equal; and that is something only religion can achieve.[111]

Of course, in general, the attitude of these early Christians was that pride and selfishness were evil because they obstructed the establishment of God's equality, and not (or not primarily) for reasons of their intrinsic moral impurity. But the moral dangers associated with pride and self-ishness were very real, these thinkers believed, whether they were posed directly in their own right or (more frequently) by means of their associ-ation with wealth and inequality. Furthermore, these thinkers shared the belief that, whether or not pride was at the center of what was morally objectionable about wealth and inequality, it was pride that was *motiva-tionally* fundamental in driving the disruptive and insatiable features of human avarice that dominated ancient and especially Roman culture.

Thus these early Christian thinkers converged in finding that the vice of avarice or greed was among the central causes of the moral and political problems of the ancient world. For the author of "On Riches," the vice of greed is "the occasion of all evils, the root of crimes, the fuel of wrongdoing, the source of transgressions."[112] Moreover, these thinkers saw such social ills as natural outcomes of the Roman social and imperial system. This is captured especially clearly in a piece of wordplay in common use through-out the early Christian world, one which implicated Roman society directly in these excesses. Those who condemned the vices of greed and avarice could have found no more succinct scriptural warrant for their view than the pronouncement of the second letter to Timothy (attributed by tradition to St. Paul) that "avarice is the root of all evil" – or in the commonly used Latin translation, "radix omnium malorum avaritia." Early Christians, however, displayed their view that Roman society itself was directly to blame for this moral failing by employing the acronym ROMA (the Latin spelling of "Rome") to reiterate the message that "*R*adix *O*mnium *M*alorum *A*varitia." For these early Christians, then, Rome itself was the most powerful evidence that the root of all evil was avarice, and the root of that avarice was in turn to be found in the character of Roman society and culture itself.

Thus the early Christians held that politics, especially in the Roman world, was a place of great moral peril, because political activity necessarily

---

[111] Lactantius, *Divine Institutes*, in O'Donovan and O'Donovan, *From Irenaeus to Grotius*, p. 49.
[112] "On Riches" 17.3, p. 199.

implicated one with the impure world of Roman military empire and a Roman culture centered on pride and insatiable greed. It was for these reasons that the early Christians (like the ancient schools of philosophy) tended to urge withdrawal and separation from the impure means and ends of Roman politics and society. Fraught with moral peril, political activity tended to require secrecy and hypocrisy from its practitioners, and thus no one can be pure in politics, they held. Courtiers, Lactantius explained, are expected to "imitate the customs and vices of the king," and as a consequence all actors in politics learn quickly to surrender their moral purity "lest, if they should live piously, they might seem to upbraid the wickedness of the king."[113] By this means, political actors invariably find themselves "being corrupted by continual imitation," and so "the practice of living wickedly by degrees [becomes] a habit."[114] It is thus in the nature of politics that political actors

by a pretence of goodness, prepare the way for themselves to power, and do many things which the good are accustomed to do, and that the more readily because they do them for the sake of deceiving; and I wish that it were as easy to carry out the goodness in action as it is to pretend to it. But when they have begun to attain to their purpose and their wish in reaching the highest step of power, then, truly laying aside pretence, these men discover their character; they seize upon everything, and offer violence, and lay waste; and they press upon the good themselves, whose cause they had undertaken; and they cut away the steps by which they mounted, that no one may be able to imitate them against themselves.[115]

While these early Christians disapproved of the active political life (at least in the Roman context), however, their disapproval hinged in part on the Roman (and particularly Ciceronian) account of the moral claims politics asserted over its subjects. Part of the reason, that is, why politics requires these kinds of evil actions on the part of its practitioners, according to these early Christian writers, derives from the peculiar character of the tasks that politics sets itself. Lactantius observes that, in contrast to divine laws, the laws of nations are always devised "not by justice, but by utility," since each nation has enacted those laws "which it deemed useful for its own affairs."[116] And the most conspicuous instance of this focus of politics on utility rather than justice is to be found in the affairs of Rome itself, whose people, "by always desiring and carrying off the property of others, have gained for themselves the possession of the whole world."[117] Indeed,

---

[113] *DI* v.vi, p. 306. [114] Ibid. [115] *DI* vi.vi, pp. 365–366.
[116] *DI* vi.ix, p. 371. [117] Ibid.

when the agreement of men is taken away, virtue has no existence at all; for what are the interests of our country, but the inconveniences of another state or nation? – that is, to extend the boundaries which are violently taken from others, to increase the power of the state, to improve the revenues – all which things are not virtues, but the overthrowing of virtues ... For how can a man be just who injures, who hates, who despoils, who puts to death? And they who strive to be serviceable to their country do all these things: for they are ignorant of what this being serviceable is, who think nothing useful, nothing advantageous, but that which can be held by the hand; and this alone cannot be held, because it may be snatched away. Whoever, then, has gained for the country these goods (as they call them) – that is, who by the overthrow of cities and the destruction of nations has filled the treasury with money, has taken lands and enriched his countrymen – he is extolled with praises to the heaven[s]: in him there is said to be the greatest and perfect virtue.[118]

This is, at its root, the core problem of political ethics in the ancient world, from the early Christians' perspective. The demands of life in a society of imperial ambition are such that they cannot be reconciled easily, if at all, with the requirements of an emerging Christian morality.

It is important to notice, however, that in calling urgently for social change such as the promotion of equality the early Christians explicitly disavowed the position that they were themselves responsible for taking the causal steps necessary to bring about this transformation in reality. On the contrary, they held that what was required of Christians was not that they provide for the needs of the poor, for example, but rather that they themselves not live in a relation of *inequality* with the poor.[119] The Pelagian author of "On Riches," for example, mocks the idea that Christians could ever have been required "to possess superfluous riches so as to always be giving them," an excuse sometimes used by modestly philanthropic Christians to justify their possession of wealth. The Pelagian mocks:

Great indeed is their love of compassion and godliness, if they care more for the poor than for God! And I would they really cared for the poor and not rather for

---

[118] *DI* vi.vi, pp. 366–367. Cf. Cochrane, *Christianity and Classical Culture*, p. 194.

[119] As John Chrysostom explains, in the earliest church practices of the apostles, believers "contributed with such enthusiasm that nobody was left in need. They did not give a part of what they had, and save the rest. Nor did they give it, even all of it, as *private* charity. They ironed out the unevenness from the center, and lived altogether free of odious comparisons, so treating one another with great respect. They would never place a gift directly in someone's hand or make a ceremonious presentation, but they 'laid it at the apostles' feet,' leaving them to dispose of it at their discretion, so that it came from the common fund and not from private donation ... It is perfectly plain from the way things turned out that by selling their possessions they did not end up in want, but simply enriched the poor." John Chrysostom, 11th Homily, s. 3, p. 100.

riches, which they try to defend on the pretext of helping the poor and under the pretense of being obliged to practice godliness, not realizing that some are in need because others have more than they need. Get rid of the rich man, and you will not be able to find a poor one. Let no man have more than he really needs, and everyone will have as much as they need, since the few who are rich are the reason for the many who are poor.[120]

So the ethic of the early Church, rather than placing the providential burden for meeting the needs of others directly on the shoulders of the community's members, instead sought as far as possible to eliminate individual agency from the process of meeting communal needs. This was of course in sharp contrast to the Roman ethic, which authorized its exceptions to ordinary morality precisely on the grounds of the providential responsibility held by the community's political leaders. In making this move, the Christians relied heavily on the idea that divine providence would meet these needs, particularly for the righteous: and this was reflected too, as we observed above, in the tremendous utopian confidence of the early Christians in the practical social efficacy of the Christian way of living.

But the changing circumstances of ancient culture would soon confront these moral commitments of the early Christians with a rival set of ethical burdens imposed by the responsibilities of practical politics. For a time, it was easy for them to stake out more hostile ground. The Christian religion, having emerged in the midst of a conquered culture, had never been required to contemplate the claims of public responsibility, beyond the question of providing for the needs of its own members. Consequently, in the post-Constantinian world, when Christians suddenly found themselves consulted by rulers – or even exercising political authority themselves – it became necessary to consider how Christian moral teachings might be combined with the effective exercise of political power, and thus how (if at all) Christianity might hope to shape itself into a responsible political creed. It is that question above all which formed the central motivation behind the moral and political theory of St. Augustine, to which we will turn in the next chapter.

---

[120] "On Riches" 12.1, p. 194.

CHAPTER 2

Two cities and two loves

Now we see through a glass darkly . . .   1 Corinthians 13:12

As we saw in Chapter 1, the earliest intimations of the problem of dirty hands arose from conflicts of value felt within ancient philosophy and culture. But the most urgent – and most problematic – formulation of the problem emerged as the value commitments of ancient politics began to confront the uncompromising new moral claims associated with the Christian religion.

The most influential ancient response to this value conflict – and to the version of the dirty hands problem it engendered – was voiced by the Christian theologian St. Augustine. No stranger to the problematic aspects of power, St. Augustine exercised considerable worldly authority in his role as bishop of the North African diocese of Hippo. Augustine's writings did more than any other philosopher to confront this challenge and to reconcile, so far as he thought possible, the moral values that animated ancient culture and politics with the Christian faith.

In approaching the conflict between ancient culture and early Christianity, Augustine made no attempt to suggest that the claims of ancient politics could compare in significance to what the Christian religion promised; nor did he suggest that the priorities of Roman political and military life could possibly be made to agree with the austerity and meekness of Christ's moral teachings. Instead, Augustine ingeniously based his attempted reconciliation not on a compromise between these two antagonistic value systems, but rather on their metaphorical resemblance. His approach emphasized not the similarities of the two antagonists, but rather the seemingly infinite distance between them. By means of this analogy, Augustine sought to recognize the claims of the earthly realm as significant and worthy of attention in their own right, while retaining a higher claim for God's own higher righteousness.

It is a version of this ingenious synthesis that lies at the heart of Augustine's proposed solution to the ancient problem of dirty hands. Throughout his voluminous writings, Augustine sought to identify what was good and useful within ancient culture in order to redeem it for the Christian religion. In his masterwork the *City of God*, he employs the metaphor of "two cities" to describe the morally diverse and intermingled character of human existence. Augustine declares at the outset of that work that his ambition is to describe the relation between two cities: the city of God and the earthly city. Augustine offers several explanations of the two cities metaphor and its constituent elements. On different occasions he says that what constitutes the difference between the two cities is that they "owe their existence to the fact that some men live by the standard of the flesh, others by the standard of the spirit," or alternatively that "some live by man's standard, others by God's."[1] But his most famous explanation comes at the end of Book XIV of the *City of God*, where he observes that "the two cities were created by two kinds of love: the earthly city was created by self-love reaching the point of contempt for God, the Heavenly City by the love of God carried as far as contempt for self."[2] Since this is so, it is natural to suppose that to grasp how Augustine conceived of the two cities, we must first understand how he conceived the natures of – and the dynamics of the relations between – the two principal forms of love in his moral psychology, pride and charity.

As we will see, Augustine's understanding of the relationship between the earthly city and the heavenly city closely tracks his account of the fundamentally *imitative* relationship between pride and charity. In turn, this natural inclination of both pride and the earthly city to imitate their higher counterparts is what underlies some of the most significant features of Augustine's political theory and political ethics. For it is because he recognizes this imitative impulse that Augustine comes to view human moral behavior as radically opaque to human judgment with respect to its inward dimensions. Because pride imitates charity, human beings are profoundly limited with respect to their ability to evaluate one another's motivations and intentions – since one and the same action can issue from either pride or charity. Thus, for Augustine, we cannot look to external actions as the center of moral action: instead, he locates morality exclusively in interior dispositions and states of mind.

This move to interiorize morally significant action exercised a crucial influence not only on the development of Western moral psychology, but also on the way human beings thought about the significance of that psychology

---

[1] Augustine, *Concerning the City of God against the Pagans* (hereafter *CG*), trans. Henry Bettensen (Penguin, 1972), XIV.4, p. 553.
[2] *CG* XIV.28, p. 593.

for questions of political ethics.[3] For by arguing that moral phenomena should be evaluated apart from their outward effects, Augustine helped to sharply disconnect intentions from consequences in the traditions of moral inquiry that he influenced. That separation in turn opened the door to a much wider range of plausible moral excuses for those charged with public responsibilities, and added an additional layer of complexity to analyzing what precisely those responsibilities required of those agents morally. Human reason, Augustine held, is profoundly limited in its capacity to exercise moral judgment with any degree of certainty; yet human beings *must* make judgments, especially in the sphere of politics and social life – and so a greater degree of latitude is appropriate in evaluating their actions morally.

Because of this opacity of the moral world, human beings (according to Augustine) are left cut off from their most important moral sources with respect to precisely those actions carrying the most significant earthly consequences.[4] Yet this same opacity, Augustine believes, offers a compelling form of excuse – grounded in their responsibility for others, and heightened by the cloudiness of human understanding in the earthly realm. This understanding of the moral problems of political life led Augustine to urge Christians in public office to do their best, and to trust to God for absolution if they sinned unwillingly in the performance of their duties.

Augustine's interiorized ethic, combined with his metaphor of the two cities, served in a variety of forms as the dominant response to intimations of anxieties about dirty hands throughout the succeeding millennium. To see how this worked, however, we need to first address certain features of Augustine's general theological framework, before turning to see more precisely how he employed this framework to produce such an innovative and influential argument with respect to the ethics of political action.

LOVE AND MORAL ORDER

Augustine places the concept of love at the center of his moral philosophy in a way that no previous thinker, Christian or pagan, had ever done before.[5] Love is the key to understanding human beings: it is the purpose

---

[3] On the interiorization of moral action in Western philosophy, see again Charles Taylor, *Sources of the Self* (Harvard University Press, 1989).
[4] On the concept of "moral sources," see ibid., esp. ch. 4.
[5] On this point see the Introduction to Oliver O'Donovan, *The Problem of Self-Love in St. Augustine* (Yale University Press, 1980). O'Donovan's work is the most careful and insightful treatment of the general themes I discuss in this section, though he does not consider the particular issue of imitation on which this chapter focuses.

and function for which they were created, and in one form or another it is destined to dominate their existence. The highest attainments of human life, its deepest passions, its greatest tragedies, are explicable only in terms of the fact that human beings are made to be lovers. However misguided, it is some form of love that inevitably drives their every thought and action.

But human beings are created for the purpose not just of loving, but of loving in a certain way: there are particular objects, in a particular order, that they are meant to love, and it is the misidentification and disordering of these objects, which Augustine calls *lust*, that leads to all the great miseries of the human condition. Lust is the opposite of love: "by love," Augustine says, "I mean the impulse of one's mind to enjoy God on his own account and to enjoy oneself and one's neighbour on account of God; and by lust I mean the impulse of one's mind to enjoy oneself and one's neighbour and any corporeal thing not on account of God."[6] Augustine therefore makes central to his moral theory not just the concept of love, but also a theory about correct *ordering* of loves.[7] Indeed, for Augustine "a brief and true definition of virtue is 'rightly ordered love.' "[8]

Augustine outlines this ordering along predictable lines. First among the proper objects of human love is humanity's Creator; at some remove from this summit of love's objects, we find human love for one's neighbor and for one's self.[9] Some simplistic understandings of Augustine characterize him as opposing love of God to love of self, but this is flatly to ignore Augustine's claim that, in the proper form, self-love is far from being necessarily vicious.[10] If we are to love our neighbours as ourselves, a degree of self-love is both necessary and proper. Indeed, Augustine gives self-love a kind of priority among various instances of neighbor love, because for Augustine loves are ordered in part by proximity. "All people," he claims, "should be loved equally. But you cannot do good to all people equally, so you should take particular thought for those who, as if by lot, happen to be particularly close to you in terms of place, time, or any other circumstances."[11] For Augustine, then, our self-love must be strictly limited to a

---

[6] Augustine, *On Christian Doctrine* (hereafter *OCD*), translated and edited by R. P. Green as *On Christian Teaching* (Oxford University Press, 1997), III.36–37, p. 76.

[7] Hannah Arendt, *Love and Saint Augustine* (University of Chicago Press, 1996), Pt. I, ch. 3, gives an important treatment of the concept of ordered loves in Augustine.

[8] *CG* XV.22, p. 637.

[9] See further Augustine, *Against Faustus the Manichean*, in Augustine, *Political Writings*, ed. Michael W. Tkacz and Douglas Kries (Hackett, 1994), XXII.73–79, p. 226.

[10] *CG* XIX.14, p. 873, and *OCD* I.67, p. 22. Augustine's relentless hostility toward pride does have a tendency to encourage this misunderstanding, however. See for example *CG* XIV.28, pp. 593–594.

[11] *OCD* I.61–62, p. 21; cf. *OCD* III.38, p. 76.

state of equality with our love for other human beings (lest we neglect our duties of charity), but under ideal conditions it is first among these equals. This is so natural that the moral law does not even need to address it: there is, Augustine observes, "no need of a commandment to love oneself."[12]

This is the first key step in Augustine's revision of classical moral psychology. For, as we will see, the effect of construing morality as an ordering of loves, as Augustine's framework does, is to relocate the center of morality in a set of internal dispositions rather than outward actions. This kind of reorientation was not of course without precedent: we find it in particular in the Sermon on the Mount as well as in the writings of the early Christians. But Augustine moves more decisively (or at least more systematically) than any of his predecessors to reposition the analytical location of moral phenomena *inside* the dispositions and states of mind of human beings, rather than in their outward actions.[13]

Since for Augustine morality is essentially a question of the right ordering of our loves, it follows that vice or sin consists in our failure to make these judgments correctly. Vice then does not "consist in defection to things which are evil in themselves; it is the defection itself which is evil . . . contrary to the order of nature."[14] For instance, greed

is not something wrong with gold; the fault is in a man who perversely loves gold and for its sake abandons justice, which ought to be put beyond comparison above gold. Lust is not something wrong in a beautiful and attractive body; the fault is in a soul which perversely delights in sensual pleasures . . . Pride is not something wrong in the one who loves power, or in the power itself; the fault is in the soul which perversely loves its own power, and has no thought for the justice of the Omnipotent . . .[15]

---

[12] *OCD* 1.84–85, pp. 26–27.

[13] See further Augustine, *Against Faustus* XXII.73–79, p. 229.

[14] *CG* XII.8, p. 480. On this point see further Augustine, *On Free Choice of the Will* (hereafter *FW*), trans. and ed. Thomas Williams (Hackett, 1993), pp. 5–6.

[15] *CG* XII.8, pp. 480–481. See also Augustine's remarks in *FW* 1.15, p. 26: "Therefore, the very same things are used in different ways by different people; some use them badly and others use them well. Someone who uses them badly clings to them and becomes entangled with them. He serves things that ought to serve him, fixing on goods that he cannot even use properly because he is not himself good. But one who uses these things rightly shows that they are good, although not good for himself. For those things do not make the one who uses them good or better; in fact, they become good by being put to good use. And so someone who uses them well does not become attached to them. They don't become limbs of his soul, as it were (which is what happens when one loves them), so that when these things begin to be amputated he is not disfigured by any pain or decay. He is completely above such things, ready to possess and make use of them when there is need, and even readier to lose them and do without them. Since this is the case, you must realize that we should not find fault with silver and gold because of the greedy, or food because of gluttons, or wine because of drunkards, or womanly beauty because of fornicators and adulterers, and so on, especially since you know that fire can be used to heal and bread to poison."

Moreover, as a consequence of this framework of precisely ordered loves, Augustine's theory opens up the possibility that the very same qualities may at one moment be virtues, at other moments vices, depending on their position within this divine ordering.

> The virtues which the mind imagines it possesses, by means of which it rules the body and the vicious elements, are themselves vices rather than virtues, if the mind does not bring them into relation with God in order to achieve anything whatsoever and to maintain that achievement. For although the virtues are to be reckoned by some people to be genuine and honourable when they are related only to themselves and are sought for no other end, even then they are puffed up and proud, and so are to be accounted vices rather than virtues.[16]

As we shall see, part of the effect of this relocation of moral action is thus to blur and confuse our confidence in the precision of our moral judgments, since whether an action is virtuous or vicious comes on this view to depend on factors outside of our ability to perceive.

Taken by itself, then, Augustine's view of self-love is basically positive.[17] His reputation as a critic of self-love rests largely on the close association he drew between the intrinsically benign phenomenon of self-love, on the one hand, and, on the other, its frequent transformation into pride, which for Augustine constitutes the chief of our vices.[18] So closely are the two matters associated, indeed, that Augustine sometimes appears to conflate them: he speaks, for example, of pride or exaltation being "assuredly the great difference that sunders the two cities of which we are speaking . . ., [for] in one city love of God has been given first place, in the other, love of self."[19] Nevertheless, as we have seen in the preceding analysis, self-love is on Augustine's account not intrinsically evil, which is not the case with pride: on the contrary, pride is "the original evil"[20] and "the start of every kind of sin."[21] Augustine goes on to define pride as "a longing for a perverse kind of exaltation."[22] It begins with the benign phenomenon of self-love,

---

[16] *CG* XIX.25, p. 891.

[17] For a closer consideration of this complex problem, see further O'Donovan, *The Problem of Self-Love*, particularly ch. 3. O'Donovan argues for an important change over time in Augustine's works, with the concept of disordered self-love in the form of pride becoming increasingly predominant in his thinking as work proceeded on the *City of God*.

[18] On the destructive effects of pride, see further O'Donovan, *The Problem of Self-Love*, ch. 4; D. J. MacQueen, "Contemptus Dei: St. Augustine on the Disorder of Pride in Society and its Remedies," *Recherches Augustiniennes* 9 (1973): 227–293; and R. A. Markus, "*De Civitate Dei*: Pride and the common good," in Joseph C. Schnaubelt and Friederich Van Fleteren, eds., *Augustine: Second Founder of the Faith* (P. Lang, 1990).

[19] *CG* XIV.13, p. 573. On Augustine's occasional conflation of self-love and pride, see further O'Donovan, *The Problem of Self-Love*, esp. pp. 94–95.

[20] *CG* XIV.13, p. 573. [21] Ibid., p. 571. [22] Ibid.

but transforms itself into a perverse exaltation of that love. Pride is thus ultimately a matter of the self's improper claim to the highest loyalty of its own love, and it is therefore a matter not only of right direction but also of natural justice, since the corrupt mind covets and claims "as its due what is really due to God alone."[23] Self-love in this form is fundamentally unjust "because it wants what is beneath it to serve it while itself refusing to serve what is above it; and it has been very well said that 'the person who loves injustice hates his own soul.' "[24]

IMITATION IN AUGUSTINE'S MORAL PSYCHOLOGY

At first glance there might appear to be nothing extraordinary about this moral theory. Augustine, it might be thought, though novel in his emphasis on love, should be seen primarily as a theorist of moral order: he is adapting to the new terrain of love the familiar Platonic notion that moral philosophy is simply a matter of bringing about conformity on an earthly scale to a particular and knowable pattern of cosmic hierarchy. What differentiates Augustine's theory from this more traditional model of moral ordering is the complexity of his moral psychology. For, as a moral psychologist, Augustine developed a far more lively sense than any of his predecessors of the depth of moral ambiguity endemic to matters of human conduct.[25]

There is, moreover, a rather peculiar and little-noticed reason why Augustine's sensitivity to moral ambiguity was able to run so deep. As we have seen, Augustine believed that all good was derived from a correct ordering of proper loves, and that the human epidemic of sin found its origin in a disordering of loves, namely pride. But at the same time he perceived, partly through the well-known intensity of his own introspective endeavors and partly through the sheer distance he ascribed to God as set against all human goodness, that self-love in the form of pride (and particularly in this form) possessed an almost limitless capacity for *mimicking love itself* in human life and behavior: and, further, that the great curse of human moral existence was our incapability, not just to choose to be loving rather than to be proud, but of reliably knowing which was which.

[23] *OCD* 1.46, p. 18. For a general exposition of Augustine's view of pride and the lust for domination, especially in its political implications, the standard account is that of Herbert A. Deane, *The Political and Social Ideas of St. Augustine* (Columbia University Press, 1963).

[24] *OCD* 1.46, p. 18.

[25] For an eloquent contemplation of this theme, see Oliver O'Donovan, "Augustine's *City of God* XIX and Western Political Thought," *Dionysius* 11 (1987): 89–110, esp. p. 109.

Augustine specifically identifies pride's *imitative* character as central to its functioning, so central, indeed, that he offers as an alternative definition the claim that "pride is a perverted imitation of God."[26] This imitative quality, on Augustine's account, is fundamental to the very nature of pride. "Pride imitates what is lofty":[27] and since the loftiest of all things is God, it is in the nature of pride to imitate God. From this it follows, according to Augustine, that all those vices of which pride is the fountainhead are in their very nature imitative of God. "Ambition [seeks] ... honour and glory," which are truly attributes of God alone.[28] "The cruelty of powerful people aims to arouse fear," while God alone is truly to be feared.[29] "Soft endearments are intended to arouse love," but there is no affection more tender than God's.[30] "Curiosity appears to be a zeal for knowledge"; "idleness appears as desire for a quiet life"; "luxury wants to be called abundance and satiety"; yet we find true knowledge, true rest, true abundance in God alone.[31] Above all, pride aspires and longs to imitate God's *power*. "For pride hates a fellowship of equality under God, and seeks to impose its own dominion on fellow men, in place of God's rule."[32] So pride and its subsidiary vices seek to imitate God himself; but, Augustine observes, there is something necessarily *false* about this imitation. The vices must masquerade as virtues in order to bolster their own lofty aspirations, but the falseness of their imitation is inevitably shown by comparison with the virtues of God himself.

This imitative impulse of pride not only accords with the vice's nature, but also serves the pragmatic function of concealing its true motivation. Naked pride threatens to engage not only the moral censure of the good, but also the resentment of the wicked.[33] As a consequence, the works that proceed from human pride will to a very considerable extent disguise themselves as the works of love:

Consider now the works that pride may do: notice how they may resemble or even equal those of charity. Charity feeds the hungry, so does pride; charity, to the praise of God, pride, to the praise of itself. Charity clothes the naked, so does pride; charity fasts, so does pride; charity buries the dead, so does pride. All the

---

[26] *CG* XIX.12, pp. 868–869.
[27] Augustine, *Confessions* (hereafter *C*), trans. and ed. Henry Chadwick (Oxford University Press, 1991), II.vi.13, p. 31.
[28] Ibid.   [29] Ibid.   [30] Ibid.
[31] Ibid. The catalog of vices continues, with prodigality mimicking God's true generosity, avarice aspiring to God's true possession of all, envy and anger and fear imitating God's true claim to excellence and vengeance and awe (ibid.).
[32] *CG* XIX.12, pp. 868–869.   [33] *OCD* I.47, p. 18.

good works that are willed and done by charity, may be set in motion by its contrary pride, like horses harnessed to a car.[34]

The capacity of pride to imitate love or charity constitutes for Augustine the greatest obstacle to pursuing a moral life in our sinful world. It is this which as much as any other factor creates for Augustine the persistent problem of moral uncertainty, the opacity of human moral psychology that he laments as the "wretched" epistemological blindness of the human condition.

How can we know or see that it be not pride which governs the good deed? Where is the proof? We see the works: hunger is fed by compassion, but also by pride; strangers are entertained by compassion, but also by pride; poverty is protected by compassion, but also by pride. In the works themselves we can see no difference.[35]

Instead, Augustine tells us, we need to recall ourselves constantly "from all this outward showing, . . . from the surface appearance displayed before men, to the inward truth."[36] This is what motivates the intensely intro-spective bent of Augustine's moral psychology; we are required to question our consciences vigorously, to "pay heed, not to the visible flowering but to the root beneath the ground," where covetousness or pride may lurk.[37]

That human beings are to a great extent incapable of distinguishing between charity and pride is a theme Augustine returns to repeatedly.[38] It emerges most clearly in the pages of Augustine's *Homilies on First John*. There he asks: "can there be a work more apparent than giving to the poor? Yet many do it for display and not for love. Can there be a greater work than dying for the brethren? Yet even of this many seek only the reputation, ambitious of acquiring the name, and not in truly heartfelt love."[39] Ultimately, for Augustine,

[34] Augustine, *Ten Homilies on the First Epistle of St. John* (hereafter *H1J*), in *Augustine: Later Works*, ed. John Burnaby (Westminster Press, 1955), 8.9, p. 322. This effect of pride is discussed most extensively in Augustine's *Homilies on 1ˢᵗ John*, from which the treatment here is principally derived. But there are other evidences of the same view elsewhere in Augustine's writings. In addition to those noted directly here, see for example Augustine, Sermon 335c, in Augustine, *Political Writings*, ed. E. M. Adkins and R. J. Dodaro (Cambridge University Press, 2001), p. 53; Augustine, Letter 138, Augustine to Marcellinus, in ibid., p. 38; Augustine, *Against Faustus* XXII.73–79, p. 227.

[35] *H1J* 8.9, p. 322. Even martyrdom may be the result of pride, a claim for which Augustine cites no less than the authority of St. Paul. (Indeed it may not be accidental that Augustine's citation of St. Paul here comes in such close proximity to the apostle's famous remark about seeing "through a glass darkly." See 1 Corinthians 13:3 and 13:12, respectively.)

[36] *H1J* 8.9, p. 322.   [37] Ibid., pp. 322–323.

[38] For the very interesting suggestion that an impulse toward concealment and privacy is central to Augustine's conception of pride, see further Markus, "*De Civitate Dei*," pp. 250–251.

[39] *H1J* 6.2, p. 303.

Love is the only final distinction between the sons of God and the sons of the devil. All may sign themselves with the sign of Christ's cross; all may answer Amen, and sing Alleluia; all may be baptized, all may come to church, and line the walls of our places of meeting. But there is nothing to distinguish the sons of God from the sons of the devil, save charity. They that have charity, are born of God; they that have not charity, are not. There is the great token, the great dividing mark. Have what else you will; if this one thing you have not, all is to no purpose. If you lack all the rest, have this, and you have fulfilled the law. "For he that loveth another," says the apostle, "hath fulfilled the law"; and "charity is the fullness of the law."[40]

There is a similar discussion of the problem in Augustine's *Confessions*. There he comments that there are

acts which resemble a vicious or injurious act but are not sins, because they do not offend against you, Lord our God, nor the consensus of the community. People accumulate resources for use as may be appropriate for the situation and the time; and it is uncertain whether or not the accumulating is done for mere lust for possession. Or with a zealous intention for improvement, proper authority may inflict punishment, and it is uncertain whether the motive was a mere desire to hurt people. Accordingly, there are many actions which people do not approve but which are attested by you to be right; and there are many actions praised by mankind which on your testimony are to be censured. Frequently the overt act has one face, the intention of the person doing it has quite another, and the critical circumstances of the moment cannot be known to us.[41]

---

[40] *HiJ* 5.7, p. 298. Augustine is even willing to go so far as to argue that the actions of God and Judas Iscariot, respectively, in giving up Christ to be crucified, can be distinguished only in terms of their inner character since they had identical outward effects. "But what makes the difference between the Father delivering up the Son, the Son delivering up himself, and Judas the disciple delivering up his master? In that the Father and the Son did it in charity, Judas in treachery. You see, we have to look, not at what a man does, but with what mind and will he does it . . . The difference in intention makes a difference in the acts. Though the thing is one, yet when we measure it by the difference of intention, the one lovable, the other damnable, we find that one is to be glorified and the other execrated. Such great virtue has charity: you see that it alone divides, it alone distinguishes the actions of men" (*HiJ* 7.7, pp. 315–316). Similarly, in Sermon 335c, p. 57, Augustine stresses the outward indistinguishability of Jesus and the two thieves with whom he was crucified in the Gospel account.

[41] *C* III.ix.17, p. 48. There is some ambiguity in Augustine as to whether the true motivating principles of human action are visible only to God, or whether they are capable of being reviewed by personal introspection. It is clear that such motivation is opaque to external viewers (*C* XIII.xxiii.33, p. 293; XIII.xiv.15, p. 282). But, despite the external opacity of human motivation, Augustine at times seems to suggest that the agents themselves may have access to the truth of their own intentions (*HiJ* 6.2, pp. 303–304). At the same time, it is a special feature of pride as opposed to other sins that it is especially resistant to introspective analysis of this sort. "I cannot easily be sure how far I am cleansed from that plague [pride]," Augustine says, for, with regard to other temptations, "I have some capacity for self-exploration, but in this matter almost none" (*C* X.xxxvii.60, pp. 214–215). Even more troublingly, pride "is a temptation to me even when I reject it, because of the very fact that I am rejecting it. Often the contempt of vainglory becomes a source of even more vainglory. For it is not

In such remarks as these we can get a sense of the dizzying set of theoretical challenges Augustine set himself by trying to couple his strict sense of moral order with the radical evaluative uncertainties, both external and internal, implicit in his moral psychology. Yet because of this very complexity, Augustine found that his moral theory must ultimately issue in a kind of moral simplicity. Knowing that "many things can be done that look well, yet do not issue from the root of charity," and that "some actions seem harsh or savage, but are performed for our discipline at the dictate of charity," Augustine is willing to state that "a short and simple precept is given you once for all: Love, and do what you will. Whether you keep silence, keep silence in love; whether you exclaim, exclaim in love; whether you correct, correct in love; whether you forbear, forbear in love. Let love's root be within you, and from that root nothing but good can spring."[42]

As we have seen, Augustine's peculiar understanding of the imitative relationship between pride and charity is at the root of the influential inward turn of his moral psychology. This alone would be of great significance to our investigation, since it is this mechanism that allows Augustine to prise apart the morality of intentions and states of mind on the one hand from the outward effects of action on the other. But the opacity and uncertainty engendered by pride's ability to imitate charity was not for Augustine merely a problem residing in the deepest recesses of psychological analysis or spiritual confession. Instead, as we will now see, it is also a centrally important feature of Augustine's political theory, carrying profound consequences for his account of the proper ends of politics as well as of the actions necessary to achieve those ends.

There are thus two implications of the imitative relationship between pride and charity that are of special importance to Augustine's proposed solution to the problem of dirty hands. First, Augustine's understanding of the imitative relationship between pride and charity served as the basis of his belief in the mutually informing and sometimes even tenuously cooperative relationship between the otherwise seemingly antagonistic forces of the earthly city and the heavenly city, a relationship that is ultimately as much as anything else one of *mutual reflection*. And, second, Augustine's conception of *moral opacity* in human life, discussed above, lays the

---

being scorned when the contempt is something one is proud of" (*C* x.xxxviii.63, p. 217). So the greatest evil in Augustine's philosophical system is all the more dangerous because it is the most resistant to our powers of knowledge and self-examination.

[42] *HiJ* 7.8, p. 316.

groundwork not only for his influential moral psychology but also (as we will see) for the core of his account of political life and political action.

AUGUSTINE'S TWO CITIES

The most immediate implications of this imitative dynamic for our understanding of Augustine's political theory can be seen in Augustine's account of the relationship between the heavenly city on the one hand and the city of Rome on the other. While Rome is not straightforwardly equivalent to the earthly city in Augustine's thought, it is nevertheless the most compelling visible exemplar of that city's character, and what Augustine says about Rome must go a long way toward explaining what he thinks about the relation between the earthly city and the heavenly city.[43] What emerges from Augustine's intriguing analysis of the Roman republic is that, in a fashion very similar to the imitative relationship of pride and charity, Rome, too, forms a kind of shadowy imitation of the heavenly city, in one sense quite distinct, but in another quite difficult to distinguish.

The Roman people, Augustine tells us, were "passionately devoted to glory; it was for this that they desired to live, for this they did not hesitate to die."[44] This desire for glory was the motivating factor behind all the Romans' impressive political achievements. First, it was the passion for glory that led the Romans to achieve their political freedom, since they found servitude to constitute the most shameful kind of political existence.[45] Then, finding that "liberty alone did not satisfy," they decided that "they had to acquire dominion" and the glory of power and empire that came with external expansion.[46] So according to Augustine the celebrated myth of the Roman attainment of liberty and empire had at its root the citizens' collective addiction to the praise of their fellow citizens and of the world.

Furthermore, Augustine makes clear, the Roman love of glory is a vice, indeed a vice closely connected to, if less dangerous than, the fundamental evil of pride. Augustine distinguishes the desire for glory from the *libido dominandi* that was central to his analysis of human evil. Even though he acknowledges that an excessive appetite for praise has a tendency to develop into a "burning passion for domination," he insists that true lovers of glory

---

[43] On this relationship, see particularly R. A. Markus, *Saeculum: History and Society in the Theology of St. Augustine* (Cambridge University Press, 1970), ch. 3, as well as J. M. Rist, *Augustine: Ancient Thought Baptized* (Cambridge University Press, 1994), ch. 6.

[44] *CG* V.12, p. 197.   [45] Ibid.   [46] Ibid. p. 198.

will not be as fully depraved as those driven by the desire for power, since they will always be anxious, not just for praise, but for the well-earned praise of good men.[47] Nevertheless, the love of glory is decidedly inferior to true virtue, Augustine claims, precisely because virtue itself "is not content with the testimony of men, without the witness of a man's own conscience."[48] Instead, this glory-seeking passion is wrong because it has an earthly rather than a heavenly object: consequently "the virtue which is employed in the service of human glory is not true virtue" in the fullest sense of the term.[49] It is instead a false virtue or quasi-virtue, an imitation of virtue that is only partially successful. The love of glory thus constitutes ultimately yet another instance of the disruption of true moral order and thus of moral failure.[50]

But while the desire for glory might be morally inferior to virtue, it nevertheless had its good effects, since it was from "the moral quality of those who stride towards glory, honour, and power by the right path, that is, by virtue itself" that true benefits came to the city.[51] This useful propensity of the Roman hunger for glory to generate publicly beneficial actions and outcomes manifested itself in two important ways, both of which were to become central features of the view that vice as well as virtue could help produce public benefits. First, the desire for glory, according to Augustine, tended to have a restraining effect on other human vices: it was the Romans' "unbounded passion for glory, above all else, [that] checked their other appetites," causing them to forego other sinful gratifications in favor of their one overarching passion.[52] This created citizens of courage and self-control, and thus of at least partly virtuous character. It would of course be preferable to have fully virtuous citizens: but since true virtue is not always available, Augustine asserts, if men have not learned to suppress their vices entirely, "at least it is good that the desire for human praise and glory makes them, not indeed saints, but less depraved men."[53]

In addition, Augustine believed, the desire for glory tended to restrain the ruthless conduct of ambitious men. Because glory requires the good opinion of others, those who pursued it needed at least to appear to have

---

[47] *CG* v.19, p. 212.   [48] *CG* v.12, p. 199.   [49] *CG* v.19, p. 213.

[50] According to Augustine, even the most "morally clear-sighted" of the Romans themselves recognized that the love of praise was indeed a fault. Such Roman thinkers acknowledged that "it is better to resist this passion [for praise] than to yield to it," and that "a man is more like God, the purer he is from this contamination," though according to Augustine they equally recognized that "in this life it cannot be wholly rooted out from the heart," because all are vulnerable to the temptation of pride (*CG* v.13–14, pp. 202–203). On the background of these ideas in Roman historical thought, see further Rist, *Augustine*, ch. 6.

[51] *CG* v.12, p. 201.   [52] Ibid. p. 197.   [53] *CG* v.13, p. 202.

those virtuous qualities for which men are praised (as Machiavelli was later to make much of).[54] As a consequence, their pursuit of glory tended to forestall their willingness to do great harm in seeking their advancement. Anyone who aims at power without regard for glory, Augustine claims, "generally seeks to accomplish his heart's desire by the most barefaced crimes," whereas the desire for glory tends to moderate one's actions.[55] By this means, the Roman passion for glory helped to generate "the energy at home ... that brought riches to the public treasure, while private fortunes remained straitened," in contrast to "the perverted situation after the moral corruption [from luxury and idleness] had set in, when we find the public purse empty and private pockets well lined."[56]

Augustine, then, recognizes that the Romans' passion for glory, while ultimately sinful, nevertheless had beneficial effects that contributed in the short term to the political well-being of the Roman state. In particular, Augustine tells us that it was because of the Romans' quasi-virtuous acts in pursuit of earthly glory that God favored them with such an extensive earthly dominion and used them as his agents in subduing and disciplining the nations of the world. It was for this reason that God, in order

to suppress the grievous evils of many nations ... entrusted this dominion to [the Romans], who served their country for the sake of honour, praise and glory, who looked to find that glory in their country's safety above their own and who suppressed greed for money and many other faults in favour of that one fault of theirs, the love of praise.[57]

This semblance of virtue which the love of glory affects, Augustine presumes, is the main reason why God has assisted the Romans, "who are good according to the standards of the earthly city, to the attainment of the glory of so great an empire."[58]

Thus Augustine suggests that the reason the Romans received divine favor in their acts of earthly conquest was the fact that their actions in pursuit of their own glory bore a genuine if imperfect resemblance to the true human virtue exercised in pursuit of God's glory. Because of this resemblance between the Romans' imitated virtue and real virtue, Augustine claims, they deserved, as the consequence of a kind of natural justice, to receive the glory they sought "as a reward for such virtues," even though their city was of infinitely lesser worth.[59] Since God refused to grant

---

[54] See Chapter 3, pp. 113–114.
[55] *CG* V.19, p. 212. The limiting factor to this beneficial feature of the vice of glory-loving is that it must at least "be overcome by the love of justice." See *CG* V.14, p. 203.
[56] *CG* V.12, p. 201. [57] *CG* V.13, pp. 201–202. [58] *CG* V.19, p. 213. [59] *CG* V.17, pp. 206–207.

true eternal life or heavenly citizenship to these Roman glory-seekers, it was only through glory that they could be "rewarded in full," paid in Caesar's coin, and thus to Augustine there is a certain natural justice to the fact that "men of this stamp should be accorded this kind of reward."[60]

In discussing pride's disposition to imitate charity, Augustine had invoked Christ's injunction about giving alms to the poor, warning the giver not to let one's left hand know what one's right hand is doing, lest one's charitable action be corrupted by one's impure motive. That passage ends with the thought that those who do good deeds solely for the praise of men "have their reward in full," and this thought seems to have been the dominant image for Augustine in conceptualizing God's providential purpose in granting dominion to the Roman people. He explains:

> If God had not granted to them the earthly glory of an empire which surpassed all others, they would have received no reward for the good qualities, the virtues, that is, by means of which they laboured to attain that great glory. When such men do anything good, their sole motive is the hope of receiving glory from their fellow men; and the Lord refers to them when he says, "I tell you in truth, they have received their reward in full." They took no account of their own material interests compared with the common good, that is the commonwealth and the public purse; they resisted the temptations of avarice; they acted for their country's well-being with disinterested concern; they were guilty of no offence against the law; they succumbed to no sensual indulgence. By such immaculate conduct they laboured towards honours, power, and glory, by what they took to be the true way. And they were honoured in almost all nations; they imposed their laws on many peoples; and today they enjoy renown in the history and literature of nearly all races. They have no reason to complain of the justice of God, the supreme and true. "They have received their reward in full."[61]

So for Augustine there is a kind of limited natural justice which explains the Romans' dominion: because their (sinful) love of glory was nevertheless strong enough to suppress their baser vices, they are rewarded, in a strictly limited sense, with the lesser gain of earthly dominion, even while the greater gain of the heavenly city's majesty is denied them.

In one sense, then, the heavenly city is a kind of higher standard against which the earthly city pales in comparison.[62] But the reflective relationship between the two cities implied by this reading of the metaphor is not a one-way transaction, as Augustine's later explanations make clear. For

---

[60] *CG* v.16, p. 205.   [61] *CG* v.17, pp. 204–205.
[62] This relationship is discussed in greater detail in Markus, *Saeculum*. See also Rex Martin, "The Two Cities in Augustine's Political Philosophy," *Journal of the History of Ideas* 33 (1972): 195–216.

Augustine, the earthly city also and importantly serves as a kind of comparative standard, a shadowy but genuine reflection of the heavenly city, able to motivate and inspire those members of the heavenly city who reside in the earthly realm.[63]

One aspect of this reflective process is familiar: Augustine always maintained that a part of the earthly city (usually that embodied either in the people of Israel or later in the Christian Church) served to represent and reflect the nature of the heavenly city here on earth. But Augustine also seems to believe that the earthly city as a whole, and not merely the part of it constituted temporarily by God's elect, can serve to signify and reflect the heavenly city by reason of its imitation of that city's true virtue. We see this most clearly in Augustine's treatment of the ways in which Rome's own imitation of virtue was able to serve as a reflection and an example of true heavenly virtue for Christians. In granting the Romans dominion, Augustine claims, God was not merely giving them their due: he also had in mind

this further purpose: that the citizens of that Eternal City, in the days of their pilgrimage, should fix their eyes steadily and soberly on those examples [of Roman virtue] and observe what love they should have towards the City on high, in view of life eternal, if the earthly city had received such devotion from her citizens, in their hope of glory in the sight of men.[64]

In order to suppress any pride they might feel in their own goodness, Augustine urges his Christian readers to "consider all the hardships these conquerors made light of, all the sufferings they endured, and the desires they suppressed to gain the glory of men."[65] For instance, countless Roman citizens sacrificed their private fortunes for the public good, and Brutus even sacrificed his children's lives for his city: what sacrifice is it then for Christians to share their property and even their children's inheritances to further the purposes of the heavenly city? As a consequence, "the citizens of so great a country should not suppose that they have achieved anything of note if, to attain that country, they have done something good, or endured some ills, seeing that those Romans did so much and suffered so much for the earthly country they already possessed."[66]

---

[63] Here I follow Richard Tuck's suggestion about Augustine in *The Rights of War and Peace* (Oxford University Press, 1999), p. 55.

[64] *CG* V.16, p. 205.

[65] Augustine, *CG* V.17, pp. 206–207.

[66] Ibid. Augustine adds that "what gives special point to this comparison is that the remission of sins, the promise which recruits the citizens for the Eternal Country, finds a kind of shadowy resemblance

The imitation of virtue inspired by the appetite for glory is not true virtue in the ultimate sense, because it is tainted by pride; yet even this sort of quasi-virtue must be given its due, he insists, since the worldly men thus inspired by glory really do come to be "of more service to the earthly city when they possess even that sort of virtue than if they are without it."[67] Thus for Augustine the imitation of true virtue by false virtue is not always *mere* vanity: on the contrary, the Romans' virtue (as far as it goes) is real virtue deserving of a real, if limited, reward at the hands of natural justice.[68]

So there is not only a kind of natural justice, but also a positive, providential purpose in Rome's acquisition of earthly dominion, Augustine claims; for

such instances as these ... would never have gained such renown, or been so often quoted, had not the Roman empire extended far and wide, coming to greatness with so impressive a record of success. Accordingly, it was that Empire, so far-spread and so long-lasting, and given lustre and glory by the heroic quality of its great men, that gave to them the return they looked for as a recompense for their resolution, while it sets before us Christians examples whose message we cannot but heed.[69]

God, then, according to Augustine, was working out his own beneficent purposes in ordaining the earthly dominion attained by the Roman people, and thus in permitting them to reach the heights attained by their own vicious appetite for glory. God was not the cause of this vice in the Roman people, but he made use of it for his own purposes.[70] This assertion is characteristic of Augustine's account of how God interacts with human vice where he encounters it. God's providence makes use of vice, but Augustine is anxious to insist that God's use of vice in this way does not implicate him in evil. He explains that God, "who is supremely good in his creation of natures that are good, is also completely just in his employment

in that refuge of Romulus, where the offer of impunity for crimes of every kind collected a multitude which was to result in the foundation of the city of Rome." See more generally *CG* v.17–18, pp. 206–211.

[67] *CG* v.19, p. 213.

[68] In reaching this conclusion, I advance a view of Augustine's evaluation of Rome and the earthly city that is substantially more positive than has been usual in Augustine scholarship. For opposed views see, for example, Charles Norris Cochrane, *Christianity and Classical Culture* (Oxford University Press, 1944), Paul Weithman, "Augustine's Political Philosophy," in Elanore Stump and Norman Kretzmann, eds., *The Cambridge Companion to Augustine* (Cambridge University Press, 2001), and Michael J. Wilks, "Roman Empire and Christian State in the *De Civitate Dei*," *Augustinus* 12 (1967), pp. 489–510.

[69] *CG* v.18, p. 211. See further Augustine, Letter 138, Augustine to Marcellinus, pp. 40–41.

[70] On this point see further Wilks, "Roman Empire and Christian State," pp. 529–530. For an important discussion of Augustine's conception of usefulness, see further O'Donovan, "Augustine's City of God XIX."

of evil choices in his design, so that whereas such evil choices make a wrong use of good natures, God turns evil choices to good use."[71] Augustine wants to claim further that even the lust for domination is frequently used by God to advance his good ends.

> The man who despises glory and is eager only for domination is worse than the beasts, in his cruelty or in his self-indulgence ... Yet even to men like this the power of domination is not given except by the providence of God, when he decides that man's condition deserves such masters. God's statement on this point is clear, when the divine Wisdom says, "It is through me that kings rule, and through me that tyrants possess the land."[72]

God, as we have seen, made similar use of the Roman people's appetite for glory, to fashion the courage and self-control they exercised in pursuit of praise into a functional imitation of virtue, something perhaps better and certainly more useful than simple lust for domination, though still ultimately vicious.[73]

Augustine's account of the good use God makes of human vice is closely related to his explanation of how vice mimics virtue, and especially how pride mimics charity. Indeed, according to Augustine, making good use of human vice is God's standard way of responding to the propensity of vice to imitate virtue. To take one example, Augustine, citing Paul's dictum, "Let Christ be preached, whether in pretence or in truth," goes on to add: "Christ is the truth, and yet the truth can be proclaimed even by untruth, in the sense that things which are right and true may be proclaimed by a wicked and deceitful heart, ... by those who seek their own and not the things of Jesus Christ."[74] Yet even this has its usefulness, Augustine tells us, since "even those that behave unprofitably are heard with profit," and consequently "they benefit many people by preaching what they do not practise," even though "they would benefit far more people if they practised what they preached."[75]

---

[71] *CG* XI.17, pp. 448–449. See further Augustine, Letter 220, Augustine to Boniface, in *Political Writings*, ed. Adkins and Dodaro, p. 222; Augustine, *Against Faustus* XXII.73–79, p. 227.

[72] *CG*, V.19, p. 213. Augustine adds: "It might be supposed that 'tyrants' here is used not in the sense of 'wicked and irresponsible rulers,' but in the ancient meaning of 'men of power' ... This suggestion is precluded by an unambiguous statement in another place, that God 'makes a hypocrite to reign, because of the perversity of the people.'"

[73] At the same time, Augustine acknowledges that "to examine the secrets of men's hearts and to decide with clear judgment on the varying merits of human kingdoms – this would be a heavy task indeed far beyond our powers," and because of this God, "who never leaves the human race unattended by his judgment or his help, granted dominion to the Romans when he willed and in the measure that he willed" (*CG* V.21, p. 215).

[74] *OCD* IV.151–152, p. 142.   [75] *OCD* IV.152–153, pp. 142–143.

PEACE AND THE LIMITS OF POLITICAL GOOD

As we have just seen, Augustine takes the imitative dynamic between pride and charity that dominates his moral psychology and transposes it to undergird the great theme of his political theory: the mutually reflective relationship between the earthly and the heavenly city. The imitative dynamic also underpins Augustine's influential response to the theological problem of evil: the claim that God systematically adapts evil actions to good uses. Taking these two insights together, we can now better understand the core proposition of Augustine's political theory. On earth, Augustine wants to claim, the political action of good people is properly directed, not toward achieving a rational ideal of political community (such as that envisioned for example by Plato), but rather toward securing the specific and limited good of temporal peace.

For Augustine, the goals of the heavenly and the earthly city converge crucially in their mutual desire for *peace*. This temporal peace is then able to serve as a shared foundation from which the two cities can pursue their ultimately differing ends. Augustine explains:

When we enjoy here, if we live rightly, such peace as can be the portion of mortal men under the conditions of mortality, virtue rightly uses the blessings of peace, and even when we do not possess that peace, virtue turns to a good use even the ills that man endures. But virtue is truly virtue when it refers all the good things of which it makes good use, all its achievements in making good use of good things and evil things, and when it refers itself also, to that end where our peace shall be so perfect and so great as to admit of neither improvement nor increase.[76]

Like the true glory sought by the Romans, temporal peace is a real but limited good which is deserving of its own reward. However imperfect this peace might be, it is the chief earthly good for which human beings in the earthly city actually do strive, and "it would be incorrect to say that the goods which this city desires are not goods, since even that city is better, in its own human way, by their possession."[77] Such goods as earthly peace "are goods and undoubtedly they are gifts of God," though they can be the source of misery if the higher goods of the heavenly city are neglected for their sake.[78] Indeed, it is precisely the fact that they *are* real goods, coupled with the (sometimes inordinate) strength of our human desire for them,

---

[76] *CG* XIX.10, pp. 864–865.
[77] *CG* XV.4, p. 599. See further Augustine, Letter 229, Augustine to Darius, in *Political Writings*, ed. Adkins and Dodaro, p. 224.
[78] *CG* XV.4, p. 600.

that makes it possible for temporal government to perform its task in the first place. As Augustine explains in his dialogue *On Free Will*:

The temporal law can punish evildoing only by taking away one or another of these goods from the one being punished. So it is by fear that the temporal law coerces human beings and bends the souls of its subjects in whatever direction it pleases. As long as they are afraid of losing those things, they use them with the kind of moderation necessary to maintain whatever sort of city can be built out of such people.[79]

Thus Augustine holds that earthly peace has real if limited moral value. "Even such a people loves a peace of its own, which is not to be rejected," Augustine tells us, "but it will not possess it in the end, because it does not make good use of it before the end."[80] Before the end, however,

it is important for us also [i.e., those in the city of God] that this people [i.e., those in the earthly city] should possess this peace in this life, since so long as the two cities are intermingled we [the citizens of the city of God] also make use of the peace of Babylon – although the People of God is by faith set free from Babylon, so that in the meantime they are only pilgrims in the midst of her.[81]

Here again we see the doctrine of the "reward in full" at work.

The two cities have very different aims in view, and this fact of course has significant moral and political implications. Those people who dwell in the earthly city are "in pursuit of an earthly peace based on the things belonging to this temporal life, and on its advantages." Those in the heavenly city, by contrast, look forward

to the blessings which are promised as eternal in the future, making use of earthly and temporal things like a pilgrim in a foreign land, who does not let himself be taken in by them or distracted from his course towards God, but rather treats them as supports which help him more easily to bear the burdens of "the corruptible body which weighs heavy on the soul"; they must on no account be allowed to increase the load.[82]

Yet the two cities remain in an important sense inseparably intermingled on earth. Augustine's favorite image for this intermingling is the Gospel parable of the wheat and the tares, in which an enemy sows weeds amidst the growing wheat in a good farmer's soil. When his servants ask whether they should pull out the tares, the farmer forbids them, lest they uproot the wheat as well; they will instead wait for the harvest, when the wheat and the tares can be cleanly separated. Augustine's preoccupation with this image seems to have arisen from his involvement with the Donatist controversy,

---

[79] *FW* 1.15, p. 26. [80] *CG* XIX.26, p. 892. [81] Ibid. [82] *CG* XIX.17, p. 877.

in which he argued against the separatists' moves to exit the institutional church to avoid entanglement with the impure elements therein. Augustine argues against the Donatist separatists by emphasizing that, as a partly human institution, the church – any church – necessarily shares in the moral opacity common to the human condition. Thus if false believers dwell in our midst unknowingly, Augustine argues, they do not contaminate us by our presence, since it is God himself who has permitted our inability to see clearly into one another's hearts. Instead, Augustine claims, we are innocent by virtue of our ignorance. "No one can be contaminated by the unknown crimes of unknown persons," he asserts, and furthermore "even well-known wrong-doers in the church do not harm its good members, if the latter have no power to prevent them from sharing communion, or if considerations of preserving peace provide a reason against this . . ."[83] Instead, Augustine teaches,

we bear with some whom we are unable to correct or even to punish; and we do not quit the Lord's threshing-floor because of the chaff which is there, nor break the Lord's net because of the bad fishes enclosed therein, nor desert the Lord's flock because of the goats which are to be in the end separated from it, nor go forth from the Lord's house because in it there are vessels destined to dishonour . . .[84]

For, according to Augustine, on earth the citizens of the heavenly kingdom, "surrounded as they are by the lost and the impious," must necessarily "be vexed by temptations, so that they can be trained and tested 'like gold in a furnace.'"[85]

So for Augustine both the city of God and the earthly city must "make use of the things essential for this mortal life; but each has its own very different end in making use of them."[86] Augustine elaborates that the "harmonious agreement" of the earthly city about "the giving and obeying of orders" is what leads to "the establishment of a kind of compromise between human wills about the things relevant to mortal life."[87] The heavenly city, however,

must needs make use of this peace also, until this mortal state, for which this kind of peace is essential, passes away. And therefore, it leads what we may call a life of

---

[83] Augustine, Letter 87, Augustine to Emeritus, in *Political Writings*, ed. Adkins and Dodaro, pp. 137–138.
[84] Augustine, Letter 189, Augustine to Boniface, s. 12, in Oliver O'Donovan and Joan Lockwood O'Donovan, eds., *From Irenaeus to Grotius: A Sourcebook in Christian Political Thought, 100–1625* (Eerdmans, 1999), p. 133.
[85] Augustine, Letter 189, Augustine to Boniface, in *Political Writings*, ed. Adkins and Dodaro, p. 217.
[86] *CG* XIX.17, p. 877.   [87] Ibid.

captivity in this earthly city as in a foreign land, although it has already received the promise of redemption, and the gift of the Spirit as a kind of pledge of it; and yet it does not hesitate to obey the laws of the earthly city by which those things which are designed for the support of this mortal life are regulated; and the purpose of this obedience is that, since this mortal condition is shared by both cities, a harmony may be preserved between them in things that are relevant to this condition.[88]

Thus Augustine's view leaves open the possibility that a political community with a real if limited common good may exist between mortals purely within the context of the earthly city. It is in this context that we ought to interpret Augustine's claim that, according to Cicero's standards in his *De Republica*, Rome never constituted a true republic. In Book II, Augustine tells us that Cicero had argued in his *De Republica* that justice is a prerequisite of harmony and flourishing in the public life: this is Cicero's basis for denying the claim that "injustice is inevitable in the government of any country."[89] The *res publica* or commonwealth can on Cicero's view only exist where there is truly "an association united by a common sense of right and a community of interest";[90] and, since such an order can only exist where there is a sound and just government, it follows that, where this does not obtain, the order that results is not an *unjust* commonwealth – which is a contradiction in terms – but rather no commonwealth at all. "For there can be no 'weal of the community' if it is unjust, since it is not 'associated by a common sense of right and a community of interest,' which was the definition of a community."[91] In particular, Augustine wants to argue, there is no community of interest – the term he uses for interest or advantage is *utilitas* – because "there are no advantages for men who live ungodly lives . . ."[92] As a consequence of this reasoning, Augustine wants to say, Cicero's own argument proves something much stronger than Cicero himself wants to acknowledge, namely that the Roman commonwealth "never existed, because there never was a real justice in the community"; the justice that appeared to exist was not "a living reality in men's behavior, but merely a fancy picture."[93]

In *City of God* Book XIX, Augustine returns to examine Cicero's argument about what constitutes a "real" *res publica*. Agreeing with Cicero that there is no true political community without true justice, Augustine goes much further to argue, on the basis of Christian religious premises, that, for there to be the kind of justice necessary to sustain a commonwealth in fact,

---

[88] Ibid. [89] *CG* II.21, p. 73.
[90] Ibid. Augustine seems to accept a version of this definition of *res publica* in Letter 138, Augustine to Marcellinus, p. 35.
[91] *CG* II.21, p. 74. [92] *CG* XIX.21, p. 883. [93] *CG* II.21, p. 75.

(1) God must rule (2) an obedient city; and due to this (3) the souls of individual people in the city must rule their bodies and (4) reason must rule the vices within their souls, in order that they may (5) live on the basis of faith and (6) show love to God and (7) to their neighbor. In other words, according to Augustine, an awful lot of pretty improbable dominoes have to fall in order to get a *true* politics off the ground at all.

But Augustine is willing to acknowledge that there is another sense in which it is appropriate to call a people a *res publica* in a weaker sense of that term, and thus that Rome "certainly was a commonwealth to some degree, according to more plausible definitions."[94] We can call a people a kind of commonwealth whenever they are "united by a common agreement on the objects of their love."[95] On this view, Rome does count as a community: the object of the Romans' love was glory, and they were in agreement on it. When applying this secondary definition of a commonwealth or people, it also follows for Augustine that "the better the objects of agreement, the better the people; and the worse the objects of this love, the worse the people."[96] Due to its sinful love of glory, Rome is far from being the best of all possible peoples. Yet at the same time, Augustine says, "I shall not make that a reason for asserting that a people is not really a people or that a state is not a commonwealth, so long as there remains an association of some kind or other between a multitude of rational beings united by a common agreement on the objects of its love."[97] Still, unless God rules in the city in the very precisely ordered and carefully calibrated sense implied in Augustine's overall moral theory, the city will remain in another sense "devoid of true justice."[98]

THE PROBLEMS OF POLITICAL ACTION

We are now prepared to turn our attention directly to the implications of Augustine's innovations in moral psychology and political theory for the development of the problem of dirty hands and the ethics of political action. As we have seen, the responsible actor in Augustine's politics undertakes to make use of an imperfect peace and of the shadowy goods of the earthly pilgrimage for higher purposes. And it is here that another aspect of pride's imitative capacity, namely its creation of a world of profound moral opacity, comes to play a role of key importance in Augustine's thinking about political ethics. For Augustine's proposed resolution of the problem of dirty hands rests on his claim that the moral opacity that characterizes humanity's sinful nature serves to justify

---

[94] *CG* II.21, p. 75.   [95] *CG* XIX.24, p. 890.   [96] Ibid.   [97] Ibid.   [98] Ibid., p. 891.

and excuse political actors in engaging in a wide range of actions that otherwise would have been morally impermissible.

In considering the problems of political ethics, Augustine displays a clear-sighted realism about the moral difficulties that may confront those who are called upon to rule. Unlike many of his early Christian predecessors, Augustine does not urge Christians to avoid public life. The claims of political responsibility, he acknowledges, may frequently compel a person to take up the active life out of love for others. "It is the compulsion of love that undertakes righteous engagement in affairs," Augustine tells us, and so if the task "is laid upon us, it is to be undertaken because of the compulsion of love."[99] God assigns us this responsibility according to his ineffable will, and it is this assignment that gives us a special moral permission grounded in our general duty of love toward others.[100]

Thus those who so act are called, Augustine believes, to a special role of political responsibility, in which they act not merely as themselves, but on behalf of their role or office. This move of Augustine's is of crucial significance for the later development of this line of thought, and in Augustine's own formulation the idea is closely tied to the actor's sense of responsible vocation, grounded in the general moral duties of love and benevolence. Augustine explains about the person called to a vocation of public responsibility that

as a man, he serves in one way, as a king in another. As a man, he serves by living faithfully, as a king by sanctioning with suitable vigour laws that order just behaviour and prevent its opposite. All kings serve the Lord in this way in so far as they are kings, performing in his service deeds that they could not perform unless they were kings . . .[101]

We can see this same idea about the moral implications of political roles further developed in the thought of Martin Luther, who in this as in so much else follows the lead of Augustine's theology to its logical conclusion. Explaining to his followers that the ethical teachings of the Sermon on the

---

[99] *CG* XIX.19, p. 880. See also Augustine, Sermon 302, s. 17, in *Political Writings*, ed. Adkins and Dodaro, p. 116.

[100] Augustine explains: "The eternal law, which commands maintaining the natural order and forbids disturbing it, places some human actions in a middle position, so that when human beings take it upon themselves to do these actions, their audacity is rightly blamed, but when they do them in carrying out a command, their obedience is justly praised. In considering the natural order, one must consider what is done, by whom it is done, and under whose command it is done. If Abraham had sacrificed his son of his own accord, what would he have shown himself to be except horrible and insane? As God was commanding him, however, did it not prove him to be faithful and devoted?" Augustine, *Against Faustus* XXII.73–79, pp. 220–221.

[101] Augustine, Letter 185, Augustine to Boniface, in *Political Writings*, ed. Adkins and Dodaro, p. 185.

Mount apply only to "how individuals are to live in relation to others, apart from official position," Luther tells us:

> We must distinguish sharply between these two, the office and the person. The man who is called Hans or Martin is a man quite different from the one who is called elector or doctor or preacher. Here we have two persons in one man ... God adorns and dresses you up as another person. He makes you a child and me a father, one a master and another a servant, one a prince and another a citizen ...[102]

In developing this influential line of reasoning, Luther appeals exactly as Augustine had to the limited, temporal necessity of establishing peace. "God himself," Luther argues, "has ordained and established this secular realm and its distinctions ... For without them this life could not endure. We are all included in them ... [and] we must also remain in them as long as we are on earth ... There is no getting around it, a Christian has to be a secular person of some sort ..."[103] The reason, moreover, that this simultaneous, dual existence is necessary, is that the Christian

> lives in human society and has to make use of secular and imperial things, the same way that heathen do. For until he has been transferred bodily from this life to another one, his flesh and blood is identical with theirs; and what he needs to provide for it does not come from the spiritual realm, but from the land and soil, which belongs to the emperor ..."[104]

Still, Luther cautions, Christians are to inhabit this dual existence "only according to our outward life and our physical existence," appealing again to a distinction made far more plausible by Augustine's inward turn. Thus Luther argues:

> When a Christian goes to war or when he sits on a judge's bench, punishing his neighbor, or when he registers an official complaint, he is not doing this as a Christian, but as a soldier or judge or lawyer. At the same time he keeps a Christian heart. He does not intend to harm anyone, and it grieves him that his neighbor must suffer grief. So he lives simultaneously as a Christian toward everyone, personally suffering all sorts of things in the world, and as a secular person, maintaining, using, and performing all the functions required by the law of his territory or city, by civil law, and by domestic law ...[105]

Augustine stresses, however, that roles of political responsibility are not something to be sought for their own sake; if such roles are "not imposed on us, we should employ our freedom from business in the quest for truth and its

---

[102] Luther, "The Sermon on the Mount," in O'Donovan and O'Donovan, *From Irenaeus to Grotius*, p. 596.
[103] Ibid., pp. 598–601.   [104] Ibid., p. 600.   [105] Ibid., p. 601.

contemplation."[106] The principal reason we should avoid politics if we can, according to Augustine, is that of the grave moral dangers which politics poses for its practitioners. Nothing is more morally dangerous than the lust for domination which is an inevitable temptation for those who wield power. "Why do you want the difficult task of accounting for someone else's death ...,' Augustine asks, when "God has given you the freedom of not being a judge" and so "the burden of authority isn't yours to carry?"[107] Given this risk of moral corruption, Augustine thinks, we should prefer even to endure the rule of an unjust government rather than hazard our own moral purity unnecessarily. For "as for this mortal life, which ends after a few days' course, what does it matter under whose rule a man lives, being so soon to die, provided that the rulers do not force him to impious and wicked acts?"[108] So while the political life does not for Augustine necessarily entail moral tragedy, its avoidance of such tragedy is strictly a matter of moral luck.[109]

But it is not only these hazards of the soul that complicate Augustine's account of the ethics of political action. Perhaps even more importantly, Augustine is acutely aware that human life, especially in politics, is beset by unavoidable choices that appear, at least on the surface, to constitute genuine moral dilemmas. And the cause of these recurrent dilemmas, according to Augustine, is most frequently our blurry perceptions of human motivation and the consequent difficulties that arise in trying to render our inevitable judgments upon them.

When Augustine lists the ills of our mortal condition, he focuses sharply on those features of human life that are caused by the uncertainty of our moral knowledge. Even peace, Augustine says,

is a doubtful good, since we do not know the hearts of those with whom we would wish to maintain peace, and even if we could know them today, we should not know what they might be like tomorrow. In fact, who are, in general, more friendly, or at any rate ought to be, than those within the walls of the same home? And yet, is anyone perfectly serene in that situation, when such grievous ills have so often arisen from the secret treachery of people within those walls? And the bitterness of these ills matches the sweetness of the peace that was reckoned genuine, when it was in fact only a very clever pretence.[110]

It is precisely for this reason that Augustine uses the terms "pitiable" and "lamentable" to describe "those judgments passed by men on their

[106] *CG* XIX.19, p. 880.   [107] Augustine, Sermon 302, s. 13, p. 115.   [108] *CG* V.17, p. 205.
[109] On the concept of moral luck, see Bernard Williams, *Moral Luck* (Cambridge University Press, 1981), ch. 2.
[110] *CG* XIX. 5, p. 858.

fellow-men, which cannot be dispensed with in cities, however much peace they enjoy."[111]

Moreover, the reason for this tragic state of affairs is at root an epistemological problem, arising out of the moral opacity that creates pride's ability to imitate charity and its virtuous outward effects. We see this especially clearly in Augustine's account of the moral problems encountered by judges in the execution of their duties. Augustine explains that the judge's moral responsibilities are different from those of ordinary citizens, based on the necessary function to which the judge is called.

Usually a judge unsheathes his sword only when forced to. When he strikes, he does so unwillingly. Personally, he would have liked to have avoided bloodshed when sentencing; but maybe he did not want public order to collapse. He was obliged to act this way by his office, by his authority, by the demands of his situation.[112]

The trouble, Augustine tells us, is that "those who pronounce judgment cannot see into the consciences of those on whom they pronounce it."[113] As a consequence, those who exercise political power

are often compelled to seek the truth by torturing innocent witnesses in a case which is no concern of theirs. And what about torture employed on a man in his own case? The question is whether he is guilty. He is tortured, and, even if innocent, he suffers, for a doubtful crime, a punishment about which there is no shadow of doubt and not because he is discovered to have committed it, but because it is not certain that he did not commit it. This means that the ignorance of the judge is often a calamity for the innocent. And there is something yet more intolerable: . . . the fact that the judge tortures the accused for the sole purpose of avoiding the execution, in ignorance, of an innocent man: while his pitiable lack of knowledge leads him to put to death, tortured and innocent, the very person whom he had tortured to avoid putting the innocent to death.[114]

And if, as frequently occurs, the accused, though innocent, "confesses to a crime he has not committed," then afterwards "the judge still does not know whether it was a guilty or an innocent person he has executed, after torturing him to avoid executing the innocent in ignorance."[115]

All this might appear to the modern reader to constitute a strong argument against the employment of torture and execution as means, but

---

[111] *CG* XIX.6, p. 859.   [112] Augustine, Sermon 302, p. 116.
[113] *CG* XIX.6, p. 859.   [114] Ibid., pp. 859–860.
[115] Ibid., p. 860. Augustine seems to believe that what is crucial in this process is not punishing the offenders so much as establishing the truth – in order to spare the innocent even more than to sanction the guilty. See Augustine, Letter 135, Augustine to Marcellinus, in *Political Writings* ed. Adkins and Dodaro, p. 246.

Augustine refuses to draw this conclusion.[116] More conspicuously, Augustine resists even the claim that the Christian judge will decline to employ these methods himself. Instead, he takes for granted that the Christian who has truly been called to a life of political action will undertake to use even these extremely dubious means, given the weight of his responsibility for the public good.[117] "In view of this darkness that attends the life of human society," Augustine asks, "will our wise man take his seat on the judge's bench, or will he not have the heart to do so? Obviously he will sit; for the claims of human society constrain him and draw him to this duty; and it is unthinkable to him that he should shirk it."[118] In fact, Augustine goes on to say, "it is not to him an unthinkable horror" that innocent witnesses should be tortured in cases in which they are not accused, or that prisoners should be driven to make false confessions through torture (even torture that results in death), or that witnesses should give false evidence, or that the judge "in his ignorance, may condemn" the innocent.[119]

But despite the fact that Augustine's judge must make use of such violent and uncertain methods, Augustine consistently maintains that, when the judge does so in fulfillment of the public responsibilities to which he has been called, he incurs no moral blame. In other circumstances, Augustine shows himself to be extremely resistant to the notion that human beings might sometimes need to employ evil means to promote just ends; he argues, for example, that "anyone who believes that a lie is sometimes useful believes that injustice is sometimes useful" (which is according to Augustine "impossible.")[120] So, inverting this same line of reasoning, in the case of the judge Augustine argues that he will not only participate in these questionable processes, but will do so blamelessly. "All these serious evils our philosopher does not reckon as sins," Augustine tells us, "for the wise judge does not act in this way through a will to do harm."[121] His predicament is rather that "ignorance is unavoidable – and yet the exigencies of human society make judgment also unavoidable."[122] The wise man who acts in accordance with this reality and performs his responsibilities does not do evil "in his judicial capacity," since "it is through unavoidable

---

[116] On this point see further O'Donovan, "Augustine's *City of God* XIX," p. 107.
[117] Max Weber echoes this language of the "calling for politics," though with quite a different moral in mind, in his famous essay "Politics as a Vocation," in H. H. Gerth and C. Wright Mills, eds., *From Max Weber: Essays in Sociology* (Oxford University Press, 1946).
[118] *CG* XIX.6, p. 860.   [119] Ibid.
[120] *OCD* 1.87–88, p. 27. But see further Augustine's remarks on lying in *Enchiridion* 6, 18–19, pp. 254–255, in *Political Writings*, ed. Adkins and Dodaro.
[121] *CG* XIX.6, p. 860.   [122] Ibid.

ignorance and the unavoidable duty of judging that he tortures the inno-cent"; he is rather excused, Augustine believes, by the joint pressures exercised by his office and his ignorance.[123]

Thus, it is the opacity of human moral existence that makes the evils and tragedies characteristic of political action both necessary and endurable; it is our helplessness to distinguish definitively among inner moral phenom-ena that both requires and excuses the brutality of our public actions. And yet, in fulfilling his duty innocently, the Christian political actor is not to be deemed "happy," Augustine tells us: he is called to troubling work, and therefore is expected to be troubled by it. It is not wickedness, but rather "the wretchedness of man's situation," which accurately characterizes the judge's predicament: "How much more mature reflection it shows, how much more worthy of a human being it is when a man acknowledges this necessity as a mark of human wretchedness, when he hates that necessity in his own actions and when, if he has the wisdom of devotion, he cries out to God, 'Deliver me from my necessities!' "[124]

A different formulation of the same dynamic can be found in Augustine's influential treatment of international political action, includ-ing his pioneering theory of "just war."[125] In his most fully developed reflections on the topic, Augustine challenges the pacifist viewpoint typical of most of the preceding Christian tradition by arguing that, under the sinful and uncertain conditions of temporal reality, it will sometimes prove necessary for even Christians to use force for the purpose of resisting evil. Always of course it is preferable to avoid violence; but sometimes, Augustine believes, there are situations in which, regardless of which action one takes, someone will be harmed. Given these harsh realities of life in the earthly sphere, it will sometimes be necessary for those in political author-ity to choose whom the burden of this unavoidable harm will fall upon. Augustine's view is clear: those in authority must choose based on the least of the various evils. "It is much better," he tells us, "that one who plots against another's life should be killed rather than one who is defending his own life"; but also (and perhaps more at odds with contemporary moral intuitions), "it is much worse for someone unwillingly to suffer a sexual

---

[123] Ibid. One of the few commentators to attend to the fact that for Augustine the moral agent's actions are excused by his ignorance combined with his responsibility is Weithman, "Augustine's Political Philosophy."

[124] *CG* XIX.6, pp. 860–861.

[125] For a general account of these views, see Deane, *The Political and Social Ideas of St. Augustine*, as well as R. A. Markus, "Saint Augustine's Views on the 'Just War,'" *The Church and War: Studies in Church History* 20 (1983): 1–13, and Paul Ramsey, "The Just War According to St. Augustine," in *War and the Christian Conscience* (Duke University Press, 1961).

assault, than for the assailant to be killed by the one he was going to assault."[126]

Someone must make these difficult choices, and this burden Augustine again places on the shoulders of those called to positions of public responsibility. Citing a remark by John the Baptist to soldiers seeking moral guidance, Augustine argues that the political role that soldiers undertake distinguishes and alters the consequent morality of their actions. Even though such soldiers might be forced to use violence in the course of their work, Augustine maintains, "they are not murderers but ministers of the law, and not avengers of their own injuries but defenders of public well-being": and this distinction of role or function matters crucially for Augustine.[127]

For it makes a great difference by which causes and under which authorities men undertake the wars that must be waged. The natural order, which is suited to the peace of mortal things, requires that the authority and deliberation for undertaking war be under the control of a leader, and also that, in the executing of military commands, soldiers serve peace and the common well-being.[128]

Thus, on Augustine's view, the good person will in general wage war when doing so is just; but in doing so he will also "lament the fact that he is faced with the necessity of waging just wars; for if they were not just, he would not have to engage in them, and consequently there would be no wars for a wise man."[129] What lays the duty of waging wars on the wise man is "the injustice of the opposing side," and injustice is assuredly "to be deplored" even though "no necessity of war should arise from it."[130] For Augustine, it is significant that the soldier acts within a context which it is beyond his power to control or alter; indeed, in a sense it is this context rather than the soldier himself that can be seen as the true agent of violence. Thus, Augustine argues that, when a soldier or other authorized agent exercises violence, "it ought to be necessity, and not your will, that destroys an enemy who is fighting you . . ."[131]

These factors, emerging out of Augustine's innovative moral psychology, allow Augustine to offer to the soldier the same escape from the dirty hands predicament that he had offered elsewhere to the judge: namely, that since morality is at its core a matter of *intention* and disposition, conceivably a person could commit any external act, even killing,

---

[126] *FW* I.5, p. 8. [127] Augustine, *Against Faustus* XXII.73–79, p. 222.
[128] Ibid. [129] *CG* XIX.7, p. 862. [130] Ibid.
[131] Augustine, Letter 189, Augustine to Boniface, p. 217. For further confirmation of this element of Augustine's argument, see *Against Faustus* XXII.73–79; *CG* IV.15, p. 154.

without incurring the moral blameworthiness associated with murder. As Evodius, one of Augustine's interlocutors in his dialogue *On Free Will*, states with Augustine's apparent approval,

If murder is just killing a human being, then there can be murder that is not sinful. When a soldier kills the enemy, when a judge or his representative puts a criminal to death, or when a weapon accidentally slips out of someone's hand without his willing or noticing it: these people do not seem to be sinning when they kill someone.[132]

Thus for Augustine killing on behalf of one's community in a just cause is morally in approximately the same class as someone whose weapon injures someone by slipping from his grasp: both are outcomes of external processes that are no part of the agent's internal will.

Indeed, it turns out that, for Augustine, not only is the difference between killing and murder exclusively a matter of intention, but also war itself is mostly lamentable not because of the physical suffering it causes but rather because it tends to damage the moral *intentions* of those it involves. Augustine asks:

What is it about war that is to be blamed? Is it that those who will die someday are killed so that those who will conquer might dominate in peace? This is the complaint of the timid, not the religious. The desire for harming, the cruelty of revenge, the restless and implacable mind, the savageness of revolting, the lust for dominating, and similar things – these are what are justly blamed in wars.[133]

Thus the crucial thing about whether an act of killing can be justified is whether it occurs with pure intention: or to put it more precisely and in Augustine's own terminology, whether or not it is motivated by lust or "inordinate desire."

It is in this light that we can see what for Augustine is morally distinctive about politics, what ultimately permits those who hold political authority or enact political roles to take actions others cannot. For it is in politics especially that we find those rare cases where such actions as killing might plausibly be taken *without* inordinate desire. "A soldier who kills the enemy is acting as an agent of the law," Augustine observes, and "so he can easily perform his duty without inordinate desire."[134] Politics creates a sphere which aims to protect interests that are not merely our own, and this fact allows political actors to do what they must *without* requiring any

---

[132] *FW* I.4, pp. 6–7. See further Augustine, Letter 138, Augustine to Marcellinus, pp. 38–39.
[133] See further Augustine, *Against Faustus* XXII.73–79, p. 221.
[134] *FW* I.5, p. 8.

improper motivation. Indeed, in a sense the purpose of politics is to permit the actions necessary to secure temporal peace, while at the same time cordoning off those morally suspect motivations which typically accompany the actions. Thus Augustine holds that "the law itself, which is established with a view to protecting the people, cannot be accused of any inordinate desire."[135] In a way, the point of the kind of politics Augustine has imagined is precisely that it justifies the necessary actions of political life: first by isolating the morality of those actions in internal states of mind, and then by using the idea of politics itself as a way of purifying the intentions of the actors involved.

Exponents of Augustine's political theory often casually attribute his stance on political action to an endorsement of what is necessary in a world of fallen men, and at the most fundamental level this is of course correct. But it is important to stress that for Augustine it is not merely human sinfulness in some *general* sense that lies at the root of the special ethical problems attached to political action. This more generalized view fails to capture two of the more interesting aspects of Augustine's treatment of the problem. First, we find in Augustine's account of the mutually reflective relationship between pride and charity the basis of his insistence on the morally opaque character of human existence – an opacity that characterizes both human motivation and the workings of God's providence (from the point of view of the human moral agent). It is this dynamic of opacity that both motivates and facilitates the celebrated "inward turn" of Augustine's psychology. But it is also this dynamic that made it possible for subsequent thinkers drawing on Augustine to further extend the concept of sinfulness almost completely beyond human comprehension and differentiation (as we will see in Chapter 5). By bringing vice indoors, so to speak, and thereby radically internalizing the conceived location of moral action, Augustine is able to portray vice as both a much more widespread and a much more inconspicuous phenomenon than any previous moral theory had done.

Second, we also find that this moral opacity is what leads Augustine to single out the epistemological blindness of the human condition as the fundamental problem that plagues the ethics of political action. The imitative, reflective quality of pride as against love, the earthly city as against

---

[135] Ibid. Of course, Augustine acknowledges, either the person who enacts the law or the person who obeys the law *might* act from inordinate desire, using the law as an excuse. But if *either* the legislator or the executive power in such a case acts from a pure will, an impure will in the other party will not impugn the morality of the other's action (that is, a purely enacted law can be lustfully obeyed, and a lustfully enacted law can be innocently obeyed).

the heavenly, is precisely what makes ethical action in politics so difficult for human beings to perform. Yet at the same time, because of that reflective quality's *usefulness* in the hand of God, it also constitutes one of the most common modes of operation of God's mysterious providence. The political actor does not seek to capitalize on this usefulness himself, in Augustine's theory: that is left to the hand of God. Nor is he required to commit actual moral evils himself: the combination of his office and his ignorance excuses him. But in a strange way, Augustine's responsible political actor, while in one sense the instrument of God's providence, is also placed in the position of navigating the uncertain and treacherous moral waters of the problem of dirty hands, precisely because this is the sea God has chosen to set him adrift on: for it is God who has chosen to use the mysterious moral blurriness of the human condition as a means of providence for his human creation.[136]

As we will see in the chapters that follow, subsequent thinkers drew on these two aspects of Augustine's thought in a variety of surprising ways. But Augustine's proposed resolution of these moral problems of public action came at a cost, and resulted in a synthesis of ancient political and Christian moral motivations that was eventually to prove to be fundamentally unstable. It is to the story of the unraveling of this Augustinian synthesis in the early years of modernity, and the vivid re-emergence of some of the very problems Augustine himself had sought thus to resolve, that we will turn in Chapter 3.

---

[136] For an alternative view, see by comparison Peter Burnell, "The Problem of Service to Unjust Regimes in Augustine's *City of God*," *Journal of the History of Ideas* 54 (1993): 177–188.

PART II

Dirty hands nowhere and everywhere

CHAPTER 3

Renaissance dilemmas

You see the position to which someone who wanted to govern states strictly according to conscience would be reduced. Therefore when I talked of murdering or keeping the Pisans imprisoned, I didn't perhaps talk as a Christian; I talked according to the reason and practice of states. Nor will anyone be more of a Christian who rejects such cruelty but recommends doing everything possible to take Pisa, since this means in effect being the cause of infinite evils to occupy something that doesn't according to conscience belong to you. Anyone who doesn't acknowledge this has no excuse before God, because – as the friars like to say – it shows "crass ignorance" . . .[1]

Francesco Guicciardini, *Dialogue on the Government of Florence*

The ancient version of the problem of dirty hands met with an ingenious resolution at the hands of Augustine, whose philosophy appealed to a metaphorical relationship between Roman and Christian values in order to fulfill the responsibilities of the one without betraying the principles of the other. This synthesis created a delicate moral balance between the claims of divine providence and human necessity, of heavenly and earthly virtue, the claims of Rome and those of Christ. Yet it remained a delicate balance, one which eventually proved to be, at its heart, fundamentally unstable.

It was in the Renaissance, amidst a culture that was beginning to think of itself once more as heir to the values of both Rome and Christ, that worries about dirty hands in public life once more began to reassert themselves systematically. With the revival of interest in ancient philosophical texts, and as governments in Italy began to experiment with adapted forms of ancient political institutions, the Augustinian synthesis began to encounter serious challenges to its coherence and cogency. In response to these challenges, the Renaissance produced a distinctive new version of the

---

[1] Francesco Guicciardini, *Dialogue on the Government of Florence*, ed. Alison Brown, Bk. II, (Cambridge University Press, 1994), p. 159.

problem of dirty hands; yet it was also one that looked backwards to the ancient past, picking up where the conflict between Roman politics and Christian morality had left off. In this chapter, we will examine the forms in which the problem of dirty hands re-emerged in two of the most important Renaissance thinkers' work: first, in Machiavelli's major political writings (*The Prince* and the *Discourses on Livy*); and, second, in Thomas More's *Utopia* (or, more fully, *On the Best State of a Commonwealth and on the New Island of Utopia*).

What was new in the Renaissance version of the problem of dirty hands, and will be significant for the entire story that follows, was a sense that not only political leaders but also those citizens on whose behalf they act contribute to the dynamic that creates the problem of dirty hands – and are therefore potentially implicated in the moral responsibility for those actions taken for their sake. These texts, that is to say, share a sense that there is a "democratic" dimension to the problem, at least as a matter of the problem's diagnosis and perhaps also as a matter of its resolution. Machiavelli's approach to the problem recognizes that the moral failures of the people – their "corruption," to use his terminology – is at least one of the major factors that makes politics such a morally perilous arena for action. Yet his approach to the problem seeks to deflect moral danger away from the populace at large by nominating some aristocratic figure, a "prince" or other political leader, to assume responsibility for confronting and if necessary taking on himself the moral dangers of dirty hands. Machiavelli does not offer the moral excuses of his new political ethic to ordinary citizens, who remain bound by traditional morality. The new ethic is instead a privilege for political leaders, justified by the great ends for which they bear responsibility – in their charge to safeguard the common good of the people as a whole, and in particular in the modes of crisis politics that especially emerge at moments of political founding and refounding.

The second part of the chapter develops a related argument with respect to Thomas More's *Utopia*. Book I of *Utopia* describes a dialogue on the relative merits of the active life of political service versus the life of philosophical contemplation and retreat. This dialogue culminates in a set of rival and incompatible claims about the moral responsibilities and moral risks associated with a life of political action – a powerful articulation of the Renaissance problem of dirty hands. As we will see, the dialogue is deliberately left unresolved because More wants to point beyond the problem of dirty hands in public life to its theoretical solution, offered in the form of an ideal polity located "nowhere" – Utopia. (Accepting that

Utopia is indeed offered as a moral ideal is controversial; the argument for doing so is therefore an integral part of what will follow.) Yet if Utopia is (at least in a broad sense) More's ideal, we must then explore why More lays such emphasis on the fact that it is located "nowhere," and what implications this has for the problem in general.

Understood in this way, *Utopia* offers a distinctive advance in the development of the problem of dirty hands. Even more thoroughly than Machiavelli, More demonstrates that behind the elite problem of dirty hands we find democratic dirty hands — that is, the root causes of the problem lie in moral failures on the part of the people as a whole. But, in contrast to Machiavelli, More urges that because dirty hands is essentially a democratic problem, only a democratic solution – if anything at all – can really hope to resolve it.

MACHIAVELLI

Because the reordering of a city for a political way of life presupposes a good man, and becoming prince of a republic by violence presupposes a bad man, one will find that it very rarely happens that someone good wishes to become prince by bad ways, even though his end be good, and that someone wicked, having become prince, wishes to work well, and that it will ever occur to his mind to use well the authority that he has acquired badly.[2] (Machiavelli, *Discourses on Livy*)

Thoughtful reflection and passionate concern about the problems of ethics in political life flourished in the Renaissance, but throughout the period no treatment of the topic commanded the attention – or the wide censure – attached to the writings of Niccolo Machiavelli. Machiavelli, a professional diplomat and political operative, rose to a position of great influence in the politics of the republic of Florence before falling – first into peril and then disrepute – when the republican regime fell to the Medici rulers in 1512. His most enduringly provocative writings on politics, *The Prince* (1513) and the *Discourses on Livy* (composed throughout the following decade), respond to this set of experiences in contrasting ways. *The Prince* tries to display to the new princely regime the potential value of Machiavelli's savvy and unconventional political analysis; the *Discourses*, by contrast, applies similar principles to the analysis of a republican politics that Machiavelli hoped could in the long run supplant and replace the Medici regime.

---

[2] Niccolo Machiavelli, *Discourses on Livy*, trans. and ed. Harvey Mansfield and Nathan Tarcov (University of Chicago Press, 1996), 1.18, p. 51.

In pioneering this new ethic, Machiavelli does not exhibit great moral anguish over the choices his political actors face. Instead, he seeks leaders with the moral courage to accept the necessity of doing wrong in order to achieve what is right. But Machiavelli's brutal realism helped to dismantle the clichéd moralistic (Cicero) and spiritual (Augustine) strategies for evading the consequences of moral conflict in politics – and succeeded in leaving generations of his readers worrying about the troubling insights generated by his new modes of political analysis and action.

What was new and distinctive in Machiavelli's political ethic? To begin with, Machiavelli's writings capture better than any thinker before him the deep potential conflict between certain of the classical and Christian virtues on the one hand and the Roman political values of glory and empire on the other. As a consequence, Machiavelli radically questions these traditional moral standards, implicitly characterizing the Ciceronian virtues as ineffective and naive, and explicitly deriding the Christian virtues as weak and effeminate. Machiavelli's theory thus rejects the Augustinian approach, undercutting both its foundations in conventional classical virtue and the Christian elevation of those virtues to an otherworldly framework.

Machiavelli's status as one of history's most daring moral revisionists has led some to mistakenly characterize him as championing a fully amoral ethic of political success. But this formulation, while containing a grain of truth, misses much of what is distinctive about Machiavelli's moral view. For, rather than merely dismissing traditional moral frameworks, Machiavelli instead begins by accepting their validity, and then pointing out how on their own terms the traditional frameworks involve plural and ultimately deeply conflictual value commitments. Machiavelli thus accepts these traditional moral frameworks but urges a dramatic reprioritization among them, elevating the value of the political common good idealized in Roman moral and political thought above competing values whenever they come (as eventually they must) into conflict. Thus Machiavelli's political theory does not call for the abandonment of traditional frameworks of moral virtue: instead it preserves those frameworks, at least in part, while at the same time insisting on the existence and importance of a different virtue – an extraordinary virtue – that can when necessary transcend the claims of ordinary virtue and morality.

THE NEW ETHIC

What is Machiavelli's new virtue? It is, to begin with, something that defines itself in opposition to the platitudes associated with classical or

Christian morality. In order to survive, Machiavelli argues, a political leader must hone his vices alongside his virtues;[3] he must learn "to be able not to be good," as his fellows are not, "and to use this and not use it according to necessity."[4] Thus one of the central features of Machiavelli's ethical approach is his claim that in certain situations virtue counts as a vice, and vice virtue. Violence and cruelty, tight-fistedness and greed, and above all fraud and faithlessness are all classical or Christian vices, but as the times require they may also, Machiavelli asserts, become the indispensable virtues for effective political leadership. To master these new virtues, political leaders must undergo the profound moral re-education offered by Machiavelli in the central passages of *The Prince*.

In advancing this line of argument, Machiavelli threatens to undermine some of his readers' most cherished religious beliefs and moral intuitions. Why then is Machiavelli able to make his redefinition of virtue plausible? The answer lies in the ambiguous and multi-layered history of the concept of virtue itself. Of necessity oversimplifying, we can isolate three key strains in the development of the concept of virtue, each central to the idea as it emerges in Machiavelli's Renaissance culture, yet held together in an uneasy tension (which Machiavelli underlines and exacerbates). The first strain in the concept's development is virtue as *areté*, the ancient Greek concept of excellence: here the central focus of virtue is *capability*, with the idea of moral goodness itself being an expression of such capability. The second strain, emerging more clearly in the Roman culture preferred by Machiavelli, is of virtue as *virtus*, literally *manliness* as well as excellence: the quality of the *vir virtutis* is that of the "manly" as well as the "excellent" man, and such quintessentially "manly" traits as independence, decisiveness and violent power were, along with more ordinary goodnesses, rolled into a single conception of Roman excellence.[5] Finally, Christianity introduced a third strain of meaning to the concept of virtue, the one which Machiavelli worried had in his own day come to overpower the first two: namely, virtue as a kind of moral *purity*. This strain incorporated the Christian excellences of meekness and gentleness, chastity and humility into the concept of virtue alongside such traditional classical moral

---

[3] The notion of a "her" having "virtues" in the relevant sense Machiavelli himself would unfortunately have found implausible. Among many sources, see especially Hanna Pitkin, *Fortune is a Woman* (University of Chicago Press, 1999).

[4] Niccolo Machiavelli, *The Prince*, trans. and ed. Harvey Mansfield, 2nd edn (University of Chicago Press, 1998), ch. 15, p. 61.

[5] On this subject, see Harvey Mansfield, *Machiavelli's Virtue* (University of Chicago Press, 1996), ch. 1, and Russell Price, "The Senses of *Virtù* in Machiavelli," *European Studies Review* 3 (1973): 315–345.

excellences as wisdom and self-control, and tended to denigrate, for example, the violence and ferocity celebrated in the Roman strain.

Machiavelli's chief moral objective, voiced most directly in Book II, chapter 2 of his *Discourses on Livy*, is to prise the manly excellence that had dominated pre-Christian moral systems – celebrated by Machiavelli in his own use of the word *virtù* – clear of this rival Christian strain of purity-virtue. "This [modern Christian] mode of life thus seems to have rendered the world weak and given it in prey to criminal men, who can manage it securely, seeing that the collectivity of men, so as to go to paradise, think more of enduring their beatings than of avenging them," Machiavelli explains; thus the modern world "appears to be made effeminate and heaven disarmed . . ."[6] The alternative is not of course necessarily to become *bad*, even on Christian terms, but rather to learn *how* not to be good, and then to choose which to be according to what the times require. This raises two central questions about Machiavelli's new approach. First, what is it *about* politics, precisely, that according to Machiavelli requires us to sometimes *not* be good in the Christian sense? And, second, *when* and *how* precisely does Machiavelli think politics requires us not to be good?

Machiavelli's response to the first question hearkens back to Cicero's *On Duties*, but not to pay homage to ancient wisdom (as Machiavelli typically did) so much as to challenge and subvert it. As we observed in Chapter 1, Cicero's *On Duties* came to be as widely read as any text in the Western tradition outside the Bible; and central to its argument was the assertion that the claims of moral rightness – *honestas* – and public expediency – *utilitas* – could never truly conflict.[7]

Machiavelli's new political ethic seeks to counter this naive optimism of Cicero's argument about the ultimate coherence of the moral universe. In particular, Machiavelli challenges Cicero's claim that moral rightness and public expediency can never conflict, and asserts that the prince must always be ready when necessary to abandon the former in favor of the latter. So, in Chapter 15, Machiavelli famously distinguishes his approach from that of other moralists on the grounds that he wants "to write something *useful* to whoever understands it."[8] We see this elevation of utility over

---

[6] *Discourses* II.2, pp. 131–132. Machiavelli goes on to suggest that there is another, less effeminate way of interpreting Christianity which would permit a more aggressive conception of virtue, but it is clear that this is an apologetic afterthought: Machiavelli never seeks to develop an alternative Christian theology shorn of its timid aspects (as Hobbes was later to attempt in reverse by downplaying Christianity's more assertive strains). Instead, Machiavelli urges the wholehearted embrace of the Roman system of moral values, regardless of its implications for the Christian moral tradition.

[7] See above Chapter 1, pp. 47–58.   [8] *The Prince* ch. 15, pp. 61–62 (emphasis added).

honorableness elsewhere in *The Prince*, as in Chapter 8 where Machiavelli (defending Agathocles of Syracuse) introduces a distinction between "cruelties well-used" and "cruelties badly used." Cruelties are well-used, Machiavelli contends, when they "are done at a stroke, out of the necessity to secure oneself, and then are not persisted in but are turned to as much utility for the subjects as one can"; cruelties badly used, by contrast, are those that increase rather than diminish over time. Similarly, at the heart of Machiavelli's articulation of the new ethic in Chapters 16–18 is his systematic cross-examination of a trinity of Ciceronian virtues, including liberality, mercy, and most importantly *honestas*, here signifying both truthfulness and moral rightness. His contention is that a prince who is liberal will invoke the hatred of all those who do not benefit specially from his rule; that a prince who is merciful will invite contempt rather than exhibit strength; and that a prince who is dutifully honest and honorable will fail to capture those opportunities that are vital in securing one's political advantage.

Machiavelli's view (*contra* Cicero) that sometimes what is morally right cannot be reconciled with what is publicly beneficial lies at the heart of his new political ethic. For Machiavelli this denial does *not*, however, involve a wholesale "revaluation of values" (on the order of, for example, Nietzsche). Instead, in ordinary circumstances Machiavelli retains a more or less traditional sense of ordinary morality – with the important exception of his denigration of certain of the Christian virtues – but argues that the nature of politics is such that it is sometimes necessary to "temporize" with evil.[9] Frequently, Machiavelli tells us, it is simply not possible to "adopt safe courses" in politics, either prudentially or morally.[10] In politics "one never seeks to avoid one inconvenience without running into another," and so one must seek not to avoid evils altogether, but rather to know "how to recognize the qualities of inconveniences" and choose "the less bad as the good."[11] By this sort of approach, it is possible to effect good that cannot be achieved by a more purist method of reform.[12]

---

[9] *Discourses* 1.37, p. 81.   [10] *The Prince* ch. 21, p. 91.   [11] Ibid.

[12] Indeed, it is often the case that some of the best outcomes in politics result directly from processes that appear on their face to be evils. Machiavelli's most famous example of this is his unusual approval of Rome's "tumults" between the patrician and plebian classes. Those who condemn these tumults because of the present discomforts they engender miss their true significance, namely "the good effects" which they eventually bring about: for it was precisely the unpleasantness of the tumults, Machiavelli claims, that led to the laws that allowed Rome to shape its citizens' character in such a way as to prepare them for greatness. Such modes may appear to be "extraordinary" from the point of view of conventional evaluative discourse, but they were at the same time, Machiavelli insists, "the first cause of keeping Rome free" (*Discourses* 1.4, p. 16). As Felix Gilbert points out in his

These features of politics are the rationale for the new political ethic. What then is its character? That is, what precisely must the Machiavellian political leader learn to do in the process of learning not to be good? Here we can turn to the metaphor Machiavelli offers to describe the new form of political education his ethic will require, that of the tutelage of ancient leaders at the hands of the centaur Chiron. According to Machiavelli, the ancients taught that leaders like Achilles were given to the half-man, half-beast Chiron to be raised because politics required them to have the ability not just to be humanly excellent, but to be capable of acting as well with beastly ferocity when the times required. "Therefore it is necessary for a prince to know well how to use the beast and the man," Machiavelli says, and thus "to have as a teacher a half-beast, half-man means nothing other than that a prince needs to know how to use both natures; and the one without the other is not lasting."[13] What are the beastly characteristics a prince must learn? Here again Machiavelli specifically has Cicero in mind as his target: for in identifying the two animals leaders must learn to mimic as the lion and the fox, representing force and fraud, Machiavelli praises precisely those emblems of beastly depravity that Cicero had condemned as being beneath human dignity.[14]

Much emphasis has been placed on Machiavelli's praise of force. His awareness of military realities and the necessity of military preparations is evident throughout his works (although his specific military beliefs, such as in the thorough inefficacy of professional mercenaries, may sometimes have been none too "realistic"). His preference of fear to love, and his praise of well-used cruelty over mercy, are also familiar. But, if anything, the more striking and novel feature of Machiavelli's thought is his willingness to make *fraud* the central political virtue/vice of his system. The greatest political successes, Machiavelli observes, have come to those leaders who knew how to handle adroitly matters of truth and falsehood, and a prince who allows honesty to master him rather than himself mastering honesty will come to ruin. Therefore a political leader, on Machiavelli's account, "cannot observe faith, nor should he, when such observance turns against

---

celebrated study *Machiavelli and Guicciardini* (Princeton University Press, 1965), p. 199, Machiavelli's extraordinary departure from conventional wisdom in his praise of Rome's tumults is yet another reason why it is impossible to see Machiavelli as simply a believer in a common good directed by the pursuit of enlightened self-interest. Yet in another sense, what drives the tumults does constitute a kind of positive unintended consequence, though via a much more indirect root than previous thinkers had suggested.

[13] *The Prince* ch. 18, p. 69.
[14] Again, Machiavelli's claim is not that a prince must *be* beastly, but rather that for every political leader there is a *time* to be beastly as well as a time to display one's noble humanity.

him, and the causes that made him promise have been eliminated."[15]
Consequently, it is necessary for a prince to know how to "color" his
nature (a rhetorical term of art), and to be "a great pretender and dis-
sembler," in order to succeed in politics, and thus "it is necessary for a
prince who wishes to do great things to learn how to deceive."[16]

Fraud is thus the evil preeminently necessary for political success,
according to Machiavelli. Of the two emblems of the "beastly" virtues in
politics, the lion and the fox, Machiavelli believes that the cunning deception of the fox is both rarer and more effective than even the ferocity of the
lion.[17] No one rises to greatness "without force and without fraud,"
Machiavelli observes, but he goes on to add that "force alone is [never]
found to be enough, but fraud alone will be found to be quite enough."[18]
This necessity of reliance on fraud holds true not only for princes but also
for republics. Like the prince establishing himself, republics also find
themselves "necessitated" to rely upon fraud as a constant policy option
"until they have become powerful and force alone is enough."[19] So the
Romans, for example, in their beginnings employed fraud, "which it is
always necessary for those who wish to climb from small beginnings to
sublime ranks to use"; yet their use of fraud, because it was more "covert,"
was just to that extent "less worthy of reproach."[20]

Still, this fraud must be used with the greatest caution in order to avoid
the contamination of the prince's other goals. In particular, the great
danger of fraud as a tool in political life is that more than any other weapon
in the prince's arsenal it has the capacity to tarnish the glory of a prince's
achievements. Machiavelli warns that for princes to break their faith
with others and betray their promises "may at some time acquire state
and kingdom," but it "will never acquire glory."[21] Consequently, the prince
finds himself under yet a further and deeper necessity to employ fraud
in his dealings: for he must employ fraud itself to *conceal* wherever possible
those actions that might appear at odds with the traditional conception
of virtue.

In the central passages of *The Prince*, Machiavelli famously urges that it
is the *appearance* of morality, and not the reality of it, that is fundamentally
necessary for political success. Morality is of course a powerful force in

---

[15] *The Prince* ch. 18, pp. 68–70. [16] Ibid., pp. 69–70; Machiavelli, *Discourses* II.13, p. 155.

[17] See further J. J. Barlow, "The Lion and the Fox: Machiavelli Replies to Cicero," *History of Political Thought* 20 (1999): 627–645, esp. p. 637.

[18] *Discourses* II.13, p. 155. [19] Ibid. [20] Ibid., p. 156.

[21] *Discourses* III.40, p. 299. A similar thought is voiced, though with greater ambiguity, in *The Prince* ch. 8, p. 35.

political life, and princes must pay it lip service. But since "human conditions do not permit" the prince "wholly" to possess or observe the conventional virtues, it is necessary for him both sometimes not to have those virtues and (if at all possible) always to appear to have them.[22] Even if it is not possible for political leaders always to *be* merciful, honest, humane, and pious, they should endeavor at least to be perceived as being "all mercy, all faith, all honesty, all humanity, all religion."[23] To have these qualities "in fact" and to consistently observe them is positively "harmful" to the prince; but merely *appearing* to have them is always useful, provided that "if you need not to be those things, you are able and know how to change to the contrary."[24]

Further, Machiavelli wants to argue, there are some virtues that are more important to appear to have than others. In the event that a conflict arises such that the prince cannot credibly maintain even the appearance of having all the virtues at once, Machiavelli's further advice is for him not to worry about appearing to have *politically useful* vices: those vices "without which it is difficult to save one's state."[25] Since it is often necessary for a prince, in order to maintain his state, to act "against faith, against charity, against humanity, against religion," he will invariably need to know "how to enter into evil, when forced by necessity," though he will also "not depart from good, when possible."[26] Also, should it prove necessary along the way to abandon this moral pose, the political leader must always be careful to "do it by due degrees" to ensure that "before your different nature takes away old favor from you, it has given you so much new that you do not come to diminish your authority."[27]

But even these occasions in which one's politically useful vices must be publicly acknowledged will not be very common, Machiavelli claims, for two reasons. First, there are the weaknesses of human nature itself. Human beings on Machiavelli's view are not only craven but also credulous, and moreover are also very "obedient to present necessities"; consequently, "he who deceives will always find someone who will let himself be deceived."[28] And, second, the prince enjoys a variety of strategic advantages in the attempt to conceal truths about his own policies, motivations and virtues from his subjects. Machiavelli outlines these advantages in Chapter 18 of *The Prince*:

Men in general judge more by their eyes than by their hands, because seeing is given to everyone, touching to a few. Everyone sees how you appear, few touch

---

[22] *The Prince* ch. 15, p. 62.   [23] *The Prince* ch. 18, pp. 70–71.   [24] Ibid.   [25] *The Prince* ch. 15, p. 62.
[26] *The Prince* ch. 18, p. 70.   [27] *Discourses* 1.41, p. 90.   [28] *The Prince* ch. 18, pp. 69–70.

what you are; and these few dare not oppose the opinion of many, who have the majesty of the state to defend them; and in the actions of all men, and especially of princes, where there is no court to appeal to, one looks to the end. So let a prince win and maintain his state: the means will always be judged honorable [*onesto*], and will be praised by everyone. For the vulgar are taken in by the appearance and the outcome of a thing, and in the world there is no one but the vulgar; the few have a place there when the many have somewhere to lean on.[29]

For the prince who must of necessity depart from conventional judgments of virtue, politics – with its carefully crafted displays of appealing images and its much rarer and more distant glimpses of naked authenticity – will always constitute a terrain uniquely well suited to the art of camouflage and concealment.

ARISTOCRATIC DIRTY HANDS

This, then, in rough outline, is Machiavelli's new ethic for political leadership. It unquestionably proposed significant revisions in the traditional theory of the virtues, casting doubt on its applicability to situations of great political consequence. It is important to understand, however, that in so arguing Machiavelli was not necessarily trying to undermine the theory of the virtues in its ordinary function. On the contrary, almost everything Machiavelli says on the subject indicates that he believed the standard account of virtues and vice remains morally authoritative for ordinary citizens.[30] Instead, what Machiavelli's new political ethic announced was a special privilege for princes and other political leaders, justified by the great ends for which they bear responsibility. Thus Machiavelli's famous formulation of this dynamic in his *Discourses on Livy*: "When the deed accuses him," Machiavelli says, "the effect excuses him; and when the effect is good . . . it will always excuse the deed . . . ."[31]

Machiavelli's new political ethic, therefore, is significant not just for its compelling depiction of the moral pressures that inevitably confront the serious practitioner of politics, but also because of the distinctive character of the solution he offers. That solution is a paradigmatically *aristocratic* approach to the problem of dirty hands. For Machiavelli, the moral problems attendant upon public life are burdens to be borne by political

---

[29] Ibid., p. 71.

[30] In so arguing, I associate my own interpretation of Machiavelli with Berlin's argument in "The Originality of Machiavelli," in Isaiah Berlin, *The Proper Study of Mankind* (Farrar Straus Giroux, 2000).

[31] *Discourses* 1.9, p. 29.

leaders, not ordinary citizens, and consequently also the moral privileges of
the new political ethic are justified, not for all, but only for those morally
heroic figures who undertake the necessary evils on behalf of the commonwealth. Machiavelli expresses his admiration for those willing to assume
such moral risks in his famous remark in the *Histories of Florence* about
those individuals willing not merely to die but to hazard their eternal
salvation for the sake of their native land.[32] But this aristocratic conception
of dirty hands in Machiavelli also profoundly limits the scope of the new
ethic's application. The new ethic is a specific and limited *exception* to the
traditional ethic, one carved out by what the sphere of politics represents,
and by the fact that the nature of politics itself is such that it is impossible
for the community to flourish without at least a few of its members
undertaking to perform necessary but real evils.

This aspect of Machiavelli's thought is easily obscured by several factors,
perhaps the most important of which is his seemingly "pessimistic" characterization of human nature generally. According to this line of interpretation, the ordinary human being in Machiavelli's world closely resembles
the character of the prince to whom he offers his advice. Like that prince,
the ordinary Machiavellian citizen is likely to be selfish, violent, and
dishonest, and certain to be untrustworthy. In *The Prince*, Machiavelli
famously characterizes his fellow human beings as "ungrateful, fickle,
pretenders and dissemblers, evaders of danger, eager for gain," friends in
good times but utterly unreliable in moments of crisis. In the *Discourses on
Livy*, Machiavelli again instructs us that political leaders must presuppose
"that all men are bad" and "never work any good unless through necessity,"
and that we must guard against the many outward signs that might appear
the result of virtue but are in fact the false appearances given off by those
"hidden causes" which really motivate political action.[33]

But while it is true that Machiavelli frequently has negative things to
say about human nature, he (significantly) does not seek to ground the
justification for his new ethic primarily in the kinds of evil he describes as
being endemic to human nature. When we turn to consider the justifications Machiavelli offers for the prince's violation of virtue, we find instead
that in general those justifications do not appeal to a common "pessimistic"
theory of human nature that applies to both princes and citizens alike. It is

---

32 Max Weber draws attention to this quotation of Machiavelli's in particular in developing his own
related argument in his celebrated essay on "Politics as a Vocation." In H. H. Gerth and C. Wright
Mills, eds., *From Max Weber: Essays in Sociology* (Oxford University Press, 1946), p. 126.
[33] *Discourses* 1.3, p. 15.

true that Machiavelli does say that the wickedness of other people is among the factors that ultimately necessitates the prince's violations of conventional morality. "A man who wants to make a profession of good in all regards," Machiavelli says, "must come to ruin among so many who are not good," and so because other men "are wicked and do not observe faith with you, you also do not have to observe it with them."[34] But, in so arguing, Machiavelli never implies that what the prince must do in learning "not to be good" is merely to mimic the badness of those around him. On the contrary, Machiavelli's prince elevates such vice from inglorious weakness to glorious strength, from the lack of self-control found in ordinary intemperance to the ultimate self-command found in Machiavellian *virtù*. Evils are necessary in politics, but the privilege of performing these necessary evils must not be widely held. On the contrary, Machiavelli urges that a republic must take care to ensure "that its citizens cannot do evil under the shadow of good."[35]

If Machiavelli's ethic is an aristocratic moral privilege rather than merely a descent to match the moral failures of his subjects, then what grounds of justification does Machiavelli offer for the violations of ordinary morality which he clearly does recommend? To begin with, in Machiavelli's scheme the crimes of the prince are justified, or rather excused, because they are necessary means to the achievement of the common good, and not (except instrumentally) to the achievement of personal ambition. Machiavelli's account of the new ethic of political leadership frames its justification in terms that ultimately point toward the concept of the common good. It is this moral privileging of the political common good, shared with the whole Roman tradition and especially with Cicero, that Machiavelli cites in justifying his general preference for republican over princely government.[36] "It is not the particular good but the common good that makes cities great," Machiavelli explains, and "without doubt this common good is not observed if not in republics, since all that is for that purpose is executed."[37]

The same rationale is also present, though in a more muted and ambiguous form, throughout *The Prince*. Generally Machiavelli frames his advice to the prince in terms of advancing that leader's own interests: he recommends the new ethic on the grounds that such actions are necessary in order for a prince to "maintain his state" in power, and not explicitly on the grounds that doing so advances the common good. But Machiavelli's underlying rationale for the new ethic in *The Prince* equally relies on

<hr/>

[34] *The Prince* ch. 15, p. 61; ch. 18, p. 69.   [35] *Discourses* 1.46, p. 96.
[36] See further *Discourses* I.2, pp. 10–14.   [37] Ibid., p. 130.

the claim that the moral privileges accorded to political leaders draw their justification from what the prince in turn is able to do for the common good.

To see this, it is important to remember that Machiavelli's *Prince*, though seemingly a systematic treatise on princely leadership, is in fact specifically limited in most of its pronouncements to one particular case: the prince who has attained power in a newly acquired monarchical regime that was formerly a republic, and who, further, has acquired his dominion not by virtue and his own arms but by fortune and the arms of others. It is this most difficult of political situations to which Machiavelli's advice in *The Prince* – including the new ethic – is principally directed. Machiavelli's new ethic seeks to justify the use of extraordinary political tactics in that particular, extreme political situation, because that situation above all others requires strong princely leadership. But it is ultimately the fact that such a situation requires the prince to be unusually secure and powerful that justifies his extraordinary moral permissions to "maintain his state" in power, as is evidenced by Machiavelli's call in Chapter 26 to use his advice to consolidate power – because he will need that power in order to unite Italy and expel the foreign invaders from her soil.

But there is a further reason why the pursuit of the common good invariably needs someone to do its evils, which is that the conception of the common good itself, especially in republics, is one that implies a fundamental insatiability. Politics, Machiavelli claims, by its very nature involves expense at the gain of others, and since republics are the purest form of politics this is most purely true in the republican case. The nature of republics, Machiavelli argues in the *Discourses*, is to seek "to enervate and to weaken all other bodies so as to increase its own body."[38] Here we encounter a striking articulation in the Christian period of that more ancient conception of the state as characterized by a supreme and self-justifying hunger, a conception later captured (as we will see in Chapter 4) by Hobbes in his observation that a "Common-Wealth can endure no Diet."[39] For Machiavelli a republic even more than a principality can achieve the highest form of political greatness because of its purity of self-oriented ambition. Machiavelli explains:

It is not the particular good but the common good that makes cities great. And without doubt this common good is not observed if not in republics, since all that is for that purpose is executed, and although it may turn out to harm this or that private individual, those for whom the aforesaid does good are so many that they

---

[38] Ibid., p. 133.   [39] See Chapter 4, pp. 177–181.

can go ahead with it against the disposition of the few crushed by it. The contrary happens when there is a prince, in which case what suits him usually offends the city and what suits the city offends him.[40]

This self-oriented and insatiable character of all cities, but especially republics, fuels the drive toward imperial expansion which for Machiavelli lies at the summit of political achievement. And successful imperial expansion in turn satisfies and enlarges that individual and social passion for acquisition that lies at the heart of the Machiavellian political ethic.[41] Since in republics each citizen "willingly multiplies that thing and seeks to acquire those goods he believes he can enjoy once acquired," it follows that in republics also "men in rivalry think of private and public advantages, and both the one and the other come to grow marvelously."[42]

Not only is the justification for Machiavelli's new political ethic grounded in the pursuit of the common good, but that justification is also most compelling in those circumstances of political instability characteristic of the founding moments of a state. As we observed before, Machiavelli's advice in *The Prince* focuses on the extreme circumstances of an attempt to found princely authority in an unfavorable political climate. Thus Machiavelli tells us that "of all princes, it is impossible for the new prince to escape a name for cruelty because new states are full of dangers"; and we find this borne out, for example, in his approving account of the actions of Cesare Borgia in Chapter 7 and his (relatively) forgiving account of the crimes of Agathocles of Syracuse at the conclusion of Chapter 8.[43]

We find the same rationale underlying Machiavelli's analysis of most of the necessary political evils discussed in the *Discourses* (with its more explicit republican orientation). Perhaps the most famous example of the unconventional new political ethic in the *Discourses* is found in Machiavelli's discussion of Romulus's murder of his brother Remus in the mythical founding of Rome. Commenting on those who condemn Romulus, Machiavelli says that their judgment "would be true if one did not consider what end had induced him to commit such a homicide."[44]

---

[40] *Discourses* II.2, p. 130.

[41] This acquisitiveness of republics, discussed further below, is a theme at the center of Mark Hulliung's study *Citizen Machiavelli* (Princeton University Press, 1983).

[42] *Discourses* II.2, p. 132. Machiavelli here alludes to Sallust, *The Conspiracy of Catiline*, ch. 1. In Sallust, *The Jugurthine War and the Conspiracy of Catiline*, trans. S. A. Handford (Penguin, 1963).

[43] *The Prince* ch. 17, p. 66; cf. chs. 7–8, pp. 25–38. Though Machiavelli condemns Agathocles' actions, he nevertheless states that the tyrant was able to find "some remedy for [his] state with God and with men" because he had used his cruelties well and efficiently, not badly or hesitantly.

[44] *Discourses* I.9, p. 29.

Though on its face morally questionable, Romulus's action finds justification in a brutal political necessity, namely the fact that political stability requires that "one alone give the mode" in founding a political community.[45] Furthermore, Machiavelli makes it clear that the justifying "necessity" here is not *Romulus's* necessity, but rather *Rome's*: "a prudent orderer of a republic, who has the intent to wish to help not himself but the common good, not for his own succession but for the common fatherland, should contrive to have authority alone."[46] Later in the passage, Machiavelli again claims that Romulus "deserves excuse" for his fratricide because "what he did was for the common good and not for his own ambition."[47] The story of Romulus shows that "a wise understanding" will never "reprove anyone for any extraordinary action that he uses to order a kingdom or constitute a republic," Machiavelli argues, "for he who is violent to spoil, not he who is violent to mend, should be reproved."[48]

A similar example is found in Machiavelli's insistence in the *Discourses* that, if one wishes to avoid the dangers of an anarchic founding period, "there is no remedy more powerful, and more necessary, than to kill the sons of Brutus."[49] The legendary founder of the republican regime showed a severity "not less necessary than useful" when he ordered the execution of his own sons after they showed their counter-revolutionary sympathies.[50] The unifying element here justifying these serious – even epic – breaches of conventional morality is that they are judged necessary to found a state securely. Unless one is fortunate enough to have some "strong and difficult accident" that leads men to submit to one's leadership voluntarily, one must do whatever it takes to establish political control and acquire "the authority that it is necessary to have in things of importance":[51] for in such cases "there is no remedy other than the death of those who have it," and consequently "he must think of every way of removing them . . ."[52]

Finally, for Machiavelli the justification for the moral permissions of the new political ethic is found in its underlying cause. A different sort of virtue, Machiavelli believes, is needed for a political society in which citizen virtue is deficient, a circumstance Machiavelli repeatedly refers to as the "corruption" of the people. By calling the people "corrupt," Machiavelli is not of course invoking the concept of corruption as it is employed in

---

[45] Ibid.   [46] Ibid.   [47] Ibid.
[48] Ibid. But see Maurizio Viroli's study *Machiavelli* (Oxford University Press, 1998) for an interpretation of the Romulus episode at odds with the one I advance here.
[49] *Discourses* I.16, p. 45. Machiavelli advances a similar argument with reference to his contemporary Piero Soderini at *Discourses* III.3, p. 215.
[50] *Discourses* III.3, p. 214.   [51] *Discourses* III.30, p. 279.   [52] Ibid., p. 280.

contemporary political discourse – matters of financial impropriety, graft, and the like. He has in mind rather the sense of corruption we use in speaking of the corruption of the body: it is a kind of sickness evidenced by the absence of those citizen virtues that make a body politic healthy and lively (as evidenced by Machiavelli's repeated use of medical metaphors in describing this political corruption). For Machiavelli, the new political ethic finds its justification in the absence of the proper moral health in the citizens and consequently in the body politic; in certain periods of their history, the citizens of a republic invariably lose or betray those virtues of mind and character necessary to meet the challenges of the moment. The new Machiavellian ethic is in this sense a special non-ideal ethic designed especially for dealing with corrupt circumstances.[53]

This explanation for the necessity of the new ethic emerges in Chapter 19 of *The Prince*. Recalling specifically his claim in Chapter 15 that the effective political leader must learn how "not to be good," Machiavelli elaborates on the reason for this necessity:

> As I said above, a prince who wants to maintain his state is often forced not to be good. For when that community of which you judge you have need to maintain yourself is corrupt, whether they are the people or the soldiers or the great, you must follow their humor to satisfy them, and then good deeds are your enemy.[54]

This corruption on the part of the citizenry forces the ruler to adopt the new political ethic: and, for Machiavelli, all nations or polities inevitably undergo a process of corruption over time.

Some of Machiavelli's moralistic predecessors might have argued that there would always exist honorable means to cure such corruption, but Machiavelli argues that we have no assurance that this will be the case. Indeed, the systemic nature of the phenomenon of corruption leads us to believe the opposite, that it will be impossible to make the appropriate corrections through ordinary modes, since in a corrupt society the modes are themselves corrupt. For this reason, Machiavelli explains in the *Discourses*, it becomes impossible to cure this corruption and deal with political problems as they arise by means of *ordinary* modes. Instead, a political leader in such a polity invariably finds that it is necessary to go

---

[53] Here I allude to the conceptual distinction (unfamiliar to Machiavelli) between ideal and non-ideal ethics, introduced by John Rawls in, for example, *The Law of Peoples* (Harvard University Press, 2001) and elaborated in a related context by Christine Korsgaard in "The Right to Lie: Kant on dealing with evil," in her book *Creating the Kingdom of Ends* (Cambridge University Press, 1996).

[54] *The Prince* ch. 19, p. 77.

beyond ordinary modes "to the extraordinary, such as violence and arms, and before everything else become prince of that city, able to dispose of it in one's own mode."[55] Polities will always need such extraordinary things done for them, at least when their ordinary modes are no longer adequate, Machiavelli suggests.

Thus, although Machiavelli has been offering the quintessential aristocratic *solution* to the problem of dirty hands, as a matter of *diagnosis* he is prepared to see the problem as originating in a moral deficiency located in the people in general rather than in some more metaphysical cause. Likewise, the extremity of the solution he offers – the new political ethic – can then be seen as a response to precisely the *democratically* grounded dimensions of the dirty hands problem he envisions. Because Machiavelli's dirty hands problem is driven by the moral failures of the people and grounded in the well-being of the people, he is able to suggest that anything at all is in principle permissible for the prince on the grounds of necessity. The prince's moral permissions in pursuit of his subjects' well-being transcend limits which the people might even be unable to cross themselves on the strength of their own moral entitlements.

Many of Machiavelli's interpreters have rightly stressed, for example, the role which the concept of glory plays in motivating Machiavelli's leaders. We see its importance in the passage of *The Prince* where Machiavelli condemns Agathocles of Syracuse for his crimes on the grounds that one can win "empire, but not glory" by means of the morally dubious methods Agathocles employs.[56] But however much Machiavelli may stress glory as a political motivation, it is not (as these commentators sometimes seem to suggest) the *summum bonum* of Machiavelli's politics. On the contrary, in the *Discourses* Machiavelli states clearly that the people's moral admiration remains one among many moral and political goods which the political leader must be willing to sacrifice on the altar of necessity.

For where one deliberates entirely on the safety of his fatherland, there ought not to enter any consideration of either just or unjust, merciful or cruel, praiseworthy or ignominious; indeed every other concern put aside, one ought to follow entirely the policy that saves its life and maintains its liberty.[57]

---

[55] *Discourses* I.18, p. 51.
[56] I have in mind here particularly Quentin Skinner, *Machiavelli: A Very Short Introduction* (Oxford University Press, 2000), and Viroli, *Machiavelli*, among many related commentaries that emphasize the limits which the desire for glory supposedly places on Machiavelli's new political ethic.
[57] *Discourses* III.41, p. 301.

Instead, Machiavelli asserts, political leaders must follow the rule that the fatherland is "to be saved in every mode" and is "well-defended in whatever mode one defends it, whether with ignominy or with glory."[58]

Machiavelli's new political ethic is thus limited not just by the ends which it pursues but also by the times and circumstances in which it is employed. Machiavelli does not call on the prince simply *not* to be good, but rather "to learn to be able not to be good, and to use this and not use it according to necessity."[59] This thought is connected to his celebrated remarks in Chapter 25 of *The Prince* about the power of Fortune. The political leader, Machiavelli remarks there, must learn to vary his mode of proceeding in accordance with what the times require, or he will invariably come to ruin. But human beings are ill suited to respond to the changing requirements of the times. A prince, Machiavelli tells us, tends to stick to his preferred mode of proceeding no matter what the circumstances, "whether because he cannot deviate from what nature inclines him to or also because, when one has always flourished by walking on some path, he cannot be persuaded to depart from it," and thus "when the times change not in conformity with his mode, he is ruined ..."[60] In the *Discourses*, Machiavelli expands on this line of thought to argue that the limited ability of individual men to vary their mode of proceeding with the times is one of the reasons that, in the long run, republics are preferable to principalities. "Hence it arises that a republic has a greater life and has good fortune longer than a principality," he explains, "for it can accommodate itself better than one prince can to the diversity of times through the diversity of citizens that are in it."[61]

Yet this advantage of republics carries with it its own problems. When necessary, republics can provide the appropriate form of aristocratic leadership more easily than principalities; but as a whole republics are "slower" to change with respect to citizen virtue, "for they have trouble varying because they need times to come that move the whole republic, for which one alone is not enough to vary the mode of proceeding."[62] Furthermore, because republics place lone princely figures in the position of performing the necessary evils of society, Machiavelli recognizes that republics frequently

---

[58] Ibid.
[59] *The Prince* ch. 15, p. 61. This is also Guicciardini's formulation. He puts the point this way: "If it were said that by doing this one would acquire a name for cruelty and also lack of conscience, I would admit to both; but I would go on to say that anyone who wants to hold dominions and states in this day and age should show mercy and kindness where possible, and where there is no other alternative, one must use cruelty and unscrupulousness." Guicciardini, *Dialogue*, Bk. II, p. 158.
[60] *The Prince* ch. 25, p. 100; *Discourses* III.9, p. 240.   [61] *Discourses* III.9, p. 240.   [62] Ibid.

find themselves encumbered with an indecisiveness and squeamishness that is ill suited to meeting their ends, even when it is their needs and appetites that ultimately fuel the need for these evils (conventionally understood). On this point Machiavelli seems to share the view of his contemporary Guicciardini that princes, even tyrants, are much better than republics will ever be at performing necessary evils with the requisite cruelty, secrecy, and dispatch.[63]

Thus effective politics requires a mixture of aristocratic and democratic virtues distributed not primarily across institutions, as in the classical theories of mixed government, but rather over *time*. The republic must provide a diversity of leaders so that it can produce the right mode of proceeding at the right time – a Henry Clay at one moment, a Lincoln at another – and these leaders must themselves be capable, when their number is called, of transcending the ordinary modes of the moment – including its conventional morality – to save the fatherland "in whatever mode" the times require.

At the same time, this way of proceeding, though eminently necessary, possesses its own set of distinctive political risks. For what this peculiar form of mixed government ultimately requires is morally unconventional leadership aimed at the conventional good of the community. Rather than a person who possesses a capacity for vicious action *alone*, what politics seems to require, paradoxically, is political leadership from someone who both *is* and *is not* virtuous in the conventional sense of the term. Machiavelli puts the dilemma starkly in the *Discourses*:

> Because the reordering of a city for a political way of life presupposes a good man, and becoming prince of a republic by violence presupposes a bad man, one will find that it very rarely happens that someone good wishes to become prince by bad ways, even though his end be good, and that someone wicked, having become prince, wishes to work well, and that it will ever occur to his mind to use well the authority that he has acquired badly.[64]

Thus, according to Machiavelli, the species of leader that politics requires involves a complex moral schizophrenia of the kind that, even if conceivable, is perhaps inherently unstable. As Max Weber later frames the point, we can only place our trust in a truly *good* person to undertake the evils necessary for political life.

Thus Machiavelli offers an analysis of the problem of dirty hands that searches for its root causes along a democratic dimension. He identifies the

[63] Guicciardini, *Dialogue*, Bk. II, pp. 157, 163.   [64] *Discourses* 1.18, p. 51.

corruption of the people at large, their inevitable failures of political virtue over time, as among the most important of the origins of those recurring moral dilemmas that confront political actors. But whereas Machiavelli offers a (partly) democratic diagnosis of the Renaissance problem of dirty hands, his solution is a quintessentially aristocratic one. A chosen few with the necessary political virtue step in to do what must be done, gambling their souls in the process, but also qualifying for potentially greater glory on a higher plane of virtue. This aristocratic solution is Machiavelli's great contribution to the development of thinking about this complex of problems, so much so that the problem to this day is often reflexively defined in Machiavelli's terms.

MORE'S *UTOPIA*

In other places men talk all the time about the commonwealth, but what they mean is simply their own wealth; here, where there is no private business, every man zealously pursues the public business. And in both places people are right to act as they do ... (Thomas More, *Utopia*, Book II)

Another major work of political theory of the same decade, Thomas More's *Utopia*, tackles a similar set of themes and concerns – strikingly similar, given that More almost certainly had not encountered Machiavelli's texts before writing *Utopia*. Even more than Machiavelli's writings, *Utopia* presses beyond a mere articulation of the problem of dirty hands in public life to try to analyze those structural features of society which help to cause and sustain that problem. But whereas Machiavelli offers an aristocratic solution to a democratically driven problem of dirty hands, More's *Utopia* suggests that precisely because the problem is democratically driven, only a truly democratic solution – to the extent that one is available – can hope adequately to resolve the problem.

A DIALOGUE OF DIRTY HANDS

The problems of political ethics that dominate Book I of *Utopia* are framed in terms of a literary genre and topic familiar to the ancients as well as to Renaissance humanists: a dialogue on the relative merits of the life of public activity versus that of philosophical contemplation and leisure. What emerges from *Utopia*'s dialogue are two rival sets of moral claims, neither of which seems clearly to prevail: first, that the public good requires wise and honest counselors to engage in politics, with all its moral compromises and even outright evils; and, second, that the wise and good person cannot participate in political life, whatever goods might be achieved thereby, without becoming both hopelessly corrupted and a potential facilitator of even greater evils. The collision of these claims in the dialogue articulates the tensions between (Christian) ethics and politics in the world of the Renaissance. In confronting these tensions, *Utopia* arrives at a set of conclusions different from Machiavelli's, yet, rightly understood, no less far-reaching in their prescriptions for remedying the ethical problems of politics in Renaissance Europe.

The main proponent of the active life in the dialogue is the narrator, "Thomas More," who argues that wise and good men have a responsibility to join the councils of kings to ensure that the best possible courses are taken by political leaders. His (at first friendly) opponent in the dialogue is the traveler "Raphael Hythloday," a stranger who has knowledge of both philosophy and the world, and who has traveled with Vespucci and others to the New World and seen strange customs and practices among its many different peoples.

Hythloday, who speaks the most in the dialogue (and is the only speaker in the discourse in Book II), challenges "More's" assumption that the active life can be a good means to good ends. He bases his argument on two main claims: first, that Renaissance politics regrettably centers on war, whereas the wise man is more knowledgeable about what is relevant to peace; and, second, that any king's court will be filled with rival bad advisers who will thwart whatever good advice the wise man may offer. As one of his key illustrations, Hythloday imagines a meeting of the council of the French king in which Hythloday tries to offer genuinely philosophical advice. He envisions himself addressing a council whose discussions have been focused exclusively on war and imperial contrivance: Hythloday urges the king to eschew foreign ambitions and to concentrate instead on pursuing generous domestic policies. In the course of his argument, he draws on his (fictitious) knowledge of the New World to praise the (imaginary) Achorians, whose laws forbid the king from pursuing foreign entanglements, and the (make-believe) Macarians, whose laws prescribe a limit on the prince's personal wealth. Such advice, Hythloday urges, would be ridiculed and ignored in a king's council.[65]

---

[65] More's contemporary Guicciardini apparently agreed. He asserts that "if someone stood up in a senate and argued" solely on the basis of claims of conscience "against undertaking some entirely feasible and useful enterprise," that "he would be repudiated" or "made fun of" by everyone. Guicciardini, *Dialogue*, BK. II, p. 158.

In describing the moral problems that would confront the good person in political life, Hythloday frames the problem in the familiar rhetorical terms of *honestas* and *utilitas*. The narrator "More" urges Hythloday that joining the king's council would be not only "noble" and "worthy" but would also help influence the actions of the prince, from whom "a people's welfare or misery flows in a stream … as from a never-failing spring."[66] Hythloday denies this, portraying politics instead as an arena in which the good adviser is not only at risk of moral corruption, but is also unable to do any real good. Seeking to illustrate this, he tells the story of a debate about capital punishment he once engaged in at Cardinal Morton's court, a discussion in which these same categories were centrally at issue. Hythloday argues to Morton and his courtiers that the English policy of punishing theft with execution "goes beyond the call of justice, and is not in any case for the public good."[67] Hythloday then demonstrates both these points, arguing the disproportionality between the punishment of death and the crime of theft (as a question of justice or moral rightness) as well as the ineffectiveness of capital punishment as a deterrent to theft (which in fact, Hythloday argues, raises the stakes of crime and thus logically encourages thieves to murder their victims).

"More" the narrator responds to Hythloday's presentation of these concerns by employing exactly the same ethical framework as Hythloday. But, applying the same criteria, "More" defends the orthodox "Ciceronian" position in favor of public service, with its implicit assumption that what is morally right and what is expedient cannot really be said to be contradictory. In response to Hythloday's imaginary depiction of the French king's council, "More" responds that these politicians would of course refuse Hythloday's advice, and goes on to assert that an adviser should not offer advice that he knows will never be listened to. He scornfully characterizes the sort of advice Hythloday has offered as "academic philosophy,"[68] and asserts that "in the councils of kings, where great matters are debated with great authority, there is no room for it."[69] Instead, "More" urges that Hythloday employ "another philosophy, better suited for the role of a citizen, that takes its cue, adapts itself to the drama at hand and acts its part neatly and appropriately."[70]

---

[66] Thomas More, *Utopia*, ed. George M. Logan and Robert M. Adams, revised edition (Cambridge University Press, 2002), p. 13.
[67] Ibid., p. 15.
[68] Or "School philosophy." In either case, the clear reference is to the sort of impractical speculation of medieval scholastic philosophy the Renaissance humanists detested.
[69] *Utopia*, p. 34.   [70] Ibid., pp. 34–35.

More the author, then, has chosen to associate the narrator "More" with the concept of a "civil philosophy" exhibiting the flexibility and role-oriented viewpoint celebrated in the classical texts of rhetorical theory, especially Cicero's. In doing so, he employs the metaphor of the stage, a commonplace among ancient texts on rhetoric, and in particular an intriguingly specific version of it: one depicting a stranger who indecorously intervenes in the midst of a play whose reality he refuses to recognize.

When a comedy of Plautus is being played, and the household slaves are cracking trivial jokes together, you come onstage in the garb of a philosopher and repeat Seneca's speech to Nero from the *Octavia*. Wouldn't it be better to take a silent role than to say something inappropriate and thus turn the play into a tragicomedy? You pervert a play and ruin it when you add irrelevant speeches, even if they are better than the play itself. So go through with the drama at hand as best you can, and don't spoil it all just because you happen to think of a play by someone else that might be more elegant.[71]

More himself was extremely interested in this particular application of the stage metaphor, employing it several times in his own writings.[72] In his *History of Richard III* (the partial basis for Shakespeare's tragedy), More has some of the observers of Richard's false reluctance to accept the throne excuse his disingenous behavior on the grounds that

Menne must sommetime for the manner sake not bee a knowen what they knowe . . . [For] in a stage play all the people know right wel, that he that playeth the sowdane is percase a sowter.[73] Yet if one should can so little good, to shewe out of seasonne what acquaintance he hath with him, and calle him by his owne name whyle he standeth in his majestie, one of his tormenters might hap to breake his head, and worthy for marring of the play. And so they said that these matters be Kynge's games, as it were stage playes, and for the more part plaied vpon scafoldes. In which pore men be but ye lookers on. And they yt wise be, will meddle no

---

[71] Ibid., p. 35.

[72] In addition to the one I consider at length, More employs this metaphor in *The Four Last Things*, in *The English Works of Sir Thomas More* (hereafter *EW*) (Dial Press, 1931), vol. I, p. 84 and in the *Treatise on the Passion*, in *The Complete Works of St. Thomas More* (hereafter *CWM*) (Yale University Press, 1963–1997), vol. XIII, p. 156. It seems to have had a special resonance for him due to a curious fact of his biography. His earliest biographer, William Roper, tells us that, when More was a youth and served as a page in the house of Cardinal Morton (the same Cardinal that appears in *Utopia* Book I), young More would "at Christmas-tide suddenly sometimes step in among the players, and never studying for the matter, make a part of his own there presently among them, which made the lookers-on more sport than all the players beside." Roper, "Life of More," in R. S. Sylvester and Davis P. Harding, eds., *Two Early Tudor Lives* (Yale University Press, 1967), p. 198. His literary inspiration for this metaphor may have been Lucian's *Menippus*, trans. A. M. Harmon, Loeb Classical Library (Harvard University Press, 1925), pp. 97–99.

[73] "Sowdane" here means roughly "sultan" and "sowter" means roughly "shoemaker" or cobbler.

farther. For they that sometyme step vp and play wyt them, when they cannot play their partes, they disorder the play and do themself no good.[74]

Another notable employment of this particular variation of the classic stage metaphor occurs in Erasmus's *Praise of Folly*. Folly is discussing how wise men are really fools. She evokes the image of life as a play, noting that "if anyone tries to take the masks off the actors when they're playing a scene on the stage and show their true, natural faces to the audience, he'll certainly spoil the whole play and deserve to be stoned and thrown out of the theatre for a menace." The image offered next is that of a mistimed interruption:

At this point let us suppose some wise man dropped from heaven confronts me and insists that the man whom all look up to as a god and master is not even human, he is ruled by his passions, like an animal, and no more than the lowest slave for serving so many evil masters of his own accord ... If he had this sort of thing to say about everyone else, what would happen? We should think him a crazy madman. Nothing is so foolish as mistimed wisdom, and nothing less sensible than misplaced sense. A man's conduct is misplaced if he doesn't adapt himself to things as they are ... and asks for the play to stop being a play. On the other hand, it's a true sign of prudence not to want wisdom which extends beyond your share as an ordinary mortal, to be willing to overlook things along with the rest of the world or to wear your illusions with good grace. People say that this is really a sign of folly, and I'm not setting out to deny it – so long as they'll admit on their side that this is the way to play the comedy of life.[75]

Unfortunately this line is also delivered by the character of Folly in one of the few Renaissance works that may be even *more* ambiguous than *Utopia*, and it is if anything more dangerous to attribute any view to Erasmus on the grounds that it is spoken by Folly than to attribute a view to More on the grounds that it was held by More's associate Erasmus. What we *can* conclude, however, from the metaphor's ubiquity in More's writings and those of his literary circle, is that it was a viewpoint which fascinated him and which he believed deserved serious consideration, even if ultimately for the purpose of being refuted.

Not only does the theatrical metaphor "More" employs draw strongly on the imagery of Cicero's rhetorical theory, but the political message that "More" infers from it is a thoroughly Ciceronian sentiment:

That's how things go in the commonwealth, and in the councils of princes. If you cannot pluck up bad ideas by the root, or cure long-standing evils to your heart's

---

[74] Thomas More, *History of King Richard III*, *CWM* vol. II, 80/26–81/10.
[75] Erasmus, *The Praise of Folly*, in *Collected Works of Erasmus*, trans. R. A. B. Mynors and D. F. S. Thompson (hereafter *CWE*) (Toronto, 1974–), vol. XXVII, p. 103.

content, you must not therefore abandon the commonwealth. Don't give up the ship in a storm because you cannot hold back the winds. You must not deliver strange and out-of-the-way speeches to people with whom they will carry no weight because they are firmly persuaded the other way. Instead, by an indirect approach, you must strive and struggle as best you can to handle everything tactfully – and thus what you cannot turn to good, you may at least make as little bad as possible. For it is impossible to make everything good unless all men are good, and that I don't expect to see for quite a few years yet.[76]

As a whole, the set of arguments put in the mouth of "More" constitute a paradigm example of the rhetoricians' emphasis on context and circumstance, as well as of the Ciceronian exhortation to the active life of public service – underwritten by a belief in the priority of the claims of the public sphere. Yet despite the fact that "More" assumes that moral rightness and utility are compatible, his argument here leans much more heavily on appeals to public expediency than on the claims of moral rightness. In any event, the utility-oriented arguments that "More" presents are powerful ones: they invoke themes and images More the author employed repeatedly throughout his career, first as a humanist and later as a polemicist. There is an added resonance to these arguments because the choice of a life of public service being advocated by "More" is in fact the path that More the author himself followed (eventually encountering, ironically, just those dangers to himself that Hythloday had warned against).

Many of *Utopia*'s commentators have taken this passage to constitute More the author's own view of the problem of political ethics, and have thus cast Hythloday in the role of a fanatical idealist. But this interpretation cannot withstand scrutiny of the way More the author frames Hythloday's rejoinder. Hythloday's reply runs substantially longer than "More's," and it is given the final position in the dialogue, a strategic location that was conventionally reserved for the strongest argument. But, most importantly, Hythloday's argument possesses no less of the mix of vehemence and argumentative skill which makes us believe that the words of "More" are not merely those of a straw man. In trying to change public life from within, Hythloday says, rather than curing the madness of others, he would

---

[76] *Utopia*, p. 35. On the face of it the sentiment in this passage sounds laudable. But the fact that More uses a very similarly constructed argument to "justify" the actions of Richard III's co-conspirator Buckingham in his *History of King Richard III* (*CWM* vol. II, 43/31–43/35) should caution us that More himself may have recognized something rather sneaky about the viewpoint he puts in the mouth of his namesake "More." Also notice "More's" rhetorical sleight of hand in his allusion to the *Republic*: the objection of Plato's philosopher does not rest on the fact that he cannot control the winds, but rather that he cannot control the *helm*.

merely be "raving along with them."[77] Indeed, Hythloday accuses "More's" "civil philosophy" of being nothing more than outright deception: "Whether it's the business of a philosopher to tell lies, I don't know, but it certainly isn't mine."[78] Most strikingly, More the author has Hythloday twice invoke the name of Christ (in the standard all-capitals form of the period) in support of his position.

Indeed, if we dismiss as outlandish and absurd everything that the perverse customs of men have made to seem alien to us, we shall have to set aside, even in a community of Christians, most of the teachings of CHRIST. Yet he forbade us to dissemble them, and even ordered that what he had whispered in the ears of his disciples should be preached openly from the housetops. Most of his teachings are far more alien from the common customs of mankind than my discourse was. But preachers, like the crafty fellows they are, have found that people would rather not change their lives to fit CHRIST'S rule, and so, following your advice, I suppose, they have adjusted his teaching to the way people live, as if it were a leaden yardstick. At least in that way they can get the two things to correspond in some way or other. The only real thing they accomplish that I can see is to make people feel more secure about doing evil.[79]

In his other writings, More might occasionally have permitted the devil to cite Scripture, as it were, but never in a passage where the strength of the invocation was so compelling. As it stands, the powerful nature of this appeal to religious authority serves as an indication of, at a minimum, More the author's profound respect for Hythloday's position.

The moral dangers of political service are real and extensive, Hythloday argues. In a royal council, he asserts,

there is no way to dissemble or look the other way. You must openly approve the worst proposals and endorse the most vicious policies. A man who praised wicked counsels only half-heartedly would be suspected as a spy, perhaps a traitor. And there is no way for you to do any good when you are thrown among colleagues who would more readily corrupt the best of men than be reformed themselves. Either way, they will seduce you by their evil ways, or, if you remain honest and innocent, you will be made a screen for the knavery and folly of others. You wouldn't stand a chance of changing anything for the better by that "indirect approach."[80]

Thus, according to Hythloday, compromise of the sort that the Ciceronian approach encourages must at least sometimes involve morally abhorrent concessions to evil, requiring one to approve or shield evil policies (i.e., it is not *morally right* to compromise); and, even if it were not, compromise

---

[77] *Utopia*, p. 35. [78] Ibid. [79] Ibid., p. 36. [80] Ibid., pp. 36–37.

would be an ineffective strategy that would not improve any of the most important things in politics for the better (i.e., it is *inexpedient* to compromise). Thus Hythloday's argument accepts the implicit Ciceronian premise that what is truly morally right will never ultimately conflict with what is truly expedient for the commonwealth – but his conclusions from this assumption run in precisely the opposite direction from that of "More" the narrator. For Hythloday, claims about the public utility or disutility of his actions fall by the wayside, trumped by the claim that the actions in question are morally wrong.

What then are we to make of the clash of powerful views on each side of this dialogue? Each interlocutor's position has undeniable rhetorical and philosophical appeal, which has led most commentators to assume that either "More" the narrator, on the one hand, or Hythloday, on the other, speaks in the end directly for More the author. But for the reasons we have just considered, it is difficult on the grounds of the argument itself to award the palm clearly to either discussant. Instead, we are meant (as a few interpreters of *Utopia* have suggested) to understand the argument between "More" and Hythloday as coming to something of a draw.[81] Understandably, many commentators have been unwilling to endorse this view, perhaps thinking it is too easy a way out of an undeniably knotty interpretive problem. But of course another way of looking at it is that the problem of adjudicating the dialogue of Book I in favor of one party or another is knotty for a reason: namely, that the author has structured the dialogue such that there are too many good arguments on each side of the question to dismiss either viewpoint completely.

Where other interpretations of Book I of *Utopia* as an unresolved dialogue have failed to convince, however, is in their explanation of *why* More would choose to write a dialogue in such a way as to leave it ultimately indeterminate. There are a variety of reasons one might adduce to explain this. More's own practical view of the matter may have been conflicted, perhaps in part because of the immediate circumstances of his own life.[82] More may also have been giving voice to the instability at the heart of Cicero's own attempt to reconcile the morally right with the beneficial, an instability echoed in Erasmian humanism's attempt to unravel and as far as possible reconcile the conflicts between classical values

---

[81] My precedents for thinking of the dialogue in this way include, for example, David M. Bevington, "The Dialogue in *Utopia*: Two Sides to the Question," *Studies in Philology* 58: 496–509, and R. J. Schoeck, "A Nursery of Correct and Useful Institutions," *Moreana* 22 (1969): 19–32.

[82] At the time he composed *Utopia*, More had been offered a position in the king's service and was apparently of two minds about the wisdom of accepting.

and the Christian religion. But, more fundamentally, the decision to represent the dialogue as ultimately unresolved either way is intended to show the incompatibility in the real world of the powerful competing claims of responsibility and the public good (captured in Ciceronian humanism) versus the absolutist moral claims derived from both philosophical ethics and the Christian religion. In actual practice, the dialogue suggests, those who seek to participate in politics in More's Europe find there to be a real dilemma of dirty hands in politics; and thus, in the political world that Book I has described, the claims of moral rightness on the one hand and of political efficacy on the other begin to look disturbingly incompatible.

THE UTOPIAN SOLUTION

Thus Book I's dialogue about political ethics has led More (the author) to the conclusion that what is politically efficacious not only can but inevitably will conflict with what is morally right in a way that leaves the wise and good man in a moral dilemma – torn between the political good he can do, on the one hand, and the moral purity he must compromise to achieve that good, on the other. More's analysis in Book I has thus achieved, with a clarity of moral insight rivaled only by Machiavelli among More's contemporaries, a striking sense of the moral costs inherent in the problems of political action.

But *Utopia* does not leave the matter there. On the contrary, while Book I has worked to a climax of paradox and irresolution, Book II is now going to offer a resolution – of sorts – to the problems that have so far been raised, showing by implication that these problems do admit of a *theoretical* resolution, provided we are willing to be sufficiently imaginative – even ridiculously so – in the pursuit of a solution. Thus, in Book II, More, employing Hythloday's discourse on the society of "Utopia," will offer both a theoretical account of how the conflict between political morality and public utility can be resolved and, by implication, a holistic social diagnosis of the conflict's origin.

The point of departure for this Utopian prescription is offered by a seemingly chance remark of Hythloday's, a tangential explanation of what he takes to be the ultimate cause of the futility of involvement in the European political scene. Hythloday explains:

To tell you what I really think, wherever you have private property, and money is the measure of all things, it is hardly ever possible for a commonwealth to be just or prosperous – unless you think justice can exist where all the best things are held by the worst citizens, or suppose happiness can be found where the good things of life are divided among very few, where even those few are always uneasy, and where the rest are utterly wretched.[83]

In contrast, Hythloday endorses the "wonderfully wise and sacred institutions of the Utopians," among whom virtue has its reward, and who, in striking contrast to the Europeans as depicted in Book I, have made equality compatible with abundance.[84] Property, Hythloday asserts, is a fundamental obstacle to the achievement of well-being for all, since, no matter how much abundance there is, "when everyone, by whatever pretexts, tries to scrape together for himself as much as he can, a handful of men end up sharing the whole pile, and the rest are left in poverty."[85] He thus draws the conclusion that "unless private property is entirely abolished, there can be no fair or just distribution of goods, nor can the business of mortals be conducted happily."[86]

This is the line of argument Hythloday advances in favor of Utopian as against European society. But he does not advance it very far before encountering substantial resistance, initially from "More," and then subtly but persistently from the overall tone of the book, perhaps indicating the resistance of the author More himself. It is important to distinguish these two forms of resistance that Hythloday's claim to resolve the problem encounters, because there is evidence that More means us to have two quite different responses to them. The first set of objections, offered on the spot by "More," encompass what were the standard objections that had been offered throughout Western history, from Aristotle through his medieval and Renaissance successors, against the desirability and practicability of communism. These objections "More" advances in a tone of high seriousness. First, he argues, without the motivation of personal gain, human beings will become lazy and grow to depend upon the work of others. This reduction in productivity will lead to an insufficient supply of goods and a consequent plummeting of the standard of living. Moreover, since men will continue to be driven by personal desire, the absence of property rights will merely result in insecurity of possessions, and consequently "bloodshed and turmoil."[87] And this situation will be further exacerbated by an inevitable crisis of political authority, since it is impossible for any class of leaders to hold the respect of their fellows without the social gradations underwritten by a system of unequal property. This is the first wave of worries about the abolition of property, voiced by "More"; and there is

---

[83] *Utopia*, p. 37.   [84] Ibid.   [85] Ibid., p. 38.   [86] Ibid.   [87] Ibid., p. 39.

reason to believe (based on factors we will consider shortly) that More the author introduces them only in order to see them successfully refuted by the story about Utopia that Hythloday is about to tell.

But there is also, in addition to this explicit and systematic wave of objections to Utopian communism, a second and subtler form of resistance which Hythloday's Utopian argument encounters, one that emerges instead from a variety of textual indications not explicitly tied to the question of the practicability of Utopian communism *per se*. These kinds of worries come in two main forms. First, there is a persistent concern throughout the remainder of *Utopia* that Hythloday's radicalism – though as a *moral* matter well founded and even superior to "More's" Ciceronian incrementalism – may not be the most effective way to get from here to there and thus to achieve meaningful if imperfect reform. Hythloday tries to pre-empt this line of criticism by launching a powerful prudential and moral argument against incremental reform. He argues that such half-measures

may have as much effect as poultices continually applied to sick bodies that are past cure. The social evils I mentioned may be alleviated and their effects mitigated for a while, but so long as private property remains, there is no hope at all of effecting a cure and restoring society to good health. While you try to cure one part, you aggravate the wound in other parts. Suppressing the disease in one place causes it to break out in another, since you cannot give something to one person without taking it away from someone else.[88]

Thus framed, the holism of Hythloday's analysis is one of its most powerful attractions. But there are important reasons to doubt whether the argument of *Utopia* as a whole signifies that More the author is completely prepared to abandon incrementalism as a solution. One such indication is the fact that the passage just cited is preceded by a litany of very plausible-sounding incrementalist reforms, which Hythloday himself acknowledges might constitute a genuine improvement over present conditions. In discussing possible remedies, Hythloday canvasses proposed laws limiting land ownership and income, checking the power of the prince, outlawing financial improprieties by public officials and providing greater financial support for honest officeholders. Hythloday ultimately dismisses all these as insufficient remedies; but More the author seems to be offering them as (at least) genuinely good suggestions for improvement over the status quo. Similarly, the radical proposals of the Utopians are not the only

[88] Ibid., p. 38.

possibilities for reform considered in the book: the somewhat less far-reaching policies of the so-called Polylerites, Achorians and Macarians[89] might all lead to genuine improvements, as might Hythloday's own practical proposals for reducing crime in the dialogue with Cardinal Morton (which Morton himself says are worthy of a trial experiment).[90] These and other indications suggest that the radical holism of the Utopian approach may not be the only worthy approach to political reform.

The second main category of worries consists of a set of ambiguous authorial hints throughout *Utopia* that Hythloday's proposals, though admirable and perhaps even well suited to answer the traditional objections to private property, remain at some level impracticable and even ridiculous. Throughout the discourse (related by Hythloday the "nonsense-speaker") More constantly lets slip remarks about how some readers might find the institutions described to be "ridiculous" or "absurd" (including for example such practice as nude inspections of marital partners before betrothal; the use of gold and silver in making chamber-pots; and the employment of fancy jewelry to mark criminal offenders as slaves). The prefatory letters and verses by More's friends and earliest critics, too, can barely contain their smirks and chuckles at the apparent absurdity of Utopian customs. And when the narrator "More" pronounces his final judgment after Hythloday's lengthy discourse, he tells us he still thinks that many of the Utopian laws and customs are "really absurd."[91] None of this is conclusive grounds for dismissing anything endorsed by Hythloday or his Utopians without careful consideration: but this motif tends to cast at least a shadow of doubt over everything that might otherwise seem plausible and even appealing in Utopian society.

Let us review the stages in the argument so far. According to the interpretation of Book I that we have been considering, More has produced in his dialogue of counsel a genuinely unresolved – and perhaps irresolvable – conflict between the demands of public utility and moral rightness,

---

[89] Meaning, respectively, "People of Much Nonsense," "People Without a Country," and "Blessed People."

[90] Hythloday's proposal: "Banish [gambling and other idle practices], make those who have ruined farmhouses and villages restore them or hand them over to someone who will restore and rebuild. Restrict the rights of the rich to buy up anything and everything, and then to exercise a kind of monopoly. Let fewer people be brought up in idleness. Let agriculture be restored, and the wool-manufacture revived as an honest trade, so there will be useful work for the idle throng, whether those whom poverty has already made thieves or those who are only vagabonds or idle servants now, but are bound to become thieves in the future" (*Utopia*, p. 20). Morton endorses a trial experiment at ibid., p. 25.

[91] Ibid., p. 106.

championed by "More" and Hythloday respectively. There seems to be no basis for awarding the victory to one over the other on the terms of the debate itself. But, at the climax of this conflict, More (the author) introduces (through Hythloday) the possibility of a genuine resolution to the problems of Book I – and therefore also, implicitly, to the paradoxes of political ethics to which those problems give rise. In a true commonwealth, Hythloday argues – such as the commonwealth he has seen in Utopia – the values of public utility and moral rightness, of political action and philosophical rectitude, are in fact not contradictory but compatible. But that possibility, however hopeful, remains shrouded in ambiguity, since the proof that these values are theoretically reconcilable is supposed to be found in a place called Utopia – that is, in a place called "Nowhere." From the irresolution of the dialogue's conclusion, it seems, the only way forward is along the murky path that leads through Utopia.

THE BEST STATE OF A COMMONWEALTH

However, the fact that *Hythloday* offers Utopia as a resolution to this set of problems does not of course imply that More the author believes the example of Utopia is adequate to resolve it. But there is significant reason to think that the author himself is in at least partial agreement with Hythloday on this point: that is, that, whatever worries we may retain about Utopia, More the author wants Hythloday to convince us that Utopia demonstrates that moral rightness and public utility are *in principle* compatible. But for this interpretation to be persuasive it is necessary to offer an interlude (as brief as possible) on the special – even unique – interpretive problems which must be overcome by any reading of *Utopia*.

Utopia is, to begin with, a self-consciously ambiguous work in a self-consciously ambiguous genre (or pair of genres). The dialogue form is inherently evasive as to authorial intention – as had been evinced to great effect by More's contemporary Erasmus – and the dialogue of Book I in particular, as we have seen, comes to a far more unclear resolution than most. Hythloday's discourse, in which we get the full description of *Utopia*, frequently appears to be part of the self-consciously ironic tradition of speeches of mocking praise encountered throughout classical antiquity (for example, in Lucian) and the Renaissance (in the works of Valla, Erasmus, etc.). The story of Utopia is related by a narrator whose name suggests both "guiding angel" (Raphael) and "nonsense-peddler" (Hythloday). That story itself is framed within a dialogue related by a narrator named after the author ("More") whose opinions often seem at odds with what More himself likely believed, and whose own name signifies "fool" (*Morus*).

"More" criticizes the description of Utopia twice – but on the basis of arguments that are either disproved (the end of Book I) or rely on evaluative premises that have already been profoundly undermined (the end of Book II). Hythloday, by contrast, praises Utopia almost entirely without reservation, but there are a variety of indications that we ought not to accept his evaluation too quickly (not least the fact that Utopian society includes such practices as divorce and euthanasia which it is difficult to believe More the author would have approved). And finally, in the prefatory letters to *Utopia*, More's editors and his earliest reviewers – a veritable *Who's Who* of Northern Renaissance humanism – praise the institutions of Utopia unstintingly; but they also never tire of hinting that these institutions, even more than they are praiseworthy, are in some sense also preposterous. Countless pages have been written trying to sort through these various ambiguities, and in this chapter, with our eyes on a limited set of substantive issues, we cannot hope to settle definitively any interpretive questions. Rather, we will have to proceed by adopting one coherent interpretive approach, and offering some broad (and necessarily incomplete) indications as to why that approach is to be preferred.

The interpretive premise we will pursue is that More means us to take Utopia quite seriously as a basis for the diagnosis of the social problems of Europe, and as a source of prescriptions for their solution; but that Utopia is not itself a description of More's own definite statements as to what the *ideal* prescriptions would be. Utopia is rather a very specialized sort of thought-experiment, conducted according to particular rules and therefore not at liberty to be changed according to the author's own preferences.[92] In particular, Utopia is a diagnosis based on the wisdom of ancient philosophy and ancient political practice: one deliberately limited to *exclude* the conclusions of Christian revelation, much as that revelation was not available to the pre-Christian philosophers.[93] Following the rules of the ancient philosophical exercise for discovering the "best state of a commonwealth" (which is of course the full title of *Utopia*), More raises the same questions confronted by Plato in the *Republic* and by Aristotle in the *Politics*. He arrives, however, at somewhat different conclusions, derived

---

[92] George M. Logan, *The Meaning of More's Utopia* (Princeton University Press, 1983), gives the most systematic and persuasive account of what precisely this project consists of.

[93] On this see further Eric Nelson, *The Greek Tradition in Republican Thought* (Cambridge University Press, 2004), ch. 1.

from a more eclectic approach that picks and chooses from all the ancient philosophical schools (including the Epicureans, the Cynics, and especially the Stoics). More's point is to demonstrate that the conclusions arrived at by this means are not only internally consistent, but are in addition more consistent with the true spirit of Christianity – in particular, more charitable, more humble, and more egalitarian – than those arrived at in Europe even by those with full access to the divine revelation of the Christian religion. Consequently, we can expect that some of the institutions we encounter in Utopia may not be consistent with More the author's own "ideal," strictly speaking; but that at the same time it might very well constitute both an improvement over contemporary European practices and a model for contemporary reform.

We can observe one indication that this interpretation captures More's intentions in a kind of interpretive guide offered by More himself in his second prefatory letter to Peter Giles, published with *Utopia* in its 1517 edition. In the letter, More declares himself "absolutely delighted" with the dilemma posed by a "very sharp" reader of *Utopia*. If the work is presented as fact, the reader says, then he finds "a number of absurdities" in the account; but if it is fictitious, then he finds "More's usual good judgment ... wanting in some matters."[94] This reader, More claims, has especially gratified him because, having read the book fully and carefully and considered its claims thoughtfully, he has then, "having selected certain elements to criticise, and not very many of them, [said] that he approves, not rashly but deliberately, of all the rest."[95] This seems to suggest an approach in which readers take *Utopia*'s discrepancies with Christian doctrine to be deliberate but also essentially peripheral aberrations; and in which they focus instead on the core issue of Hythloday's discourse, namely, whether the fundamental institution of Utopian society – its communal life – is truly desirable.[96] With characteristic ambiguity, More seems to turn immediately to undercut

---

[94] *Utopia*, p. 108.   [95] Ibid.

[96] Further evidence for this interpretation can be found in the fact that, in introducing each of these "dubious institutions" in the narrative, More has Hythloday employ a common pattern of description. He begins by explaining some desirable practice of the Utopians; but, having done so, he then introduces a series of exceptions to the policy which reason has suggested to the Utopians to modify their rule (exceptions which might occur to a benevolent natural reason lacking the benefits of Christian revelation as the best solutions to admittedly difficult problems). Whether More thought these exceptions permissible for virtuous pagans is probably an unanswerable question. But if the dubious institutions are in fact just what one would expect to find in an imaginary society of virtuous pagans drawn by a late medieval Catholic of a relatively broad mind, then there is in principle nothing in the presence of such institutions to discount the claim that those pagans have achieved "the best state of a commonwealth" as More would have understood that expression.

this interpretation by declaring that he would be glad if he had merely been able "to set down just a few things out of many that were not altogether absurd."[97] But he then points out that there is nothing unusual about this, for:

Aren't there absurdities elsewhere in the world? And did any one of all the philosophers who have offered a pattern of a society, a ruler, or a private household set down everything so well that nothing ought to be changed? Actually, if it weren't for the great respect I retain for certain highly distinguished names, I could easily produce from each of them a number of notions which I can hardly doubt would be universally condemned as absurd.[98]

The final irony is that this is exactly what More himself has been doing through Hythloday's description of Utopia's institutions.

On this interpretive approach, then, the central institution we need to evaluate is Utopian communism itself. Everything in Utopian life depends upon it: their labor system, their social customs, their methods of waging war and even their religious practices are premised ultimately on their principles of equality, true pleasure and common ownership. Both at the end of Book I and at the conclusion of Book II, the narrator bases his criticisms of Utopia centrally on the institution of Utopian communism alone. Thus, on this interpretation, the light in which *Utopia* presents Utopian communism (and the principles that justify it) should carry far more weight than the presence of specific unorthodox institutions in evaluating the work's ultimate purpose. If on balance Hythloday's arguments for Utopian communism are persuasive, then we have reason to think that on balance More means to offer Utopia as a serious model for reform; if they seem to be offered in a style of irony and ambiguity, then we should retain serious doubts about Utopia as a model for reform.

What then is the evidence for and against Utopian communism? To begin with, let us consider the arguments against communism, which More the author puts in the mouth of "More" the narrator. "More" first objects to communism at the end of Book I, before Hythloday has told his story, and the objections he mobilizes there are not moral but rather pragmatic objections (drawn from Aristotle's criticisms of Plato in the *Politics,* Book II). The moral values implicated by these pragmatic objections are put in jeopardy in a purely conditional way: any normative criticism would dissolve if the undesirable consequences "More" predicts did not follow. And that of course is precisely what the account of Utopia is

---

[97] *Utopia*, p. 108.   [98] Ibid., p. 109.

meant to prove. Hythloday explains that "More" only raises these objections because he has not seen what Hythloday has seen: "You should have been with me in Utopia, and seen with your own eyes their manners and customs, as I did.... If you had seen them, you would frankly confess that you had never seen a well-governed people anywhere but there."[99] In doing so, Hythloday offers up his discourse on Utopia as evidence the reader must assess in deciding whether or not these pragmatic criticisms are well grounded – though ambiguous evidence, to be sure, since its force supposedly resides in its real instantiation in a non-existent place.

When the narrator "More" reappears at the end of Book II, however, his grounds for objection have substantially changed. Gone are the pragmatic objections based on Aristotelian philosophy: we are left to think that Hythloday has satisfied "More" that these objections do not apply to Utopian communism. In their place is a new "chief objection" to the Utopians' communism: that it "utterly subverts all the nobility, magnificence, splendour, and majesty which (in the popular view) are the true ornaments and glory of any commonwealth."[100] The irony here could hardly be thicker. If there is one thing which Hythloday's account has unquestionably established, it is that the prevailing European conceptions of "nobility, magnificence, splendour, and majesty" are positively shameful by comparison with the "true nobility" seen in the Utopian system of values.[101] More the author's irony here tends to underscore the insincerity of "his" claim that "his" chief objection is to the Utopians' "communal living" and "moneyless economy." In any event, this linkage reinforces the idea that Utopian communism is the central institution we must evaluate in assessing the irony of *Utopia* as a whole.

There are a variety of other reasons external to the text for believing that Utopian communism was something toward which More might be sympathetic. First, the book as a whole is a tribute – and at times at least clearly an affectionate tribute – to that most famous of pre-modern arguments for communal living, Plato's *Republic*. Second, Stoic philosophy – an important source of both Utopian philosophy and More the author's own moral ideals – had held that "everything belongs to the wise" and that the wise would be the sort of friends who made "common use of all that has to do

---

[99] Ibid., p. 39.   [100] Ibid., pp. 106–107.
[101] See further Quentin Skinner, "Thomas More's *Utopia* and the Virtue of True Nobility," in *Visions of Politics*, vol. II (Cambridge University Press, 2002), ch. 8.

with life,"[102] a theme the contemporary Erasmian humanists had warmly endorsed. Erasmus himself had stated that if people would just follow this adage about friends sharing all things in common, "most of the evils of our lives would promptly be removed."[103] He had gone on to express amazement at the criticisms of Plato's communal living by his contemporaries, despite the fact that "nothing ever said by a pagan philosopher is more in keeping with the mind of Christ" and communal living is something that "Christ wishes all Christians to practice."[104] Erasmus was one of the editors who helped rush *Utopia* into print, and it is difficult to imagine the thin-skinned Erasmus going to such lengths if he took More's purpose in sketching such a community to be one of ridicule and derision.

The most powerful evidence of all for More's sympathetic view of Utopian communism, however, is the fact that in Utopia (as Hythloday describes it) communal living really does work, and succeeds in solving many if not most of the social problems that plague the Europe portrayed in Book I. The Utopians do not use money; they share common stores of food and supplies, and they divide the necessary labor equally among themselves. But their principle of common life extends much farther than this, encompassing every aspect of life on the island through the elimination of anything that might be considered private. Thus the Utopians share identical houses, which they exchange every ten years by lot; they clothe themselves identically; they eat their meals in common; they cannot travel on a private whim, but only with the permission of their smaller family community, and even then they must contribute to the public good through common labor. In political matters, the same principle applies: members of the legislature cannot discuss political affairs outside of the senate house, for fear of fomenting conspiracy.

Yet this communal quality of Utopian life does not result in the realization of the worries Aristotle (and "More") had voiced about the provision of material plenty: on the contrary, Utopian communism facilitates

---

[102] Diogenes Laertius, "Life of Zeno," in *Lives of Eminent Philosophers*, trans. R. D. Hicks, Loeb Classical Library, vol. II (Harvard University Press, 1925), p. 228. The Stoics also endorsed the community of wives (p. 234), as does Plato in the *Republic*, 457d–466d. Erasmus tells us (in his "Letter to Ulrich von Hutton," *CWE* vol. VII, p. 23, lines 275–277) that More in his youth had written a paradoxical dialogue praising Plato's communism and extending it even to wives. For an intriguing possibility as to More's motivation in praising the community of wives, see the epitaph More wrote for his wives Jane and Alice. In Elizabeth Rogers, ed., *Selected Letters of St. Thomas More* (Yale University Press, 1961), Letter 46 to Erasmus, pp. 182–183. On this see further Logan, *The Meaning of More's Utopia* and my own note "A New Source for More's 'Utopia,'" *Historical Journal* 40 (1997): 493–498, as well as Nelson, *Greek Tradition*.

[103] Erasmus, *Adagia*, *CWE* vol. XXXI, 1.i.1, p. 29.   [104] Ibid.

abundance, since, in the absence of privacy, everyone can be forced to work – including women,[105] priests, and political leaders, as well as the (now non-existent) idle rich and their unproductive retainers. As a consequence of these arrangements, there is in Utopia

Nowhere any chance to loaf or any pretext for evading work; there are no wine-bars or ale-houses, or brothels; no chances for corruption; no hiding places; no spots for secret meetings. Because they live in the full view of all, they are bound to be either working at their usual trades or enjoying their leisure in a respectable way. Such customs must necessarily result in plenty of life's good things, and since they share everything equally, it follows that no one can ever be reduced to poverty or forced to beg.[106]

Yet the Utopians also value contemplative leisure, and by means of their policies they are even able to limit the number of working hours per day to six, because they focus only on producing necessities, rather than luxuries.[107] Even more important, however, their principle of common life allows each of Utopia's workers truly to consider the *common* good of the community in their political deliberations, in a way that is not possible in Europe. Thus, in Utopia, "where there is no private business, every man zealously pursues the public business."[108]

What is required to make all this work, on More's account, is a revaluation of values on the part of all citizens, coupled with a series of institutions designed to support and reinforce those values. The importance of this new moral education is underscored by Hythloday's lengthy (perhaps too lengthy) discussion of the Utopians' moral philosophy. Hythloday wants to urge that the Utopians' moral values are at least superior to those practiced in (ostensibly Christian) Europe, measured in terms of the *honestas* that Hythloday insists upon: but, to drive home the point, More the author chooses to portray the Utopian moral philosophy as grounded – at least at first glance – in the *utilitas* central to Epicurean hedonism.[109] On closer examination, however, the Utopians' hedonism turns out to place the highest value only on "true and honest pleasure": a distinction which Epicurus himself had made, but which Hythloday's Utopians use to open the door to a much more Stoic theory of virtue and moral goodness. This

---

[105] Unsurprisingly, women not only shoulder an equal share of the community's ordinary labor in Utopia but apparently do so in addition to an exclusive responsibility for more traditional house-keeping duties.

[106] *Utopia*, p. 59.   [107] Ibid., p. 51.   [108] Ibid., p. 103.

[109] There were precedents of linking true hedonism with true Christian moral values, most famously in Lorenzo Valla's treatise *On Pleasure*, trans. A. Kent Hieatt and Maristella Lorch (Abaris Books, 1977).

144   *Dirty hands nowhere and everywhere*

allows them to dismiss both those pleasures that harm others – since human beings are supposed to be naturally sociable – as well as pleasures of limited scope or duration, or pleasures that interfere with greater pleasures or cause pains.[110] It also changes their attitudes toward various everyday matters in their society, especially the value they place on gold, silver, and jewels. These attitudes attach contempt and ridicule to those things that are in contemporary Europe the focus of intense pride and interpersonal comparison. And because they hold these attitudes, the Utopians focus all their work efforts only on the most useful of productive activities: agriculture, wool-working, linen-making, masonry, metalworking, and carpentry, but no luxury goods and no idle professions.[111]

By making the surprising move of having his Utopians adopt pleasure as their moral standard, More the author is able to firmly ground the claim that Utopian policies aim exclusively at – and therefore presumably succeed in achieving – the maximum utility of its citizens. At the same time, however, Hythloday emphasizes that their conclusions comport fully with the standards of moral rightness, understood in the classical as well as the Christian senses. The Utopians themselves, at least, clearly recognize the beneficial features of their communal living as points of similarity between their own way of life and the Christian religion. Thus Hythloday tells us that, when the Utopians first heard about Christianity,

You would not believe how eagerly they assented to it, either through the secret inspiration of God or because Christianity seemed very like the sect that most prevails among them. But I think they were also much influenced by the fact that Christ approved of his followers' communal way of life, and that among the truest groups of Christians the practice still prevails.[112]

Thus the institution of Utopian communism – at least on Hythloday's account, and as we have seen there is much reason to suppose that More the author was sympathetic – has succeeded in resolving the tensions between philosophy and politics, and between moral rightness and public utility, which had characterized the political situation described in Book I. We therefore have sufficient reason to believe that More the author intended

---

[110] In following Epicurus's typology of dimensions along which pleasures vary, More manages to produce something that sounds remarkably like Bentham's theory almost three centuries before Bentham wrote it.

[111] *Utopia*, pp. 48–49. This usefulness rationale is also behind the Utopians' war policies and colonial policies: indeed, the Utopians' theories about colonization seem to be an unexpected link in the chain connecting Stoic use-right theories with modern imperial theories justifying acquisition for agricultural purposes.

[112] Ibid., pp. 93–94.

the arguments in favor of Utopian communism, in the context of Utopia itself, to be persuasive.

THE PROBLEM OF "NOWHERE"

But there is a further problem. For while it is true that these arguments succeed in the context of Utopia itself, it is also apparent that they are a long way from being easily applied to Europe as Hythloday describes it. This brings us to a second and more difficult problem. For while we have reason to think that the Utopia Hythloday has described to us may well be "the best state of a commonwealth," it is also the case that Utopia is, as More the author reminds us at every opportunity, "nowhere." There is then a further problem – not just the question of whether Utopia is "the best state of the commonwealth," but the further question of what we are to make of the fact that More keeps telling us it is "nowhere."

In More's second letter to Giles, cited above, he concludes his discussion about the dilemma proposed by the very sharp critic by suggesting that it is foolish of the critic to ask whether Utopia is real or imagined. If More had determined to write his own ideas about the best state of a commonwealth, he says, he might have employed a fiction "through which the truth, like medicine smeared with honey, might enter the mind a little more pleas-antly."[113] But had he done this, he goes on to say, he would have left a few hints to enable the more learned to see through the deception:

Thus if I had merely given such names to the governor, the river, the city and the island as would indicate to the knowing reader that the island was nowhere, the city a phantom, the river waterless and the governor without a people, it wouldn't have been hard to do, and would have been far more clever than what I actually did. If the veracity of a historian had not actually required me to do so, I am not so stupid as to have preferred those barbarous and meaningless names of Utopia, Anyder, Amourot, and Ademus.[114]

But this is of course precisely what these Latinized Greek puns More has chosen as names do mean (for the "more learned" who know Greek as well as Latin), and so in making this denial More is ironically underlining the very fictitiousness of Utopia that he is ostensibly dismissing. In line with the interpretation we have been pursuing thus far, then, what More seems to be doing here is directing our attention away from the possible flaws of

---

[113] Ibid., p. 109.   [114] Ibid.

the commonwealth Hythloday has described, and pointing instead to the fact that Utopia is *nowhere*.

When we review the other prefatory letters and verses, we find that it is this theme of Utopia's non-existence that preoccupies them more than any other. They assert that "the world has never seen" Utopia's equal, and advance the (impossible) suggestion that distinguished European theologians might go to visit Utopia. Guillaume Bude calls attention to the issue by saying that Utopia is also called "Udetopia" (a Greek coinage for "never"), although he adds the caution "if the story is to be believed." Bude also claims that he has personally investigated and discovered that "Utopia lies outside the bounds of the known world," being perhaps "one of the Fortunate Isles, near to the Elysian Fields"; More himself has said that "Hythloday has not yet told exactly where it is to be found." In the same way, More's first letter to Giles, which forms a sort of preface to *Utopia*, never tires of emphasizing the reality of Utopia, thus ironically underscoring its fictional nature. More and his servant, he tells Giles, have differing recollections of what Hythloday told them about the length of the bridge at Amaurotum. They must attempt to clarify this detail by getting in touch with Hythloday (who cannot, of course, be contacted). This is especially important because they have forgotten to inquire in what part of the world the new island of Utopia is to be found. And it has gained even greater urgency now that a certain theologian is contriving to get himself appointed bishop to the Utopians by the pope. In his own prefatory letter, Giles also repeatedly emphasizes this aspect of the joke. Hythloday's account made it readily apparent that he was describing "exactly what he had seen close to hand with his own eyes and experienced in his own person," Giles assures us. He also extends More's joke about the location of Utopia, adding that Hythloday had actually mentioned its location, but More was unluckily distracted at the crucial moment by a whispering servant, while Giles missed hearing the location thanks to an untimely cough. Perhaps most significantly, More's other letters from the period refer to the work as his *Nusquama* (nowhere).[115]

---

[115] Given the influence of Stoicism on *Utopia*, it is intriguing that one key theme associated with the Stoics in antiquity was the idea of their *unreality*: the impossibility of any person achieving the moral perfection of the Stoic sage. Interestingly, this impossibility was sometimes likened to the impossibility of Plato's Republic, which was perceived to be a similarly unattainable idea. See for example Cicero's comment about the arch-Stoic Cato that despite Cato's "unimpeachable honesty" he nevertheless "does harm to the country; for the opinions he delivers would be more in place in Plato's Republic than among the dregs of humanity collected by Romulus." Cicero, *Letters to Atticus*, trans. E. O. Winstedt, Loeb Classical Library (Harvard University Press, 1921), II.1, p. 108.

Nowhere: the thought reverberates throughout the prefatory letters and on through the text itself, haunting every word spoken in praise of Utopia.

Isolating this issue further helps to explain some of More's remarks in his later writings that seem critical of the kind of communal living praised (by Hythloday) in *Utopia*. For the doubts about communism expressed in More's later writings appear (in the light of the interpretation we have been advancing) to refer not in any instance to More's doubts about the *morality* of communism, but rather to its association in his mind with this problem of nowhere.

In his *Confutation of Tyndale's Answer*, More condemns the opinion of the Anabaptists "that no man shold haue any thynge proper of his owne, but that all landes and all goodes ought by goddes lawe to be all mennys in comen ..."[116] The key to this formulation is "by goddes lawe": for elsewhere More argues that "the law of the gospel does not apportion possessions, nor does reason alone prescribe the forms of determining property, unless reason is attended by an agreement, and this [agreement] ... is public law."[117] The Anabaptists were wrong to argue that the moral law necessitated communism, which would (like private property) be a wholly conventional arrangement. But this is to say nothing about the desirability of communism as such, which would of course depend upon its appropriateness to the society and its conformity to the principles of social justice.

More voices a similar thought in his *Responsio ad Lutherum*. There he challenges Luther's (alleged) view that:

The law of the gospel alone would ultimately be sufficient and human laws worthless if magistrates were good and the faith truly preached. As if even the best magistrates could manage either that the whole Christian people would want to live in common or that the wicked would not want to steal or that any preaching of the faith could procure that no one anywhere would be wicked. If the law of the gospel does not permit stealing, surely the human law which punishes stealing is not useless; and the human law which alone apportions ownership of goods binds

---

Of related interest is Folly's comment in Erasmus's *The Praise of Folly* that the Stoic ideal of the wise man "leaves nothing at all of the man, and has to fabricate in his place a new sort of god who never was and never will be in existence anywhere." Folly goes on to urge that those who prefer the Stoic ideal of the sage should be left to "love him without a rival, live with him in Plato's Republic or in the kingdom of Ideas, if they prefer, or else in the gardens of Tantalus." Erasmus, *The Praise of Folly*, *CWE* vol. XXVII, p. 103. See also Erasmus's explication of the term "Gardens of Tantalus" in his *Adagia*, including the statement that the term refers to "things which seem to be substantial when they are nothing" or that "both exist and do not exist." Erasmus, *Adagia*, *CWE* vol. XXXIII, II.i.46, p. 43.

[116] Thomas More, *Confutation of Tyndale's Answer*, *CWM* vol. VIII, 664/11–13.

[117] Thomas More, *Responsio Ad Lutherum*, *CWM* vol. V, 276/21–25.

Christians, if this ownership is done away with there cannot indeed be any stealing. But if he should say from this premise the argument is drawn that we would do better to be without that law from which the ownership of goods arises and would do better to live in a certain natural community with the occasion of stealing eliminated, it does not help his case even if someone should grant him this argument. For even if we could live in common with far fewer laws, we still could not live altogether without laws. For the obligation to work would have to be prescribed for certain classes, and laws would be needed to restrain crimes which would run riot even in that kind of life. But now if, with the faith most truly preached as the apostles used to preach it most truly, with, moreover, the best rulers everywhere put in charge of the Christian people, the ownership of property could yet remain, and many wicked men would remain, he cannot deny that the human law binds Christians so that no one might steal what the law has apportioned to another, nor would the law be useless in punishing anyone who committed theft.[118]

The position here is clearly reconcilable with the interpretation of *Utopia* we have been exploring. Notice that the "best magistrates" might well want to persuade their charges to live in common, just as they would want to persuade them not to steal. More even suggests that he might be willing to grant that it would be "better to live in a certain natural community." The moral objective of communism is laudable, perhaps even ideal. But in the real world of sinful men, it is also very unlikely that such a change will come about. In the meantime, some sort of political arrangement must exist, however conventional and imperfect: and to the extent that such arrangements correspond to the law of the gospel (for example, in their prohibition of theft), they must be accepted as binding upon Christians.

Somewhat more challenging to explain is the position on communism More adopts in his *Dialogue of Comfort Against Tribulation*. Addressing the question of whether Christian morality requires monastic poverty, More offers the following analysis:

Men of substance must there be / for els mo beggers shall you haue perdy then there be, & no man left able to releve an nother. For this I thinke in my mynd a very sure conclucion / that yf all the money that is in this countrey were to morrow brought to gether out of euery mans hand, & laid all vppon one hepe, and than devidid out vnto euery man a like: it wold be on the morrow after worse than it was the day before. For I suppose whan yt were all egally thus devidid among all / the best shuld be left litle bettre than almost a beggar is now / And yet he that was a begger before, all that he shall be the richer for that he shuld thereby recyve, shall not make hym mych above a beger still / but many one of the rich men yf their

---

[118] Ibid., 274/23–276/13.

riches stode but in movevable substans, shalbe safe inough from riches happely for all their life after.[119]

As the remainder of the passage reveals, More's concern here is with egalitarian reform in the context of a society that continues to desire a wide variety of luxuries and continues to distribute them through an exchange economy.[120] In the light of *Utopia*, More's point is surely that even communism is by itself an insufficient remedy for the problems of economic distribution sketched out in Book I. A radical change of social priorities, and a fully cooperative method of production as well as distribution, is required in order to make the Utopian economy abundant.[121] In the real world, it is only too likely that if nominal equality were achieved "to morrow," without any fundamental change in the citizens' attitudes toward life and its luxuries, the economic consequences would indeed be disastrous.

Thus the problem with communal living encountered throughout these later writings is not a substantive moral or political problem with the Utopian institutions, but rather an incessant reformulation of this problem of nowhere. It is not the undesirability of communal living that makes it objectionable, but rather its unlikelihood of ever existing at all.

THE DEMOCRATIC DIMENSION

What makes it unlikely ever to exist, according to Hythloday, is ultimately a moral fact about human nature itself. For it is *pride*, and the set of institutions and practices to which pride gives rise, that makes the acceptance of the good Utopian institutions impossible in practice. Hythloday explains:

I have no doubt that every man's perception of where his true interest lies, along with the authority of Christ our Savior (whose wisdom could not fail to recognize the best, and whose goodness would not fail to counsel it), would long ago have brought the whole world to adopt the laws of this commonwealth, were it not for one single monster, the prime plague and begetter of all others – I mean Pride.[122]

---

[119] Thomas More, *A Dialogue of Comfort Against Tribulation*, *CWM* vol. XII, 179/30–180/13.
[120] Ibid., 180/14–181/4.
[121] On this point as well as the issues discussed immediately below, see Thomas I. White, "The Key to Nowhere: Pride and *Utopia*," in John C. Olin, ed., *Interpreting Thomas More's Utopia*, (Fordham University Press, 1989), and Athanasios Moulakis, "Pride and the Meaning of *Utopia*," *History of Political Thought* 11 (1990): 241–256.
[122] *Utopia*, p. 106.

As we have seen, pride constituted the deadliest of the vices in the Augustinian strain of Christianity (in which More was greatly interested).[123] In the rhetorical climax of the discourse, Hythloday focuses all our attention and energy on the central role that pride plays in corrupting the political and social life of More's Europe. Pride, he says, is "a serpent from hell that twines herself around the hearts of men, acting like a suckfish to draw and hold them back from choosing a better way of life."[124]

The nature of pride's evil, furthermore, is bound up intimately with those social structures of inequality which the Utopians have eliminated. In Utopia, what one wears, what one eats, where one lodges, what one's leisure consists in: none of these can possibly serve as an occasion for envy or interpersonal comparison. Such vicious attitudes are systematically eliminated from Utopian society by rooting out the institutions and practices that give them their foothold in our everyday existence. Because all share alike in the society's common wealth, in Utopian society it is systematically the case that no one can have any better than anyone else, for there is nothing better to have; that no one can lord it over another person, for every other person is one's equal in every relevant respect. In such a world, as even Utopia's children understand, to puff oneself up because one wears a shiny chain or a sparkling rock is simply laughable.

The source of evil in politics, then, is to be found in the *souls* of the individuals in society: for it is their needs and desires, their good, that makes up the conflicted agenda of those who would serve in the public sphere. It is a systematic problem requiring a holistic solution. Only by approaching the problem systematically, Hythloday thinks, can the ultimate causes of political evil – namely the moral vices of the people at large – be treated and, when necessary, rooted out. For the crucial moral vice – indeed, the source of all the other vices – is pride; and in order to capture our hearts effectively pride needs us to differentiate ourselves comparatively in a way that truly egalitarian institutions obstruct. Hythloday explains:

Pride measures her prosperity not by what she has but by what others lack. Pride would not deign even to be made a goddess if there were no wretches for her to sneer at and domineer over. Her good fortune is dazzling only by contrast with the miseries of others; she displays her riches to torment and tantalise the poverty of others.[125]

---

[123] More's biographer tells us he taught a course on Augustine's *City of God* from a historical and political point of view.
[124] *Utopia*, p. 106.   [125] Ibid.

   This draws our attention to a sort of chicken-and-egg problem that lies at the heart of Utopia: do the Utopians hold their peculiar moral views because they have political and social institutions that restrict pride? Or do they have political and social institutions that restrict pride because their peculiar moral views are hostile to it? There is no way to settle the matter definitively on the basis of what Hythloday (or More the author) tells us. But there is an indication in the fact that Hythloday in this same passage argues that pride is "too deeply fixed in human nature to be easily plucked out," and so celebrates the (false) fact "that the Utopians at least have been lucky enough to achieve this republic" (a formulation that again echoes the problem of nowhere).[126] For More, then, it appears that the ultimate roots of political evil are the same as the roots of moral evil, the key fact that (in reality) appears on its face to make reform hopeless. "For it is impossible to make everything good until all men are good," as "More" remarks in Book I, and, despite Hythloday's confidence in the Utopian achievement, at the end of Book II that prospect still seems for the most part dismayingly distant.

   The notion that the vice of pride helped to create political as well as moral evil was not by itself a claim of great novelty in Renaissance discourse. But in More's hands the assertion takes on a much deeper meaning, for two reasons. First, More's account offers much greater analytical sophistication than any of his contemporaries in explaining precisely *how* pride operates to obstruct the good life – namely, through the institutions and practices of European society which Hythloday criticizes, and which the Utopians have eliminated from their shared life. And, second, More's text also provides a truly pioneering account of how the ethical problems confronting the citizens of a polity are systematically *interrelated* with those confronting their leaders. In closing, let us consider each of these points in turn.

   First, More's profound analysis of how pride is instantiated in and reinforced by particular social institutions reaches far beyond a glib moralism to approach something like a modern sociological insight. His examination in Book I of the roots of Europe's social problems – from the idle classes who leech off society to self-serving policies such as the enclosure of sheep, which destroys agriculture and all the economic activity that depends on it – evinces a keen understanding that subtle evaluative judgments and behavioral incentives operating well beneath the surface of our everyday life doom to failure any facile moralistic effort at reform. We

[126] Ibid.

encounter the same kind of depth of analysis in the discourse of Book II, where Hythloday's description of Utopia constitutes a marvel of internal coherence and external plausibility. If Hythloday's story is "true" – whether in fact or in essence – it shows that, while original sin may be a necessary obstacle to the attainment of full Christian virtue, it is only a contingent obstacle to the attainment of social justice. And thus, despite More's suggestion that the "best state of a commonwealth" is in fact "nowhere," he also seems at the end to want to urge that the conflicts between moral rightness and public expediency are at least *theoretically* resolvable, even in a world of sinful people.

But, second, More's greatest achievement with regard to political ethics – a central subject of the work as a whole – is his emphasis on the interrelated character of the ethical problems of political leaders and those of its citizens. Like Machiavelli's account, More's theory too ultimately rests on a democratic diagnosis of the problems of political ethics. It is a failure of virtue on the part of the people as a whole – specifically a failure to restrain the chief vice of pride – that creates the deplorable political pressures which political leaders (and advisers) in Europe must routinely face. And, also as in Machiavelli's theory, More finds that institutional factors both reflect and reinforce these failures of moral values: so that corrupt institutions breed further corruption in the citizens, and corrupt citizens make reform of the relevant institutions impossible. But unlike Machiavelli, instead of an aristocratic solution to the problem (granting special moral privileges to political leaders), More urges that only a solution of genuinely democratic moral reform – such as we find in the example of the Utopian commonwealth – can ever really eliminate the moral dilemmas that confront both political leaders and citizens in More's Europe.

Thus, however powerful Hythloday's argument for "Utopia" may be, there still remains the gaping question of how in the meantime our ethic is supposed to accommodate the real political world. More makes this contrast clear in a passage which compares the actions of Europeans directly with those of the people of Utopia. In Europe, Hythloday observes, "men talk all the time about the commonwealth, but what they mean is simply their own wealth," whereas in Utopia, as we have already observed, "where there is no private business, every man zealously pursues the public business."[127] Commentators have made much of this passage, but few have noted what Hythloday goes on to add: that "*in both places men are right to act as they do*."[128] The constraints of necessity operating on actual human

---

[127] Ibid., p. 103.   [128] Ibid. Emphasis added.

beings – somewhere as opposed to nowhere – "forces them to think that they must look out for themselves, rather than for the people, that is other people." It is only in Utopia, that is nowhere, "where everything belongs to everybody," that "no one need fear that, so long as the public warehouses are filled, anyone will ever lack for anything for his own use."[129]

If so, then More's argument is significantly more disquieting at the level of individual ethics than it is even at the level of social macro-analysis. For Hythloday's claim – that the Ciceronian ethic of political action in pursuit of the public good conflicts fundamentally with Christian morality – has not really been resolved in practice even if it has been settled in principle. It is because European social institutions are corrupted, centered on pride and selfishness, that a wise and good man cannot act safely in the political arena with respect to either his fortune or his conscience. In Utopia – that is, nowhere – virtuous political action is possible, and the tensions of the dirty hands dilemma can be relaxed by this resolution. But, given the book's final implications, this is only to point relentlessly to the fact that in the real world such a resolution is *not* possible.

And this means the responsible (Christian) political actor cannot be let off the hook. There is no special political ethic in More's world vision: Hythloday has already closed the door to this with his vehement and persuasive denial of the proposition that justice is "a humble, plebeian virtue, far beneath the dignity of kings," or that "there are two kinds of justice, one for the common herd, a lowly justice that creeps along the ground, hedged in everywhere and encumbered with chains; and the other, which is the justice of princes, much more majestic and hence more free than common justice, so that it can do anything it wants and nothing it doesn't want."[130] If the only place political morality is possible is "nowhere," then it follows that a very real problem of dirty hands exists everywhere people motivated by moral intuitions derived from Christianity try to engage in the messy realities of political life.

---

[129] Ibid.   [130] Ibid., p. 84.

CHAPTER 4

Hobbes's choice

BERNARD: *But what's wrong with open government? I mean, why shouldn't the public know more about what's going on?*

SIR ARNOLD: *Are you serious? . . . My dear boy, it's a contradiction in terms. You can be <u>open</u>, or you can have <u>government</u>.*

BERNARD: *But surely the citizens of a democracy have a right to know?*

SIR HUMPHREY: *No. They have a right to be ignorant. Knowledge only means complicity in guilt. Ignorance has a certain . . . dignity.*

Anthony Jay and Jonathan Lynn, Yes Minister, Episode One

In Machiavelli and in Thomas More, we find a common diagnosis of the problem of dirty hands – but two divergent prescriptions for dealing with its effects. Both writers argue that what drives the dirty hands dilemmas confronted by political leaders is ultimately connected to the moral failures of the people on whose behalf they act. Machiavelli's prescription is to propose an aristocratic intervention by leaders: a chosen few who take the necessary guilt of political action on themselves and in the process spare the people as a whole the resulting moral risks. Thomas More, on the other hand, asserts that the democratic dimension of the problem's origins precludes an aristocratic solution from ever truly addressing the problem's root causes. Only a democratic solution, More holds, can truly confront the problem at its source. The Renaissance version of the dirty hands problem raises fundamental questions about the moral responsibilities that states and their citizens bear for political actions and outcomes, and this problem, as we will see, is one of the central philosophical issues that Thomas Hobbes's political theory is designed to address.

Hobbes confronts a choice about how to characterize political agency that is at the same time a choice about how to assign moral responsibility for political outcomes. For Hobbes, action in pursuit of the public good requires both aristocratic and democratic agency. His political ethic urges that both sovereignty and the obedience of citizens are indispensable in order to secure the ends of society. Thus Hobbes's theory responds to the dirty hands dilemma by providing an agency collectively capable of securing the public benefit, in the form of the sovereign state and the subjects who faithfully obey its commands. This meets Machiavelli's pragmatic demand by ensuring that there is someone to make the hard calls, someone to do the killing and coercing and presumably also the lying and betraying should they become necessary. Yet Hobbes has a curious pair of arguments (which we will trace below) purporting to show that the sovereign and his subjects can *both* be exonerated from moral blame in the pursuit of their shared public ends.

The choice implied by Hobbes's solution to the problem of dirty hands has left behind a commanding modern legacy. In modern state systems, especially democratic systems, we frequently encounter the residue of Hobbes's choice in the circular pattern in which both citizens and their representatives seek to evade moral responsibility for the state's acts. Modern citizens claim to be innocent of their states' actions on the grounds that they are obligated as political subjects to obey an authority above and beyond their own moral judgments. At the same time, however, those who administer the government's authority also claim justification for their deeds – on the grounds that in acting they aim not at their own private ends but rather at the public benefit.

This is a key problem for modern democratic theory, and behind it lies another, even more fundamental, question: what kind of moral authority is implied by our conception of the representative function of the state? Is the state we envision one whose claims are preeminent over the moral values and judgments of individuals, such that it can exonerate those who obey its commands from those of their own conscience? Or is the state we envision one whose claims obligate us only to the extent that we judge those claims to be moral by our own lights, such that the state's authority offers no special moral permissions of any kind to its citizens?

By understanding Hobbes's political theory as a response to the problem of dirty hands – and in particular *democratic* as well as aristocratic dirty hands – we can see that this familiar dynamic of evasion finds its most significant origin in Hobbes's theory of state sovereignty. Central to Hobbes's system is the claim that the actions of subjects are morally excused when they result from obedience to the sovereign's commands; but also central for Hobbes is the claim that the sovereign has special moral prerogatives derived from the fact that he is the authorized representative of his subjects. This chapter inquires to what extent either sovereigns or subjects in Hobbes's world are properly held responsible morally for their actions. In particular, it focuses on one peculiarity of Hobbes's theory, namely, the unusual problem his theory of representation appears to cause for assigning moral responsibility to sovereigns and subjects respectively.

Given the nature of Hobbes's absolutist political theory, it might seem natural for him to attribute moral responsibility for political actions entirely to the sovereign. When one person is morally obliged not to resist and even to obey the commands of another, it would seem very unusual for us to attribute responsibility to the obligated person and not to the person who commands. That this captures at least part of Hobbes's view is borne out by the fact that, in cases where subjects obey their sovereign's commands rather than their own judgments and desires, Hobbes claims their actions should properly be considered "not [theirs], but [their] Soveraign's."[1] But Hobbes also takes a forceful position that seems to cut against this attribution of moral responsibility to the sovereign. For, in the theory of representation set forth in *Leviathan*, Hobbes's final articulation of his political theory, Hobbes is at pains to insist that in an important sense it is the subjects rather than the sovereign who bear moral responsibility for most if not all of the sovereign's actions.[2]

The problem is further complicated by the fact that one of Hobbes's central concerns in *Leviathan*, especially in Parts III and IV, is to establish that subjects can never have a sufficient justification of conscience for resisting the sovereign's commands. By introducing a theory of political representation that focuses on attributing moral responsibility for the sovereign's actions to the subjects, Hobbes adds an element to his theory that seems to undercut significantly his primary apologetic purpose.[3]

The problem, as we will see, can ultimately be resolved only by revisiting – and challenging – some of Hobbes's foundational claims about his own theory. In particular, we will re-examine and question Hobbes's belief in the clear moral superiority of the institution of civil society over the state of

---

[1] Thomas Hobbes, *Leviathan* ch. 42, p. 344. I cite from Richard Tuck's edition (Cambridge University Press, 1991).

[2] *Leviathan* ch. 16, pp. 111–115.

[3] There are a variety of persuasive explanations on offer in the secondary literature about why Hobbes would have been motivated to employ the language of representation, particularly in light of the use of that language in political controversies of the time. (Deborah Baumgold, *Hobbes's Political Theory* (Cambridge University Press, 1988), especially chapter 3, offers useful explanations of this kind.) Yet while Hobbes had motivations to employ this language given its implications for contemporary debate, he also encountered certain costs, particularly with respect to the casuistical purposes which I consider in detail in the middle sections of this chapter. The question I want to consider is why Hobbes would have been willing to use the language of representation given these rhetorical risks. Understood in this way, this problem has engaged surprisingly little discussion in recent Hobbes scholarship. A form of the problem is noticed obliquely, though no solution to it is offered, in A. P. Martinich, *Thomas Hobbes* (Palgrave Macmillan, 1997), pp. 46–47.

nature (due to its purported capacity to overcome and eliminate fully the moral dangers and desperations characteristic of that state). Instead, we will find, the civil state created by the social compact must, to a greater degree than Hobbes is willing to acknowledge, continually draw upon and justify its actions *directly* in terms of the expansively brutal and amoral vision of human existence depicted in Hobbes's state of nature. Consequently, and despite Hobbes's hopes, the moral dangers of the state of nature can on Hobbes's theory never fully be overcome.

MORAL RESPONSIBILITY IN HOBBES'S POLITICAL THEORY

At first glance, it might seem odd to approach Hobbes's political theory with an eye to the question of moral responsibility, since Hobbes is famous as an early and influential form of moral relativist. But, despite his moral relativism, there is unquestionably a place in Hobbes's philosophy for a certain kind of moral imperative: namely, the requirements set out in the laws of nature, and later, by means of the laws of nature, in the sovereign's laws. The laws of nature constitute authoritative and persistent rules of reason forbidding us to act in a way contrary to our self-preservation.[4] In one respect Hobbes clearly means these rules to count as morally obligatory: he says they constitute "the true and onely Morall Philosophy" and "the science of Vertue and Vice," and that we can think of them in one sense as the laws of God.[5] But in another respect, Hobbes tells us, the laws of nature are not strictly obligatory *in practice* in the state of nature – since they oblige us only *in foro interno*, to will their observance, rather than *in foro externo*, to actually observe them, so long as it is unsafe to do so.[6] So there is in practice no such thing as moral obligation or moral responsibility prior to the establishment of state sovereignty.[7]

Instead, the state of nature is characterized by the right of all people to all things – by which Hobbes means that in the absence of government each individual has a right, that is, a blameless liberty, to take or do anything at all which they might judge to be necessary to their self-preservation.[8] The extent of our blameless liberty derives from the fact that for Hobbes

---

[4] *Leviathan* ch. 14, p. 91.   [5] *Leviathan* ch. 14, pp. 110–111.   [6] *Leviathan* ch. 14, p. 110.

[7] *Leviathan* ch. 13, pp. 89–90. On the basic interchangeability of the concepts of "state" and "sovereign" in Hobbes, see a pair of articles by Quentin Skinner: "From the State of Princes to the Person of the State" and "Hobbes and the Purely Artificial Person of the State," in Skinner's *Visions of Politics* (Cambridge University Press, 2002), vol. II, ch. 14 and vol. III, ch. 6.

[8] Thomas Hobbes, *Elements of Law* ch. 14, p. 79 (I cite from J. C. A. Gaskin's edition (Oxford University Press, 1994)); *Leviathan* ch. 14, p. 91.

the state of nature is an exceedingly dangerous place. Absent government, human beings are naturally driven by their fears and their desires – especially their desire for glory and reputation – to engage in what Hobbes characterizes as a continual state of war "of every man, against every man."[9] Such a perpetual war (again, in the absence of political rule) is impossible to avoid. Everyone in the state of nature might want what you possess or also desire; or they may seek the reputational benefits they would derive from killing you, or, even if they lack all these desires, they may decide that killing you is the most prudent thing to do because they don't know if *you* want something of theirs. It is possible that there will not be constant fighting – though this certainly seems likely – but there will of necessity be the constant *threat* of fighting; and that threat is sufficient to ensure that, so long as the state of nature prevails, there will be

no place for Industry; because the fruit thereof is uncertain: and consequently no Culture of the Earth; no Navigation, nor use of the commodities that may be imported by Sea; no commodious Building; no Instruments of moving, and removing such things as require much force; no Knowledge of the face of the Earth; no account of Time; no Arts; no Letters; no Society; and which is worst of all, continuall feare, and danger of violent death; And the life of man, solitary, poore, nasty, brutish, and short.[10]

To paraphrase, then, the right to all things which all persons in the state of nature possess is then a kind of infinite moral permission – there is in the state of nature nothing you could really be *blamed* for doing. As Hobbes goes on to elaborate, "the notions of Right and Wrong, Justice and Injustice, have [in the state of nature] no place," for "where there is no common Power, there is no Law: where no Law, no Injustice."[11] Furthermore, the unlimited character of this right of all people to all things is itself the great and constant threat to peace and even survival in the state of nature – because everyone possesses it and may rightfully claim it – and consequently, even though it is described as "natural," as "liberty," and even as "right," it remains the great evil of human existence outside the political state.

Thus, when Hobbes describes what the laws of nature require *externally*, he offers man in his state of nature a set of moral exemptions that closely mirror those which Machiavelli had afforded his prince. Just as Machiavelli

---

[9] *Leviathan* ch. 13, p. 88. [10] *Leviathan* ch. 13, p. 89.

[11] *Leviathan* ch. 13, p. 90. In a similar vein, see Hobbes's remark in the same chapter (p. 90) that "the Desires, and other Passions of man, are in themselves no sin. No more are the Actions, that proceed from those Passions, till they know a Law that forbids them: which till Lawes be made they cannot know: nor can any Law be made, till they have agreed upon the Person that shall make it."

had insisted in Chapter 15 of *The Prince* that, when others act immorally, our virtues may sometimes prove to be vices, and our vices virtues, so too Hobbes argues that if in the state of nature a man were to be "modest and tractable, and performe all he promises, in such time, and place, where no man els should do so, [he] should but make himselfe a prey to others, and procure his own certain ruine, contrary to the ground of all Lawes of Nature, which tend to Nature's preservation."[12] Instead, for Hobbes the state of nature is necessarily a state of war: and, like Machiavelli, Hobbes too believes (in contradiction to Cicero's classical moralism as well as the Christian tradition generally) that "Force, and Fraud, are in warre the two Cardinall vertues."[13]

The establishment of sovereignty changes all this. Though we still derive our moral obligations from the law of nature, that law now requires us to do whatever conduces to peace, in particular to support a system of state sovereignty. The mechanism that produces this system is what Hobbes describes as "transfer of right": by means of this process, a person who possesses a right may disclaim the benefit of the right she possesses in favor of some other person by committing herself not to interfere with the other person's exercise of the liberty. (For example, in selling a piece of land, the owner must not only alienate her right to come and go as she pleases on the land, but *transfer* her right to the new owner, who now possesses this blameless liberty of entrance and egress.)

Hobbes claims that this transfer of right is what underlies the social contract.[14] In consenting to government, Hobbes explains, I "*Authorise and give up my Right of Governing my selfe, to this man, or to this Assembly of men, on this condition, that thou give up thy Right to him, and Authorise all his Actions in like Manner.*"[15] Authorization, then, is for Hobbes a way of describing the moral significance of this process of transfer of right. The transfer of our rights to the sovereign transforms our moral obligations in several ways, according to Hobbes. First, it makes our moral responsibilities genuine obligations by making it safe to perform them in practice. But, second, it gives those obligations a much more determinate content by giving subjects a new and almost unlimited duty to obey the commands of

---

[12] *Leviathan* ch. 15, p. 110. In particular, what makes human beings vulnerable to this perpetual war are two very Augustinian concepts: the limitlessness of their desires (*Leviathan* ch. 6, pp. 44–45, ch. 11, p. 70); and their overestimation of their own worth and ability relative to the worth and ability of their fellows (*Elements* ch. 9, pp. 50–51, and ch. 14, p. 78; *Leviathan* ch. 8, pp. 54–55, ch. 13, pp. 87–88, and ch. 15, p. 107, 110).

[13] *Leviathan* ch. 13, p. 90.

[14] In the case of the commonwealth by institution, on which my argument will principally focus.

[15] *Leviathan* ch. 17, p. 120.

the sovereign, even when he goes beyond the laws of nature, indeed even when he appears to contravene them. And finally, as we will see, by authorizing the sovereign's representation of us, we also acquire a strong form of moral responsibility for his actions on our behalf, even where we disapprove of those actions and would prefer to disavow them.

HOBBES AND THE CONSCIENCE

Hobbes, therefore, believes he has established that, under the state, individual moral obligations collapse into political obligations. Since the first law of nature is to seek peace and the second is to be willing to surrender our rights, there is no imaginable scenario in which our obligations under the law of nature might point us in a different direction than that specified by the sovereign's commands.

What does present a potential rival source of moral authority, however, is the possibility that God will give – or has given – commands that might conflict with the commands of the sovereign. To address this possibility, it is necessary for a moment for us to reconsider one of the classic puzzles about Hobbes's religious thought: namely, what Hobbes, whom his contemporaries viewed as obviously atheistic or at least startlingly heretical, might have been up to in mounting a defense of his theory's religious orthodoxy so extended and detailed that it takes up almost half of his *Leviathan*. The first and second parts of *Leviathan* seem to go to enormous lengths to exclude religious premises from doing any heavy lifting in Hobbes's political theory; but then the third and fourth parts of *Leviathan* devote incredibly detailed attention to religious argumentation.

A variety of possible responses to this question have arisen in the interpretive literature on Hobbes. One approach tries to see Hobbes as more sincerely theist and at least more aspirationally orthodox than is commonly supposed,[16] while an alternative view takes Hobbes's religious arguments to be insincere but nevertheless instrumentally necessary in communicating to a religiously serious seventeenth-century audience.[17] There are problems with both approaches: the former strains to accommodate the evidence at times, while the latter aims at trying to provide answers to such questions as "was Hobbes a 'true Christian?'," which are

[16] See, for example, A. P. Martinich, *The Two Gods of Leviathan: Thomas Hobbes on Religion and Politics* (Cambridge University Press, 1992).
[17] Paul D. Cooke, *Hobbes and Christianity: Reassessing the Bible in Leviathan* (Rowman and Littlefield, 1996.)

both unanswerable and beside the point. Together, they have contributed to an unhelpful focus on trying to ferret out Hobbes's inner beliefs as opposed to explaining the effects of his expressed arguments.

By contrast, we should instead approach Hobbes's use of religious argumentation as equally instrumental throughout his work: Hobbes's argument should be understood as a philosophical *and* a religious argument all the way through, not a religious argument that picks up in Parts III and IV where the philosophical argument of Parts I and II leaves off. Both sections of the work display philosophical and religious arguments aimed at securing a political purpose, seeking not only to persuade philosophically but also to resonate specially among those for whom the *Christian* religion is authoritative.

The case for the pervasiveness of religious argumentation in Hobbes's theory could be made at length but, rather than detailing those points here, we can merely notice three such aspects of his argument: namely, the attitudes toward the values of humility, equality, and obedience displayed in Parts I and II. Hobbes's argument presents the state of nature as one in which pride plays a dominant role, and sees the system of sovereignty as making possible the Christian virtue of humility. It portrays the state of nature as one in which selfishness and greed are given free reign, whereas the system of sovereignty makes possible the recognition of the Christian value of equality. And it sees the state of nature as overrun by self-assertive willfulness, whereas the system of sovereignty makes possible order through obedience and submission.

Hobbes consistently frames his appeals to these values in such a way as to highlight their religious significance.[18] He indicates that a central function of the sovereign is to subdue human pride and cultivate humility by choosing the name "Leviathan," referred to in Job as "the King of the Proud," to represent his state.[19] He frames the law of nature such that its essence is to be found in the rejection of selfishness and recognition of equality framed in Christ's Golden Rule.[20] And he argues that the whole system of the Christian religion is built upon strong and numerous "precepts of absolute obedience to human authority."[21] These appeals are not for mere show: they are instead points of deep connection between

---

[18] For this reason I cannot agree with Cooke that "the entire treatment of Christianity constitutes an exceedingly clever illusion manufactured by Hobbes." Ibid., pp. 32–33 and *passim*.
[19] *Leviathan* ch. 28, p. 221. [20] *Leviathan* ch. 15, pp. 109–110. [21] *Elements* ch. 25, p. 143.

Hobbes's system and important traditional values (though not all the important traditional values) of Christianity.[22]

The tendency to dismiss Hobbes's religious arguments as entirely disingenuous has contributed to an interpretive misrepresentation of the problem Hobbes took himself to be addressing with respect to political obligation and responsibility. Contemporary political philosophy has tended to focus on what we might call the philosophical problem of political obligation.[23] This problem is framed as that of providing adequate reasons for obedience to subjects who may question the sovereign's authority: why should a subject do what the sovereign asks rather than what she herself wishes?[24] But closer attention reveals that this is not the problem to which Hobbes himself devotes the bulk of his attention. Instead, Hobbes focuses his argument on a quite different problem: how to dispense with his subjects' excuses for disobedience grounded on scruples of *conscience*. Instead of answering why the subject has any obligation to do what the sovereign asks rather than what she wishes – the problem of political obligation – Hobbes devotes his primary attention to explaining why the subject's obligation to the sovereign should not be outweighed by an (apparently rival) obligation to God – e.g., if the sovereign commands the subject to do something she believes to be morally objectionable.[25] Hobbes's theory of political citizenship, in other words, focuses not on contemporary analytical philosophy's problem of obligation, but rather on the issue of moral responsibility: and it seeks to offer a solution to the

---

[22] This is how I interpret Henry Hammond's curious and suggestive remark that Hobbes's *Leviathan* constituted "a farrago of Christian Atheism." See further the article which drew my attention to this remark and which is very suggestive in its own right, Richard Tuck, "The 'Christian Atheism' of Thomas Hobbes," in Michael Hunter and David Wootton, eds., *Atheism from the Reformation to the Enlightenment* (Oxford University Press, 1992).

[23] See in particular Gregory S. Kavka, *Hobbesian Moral and Political Theory* (Princeton University Press, 1986) ch. 10. For an analytically careful description of the problem in contemporary philosophy, see A. John Simmons, *Moral Principles and Political Obligations* (Princeton University Press, 1979).

[24] One reason this problem has engendered so much critical attention is the fact that it is one of the softest spots in Hobbes's generally firm analytical underbelly: the notorious argument against the "Foole" in *Leviathan* chapter 15, for example, illustrates that if Hobbes has an answer to this problem it is not one that can be crisply and clearly elaborated. *Leviathan* ch. 15, pp. 101–102. See further Kinch Hoekstra, "Hobbes and the Foole," *Political Theory* 25 (1997): 620–654.

[25] On this matter see further Mary G. Dietz, "Hobbes's Subjects as Citizens," in Mary G. Dietz, ed., *Thomas Hobbes and Political Theory* (University Press of Kansas, 1990), and Margaret Sampson, "Will You Hear What a Casuist He Is? Thomas Hobbes as Director of Conscience," *History of Political Thought* 11 (1990): 721–736. I agree with Sampson that Hobbes's system is designed to meet the demands of the casuistic enterprise while at the same time providing a standard intended to make those demands obsolete.

specific problem of dirty hands *for citizens* which the issue of moral responsibility for sovereign action raises.

Hobbes frames his consideration of this problem in terms of a dilemma "which, if it be not removed, maketh it unlawful for any man to procure his own peace and preservation, because it maketh it unlawful for a man to put himself under the command of such absolute sovereignty as is required thereto."[26] He outlines the dilemma thus:

> We have amongst us the Word of God for the rule of our actions; now if we shall subject ourselves to men also, obliging ourselves to do such actions as shall be by them commanded; when the commands of God and man shall differ, we are to obey God, rather than man: and consequently the covenant of general obedience to man is unlawful.[27]

In a later formulation Hobbes puts this dilemma even more starkly by framing it as the question of "how obedience can be safely offered if an order is given to do something which CHRIST forbids."[28] For Hobbes, then, while there can be no conceivable conflict between the moral obligations of subjects based on the law of nature and the moral obligations of subjects deriving from sovereign commands (since the law of nature itself commands obedience to the sovereign in practically all instances), there can be conceivable conflicts of obligations based on conflicts between the commands of the sovereign and the commands of God.[29] The problem, as Hobbes conceives it, derives from the fact that certain Christians believe they have a right or even a responsibility to make their actions conform to their own moral judgments or their own interpretations of

---

[26] *Elements* ch. 25, p. 141. In stating Hobbes's argument about conscience I draw freely on the full range of explanations he offers in *The Elements of Law* and *De Cive* as well as in *Leviathan*. There are of course inconsistencies between Hobbes's articulation of his theory in the three works; but I think it can be shown (though I do not undertake to show it here) that Hobbes's earlier expressions are consistent with the argument about conscience as stated in *Leviathan* in all relevant respects.

[27] *Elements* ch. 25, p. 141.

[28] Thomas Hobbes, *De Cive* ch. 18, p. 234. I cite from the edition of Richard Tuck and Michael Silverthorne (Cambridge University Press, 1998).

[29] The one instance in which the law of nature does not *command* obedience to the sovereign is in the case of a direct and incontrovertible risk to one's own life, in which instance one is rightfully at liberty to disobey and even to resist the sovereign. *Leviathan* ch. 21, pp. 151–154. But even in this instance the law of nature does not *conflict* with the sovereign's commands. This is true because the law of nature does not require disobedience or resistance, though it does permit it. Further, in Hobbes's system, a circumstance in which the right of nature can correctly be invoked is a circumstance in which *ipso facto* the law of nature can't apply. For Hobbes, a right is a blameless liberty: consequently, if the sovereign is out to kill us, we cannot be *blamed* for defending ourselves, but we are not necessarily obliged to do so. In any event, this exception applies in such an extreme circumstance that as a matter of moral requirement it cannot really be addressed to anyone who still meaningfully plays the role of *citizen*.

Scripture, a mandate which they equate with "liberty of conscience." In response, Hobbes's own purpose, as he clearly asserts, is to "take away this scruple of conscience" from the Christian mind.[30]

So Hobbes finds himself confronting a profound danger of political instability in his commonwealth: one posed by the plurality of reasonable moral judgments about the world coupled with his subjects' feelings of moral responsibility for the actions they may have to take in response to their sovereign's commands. Consequently, Hobbes is powerfully motivated to try to defuse this threat by any means at his disposal – and to succeed he needs to find a solution to what is in essence a kind of "democratic" version of the problem of dirty hands, one in which the subjects themselves must be cleared of the guilt associated with their performing, or permitting the sovereign to perform on their behalf, actions which they themselves might judge to be morally wrong.

Hobbes begins by trying to deflate the special moral authority which conscience tries to claim for itself. His argument for this turns on equating conscience with *judgment*: when we say our conscience tells us we ought to do something, Hobbes claims, we really mean only that we *think* or *judge* that we ought to do it.[31] But this, Hobbes points out, is quite problematic: judgments can be mistaken, and judgments certainly differ.[32] Part of the rationale for sovereignty was that it eliminated the latter of these problematic features of our judgment, by substituting for the judgment of each individual the single judgment of the sovereign.[33] This transfer of judgment extends to moral matters as well, such that claims of conscience have no special standing of moral authority.

This occurs, moreover, by means of a substitution of the sovereign's agency for the agency of his subject. Hobbes explains that when a subject "hath once transferred his right of judging to another, that which shall be commanded, is no less his judgment, than the judgment of that other; so that in obedience to laws, a man doth still according to his conscience, but

---

[30] *Elements* ch. 25, p. 142. As this passage goes on to make clear, Hobbes conceives of this as a peculiarly Protestant moral problem, one that cannot be generated by the ancient Judaic theocracy, the ancient Greek or Roman polytheisms, or the modern Catholic Church, each of which possessed sufficient structures of authority for mediating controversial issues of interpretation and moral judgment. This makes Hobbes's discussion of this issue especially relevant to modern readers, most of whom will have inherited some secularized form of this Protestant responsibility for individual judgment fully intact.

[31] *Elements* ch. 6, p. 42; *Leviathan* ch. 29, p. 223.   [32] *Elements* ch. 29, pp. 180–181.

[33] This is the major theme of many of Richard Tuck's recent treatments of Hobbes, especially *Hobbes* (Oxford University Press, 1989) and *Philosophy and Government, 1572–1651* (Cambridge University Press, 1993).

not his private conscience."[34] So Hobbes thinks we must in all cases substitute the sovereign's conscience or judgment for our own, creating what Hobbes calls a "publique Conscience."[35] So we can still obey our conscience, only it is now our public conscience, the conscience we have authorized in our sovereign, rather than our own private conscience, which we obey. This latter individual conscience is to be eradicated or at least ignored,[36] lest it be used not literally but "metaphorically" to justify following such judgment and moral authority as we have already ceded to the sovereign's control.[37]

The fact that Hobbes's attention is focused on this dilemma of conscience, rather than the more general philosophical problem of political obligation, helps to clarify why Hobbes's argument in *Leviathan* takes its peculiar structure. He has already demonstrated, in Parts I and II, that there are powerful Christian reasons for obedience to political authority in every case: namely, the tendency of obedience to promote such Christian values as humility, equality, and most of all peace.[38] This enables him to isolate a much narrower range of cases in which he still needs to justify obedience, namely, those in which we might appear to have a more powerful Christian reason to deny or resist the authority we would otherwise have strong reasons to obey.

In pursuing this isolative strategy Hobbes employs two main tactics. The first is to undermine through epistemological arguments the range of knowledge that we can possibly have about what God intends for us to do. It is practically impossible, Hobbes argues, ever to know with certainty either that God is talking to you or that God has talked to someone else, and therefore it is also practically impossible for you ever to know that God wants you to resist the sovereign (particularly since we have powerful natural and religious reasons for thinking that God wants us to obey the sovereign).[39] The second and related tactic is to argue that, since resistance to the sovereign typically puts us in danger of our life, only something worse than losing our life could ever motivate us to resist the sovereign.

---

[34] *Elements* ch. 25, p. 153.   [35] *Leviathan* ch. 29. p. 223.

[36] This is my major reason for doubting the otherwise attractive characterization of Hobbes as a kind of individualist proto-liberal in Richard Flathman's *Thomas Hobbes: Skepticism, Individuality, and Chastened Politics* (Sage, 1993).

[37] *Leviathan* ch. 7, p. 48.   [38] *Leviathan* ch. 15, p. 111.

[39] Of course, this makes it equally difficult for the sovereign to argue persuasively that God has commanded him directly; but Hobbes's theory does not depend upon the sovereign being the recipient of special revelation from God, only of the natural revelation found in the laws of nature.

And the only thing worse than losing our life, on Hobbes's account, is that God might send us to hell or deny us salvation.[40] To forestall the possibility of justified or reasonable resistance to the sovereign, Hobbes therefore merely needs to eliminate – or at least reconfigure and vastly reduce in scope – the range of things for which God might be willing to send us to hell or deny us salvation.[41] This is what Hobbes's arguments about the "essence of Christianity" are aimed at.

The only limits on the state's authority to command, then, are to be found in those things which are fundamental to salvation, part of the essence of Christianity. For Hobbes, the core proposition of the religion, and the sole belief necessary to salvation, is the claim "that Jesus is the Messiah, that is, the Christ," as well as that claim's derivative "explications," which appear to include such beliefs as the authority of Scripture, the immortality of the soul, and belief in the persons of the Trinity (though apparently not the doctrine of the Trinity itself, to which it is doubtful Hobbes himself subscribed). But the true force of this new theology is to be found in Hobbes's claim that one of the necessary "explications" of this fundamental Christian premise about Jesus's messianic identity is that Christians ought to obey their respective earthly sovereigns. This Hobbes derives specifically from God's normative authority (implied in the claim that Christ is "Lord,") which according to Hobbes implies a sincere "endeavour to obey [God's] laws," including specifically the laws of nature, since these are "the moral law taught by our Saviour himself."[42] And at this point the trap is sprung. For if the laws of nature, including their requirement of absolute obedience to the sovereign, are tied this closely to the fundamental tenets of the Christian faith, then it follows that only direct conflict with the most explicit formulations of the fundamental belief could possibly constitute a greater moral (not to mention physical) danger than that we encounter by defying the sovereign's divinely sanctioned will.

---

[40] Hobbes more or less takes it for granted that there can be no moral requirement that is not backed up by fear of eternal punishment; no kind of vague desire to do the right thing or maintain one's integrity can generate the kind of nerve needed to defy the sovereign and his wrath. *Elements* ch. 25, pp. 143–144.

[41] It is of course this same motivation that lies behind Hobbes's theological reconfigurations about the nature of hell and divine punishment, which further serves to weaken the fear of hell as an alternative to fear of the sovereign. On this point see further Richard Tuck, "The Civil Religion of Thomas Hobbes," in Nicholas Phillipson and Quentin Skinner, eds., *Political Discourse in Early Modern Britain* (Cambridge University Press, 1993), together with Lodi Nauta, "Hobbes on Religion and the Church between *The Elements of Law* and *Leviathan*: A Dramatic Change of Direction?," *Journal of the History of Ideas* 63 (2002): 577–598.

[42] *Elements* ch. 25, pp. 151, 153.

Thus on Hobbes's account the moral requirement to obey the sovereign derives directly from the fundamental premise of Christianity necessary to guarantee salvation.[43] This is why Hobbes believes that the special claim to an alternate and direct rule by God implied by Christian doctrine and practice, specifically in the form of the doctrine of a "Kingdom of God by Prophecy," does not constitute a major problem for his system of absolutist politics. For, even when Christianity is added to the picture, it is still the laws of nature alone, together with the corollary responsibilities they imply with respect to obeying the laws of their sovereigns, that Christian subjects are responsible for obeying. Indeed, for Hobbes the central moral significance of the Gospel teaching was that it made individual conduct maximally amenable to sovereign direction. "Our Saviour Christ," Hobbes insists, "hath not given us new Laws, but Counsell to observe those wee are subject to; that is to say, the Laws of Nature, and the Laws of our severall Sovereigns."[44] For subjects in a commonwealth, then, there is no additional law of God beyond the laws of nature: rather, Hobbes asserts that "the Laws of God therefore are none but the Laws of Nature, whereof the principall is . . . [the] commandement to obey our Civill Soveraigns,"[45] and consequently "there can . . . be no contradiction between the Laws of God, and the Laws of a Christian Common-wealth."[46]

THE ACTIONS OF STATES AND THEIR SUBJECTS

Hobbes, then, believes that the institution of sovereignty grants the state's citizens extraordinarily extensive rationales for deferring their own moral judgments to the sovereign's judgment, and thus for substituting throughout almost every aspect of their lives the sovereign's judgment for their own private conscience. This has the effect of offering a solution of sorts to the subjects' apparent problem of dirty hands. By substituting the sovereign's judgments for their own, Hobbes's subjects are (on this set of premises)

---

[43] This is a compelling reason, incidentally, for thinking that such commentators as A. E. Taylor, "The Ethical Doctrine of Hobbes," *Philosophy* 13 (1938): 406–424, and Howard Warrender, *The Political Philosophy of Hobbes: His Theory of Obligation* (Oxford University Press, 1957), had more of a point than recent scholarship has tended to recognize. These commentators claimed that Hobbes's well-known assertion that the laws of nature were in an important sense God's laws constituted more than just window dressing aimed at mitigating criticism of his heterodoxy. Though Hobbes may not have needed the claim that the laws of nature were God's laws in order to ground much of his philosophical system, as Taylor and Warrender seemed to think, he *did* need to substantiate that claim in a serious way for the purpose of holding at bay possible challenges to his philosophical system from certain strains of Christian doctrine and practice.

[44] *Leviathan* ch. 43, p. 404.   [45] Ibid.   [46] Ibid., p. 414.

cleared of any guilt associated with what the sovereign does on their behalf, or what they do in obedience to the sovereign's command.

What is very curious about this claim, however, is that Hobbes seems to hold views that are contradictory, or at least very difficult to reconcile, about the extent to which this substitution in fact makes the resulting actions the sovereign's moral responsibility rather than the responsibility of his subjects. This emerges most clearly in Hobbes's treatment in *Leviathan* of the issue of obedience to a non-Christian sovereign in matters of worship, and especially in his revealing treatment of the biblical story of Naaman the Syrian.

Whereas in a Christian commonwealth subjects can never face a genuine moral dilemma with respect to political obedience, Hobbes acknowledges that there are greater possibilities for genuine moral conflict in a non-Christian[47] commonwealth. Under a non-Christian sovereign, it is of course conceivable that the sovereign will order his subjects to deny the fundamental premise of the Christian faith, that Jesus is the Christ. Hobbes concedes that, in such circumstances, cases may arise where accepting martyrdom (though not instigating armed resistance) may be warranted (though he also seems to believe that, given the right to self-preservation, no one can be morally required to accept martyrdom). But he goes on to argue that this fact is most unlikely to prove a significant political problem for several reasons. First, all that is required on Hobbes's account is inward acceptance of the truth of the fundamental premise of Christianity, rather than any outward defense or proclamation of it: the relevant faith is "internall, and invisible."[48] And, second, given this framework, Hobbes points out that it is only possible to reach this quandary if the sovereign himself is not following the laws of nature. As Hobbes points out, it is an extraordinarily unreasonable sovereign who will not buy the unstinting and slavish obedience of a Hobbesian citizen at the paltry price of permitting them to believe privately what they like so long as they publicly toe the sovereign's line.[49]

It is in this context that Hobbes introduces his very telling description of the relationship between sovereign and subject agency illustrated in the case of Naaman the Syrian. In the biblical story Naaman, a Gentile converted to the religion of Judaism, asks the prophet Elisha for a special permission related to the responsibilities he bears to his sovereign. " '*In this thing the Lord pardon thy servant, that when my Master goeth into the house of [the idol] Rimmon to worship there, and he leaneth on my hand, and I bow my selfe, in the house of Rimmon; when I bow my selfe in the house of Rimmon, the*

---

[47] A term I substitute for Hobbes's actual "Infidel."   [48] *Leviathan* ch. 43, p. 414.   [49] Ibid.

Lord pardon thy servant in this thing.' "[50] The prophet grants this permission, even though according to Hobbes the act itself unquestionably constitutes idolatry.[51]

Hobbes goes on to explain that there are two reasons God is willing in such circumstances to permit such conduct. The first reason is the fact that, regardless of the external action taken, the internal action is consistent with religious truth, and only internal actions can in religious matters be relevant to salvation.[52] "No human law is intended to oblige the conscience of a man, but the actions only," Hobbes claims, and furthermore "no man (but God alone) knoweth the heart or conscience of a man, unless it break out into action."[53] The basis for this claim seems to be related to Hobbes's distinction between obligations *in foro interno* and obligations *in foro externo*: there is one form of obligation that requires only our inward willingness, another that requires our outward conformity of action. Laws can certainly be made that *claim* to lay an imperative on internal states of mind, but these according to Hobbes are not really laws. Such directives lack true legal force, or are "of none effect," since "no man is able to discern but by word or other action whether such law be kept or broken."[54] In calling on this now traditional inward orientation of Christian moral doctrine, Hobbes draws upon Augustine's conception of human motivation as morally opaque in order to justify and purify the private conscience. The sovereign is sovereign absolutely – but also exclusively – over the sphere of visible action, because nothing that is done in that sphere in obedience to his commands could (by definition) ever constitute a moral wrong. At the same time, the sphere of invisible thought – in which alone are performed those actions of true religious moral significance – remains by the same principle absolutely insulated from his dominion.

The second and related reason, on Hobbes's view, is that the external worship of the false god counts, not as Naaman's action, but rather as the action of his *sovereign*. The image vividly captures the relationships of agency and responsibility between sovereign and subject: the sovereign is the one doing the kneeling, while the subject is just someone on whose arm the sovereign happens to be leaning; the sovereign's agency is primary, and the subject's is instrumental. Hobbes himself draws the consequence unambiguously:

Whatsoever a Subject, as Naaman was, is compelled to in obedience to his Soveraign, and doth it not in order to his own mind, but in order to the laws of

---

[50] *Leviathan* ch. 42, p. 343. The biblical reference is to 2 Kings 5.   [51] *Leviathan* ch. 42, p. 344.
[52] Ibid., p. 343.   [53] *Elements* ch. 25, p. 142.   [54] Ibid.

his country, *that action is not his, but his Soveraign's*; nor is it he that in this case denyeth Christ before men, but his Governour, and the law of his countrey.[55]

In this way, Hobbes's conception of the state follows Machiavelli in assigning to the sovereign those actions that would certainly be morally disastrous if they were permitted to all citizens. The subjects are morally forbidden to resist or disobey the sovereign's decisions except in the rarest and most isolated of circumstances. Yet at the same time, Hobbes seems to argue, from a moral point of view none of these subjects have committed any of these necessary political evils themselves, and thus they need only report to their God that, immediately subsequent to becoming cognitive religious believers, they have acted outwardly as consistently obedient citizens.[56]

REPRESENTATION AND MORAL RESPONSIBILITY

As we observed at the outset, however, this is a problematic formulation for Hobbes, since earlier in *Leviathan* he had committed himself to the claim that, whenever the sovereign acts, it is not he himself but rather the people whom he represents who bear the responsibility for his actions. The sovereign properly acts in their name, for their sake, and by their authority. This leaves us with an apparent contradiction.[57] For if all the sovereign's actions are authorized by and therefore properly attributed to his subjects,

---

[55] *Leviathan* ch. 42, p. 344. Emphasis added. In a similar vein, Hobbes elsewhere maintained that even sins committed at the command of the sovereign do not count as the sins of the person who acts. "If someone sins at another's command, both sin, since neither did right; unless, by chance, the state commanded it to be done, so that the actor ought not to refuse." *De Homine* ch. 15, p. 84. I cite from the sections of *De Homine* translated in *Man and Citizen*, ed. Bernard Gert (Hackett, 1991).

[56] Some readers might wonder if too much importance is given here to the Naaman passage, which after all appears only once in Hobbes's writings and in the theological sections of *Leviathan* at that. There are several responses to this. First, Hobbes's theory of representation itself appears only in one passage in *Leviathan*, yet interpreters have had no difficulty assigning great importance to that passage. (And it is only by pure anachronism that contemporary readers might feel that something in Part I somehow "outranks" a claim made in the more theologically oriented Part III.) More substantially, as I have tried to show throughout this chapter, the Naaman story is merely the most explicit formulation of a position Hobbes relied on throughout his writings – namely, that subjects could defer their own moral judgments to the sovereign's judgment and substitute the sovereign's conscience for their own consciences.

[57] Deborah Baumgold, in "The Composition of Hobbes's *Elements of Law*," *History of Political Thought* 25 (2004): 16–43, argues that we should not be surprised to discover such minor contradictions in Hobbes's political theory, especially given his unsystematic method of composition. Despite this salutary warning, I proceed here on the hypothesis that this apparent contradiction requires every effort of interpretive charity to resolve it, especially given the deliberate introduction and strategic positioning of the passage on representation in the new version of Hobbes's theory advanced in *Leviathan*.

how can it possibly be the case that actions which the sovereign compels the subject to take are always morally permissible because they are the sovereign's actions and *not* the subjects'?

To make sense of this, we need to examine more closely what kind of responsibility is acquired in the case of *authorized* representation, such as a sovereign has with his subjects.[58] According to Hobbes, a representative is someone who "acteth another" or "is said to beare his Person, or act in his name."[59] Such relations of representation, further, can be either authorized or unauthorized. Just because someone is taken to act my part, or to act in my name, does not necessarily mean they are truly exercising my rights, or that I am responsible for their actions. What is further needed, according to Hobbes, is some sense that the words and actions of the representative are "*Owned* by those whom they represent."[60] When this condition obtains, the (artificial) person who owns the representative's actions is said to be the "author" of his deeds, and his actions are consequently said to be characterized by "authority." For example, if the representative enters into a contract on behalf of the person he represents, that person is properly described as the "author" of that contract and as having "authorized" its terms. In such a case, Hobbes says, the representative "bindeth thereby the Author, no lesse, than if he had made it himselfe; and no lesse subjecteth him to all the consequences of the same."[61]

Hobbes then goes on to make clear that in civil society the sovereign is not only the representative but the authorized representative of his subjects. It remains somewhat obscure exactly how we are to understand their authorization of him. On the one hand, it seems clear that they do so by means of the intermediate mechanism of the creation of the commonwealth or state. Thus "a multitude of men, are made *One* [artificial] Person, when they are by one man, or one Person, Represented ... For it is the *Unity* of the Representer, not the *Unity* of the Represented, that maketh the Person *One* ... "[62] Thus Hobbes wants to say that the sovereign's task is

---

[58] In treating this subject, I have been helped greatly by the discussion in Jean Hampton, *Hobbes and the Social Contract Tradition* (Cambridge University Press, 1986), ch. 5, though I ultimately take issue with her conclusions. See also the related discussions in David Gauthier, *The Logic of Leviathan* (Oxford University Press, 1969) and Kavka, *Hobbesian Moral and Political Theory*, ch. 10.

[59] *Leviathan* ch. 16, p. 112.

[60] Ibid. Hobbes's use of the term "own" here makes use of its connotations of "confessing" or "acknowledging" as well as possessing, as for example in the case of a father "owning" his paternity of a child, or a penitent "owning up" to a sin or mistake.

[61] Ibid.

[62] Ibid., p. 114. There is considerable ambiguity in the text of chapter 16 itself as to whether Hobbes means the artificial person to be the representative or the person being represented. Quentin Skinner, in his essay "Hobbes and the Purely Artificial Person of the State," unravels the knot

to represent the people not only individually, but also collectively: indeed, he makes possible their collective identity in a way that is not pre-politically possible, in precisely the same way that a national state may be said to make possible the nation that it represents simply by its existence as a state.[63] On the other hand, he is concerned to insist that the subjects remain separately and individually responsible for every one of the sovereign's actions.

> Because the Multitude naturally is not *One* but *Many*; they cannot be understood for one; but many Authors, of every thing their Representative saith, or doth in their name; Every man giving their common Representer, Authority from him-selfe in particular; and owning all the actions, the Representer doth . . .[64]

On its face, this appears to be a very problematic formulation for Hobbes: for though he wants to insist that the sovereign's actions are properly to be attributed to the subjects, his casuistic agenda commits him also to being able to say that the subjects cannot properly be blamed for or do wrong by means of the actions they take through the sovereign's agency.[65] How can these two claims be reconciled? Hobbes seems to need to be able to claim that the subjects can somehow *own* their sovereign's actions without thereby coming to *own* the blame (or moral responsibility) attached to his actions as wrongs.[66] There are a variety of different ways in which such a distinction could be drawn: for example, one possible

---

with characteristic dexterity and demonstrates convincingly that it is the person represented rather than the representative that Hobbes means to designate with the term "artificial person." See especially pp. 187–190 of Skinner's essay.

[63] See further Baumgold, *Hobbes's Political Theory*, ch. 3.

[64] *Leviathan* ch. 16, p. 114. This is not true if authors limit the scope of his representative commission, in which case "none of them owneth more, than they gave him commission to act" (ibid.). But Hobbes is clear that this is never true of the kind of commission which subjects give to their sovereign.

[65] There is one passage in chapter 16 which might appear to suggest that they *can* be blamed for the sovereign's actions, but this appearance is misleading. Hobbes tells us: "When the Actor doth any thing against the Law of Nature, by command of the Author, if he be obliged by former Covenant to obey him, not he, but the Author breaketh the Law of Nature: for though the Action be against the Law of Nature; yet it is not his: but contrarily, to refuse to do it, is against the Law of Nature, that forbiddeth breach of Covenant" (*Leviathan* ch. 16, p. 113). Whatever sort of situation Hobbes may have in mind here, it is not that of subjects rather than sovereigns being held responsible for breaches of the law of nature, since Hobbes's condition on this occurrence, "if he be obliged by former Covenant to obey him," is one that cannot apply to a Hobbesian sovereign. Hobbes is at pains throughout his writings to insist both that the sovereign cannot be party to a binding covenant with his subjects, and that, covenant or no, sovereigns cannot in any case be obliged to obey their subjects. On this point see further *Leviathan* ch. 15, pp. 104–105.

[66] Though Hobbes often sounds as though the sovereign can do no wrong, this is not of course his real position. The sovereign cannot wrong his *subjects*, in the sense of doing them injury. But he can certainly violate the law of nature, either by getting (objectively) wrong what the law of nature requires or by choosing to ignore what the law of nature seems to require. Under such circumstances, we (though not his subjects) may fairly characterize his actions as a violation of the law of

mechanism can be found in the fact that the same action can bear more than one moral description.[67] Thus an act of murder ordered by the sovereign may count as a moral wrong and a violation of the law of nature on the sovereign's part, in that it is provocative and contrary to peace; yet the same act on the part of his subjects who authorize his sovereignty may count as a moral right and as obedience to the law of nature. But, to sustain such a distinction, Hobbes would need to provide us with a basis for supposing that the "ownership" responsibility for an action, held by one who *owns* that action, can properly be separated from the *moral* responsibility, i.e., the proper praise or blame attached to, the very same action.

To clarify this seeming tension, we need to consider further the specific sense in which Hobbes thinks that authorized actions are "owned" by the persons represented. Despite his remark that the status of the "author" of an action is analogous to the status of an "owner" or "*dominus*" (master) in the theory of property,[68] Hobbes does not mean that the author is in a position of *control* over her representative's actions (at least in the case of primary interest, that of the sovereign representative).[69] What Hobbes instead wants to say is that the subject is the owner or master of the *right* by which the actions of the representative are performed.

As the Right of possession, is called Dominion; so the Right of doing any Action, is called AUTHORITY and sometimes *warrant*. So that by Authority, is always understood a Right of doing any act: and *done by Authority*, done by Commission, or Licence from him whose right it is.[70]

So whatever moral responsibility the subjects hold for the sovereign's actions, it results in some way from the fact that the sovereign acts on the basis of their rights. And since rights are "blameless liberties," this would offer the beginning of an explanation as to how the subjects could be both

nature, and therefore also as an (objective) moral wrong (*Leviathan* ch. 24, p. 172). Hobbes cautions only that we are not to infer that such moral wrongs can constitute a legitimate pretext for resistance or disobedience (or even public criticism) by his subjects.

[67] On Hobbes's awareness of a related complex of issues, see further Quentin Skinner, *Reason and Rhetoric in the Philosophy of Hobbes* (Cambridge University Press, 1996).

[68] Thus Hobbes finds himself in the curious position of casting his citizen/subject, who is the "author" he is particularly interested in, in the role of *dominus* or master over the sovereign's actions.

[69] It is possible, Hobbes acknowledges, to have conditional as well as unconditional forms of authorization, but Hobbes insists throughout *Leviathan* that the form of authorization which the sovereign receives as a result of the social contract is an entirely unconditional grant of power. *Leviathan* ch. 16, p. 115; ch. 18, *passim*.

[70] *Leviathan* ch. 16, p. 112. Sometimes, though apparently not always, someone authorized in this way can be responsible *jointly* with the action's author. See further *De Homine* ch. 15, p. 84. "What he doth at the command of another is always the act of the one commanding, though sometimes of the representative also, that is, of both author and actor."

authors of the sovereign's actions and yet not responsible for his moral wrongs: because so long as he acts on the basis of their rights, that is, their blameless liberties, it is (by definition) impossible to *blame* them for the actions he takes.[71] Since they are blameless in executing their rights, so is he.

THE PUZZLE OF HOBBESIAN REPRESENTATION

This explanation, in essence, correctly captures Hobbes's view. But a complication arises, because this way of understanding Hobbes's conception of political agency highlights a largely unexamined problem in Hobbes's use of the term "transfer of right." This expression implies that the sovereign acts on the basis of his subjects' rights *rather than*, or at least in addition to, his own rights: and of course, in order for the idea of the transfer of right to constitute a solution to the problem we are considering, this needs to be true in a quite literal sense. Yet, throughout the development of his political theory, Hobbes had been resolute in insisting that what justifies the sovereign's action is *not* any new right he receives from the process of the transfer of right, but rather his *own* pre-political rights. Since he possesses in the state of nature the right to all things, Hobbes maintained, the sovereign needs no grant of rights from his subjects to justify anything he might do, and consequently is neither indebted nor accountable to them for the exercise of the rights in question. According to Hobbes's account in *De Cive*, the whole meaning of the transfer of right envisioned in the social contract is not that the sovereign acquires any new rights from his subjects, but rather that they permit him to continue to exercise the right which he himself possessed in the state of nature, that is, the unlimited right to all things.

The argument that *transfer of right* consists solely in non-resistance is that the recipient already had a right to all things *before the transfer of the right*; hence the transferor could not give him a new *right*. Justified resistance, however, on the part of the transferor, which previously prevented the recipient from enjoying his *right*, is now extinguished. Whoever therefore acquires a *right* in men's natural state, does so simply in order to enjoy his *original right* in security and without justified interference.[72]

In this sense, even though the subjects are said to "transfer" their rights, the sovereign receives no rights from his subjects that he did not possess

---

[71] On this feature of early modern theories of rights, see further Richard Tuck, *Natural Rights Theories* (Cambridge University Press, 1979).

[72] *De Cive* ch. 2, p. 34.

himself, and consequently is neither indebted nor accountable to them for the exercise of the rights in question.[73]

This remained Hobbes's theory throughout his career. In *Leviathan* he explicitly retains his premise that the transfer of right consists solely in non-resistance rather than in any positive grant.[74] We see this for example in Hobbes's explanation of the sovereign's right to punish:

> It is manifest therefore that the Right which the Common-wealth (that is, he, or they that represent it) hath to Punish, is not grounded on any concession, or gift of the Subjects. But I have also shewed formerly, that before the Institution of Common-wealth, every man had a right to every thing, and to do whatsoever he thought necessary to his own preservation; subduing, hurting, or killing any man in order thereunto. And this is the foundation of that right of Punishing, which is exercised in every Common-wealth. For the Subjects did not give the Soveraign that right; but onely in laying down theirs, strengthned him to use his own, as he should think fit, for the preservation of them all: so that it was not given, but left to him, and to him onely; and (excepting the limits set him by naturall Law) as entire, as in the condition of meer Nature, and of warre of every one against his neighbour.[75]

But in this later version of the theory, this premise is now complicated by the new element Hobbes has introduced in *Leviathan*, namely his claim that the sovereign in some sense acts in place of his subjects and on the basis of their rights, and that this makes them the true authors of the sovereign's actions and himself a mere actor only.

Much turns on what it means for the sovereign to *retain* his right to all things after the state is established. Since Hobbes defines the right to all things as a kind of blameless liberty, we can reframe Hobbes's premise as the assertion that the sovereign has a special kind of *moral permission* after the establishment of the state: unlike his subjects, he cannot be blamed for doing certain things. How far, then, does this permission extend, and what are the moral limits to be imposed on the sovereign's conduct? Hobbes tells us that, even though his subjects have no recourse to enforce it, the law of nature is binding on the sovereign even after the establishment of the commonwealth. But in the state of nature, as we have seen, the law of nature – "the science of virtue and vice" – is said to oblige only *in foro interno* and not *in foro externo*. That is to say, even after the establishment of the state, the requirements of morality, virtue, and natural justice are

---

[73] This makes it somewhat puzzling that Hobbes in this version of the theory is so insistent on the nomenclature of "transfer," since what the subjects actually do seems adequately described by the alternate terms Hobbes considers of "relinquishing" or "renouncing" their rights.

[74] *Leviathan* ch. 14, p. 92.   [75] *Leviathan* ch. 28, p. 214.

binding on the sovereign's actions to the degree, but only to the degree, that it is safe to practice them.

How safe is life for the sovereign under the social contract? At first glance it might appear that the position of the sovereign after the establishment of the social contract was far more secure than that which his subjects might enjoy in the relative stability of the commonwealth (much less in the state of nature). But this view is undercut by the fact that, according to Hobbes, the sovereign himself never entirely escapes the state of nature. Part of the reason why the sovereign is permitted to exercise the right to all things is because he still has *need* of it, because it still applies to his situation, which is, vis-à-vis the world as a whole, still very much potentially a state of misery and war.[76] Addressing himself specifically to the question of whether the state of nature as a state of war exists anywhere on earth, Hobbes replies that all sovereigns remain in the state of nature, especially with respect to other states and their sovereigns:

In all times, Kings, and Persons of Soveraigne authority, because of their Independency, are in continuall jealousies, and in the state and posture of Gladiators; having their weapons pointing, and their eyes fixed on one another; that is, their Forts, Garrisons, and Guns upon the Frontiers of their Kingdomes; and continuall Spyes upon their neighbours, which is a posture of War.[77]

So it seems to be Hobbes's view that the sovereign retains fully intact his natural right to all things – that is to say, the practically unlimited set of moral permissions that fell within the scope of the "blameless liberty" of the state of nature.

But if, as Hobbes seems to maintain, the sovereign's *own* right to all things in the state of nature is the exclusive source of the sovereign's moral warrant for his actions, it becomes very difficult to explain Hobbes's decision to use the language of authority and authorization. On this account of the matter, the sovereign, fully possessed of a right to all things, consequently also possesses a sufficient (moral) warrant for taking any action he may think necessary. Perhaps it is also the case *incidentally* that the sovereign is authorized in his actions by his subjects, but this adds nothing to the available justification from the point of view of the

---

[76] On this theme in Hobbes's writings and in the writings of his contemporaries, see Richard Tuck, *The Rights of War and Peace* (Oxford University Press, 1999).

[77] *Leviathan* ch. 13, p. 90. He goes on to add that "because they uphold thereby, the Industry of their Subjects; there does not follow from it, that misery, which accompanies the Liberty of particular men." But this surely counts as reassurance merely that we are not in the state of nature so far as the well-being or misery of the subjects themselves is concerned. This proviso would do nothing to alter the moral permissions that the sovereign has vis-à-vis his external world.

sovereign. Whatever function the language of authorization is meant to serve, then, it cannot on this interpretation be meant to shift the moral burden of the sovereign's actions off his shoulders and onto those of his citizens, since Hobbes has made him fully capable of bearing the weight himself. At the same time, however, the language of authorization seems to add nothing from the point of view of the subjects: for, as we have observed at length in the previous sections of this chapter, Hobbes's subjects are already possessed of what should be an entirely sufficient moral warrant for their obedience, on philosophical as well as (Christian) religious grounds, even when they disagree with their sovereign.

Hobbes could of course have employed a different version of representative theory, one that emphasized only the *rights* which the sovereign derived from his relationship with the people, without taking up the question of the extent to which they were *responsible* for his actions. But he makes the deliberate choice to *emphasize* the responsibilities which the subjects have for the actions the sovereign takes, even though this carried potentially enormous risks for the most elusive trick he hoped to turn, namely the elimination of plausible conflicts of conscience between the sovereign's actions and the citizens' beliefs.

THE MORAL RIGHTS OF SOVEREIGNS AND SUBJECTS

Under Hobbes's own account of the transfer of right, then, it remains difficult to explain why he would have chosen to employ the language of authority and authorization, especially given the awkward consequences this move potentially held for his theory with respect to the issue of moral responsibility. But perhaps we have been just slightly misunderstanding the kind of claim Hobbes was making about the right from which the sovereign acts, and as a consequence misunderstanding also the kind of choice Hobbes was making in locating the moral responsibility for state action. So let us now consider an alternative interpretation of Hobbes's theory which would help to eliminate this confusion, by drawing into question the extent to which his argument that the sovereign exercises only his own rights *rather than* those of his subjects is to be taken at face value as Hobbes's final word on the matter.

This hypothesis requires us to look again more closely at the question of the transfer of right at the foundation of the social contract, and to ask what if any new rights and what if any new obligations the sovereign may acquire through the transfer of his subjects' rights. In one sense the sovereign appears to acquire neither new rights nor new obligations. Before the social contract, he has a right to all things; and after the social contract, he has a right to all things. Before the social contract, he is obligated solely by the law of nature, *in foro interno*; and after the social contract, he is obligated solely by the law of nature, again, apparently, *in foro interno*. There seems to be no basis for imputing to him new moral responsibilities on the basis of the social contract itself: unlike his subjects, Hobbes insists, the sovereign himself does not submit to the terms of any contract and so acquires no contractual obligations to his subjects for which he can be held responsible.

Yet it does appear that the sovereign has acquired at least one new set of moral obligations he did not obviously possess in the state of nature. These are the moral obligations associated with what Hobbes calls the "office" or "duty" of the sovereign representative.[78] This duty of the sovereign's, Hobbes tells us in all three versions of his political theory, can be summed up in one familiar phrase: "*salus populi suprema lex*," "the safety of the people is the supreme law."[79] On its face, this might seem to suggest that the sovereign does indeed acquire a new set of more extensive moral responsibilities from the social contract: for surely in the state of nature he had no responsibility for the health and well-being of other people, but only for his own health and well-being. But this way of framing the problem reminds us that, in identifying the sovereign's responsibility as his subjects' *salus*, Hobbes would have been implicitly invoking the framework of their individual rights to self-preservation which underlay his account of the state of nature. In *The Elements of Law*, Hobbes's comments on this topic are preceded by a remark that, in treating the duties of the sovereign, he will be discussing "the preservation" of the body politic; likewise, in *Leviathan*, he feels it necessary to suggest a potentially broader scope for the sovereign's duties because he takes for granted that his readers will associate the phrase *salus populi* with the "bare Preservation" of the individuals in question.[80] In other words, when Hobbes says that the special office or duty of the sovereign is to look after the *salus populi*, he is implicitly invoking as his justification for the sovereign's actions the subjects' right to self-preservation.

---

[78] The English term "office" derives from the translation of the Latin term for "duty": in English, Hobbes uses the term "office" in *Leviathan*, but uses the term "duty" in the *Elements of Law*, which may be a translation of a previously written section of *De Cive*. On the issues surrounding the composition of the latter two works, see Richard Tuck, "Hobbes and Descartes," in G. A. Rogers and Alan Ryan, eds., *Perspectives on Thomas Hobbes* (Oxford University Press, 1991), as well as Baumgold, "The Composition of Hobbes's *Elements of Law*."

[79] *Elements* ch. 28, p. 172; *De Cive* ch. 13, p. 143; *Leviathan* ch. 30, p. 231.

[80] *Elements* ch. 28, p. 172; *Leviathan* ch. 30, p. 231.

If so, then Hobbes has been somewhat misleading in suggesting that the sovereign acquires no new rights from his subjects, only their non-resistance in the exercise of his own right.[81] It is important in this regard to consider the content of the right of self-preservation that the sovereign is supposed to exercise on his subjects' behalf. Hobbes insists that in one sense the subjects never surrender their right to self-preservation itself: in genuinely indubitable cases of danger to their own lives or souls, they always retain the right to resist.[82] What they are supposed to surrender instead is their right *to all things*: the vast range of means and methods that may be necessary to secure their lives under the uncertainty of the state of nature. So it is true in one sense that Hobbes's sovereign acquires no new rights from his subjects: in the state of nature they have a right to all things, and he also, with no grant from them, has a right to all things. With respect to the *kind* of right it is, Hobbes is entirely correct in saying that it is the *same* right.

But in the state of nature, the sovereign's right to all things applies only to himself and his own preservation: and this appears not to be true of the right he exercises after the establishment of the state. On the contrary, the view we are considering suggests that while the *kind* of right the sovereign exercises after the social contract may remain the same, the *scope* of its potential exercise has broadened massively. For it is no longer merely *his* right that he exercises. Hobbes thinks that, under the conditions created by the social contract, the sovereign exercises not merely his own right to all things but, much more extensively, the right of *all persons* to all things. In other words, when Hobbes claims that the subjects *own* the actions of the sovereign, he means that the sovereign cannot be blamed for his actions on his subjects' behalf since he acts on the basis of those blameless liberties permanently attached to *their* welfare rather than his own.

This interpretation helps to make sense of Hobbes's otherwise peculiar insistence on the language of transferred as opposed to relinquished rights. And it makes sense as well of his insistence that the subjects bear responsibility for the sovereign's actions because they are the true authors of his deeds. Indeed, this is only possible on Hobbes's theory if the acts the sovereign takes are based on his subjects' rights rather than exclusively his own: for, as he explains in *De Homine*, "unless he that is the author hath the right of acting himself, the actor hath no authority to act."[83]

---

[81] Here I offer an alternative to the claims of John Plamenatz, *Man and Society* (McGraw-Hill, 1963) vol. 1, pp. 138–148, and Hampton, *Hobbes and the Social Contract Tradition*, ch. 5, that Hobbes's account is "aberrant" or "confused" in this respect.

[82] On one important instance of this, see Baumgold, *Hobbes's Political Theory*, ch. 5.

[83] *De Homine* ch. 15, p. 84.

But this interpretation, if valid, suggests another and potentially even more troubling feature of Hobbes's theory. For, if this interpretation is correct, Hobbes's solution to the problem of dirty hands, for both sovereign and subject, comes at a formidable moral cost. As many interpreters have noted, Hobbes consistently tries to portray his Leviathan state as the solution to the countless dangers and incommodities of the state of nature, including particularly the inability of the people in it to live not merely safely but also sociably and civilly. This solution, moreover, is supposed to be made possible by the fact that the Leviathan state is able to eliminate or at least sequester and contain the boundless hunger of human beings' desire after desire and the limitless moral permission implied by their right to all things. But if the hypothesis we have been considering is correct, it suggests that in a sense the right to all things never really goes away, and that, as a consequence, human beings never entirely escape the state of nature with all its moral perils.

This is borne out by Hobbes's account of the sovereign's responsibilities after the establishment of the state. Were the sovereign to exercise merely his own individual right to all things, diminished perhaps by the relative security of his new circumstances, his demands on the world might be relatively modest. But instead he represents the needs and the rights of *all* his subjects: and these are not merely the modest rights which he continues to permit them, but the practically limitless rights they enjoyed in the state of nature. This, according to Hobbes, is why the sovereign's task permits, and even requires, apparently limitless acquisition and mastery. The sovereign, Hobbes asserts, must secure to his subjects not merely a "bare Preservation," but rather "all other Contentments of life, which every man by lawfull Industry, without danger, or hurt to the Common-wealth, shall acquire to himselfe."[84] Just as in the state of nature there is no such thing as true felicity or a *summum bonum*, because human life is driven by "a perpetuall and restlesse desire of Power after power," so also human beings after the state of nature retain their natural limitlessness of desire not individually but collectively.[85] For, Hobbes tells us, "Common-wealths can endure no Diet," and "the Publique Riches cannot be limited by other limits, than those which the emergent occasions shall require."[86] If this is so, then Hobbes derives the moral permissions he offers to subjects and sovereigns alike from the premise that some part of human beings, the part

---

[84] *Leviathan* ch. 30, p. 231.   [85] *Leviathan* ch. 11, p. 70.
[86] *Leviathan* ch. 24, p. 173. In connection with this see also *Elements* ch. 28, p. 172.

we designate as within the sphere of sovereign authority, remains forever in the state of nature: forever beastly and brutal, beyond virtue and beyond blame.[87]

This is the true moral cost of Hobbes's solution to the problem of dirty hands. And since Hobbes's theory of sovereignty is still to an extent *our* modern theory of sovereignty, relying on his solution to the moral dilemmas of political subjects and leaders alike potentially requires the same moral cost of us today. As subjects of modern states, our understanding of both our state's authority and our citizen duty bear the indelible stamp of Hobbes's influential apology for state sovereignty and the choice that lay behind it. But we must remember that on Hobbes's theory the sovereign we uphold represents *us*; and that consequently whatever he does in our name may ultimately be laid at our door. And we must remember also that, when we claim moral permission for our governments to undertake on our behalf such deeds as Hobbes's sovereign must inevitably make its business, we do so at the cost of acknowledging ourselves to be inescapably like the creatures Hobbes's state of nature envisions.

---

[87] For this reason it seems to me wrong to characterize Hobbes's political theory as "utopian," as Richard Tuck has suggested (in a qualified way) in "The Civil Religion of Thomas Hobbes" and other recent writings. If Hobbes's Leviathan state is a utopia in any sense, I am suggesting, it is a utopia for its subjects at the expense of its sovereign; and, further, it is a utopia not within the area that the state marks as its own domain, but rather exclusively in that area of individual liberty and enjoyment which lies beyond what the state designates as political.

PART III

From dirty hands to the invisible hand

CHAPTER 5

Dirty hands commercialized

> *Then Leave Complaints: Fools only strive*
> *To make a Great an Honest Hive*
> *T'enjoy the World's Conveniencies,*
> *Be fam'd in War, yet live in Ease,*
> *Without great Vices, is a vain*
> *EUTOPIA seated in the Brain.*
> *Fraud, Luxury, and Pride must live,*
> *While we the Benefits receive . . .*
>
> Bernard Mandeville, "The Grumbling Hive"

Hobbes's account of the impersonal, sovereign state has been extraordinarily influential; yet (as the preceding chapter has tried to show) his concept of the state also constitutes a proposed solution to the recurring dilemmas of political agency and value conflict that we have denoted as the problem of dirty hands. That it does constitute a response to these issues, however, is not necessarily obvious, especially to contemporary political thinkers. This is partly by happenstance and partly by design. By happenstance: for we employ the concept of the state without recalling all of the apologetic functions it was originally introduced to serve. By design: for our acceptance of the outcome of the argument for the state, whether or not we recall its premises, serves to take the question of dirty hands – whether asked of the citizens or of the state – in large part off the agenda.

In Part III we will consider another approach to the problems of political ethics: an approach that on its face is perhaps even less obvious as a response to the dynamic of dirty hands. In the end, however, this approach is no less influential as a solution to that problem: that is, as an apology for the indispensability of certain necessary evils in the fulfillment of public purposes. The characteristic mechanism of this second approach is the modern commercial market; and in the following two chapters we will explore how it came to be implicated – and ultimately, in the hands of

Adam Smith, popularly vindicated – in yet another version of the problem of dirty hands.

The commercial version of the problem of dirty hands – introduced in the Enlightenment by the writers Pierre Nicole and Bernard Mandeville, and for a time urgently topical – may not immediately appear to contemporary readers to be obviously political in nature. This is a flattering measure of the persuasive success attained by the most influential modern solution to this version of the problem: the invisible hand of Adam Smith's commercial market (as we will see in Chapter 6). Yet, from a wider perspective, the commercial reformulation of the dirty hands problem – in the form of the "private vices, public benefits" argument that so powerfully influenced Enlightenment moral discourse – merely continues a trend we observed in Machiavelli, More, and Hobbes: a further democratization of those agents potentially implicated in the problem. Like the older versions of the problem, the commercial problem of dirty hands also focuses on the pursuit of the public benefit, and wonders how to grant absolution to those who do the work necessary to its provision. But as reframed by Nicole and Mandeville, this version of the problem casts the net of those implicated in the Machiavellian dilemma yet wider – now indicting not only those who seek the public good, but those who seek their own private good as well.

At the origin of this new version of the problem, we find the relatively obscure figure of Pierre Nicole, a leading Jansenist theologian who in the late seventeenth century advanced the first description of an idea that came to preoccupy eighteenth-century moral philosophy: namely, the observation that private vices could under certain circumstances produce public benefits. Part of what enabled Nicole to advance this notion was his reconceptualization of what counted as vice: a reconceptualization that relied heavily on Augustine's account of pride. Because of this neo-Augustinian moral psychology, Nicole was able to provide a much broader account of how extensive human vice could be – and therefore open the door to viewing the necessary evils of politics as capable of being undertaken by a much wider variety of agents.

If Pierre Nicole was the progenitor of the private vices, public benefits argument, then Bernard Mandeville was its most scandalous promoter and publicist. Mandeville followed Nicole but with a radically different agenda, pioneering a distinct new territory for the Machiavellian ethic.[1] For, as we

[1] I would not have understood the importance of the connection between Nicole and Mandeville were it not for three excellent studies of these writers: Laurence Dickey's essay, "Pride, Hypocrisy and

will see, for Mandeville, it is not just princes in moments of crisis who may have to call upon the worst angels of their nature to meet the necessities of the hour: it is the ordinary citizen, in the workplace and the marketplace, whose ordinary vices are instrumental to the success of the society.

PIERRE NICOLE

No one can wear one face to himself and another to the multitude without finally getting bewildered as to which may be true. (Nathanael Hawthorne, *The Scarlet Letter*)

Nicole's private vices, public benefits argument, the first adaptation of this paradox to an economic context, arose (ironically) in the writings of the seventeenth-century Jansenist party in the French Catholic Church. The irony consists in the fact that the Jansenists were the strictest moralists of their era (and among the strictest of any Christian era), radical exponents of the Augustinian tradition, explicitly committed to eradicating what they saw as the systematic moral compromise of their arch-rivals, the Jesuits.[2] It was in the context of this attempt to draw a sharp line between the strict moral claims of Jansenist Christianity and the more relaxed evaluation of human behavior advanced by the Jesuits that one leading Jansenist figure, Pierre Nicole, put forward the first version of the private vices, public benefits argument, for the purpose of radically criticizing, not excusing, the ordinary moral behavior of his day.[3]

But it is this very insistence on severely condemning ordinary moral behavior that enabled the Jansenists to make their fateful move. The Jansenists were committed to the theological position that true Christian virtue was much less widely distributed than was commonly believed. To justify this criticism, they needed to account for why there was much more *seeming* charity and virtuous action in the world than would seem consistent with the direst of their theological pronouncements. Their solution was to recur to Augustine's insistence on the extent of the hiddenness of

Civility in Mandeville's Social and Historical Theory," *Critical Review* 4 (1990): 387–431; Dale Van Kley, "Pierre Nicole, Jansenism, and the Morality of Enlightened Self-Interest," in Alan C. Kors and Paul Korshin, eds., *Anticipations of the Enlightenment* (University of Pennsylvania Press, 1987), and E. J. Hundert, *The Enlightenment's Fable* (Cambridge University Press, 1994). I am greatly indebted to all three of these works in my treatment of Nicole and Mandeville.

[2] On Jansenism, see the excellent recent book by Leszek Kolakowski, *God Owes Us Nothing: A Brief Remark on Pascal's Religion and on the Spirit of Jansenism* (University of Chicago Press, 1995).

[3] The best source in English on Nicole is E. D. James, *Pierre Nicole, Jansenist and Humanist* (Martinus Nijhoff, 1972). There is also a helpful short exposition in Nannerl Keohane's *Philosophy and the State in France: From Renaissance to the Enlightenment* (Princeton University Press, 1980), and in J. B. Schneewind, *The Invention of Autonomy* (Cambridge University Press, 1997), pp. 276–279.

human moral phenomena (explored in Chapter 2), and in particular to his argument that the nature of pride is to imitate charity. From this, they were able to conclude that most of what was taken for virtuous moral action in the world was actually fraud, and consequently that much of what preoccupies human beings is producing the *effects* of charity so that the dispositions that tend to produce these effects might mistakenly be interpreted as their cause.

Thus Nicole helped to pioneer a further reconceptualization of the place of vice in political life. Nicole's revision sought centrally to reposition the vice of *pride* as the crucial vice of public consequence. The thinkers we considered in Part II, from Machiavelli to More to Hobbes, had all conceived of pride as in some way socially threatening; after Nicole, thinkers such as Mandeville and Smith would view pride rather as potentially beneficial to society through its commercial effects, provoking a second modern version of the dirty hands dilemma and, subsequently, a second set of solutions to it.

NICOLE'S SELF-LOVE

As we saw in Chapter 2, Augustine's moral theory had been the first to base all moral worth on the concept of charity or godly love. Morality was a matter of the right arrangement of loves: the purpose of human life was the wholehearted love of God, while the natural sinful bent of mankind was to misdirect this love toward less worthy objects (other human beings, idols, and especially one's self). Nicole's moral theory takes this as its starting point. All human actions derive from either charity or self-love. Charity relates everything to God and indeed is the unmerited, unachievable gift of God's grace; self-love, by contrast, is the direct denial of charity, the squandering of the devotion properly due to God on our own unworthy selves.

This self-love manifests itself in two principal forms: the pursuit of pleasures (the object of the self-love of the body) and the pursuit of honors (the object of the self-love of the mind).[4] Thus the corrupt human being according to Nicole

not only loves himself but loves himself beyond measure, loves only himself, and relates everything to himself. He wants every kind of property, honor,

---

[4] Pierre Nicole, "Of Conversation," in *Moral Essayes*, trans. Anonymous (London, 1696), p. 151.

and pleasure, and he wants them only for himself. Placing himself at the center of everything, he would like to rule over everything and wishes that all creatures were occupied with nothing but pleasing him, praising him, and admiring him . . .[5]

The boundlessness of this desire is for Nicole fundamental to human nature, an implication of the fact that human beings are "both mortal and immortal": immortal as created, and mortal as corrupted; proved mortal by their fears, and immortal by the boundlessness of their desires.[6]

This limitlessness of desire motivates humanity's taste for luxuries, because it is in the nature of self-love to come to require novelty and variety. We are dependent on a much wider range of objects than we would at first be willing to acknowledge: the vast number of "litle props" that we require for our happiness are invisible to us most of the time, only becoming obvious to us when we are forced to do without them.[7] Such distractions are not able to sustain our interest for long, and thus "we are forced to change them often," or "our weight would else breake them."[8] Almost everyone is willing to acknowledge that most of the things to which they are attached in the world are vain and pointless, but in spite of this knowledge human beings still find themselves preoccupied by such transient goods as beauty, honor, and reputation; their minds are "of noe solidity, nor weight: but a straw, a feather, that the least puff carrys away with it."[9] The numerousness of our needs is one of the most distinct signs of the fallen and diminished condition of human existence. Human beings may attempt "to shoare up their weaknesse, with borrowed props," but in so doing they only increase their weakness by adding a greater burden of wants and necessities which they must thereafter carry. Thus for Nicole, self-love is

the monster we carry in our bosom; it lives and reigns absolutely within us, unless God has destroyed its reign by filling our hearts with a different kind of love. It is the principle of all actions that are untouched by anything but corrupt nature; and we, far from being horrified by it, love and hate all things outside ourselves only according to whether they conform to or contradict these inclinations.[10]

---

[5] Pierre Nicole, "On Charity and Self-Love" (hereafter CSL), ch. 1, in J. B. Schneewind, ed., *Moral Philosophy from Montaigne to Kant: An Anthology*, vol. II (Cambridge University Press, 1990), p. 371.
[6] Pierre Nicole, "Of the Education of a Prince," in *Moral Essayes* II, p. 42.
[7] Pierre Nicole, "Of the Weaknesse of Man," in Jean S. Yolton, ed., *John Locke as Translator: Three of the Essais of Pierre Nicole* (Voltaire Foundation, 2000), pp. 97–99, s. 52–53.
[8] Ibid., s. 54.   [9] Ibid., p. 93, s. 49.   [10] CSL, ch. 1, p. 371.

It is the root of all evil, the cause of all wars, all injustice, "all man's crimes and profligacies."[11]

What we worship in ourselves, however, we despise in others, precisely because it interferes with our own self-love; we hate others dominated by self-love, and we are aware that others despise the same in us.[12] As a consequence, we become aware that the untrammeled pursuit of self-love is counterproductive to achieving our own selfish goals, and, though we would like nothing better than to dominate our fellows without dissimulation, we are willing to accept a great deal of compromise. We desire self-aggrandizement, but we have other, sometimes rival, selfish desires as well, Nicole tells us. Self-love "loves to dominate; it loves to subjugate everyone; but even more it loves life and possessions, and more than domination it loves the comforts of life; furthermore, it sees clearly that the rest of the world ... is ready to take away from every individual's self-love what it loves most."[13] So out of self-love men become willing, for example, to unite for mutual defense under a sovereign.[14] But beyond this initial step, the whole of humanity's mutual interdependence, especially its commercial interdependence, rests upon this foundation of self-love:

> One gives in order to be given. This is the mainspring and foundation of all business transacted among men, which is now taking a thousand forms; for trade is not only a matter of merchandise, given for other merchandise or for money but also one of labor, services, attentions, and civilities; all of this is exchanged either for things of the same nature or for more concrete goods as, for instance, when one obtains actual advantages through mere friendly words.[15]

Human beings are therefore at once "void of Charity by the disorder of Sin," and at the same time "full of wants" and mutually interdependent in a variety of ways.[16]

Thus we stand in need of others because they represent potential dangers, potential helps, and what everyone craves most, potential

---

[11] Ibid. It is also the principal element that perverts human reasoning: it is usually "some connection to self-love, interest or passion" that ultimately persuades us to adopt one view rather than another, because "for us truth and utility are the same thing." Pierre Nicole and Antoine Arnauld, *Logic or the Art of Thinking*, ed. Jill Vance Buroker (Cambridge University Press, 1996), p. 204.

[12] Pierre Nicole, "Of Grandeur," in *Moral Essayes* 1, p. 83, s. 1.   [13] CSL ch. 2, p. 372.

[14] If the story so far sounds rather Hobbesian, that is no accident: Nicole acknowledges as much explicitly, noting that if Hobbes, "who said that men are born in a state of war and that every man is by nature the enemy of all others had said this only to show the disposition of men's hearts toward one another, without claiming that this was legitimate and just, what he said would correspond to truth and experience as much as his actual contention is contrary to reason" (CSL ch. 1, p. 371).

[15] Ibid., p. 372.

[16] "Of Grandeur," p. 97, s. 29. Indeed, this interdependence is itself evidence of God's willing that human beings should live in societies, since God would not have left us under the necessities that

admiration and love. This last point is for Nicole the central feature of social psychology. The craving for others' esteem and approbation goes far deeper than its instrumental value in procuring their help: on the contrary, even more than instrumentally we value their approval intrinsically, because it offers us grounds for reinforcing our belief in our own likability, and thereby allows us to "find satisfaction in this lovely Idea of our selves."[17]

> Nothing is so natural to Man as the desire of being belov'd by others, because nothing is so natural to him as to love himself . . . We desire to be belov'd that we may love our selves the more. The love which others bear us makes us judge we deserve to be belov'd, and makes us frame of our selves a more lovely Idea . . . Our judgment, which is always weak and timid when alone, gets strength and confidence when fortified by the judgment of others . . . Our Soul is so languishing and so weak, that it cannot sustain it self without being under-propt by the approbation and love of others.[18]

This condition of mutual interdependence carries some tremendous moral and social benefits in Nicole's system. The most important of these is that it forecloses the possibility of our indifference toward others, and as a consequence also the possibility that we will retreat into our selves, and so overlook and estrange ourselves from our fellows.

And so, having realized both how much they need their fellow human beings as well as how distasteful their self-love is to others, human beings are compelled to dissimulate their self-love, at least until they have become strong enough to dispense with others' good will. Because we know by experience "that we love those who love us," we too "love or would seem to love others, that so we may purchase their affection."[19] This "traffick of Self-love," whereby we "buy the affection of others" through our kindnesses to them, is for Nicole the very "ground of humane Civility."[20]

Self-love, then, on Nicole's theory, has an almost infinite capacity for mimicking charity both in its outward characteristics and in its effects, just as it had for Augustine. Though

> nothing is more different from charity, which relates everything to God, than self-love, which relates everything to itself; yet nothing is so similar to the effects of charity as those of self-love, which follows the same paths so closely that there is

---

drive us into the societies if he had not intended us to depend upon them for our survival. So the socializing of humanity is God's will, and consequently "whatsoever then serves to the preservation of society comes from within that appointment." Pierre Nicole, "On the Ways of Preserving Peace," in Yolton, *John Locke as Translator*, Part 1, p. 191, s. 90.

[17] Pierre Nicole, "Of Christian Civility," in *Moral Essayes*, p. 139.   [18] Ibid., p. 137, ss. 1–3.

[19] Ibid., p. 138, s. 4.   [20] Ibid.

virtually no better means to ascertain where charity should lead us than to uncover the paths taken by an enlightened self-love that knows how to recognize its true interests and pursues the goals it has set for itself by reason.[21]

Because the appearance of self-love in ourselves is so hateful to other human beings, self-love takes care to "obliterate . . . with marvelous canni-ness all traces and all marks of the self-love that has given rise to it, knowing full well that it would not obtain any of the things it desires if they were noticed."[22] It is thus possible for us to be quite "exact in the practice of certain exterior Duties," even to the point of obsessive fastidiousness, and at the same time to have "only very confus'd Ideas" about our true spiritual duties and interior virtues.[23]

Of course it is not always the case that self-love is so shrewd about pursuing its goals. Our self-love may be very intense, but it is at the same time frequently very inefficient. Nevertheless the capacity for accurate imitation of the outward forms and effects of charity which self-love does display when it tries to is nothing short of astonishing. Self-love "apes" charity out of fear, or self-interest, or a desire for the favor and affection of others. Here Nicole follows Augustine almost exactly in observing that it is in the very nature of evil to imitate good.

In the end, Nicole claims, the effects of charity and those of self-love are for all practical purposes coextensive. The move Nicole makes here is at once the logical extension of Augustine's theory of moral opacity and at the same time a startling new application of it. For Nicole wants to claim that, for the purposes of providing benefits, human vice rather than human virtue is not only *sometimes* but *usually* the source of the external goods we need. Self-love can produce practically *all* the necessary, externally benefi-cial actions required to sustain a community's welfare. "There is virtually no deed inspired by charity for the sake of pleasing God that self-love could not prompt us to perform for the sake of pleasing men," Nicole claims. So far he is on safe Augustinian ground: there is no action that could not in principle be inspired by either self-love or charity. But Nicole then points out that the clear implication of this is that we can have far less confidence than we previously did in our own capacity for moral evaluation. The inclination of self-love to imitate charity is "so cunning and so subtle, and at the same time so pervasive," he suggests, that "it is almost impossible to know clearly what distinguishes" charity from self-love.[24] And if this is true

[21] CSL ch. 1, pp. 370–371.   [22] CSL ch. 4, p. 374.
[23] Pierre Nicole, "Of Profiting by Bad Sermons," in *Moral Essayes*, p. 232.   [24] CSL ch. 4, p. 374.

of charity and self-love themselves, it is even more dramatically true of the outward effects which each of these motivations produces.[25]

So it is a combination of both charity and (much more commonly) disguised self-love that gives rise to the value system of *honnêteté*, the conventions of society and manners.[26] Nicole's contemporaries regularly appealed to this idea of *honnêteté* as the key cultural source of moral standards and motivations in their society. But for Nicole this *honnêteté* is actually just "a more intelligent and more adroit self-love than that of the world at large."[27] This civility thus constitutes "a sort of commerce established & regulated by self-love which being supreme judg in the case obliges both sides to equall, & punctuall returnes; & allows us to complain, when others faile in their part of the performance."[28] Such civility is fawning, false and insincere, and as soon as our backs are turned, it turns to mockery.[29]

One of the principal marks of this decency, Nicole makes clear, is the appearance of *impartiality*: *honnêteté* prompts us "to display to the world a show of extreme impartiality, to praise willingly what deserves to be praised, to give every possible due to all the good qualities of others, and not to deny even our enemies the marks of esteem they deserve."[30] The man of selfish decency realizes that the more his kindnesses "appear disinterested and free of all self-seeking, the more they will attract the attention of the world, as they afford everyone the hope of receiving similar kindnesses."[31] In addition, by acknowledging his faults openly and not taking offense at others' noticing them, the *honnête homme* "acquires the reputation of an amiable impartiality that enables him to judge himself without blindness and passion, of being someone who knows how to do justice to himself."[32] In a way it is of course unsurprising that impartiality should come to figure prominently in a moral psychology of this kind, for

---

[25] Nicole's claim, it should be observed, is not that self-love serves the public benefit *better* than charity. He is quite clear that genuine charity exists, despite the false conclusion of some that because "frequently people hide great vices behind an appearance of piety," it therefore follows "that all devotion is only hypocrisy." And when charity does make a rare appearance in human behavior, it certainly tends to yield the proper fruits in the form of social benefits. It makes us "carefull, to keep peace with our neighbours" and to "looke on the faults we committ against others, as great, & important; & their trespasses against us, as small, & inconsiderable." *Logic or the Art of Thinking* IV, pp. 218–219; "On the Ways of Preserving Peace" I, pp. 127–129.

[26] This term, a derivative of the Latin *honestas*, was an important concept in Jansenism and seventeenth-century French philosophy generally, which can be loosely translated as "decency." On this topic see further especially Keohane, *Philosophy and the State in France*.

[27] CSL ch. 4, p. 375.   [28] Peace II, p. 247, s. 63.

[29] "Of Christian Civility," p. 149, s. 32; Peace II, p. 247.   [30] CSL ch. 9, p. 380.

[31] CSL ch. 10, p. 381.   [32] CSL ch. 7, p. 378.

in one sense self-love simply is partiality toward oneself. But it is worth noticing that *impartiality*, though on the face of it an antidote to self-love, is not yet charity: one may acquire the quality of impartiality, and even more easily the appearance of impartiality, without any true mark of charity, anything at all of positive moral worth (from the Augustinian point of view) figuring into one's action.

So great is the capacity of our self-love for imitating the fruits of charity that we are frequently successful in fooling ourselves. Often of course we simply wish to fool ourselves: we either judge our own actions and motivations to be something they are not, or we adapt our standards of judgment to alter morality to fit our own weaknesses and desires. Just as More's Hythloday had charged, Nicole too asserts that human beings, "not being willing to render their actions [to] conform to the Law of god, have endeavoured to render the Laws of God [to] conform to their actions."[33] In particular, the ideology of *honnêteté* proves useful in this regard: we make use of such terms as "*humanely speaking*" to sketch out the requirements of basic "decency" with no other purpose than "to hide, lessen, and excuse vice, and to apply our own minds as well as those of others, to a false outward appearance which makes them seem conformable to the dictates of reason, such as is to be found in the World, that is, to the dictates of deprav'd and corrupted Reason."[34] Indeed, Nicole says, self-love frequently disposes us to create our own imaginary God, a "Ghostly Father" from whom we can elicit condemnation of just those vices to which we are really indifferent, and who will turn a blind eye to those faults we are unwilling to acknowledge and abandon.

For Nicole, then, much of the extent of our self-deception can be attributed simply to the extent of our self-love. But he goes further, again following Augustine, in viewing moral phenomena generally as being characterized by an opacity that cannot be wholly explained by our moral laxity and self-bias. This confusion often begins "in our very hearts, so that we are unable to distinguish whether we are acting from charity or from self-love," and even true Christians can rarely be assured "that any specific action will be entirely free of all self-seeking."[35] The causes of our

[33] Pierre Nicole, "Of Knowledge of Self," in *Moral Essayes* 1, p. 32.
[34] "Of Conversation," p. 159, s. 25.
[35] CSL ch. 12, p. 384; ch. 13, p. 385. By the same token, one may have charity and be unaware of this fact: for example, some persons believe they do not love Jesus Christ, because they feel no particular devotion to him, but if they love God's law and justice, and shun sin in obedience to it, they in fact "truly love JESUS CHRIST as God, because he is this Justice, this Wisdom, this Eternal Law which they love." Pierre Nicole, "Of Submission to God's Will," in *Moral Essayes*, p. 41.

actions are often confusing and even more often mixed, and consequently "there is almost no one but God who is able to discriminate between them."[36]

This problem of moral opacity is for Nicole a general feature of human life, a view that, as we have seen, follows directly from the premises he had inherited from Augustine (and through Augustine, in part, from Plato). Most things in the world we admire only externally because "everything is judged by appearances" and "hardly anyone penetrates to the core and foundation of things."[37] The whole of our historical knowledge constitutes at the end of the day nothing more than "the skeleton of affairs . . . void of those secret springs . . . that gave rise, and successe to them," merely "the outside of actions, without the designe, the soule, that inlivend them."[38] Nicole is not a relativist, of course: he expressly denies the view that "truth is so similar to falsehood and virtue so similar to vice that it is impossible to tell them apart," calling this opinion "false and impious."[39] But he insists that our understanding in this area is decidedly cloudy: "in most matters there is a mixture of error and truth, vice and virtue, perfection and imperfection, and this mixture is one of the most common sources of our false judgments."[40] This is no excuse for abandoning the hard work of attempting to make these discriminations, however: "the truth is no less the truth for being mixed with lies," and so "in everything containing a mixture of good and evil we distinguish them."[41]

---

[36] CSL ch. 12, p. 384. By one and the same action, Nicole thinks, we seek both God and the world: "the heart is happy to please both, not knowing whether it is God that it means by God, for this is a judgment that can be made only by delving into a certain depth within the heart that is known clearly to no one but God alone" (ibid.). So we may always reasonably fear that God will apply to us the same judgment his prophets passed against Israel: "*This people honour me with their Lips, but their Heart is far from me*" (CSL ch. 2, p. 372).

[37] Logic I, p. 216.

[38] "Weaknesse of Man," p. 7. For Nicole, this reflects a very deep theological truth about the relation of God to the world, reflected in the Christian doctrine about Christ and the Church: Christ is to be found not only as the head, but also in the members of his church, yet in the members "he is hidden." Often we mistakenly "despise him in his Members wherein he is hid," for "it is much easier to contemn Jesus Christ in his Members than in himself, because there he is more hidden," but this is plainly to mistake Christ's true method of existing and residing in the world, hidden within the midst of the world in the form of his Church. Pierre Nicole, "Not to be Scandalized," in *Moral Essays*, p. 205. Also, Nicole tells us, it is for this reason that we ought not to be concerned about the love or hatred we may elicit from other human beings: for in love or in hatred, they engage not with us but with "an Idea, a Phantome of their own making," devised in their imagination from their fears or their desires. Peace II, p. 231, s. 41.

[39] Logic I, p. 214.   [40] Ibid.

[41] Ibid., p. 215. Even the discourse of good and virtuous people, Nicole claims, "is not free from illusion, since they in many occasions borrow from the World its Language," and sometimes must

This cloudiness of the moral world is at its most pronounced with respect to our ignorance about the internal motivations of other human beings. Part of our trouble in reasoning about this, Nicole says, is the fact that "the same outward action may spring from several different intentions" such that "we are not capable of comprehending the infinite number of hidden motions and considerations which might produce it."[42] In a telling comparison, Nicole suggests that while Christ's commands are morally strenuous, the law of the prophet Mohammed is as a matter of external performance frequently of a difficulty equal to the true precepts of Christ.[43] It follows for Nicole that "this exterior innocence, consisting only in observing the exterior duties of Christian Religion, is a very deceiptful equivocal sign of interior Grace and Innocence: Since all this may proceed from custom, a habit gotten, the love of Creatures, and a fear purely humane."[44]

PRIDE'S SOCIAL BENEFITS

Yet from the perspective of what is really morally valuable, this hiddenness of human motivation can have positive effects. In so arguing, Nicole puts at the center of his moral theory a significant extension of Augustine's theory of the providential uses of vice, explored in Chapter 2. Like Augustine, Nicole sees virtue and vice as inextricably woven together in human life in the most complex patterns. Human beings consist of "a mixture of good, and bad qualities"; and "what is a Vertue in one, may be a Vice in another."[45] The "infinite chain of causes" is so complex and so far beyond our understanding that we frequently cannot "distinguish the effects of [God's] Mercy from those of his Justice" such that "sometimes the greatest evils are attached to the greatest seeming goods, & vice versa."[46] Furthermore, it is frequently the case that certain accidents which are "the necessary consequences of our sins" will prove to have positive effects for ourselves and for others: for one of the principal marks of God's action in the world is his ability to "draw good from evil, and change into means

---

even "call good and evil which the world call so." Indeed, frequently they are "obliged to do so" since "they would not be understood, did they talke a Language so different from that of others." This serves simply to reinforce, albeit against the will of the good people involved, the world's own error. "Of Conversation," p. 161, s. 28.

[42] Pierre Nicole, "Of Rash Judgments," in *Moral Essayes*, p. 191, s. xxv.

[43] Pierre Nicole, "Of the Fear of God," in *Moral Essayes*, p. 95, s. xxxiii.   [44] Ibid., s. xxxiv.

[45] Peace 11, p. 253; "Submission to God's Will," p. 44.   [46] "Submission to God's Will," p. 71.

of saving us, that which deserv'd only chastisement."[47] It is God, in short, who "approves all that is just and necessary to the conservation of humane societies,"[48] and consequently it is impossible to evaluate any sort of human power or endowment without considering "the good or bad use that may be made thereof."

This Augustinian theory about God's tendency to use evil means to good ends helps Nicole to bring off his novel extension of Augustine's portrayal of pride as naturally inclined to imitate charity. There are two reasons, Nicole claims, why God permits pride to mimic charity: first, because pride's imitation unwittingly helps to further the cultivation of true charity; and second, because it also unwittingly aids in the work of providence. For Nicole, human motivation is hidden: consequently, the heavenly kingdom of charity is able to endure not by clear signs, but only by faith. This situation demands that "the righteous be outwardly indistinguishable from the wicked," both because God's justice requires that his "treasures of grace" be hidden from the wicked, and because God in his mercy understands that it is "useful" to the righteous "not to know themselves and not to see the righteousness that is in them," which might be a temptation to pride or sin.[49] By means of this obscurity of the moral world, God keeps human beings on the correct moral path.[50] Moreover, even among God's elect, true charity is so weakly anchored that the fear of others' disapproval can provide disciplinary restraint where charity alone would fail. Whenever charity languishes, *honnêteté* can "sustain the spirit and prevent it from falling into dangerous excesses."[51]

But it is God's second and broader providential reason for permitting this mimicry that is of most immediate significance for our purposes, because it is here that Nicole draws out the implications of Augustine's

---

[47] Ibid., pp. 72–73.
[48] Pierre Nicole, "Of the True Idea of Things," in *Moral Essayes*, p. 171, s. 14. [49] CSL ch. 13, p. 385.
[50] "Not to be Scandalized," p. 206. Citing Augustine's doctrine that the reason God permits the just to suffer along with the wicked is to forestall our directing our services to God for the purpose of avoiding temporal evils, Nicole extends the idea by arguing that God "permits us not to see the excellence of a Just Souls beauty, and the horrible Deformity of a Soul in sin, lest it should be through these interested Motives, that we should desire justice, and have a Horror for sin." Indeed, in a move that cuts against the spirit at least of Augustine's project, Nicole tells us that God desires that we know our selves no "more than is necessary to make us humble, and to govern our selves," and so all attempts at introspection which reach beyond this limit are "not agreeable to God, nor useful to us." The reverse, however, is not necessarily true: self knowledge is helpful to a person who is proud, since "the readiest way, to humble him, is to give him a view of his own weaknesse"; in such cases we must try "to prick this buble, to let the winde out that swells it," and to "remove the illusion, & pull off the disguise, that makes a man looke big to himself, by seting before him his smalnesse, & infirmitys …" "Not to be Scandalized," pp. 206–207; "Knowledge of Self" II, p. 75.
[51] CSL ch. 13, p. 386.

theory about pride and charity to produce a startling new application. Although part of God's purpose in permitting pride to mimic charity is to conceal from moral agents the motivations for their actions, God has a broader providential purpose as well, Nicole believes. Because human sinfulness is so extensive, there is just not enough charity, on Nicole's view of the world, to account for all the good deeds that human beings do to and for one another. However cruel it may sometimes appear, the world nevertheless seems to behave better than it should under the premises of a radical Augustinian theology. But this is deceptive, Nicole believes, for what we see at work in most instances is not charity but pride. God's providence, finding too little charity in the world to furnish the necessaries and conveniences of life to his human creation, chose pride itself as the unwitting agent for supplying these goods and services.

As we noted earlier, Nicole argues that it is by means of the self-love of all human beings that human beings are preserved from outward sufferings and provided with their material needs, especially in the commercial sphere. Nicole now presses the same point further, going beyond anything Augustine had suggested to argue that by means of this selfish interdependence *"all of life's needs are somehow met without involving charity."* Nicole thereby attempts to sever the connection between good works and human happiness in all but the most coincidental sense, arguing that "there is no reason that in states that have no place for charity because the true religion is banished from them one would not live as peacefully, safely, and comfortably as if one were in a republic of saints."[52] From this he presses on to a conclusion of astonishing scope, asserting that

what would be needed to reform the world entirely, that is, to banish from it all the vices and all the most glaring disorders and to make humans happy even in this life, would be nothing more than to instill in all of them, in the absence of charity, an enlightened self-love that would know how to discern its true interests and pursue them in the ways pointed out by right reason. However corrupt this society might be inwardly and in the eyes of God, outwardly nothing would be more orderly, courteous, just, peaceful, honorable, and generous; moreover, it would be an excellent thing that, everything being inspired and driven only by self-love, self-love would not show itself and that, society being entirely without charity, what one would see everywhere would be only the forms and the outward marks of charity.[53]

---

[52] CSL ch. 2, p. 372. Emphasis added. In this connection, see further Immanuel Kant's remark in his essay on "Perpetual Peace" about the capacity of a "republic of devils" to achieve good government.
[53] CSL ch. 11, p. 383.

Though his explicit articulation of the principles underlying this hidden economy of pride is unusual, Nicole argues, there is nothing new about the thing itself: it is the only economy we have ever known. Nicole offers as an example the case of an innkeeper in the country ready to serve those travelers who pass by, who has furnished a house for that purpose and is willing to obey the travelers' every command.[54] We would scarce believe it if innkeepers offered such service out of mere charity, and with good reason. Concupiscence is their true motivator, but Nicole believes that selfish desire does its work "so well and gracefully, that they would even have us [the travelers] think that they take it for a courtesie that we employ them in our service."[55] Indeed, concupiscence can reliably be enlisted to produce good results that we would hope for in vain from charity. He elaborates:

What a piece of Charity would it be, to build for another an intire House, furnish it with all necessary Houshold-stuff; and after that to deliver him up the Key? Concupiscence does this cheerfully. What Charity would it be to go and fetch Drugs from the *Indies*, to submit ones self to the meanest Offices, and serve others in the most abject and painful commands? And this Concupiscence does without ever complaining. There is therefore nothing whence Men derive greater benefits to themselves than their own Concupiscence.[56]

Pride, Nicole believes, is utterly vicious. Yet he has committed himself to the view that, from the point of view of procuring the public benefit, it is not only more reliable but also vastly more effective. At the very least, it is able to supply a great deal more labor: charity may coax some occasional efforts from a few of her knights-errant, but pride has constant access to the productive energies of whole battalions.

POLITICS AND PROVIDENCE

Nicole, then, was the first to advance a version of the view that public benefits were produced by private vices, which alone makes him an important figure in the story we have been exploring. But there is an additional contribution Nicole made to the development of thinking about this problem, one relating more directly to its political dimensions.

As we have seen, in his essay on "Charity and Self-Love," Nicole argued that self-love is capable of producing all the good effects of charity, especially on the larger scale of commercial exchange. But in his other

[54] "Of Grandeur" 1, pp. 97–98.   [55] Ibid., p. 98, s. 29.   [56] Ibid.

works Nicole acknowledges that concupiscence does not of its own volition naturally flow along these productive courses. Left to its own devices, concupiscence "keeps within no bounds"; there is "no excess it will not run into, if not held back," including being carried "to rob, kill, and create the greatest injustice and extravagances."[57] In short, undirected concupiscence, instead of being "beneficial to human Society, . . . utterly destroys it." Therefore, to ensure that self-love "may be disposed to do these [beneficial] Offices, there ought to be something to keep it within compass."[58] For this purpose, Nicole argues, it is necessary to devise an "art" by which

> to keep Concupiscence within bounds: and this art consists in that polity which by fear of punishment keeps it in, and applies it to whatsoever is necessary for human life. This polity furnishes us with Merchants, Physicians, Artificers, and generally with whatsoever contributes to our pleasure, or supplies the necessity of Life. Thus we have an Obligation to those who maintain Government, that is, to those in whom resides the authority which regulates and keeps the Body of the State together.[59]

The art of government, then, according to Nicole, is necessary in order to direct the vicious energies of human beings effectively into channels that will produce public benefits. The person who invented the art of domesticating wild beasts and taming them to human service, Nicole observes, performed nothing short of a miracle; but it is a greater wonder still that human beings should be tamed, and it is "Government" which is "the worker of this wonder." Left to their own desires, men "are worse than Lions, Bears, or Tygres. Every one would devour his Neighbour; and it is by means of Policy and Laws that these Wild Beasts are become tractable, and that from them we reap all those human services that might be had from pure Charity."[60]

For Nicole, then, the whole aim of "policy in governing" is "to furnish private Persons with those conveniences, which the greatest Kings could not have, were their Officers never so many, their Riches never so great, if this order were destroyed."[61] This policy in governing helps to procure those conveniences which "now any one of four hundred Pounds a Year enjoys," but which no amount of wealth would be able to procure without the assistance of this policy in governing.[62] The reason it is able to have such a powerful effect is the profound interdependence of social life. Each person requires the products of such a wide variety of trades that he could

---

[57] Ibid.   [58] Ibid.   [59] Ibid.   [60] Ibid., pp. 98–99, s. 30.   [61] Ibid., p. 99, s. 31.   [62] Ibid.

barely contrive to have them supply all his own needs, much less the needs of all those employees he would need to undertake such provision. But these days an ordinary person has all this, "without trouble, turmoil, or anxiety."[63] In an interdependent economy, those who work for such a person "bring him no trouble, nor is he oblig'd to supply their wants."[64] Such a system, capable of thus equalizing "the private Condition of Subjects to that of Kings, and which freeing them from all the troubles, [bestows] on them all that is to be had of good in the greatest riches," creates benefits that are truly beyond estimation.[65]

One of the necessary conditions for the effective exercise of governmental direction, Nicole argues, is the maintenance of the social structures and distinctions of *grandeur* or "greatness." The great ones of the world, though they may be entirely vicious people, are nevertheless "the Ministers God makes use of to procure Men the greatest and most essential goods this world has."[66] All our commercial benefits, all our domestic security, all the profit we derive from human industry, we hold "by the means of publick Discipline" which the structures of "greatness" uphold, and, were this to disappear, we would be plunged immediately into "an universal War" of which force could be the only final arbiter.[67] Part of the means by which the distinctions of greatness are maintained, Nicole claims, are precisely those trappings of luxury which (according to his moral theory) emerge from the free exercise of human pride. It is therefore necessary for those who have responsibilities of prominence and authority to "have Riches in proportion to the Degree ... which is requisite for their condition ..."[68]

However necessary it may be to human well-being to have a class of people exercising the offices of greatness, though, such offices are still a site of considerable moral peril, Nicole maintains. The condition of the great is, "in Christians, a state of violence," and indeed "there is almost no Christian [virtue] to which Grandeur is not in some ways opposed, and from which it does not estrange us."[69] Moreover, the particular aspect of greatness which engenders this moral danger is its close connection with self-love as opposed to charity: "the instinct of Grandeur refers all things to it self," Nicole observes, while "Charity regards not its self, but is all for others."[70] Nicole does not directly address the possibility that one might accept the duties of a station of greatness not for one's self, but rather on behalf of others; but his other views would seem to imply that this situation is far from typical, and that, even when this appears to be the case, the

[63] Ibid. [64] Ibid., p. 100, s. 31. [65] Ibid. [66] Ibid, p. 97, s. 28. [67] Ibid.
[68] Ibid., p. 92, s. 20. [69] "Of Grandeur" II, p. 122, ss. 35–36. [70] Ibid., pp. 122–123, s. 36.

person concerned ought to be very wary that he is not making excuses to justify his own prideful desires. Even if someone did undertake a station of greatness from a sense of genuine concern for others, of course, this would hardly eliminate the deeper and more ineliminable conflict between political life, on the one hand, and Christian morality, on the other.[71] The life that Christ led on earth, Nicole observes, was "in outward shew quite contrary to that of Men in Power," and "as this instinct remains in the Great, when they are truly Christians," so also "of necessity it must raise in them an interior war and opposition against the slaveries they are oblig'd to by their call."[72]

No matter who receives the reins of political leadership, certain provisions must be made to prepare them for their task. And central to these provisions, according to Nicole, is preparing the prince to produce, not the *reality* of charity for his subjects, but rather its effects. He advises those who

---

[71] This attitude might have led Nicole like many of his fellow religious conservatives to endorse a retreat from political life. But instead Nicole, following Augustine's account of the judge, acknowledges that "the commerce of life ... permits not this"; it is necessary to ground "an infinite number of things on the relation of men, and those of the greatest moment; even to give sentence thereby very often of life and death." It may seem difficult to reconcile our "indispensable obligation" to judge based on sure evidence with the necessity of relying on human sources for information. But we must make a distinction between "the knowledge sufficient, to act from that which is necessary to frame an absolute judgment of true things." Thus we can act on imperfect human sources of information "when we are oblig'd to act and cannot come to a clearer knowledge of the truth," as in the case of "a Judge passing sentence on one that's accused," who "judges not rashly, though he should condemn one that is innocent; because he does not absolutely judge that he is guilty, but that he is convicted of being so according to the forms of justice." As for Augustine in Book XIX of the *City of God*, so too for Nicole, the judge who renders an unjust verdict is rendered innocent by virtue of the conjunction of his necessity of acting with the ineliminable vagueness inherent in the human condition. "Rash Judgments," p. 195, s. xxxi.

[72] "Of Grandeur" II, pp. 122–123, s. 35. Nicole is constantly reminding his readers of the intense and difficult moral responsibilities attendant upon positions of public greatness and political leadership. It is not possible for people truly acting in a position of greatness in the world to "give something to the World, without delivering themselves totally up to it," for the world will not "be satisfied with this share," and will "look on them as ridiculous." It is thus inevitable that "a thousand occasions ... will offer themselves, wherein the World must be cross'd and thwarted; and to do this, great courage is required." Another part of the peculiar moral risk associated with positions of power lies in the special responsibility that inevitably accompanies those who take on themselves the visible position of greatness. A "woman of low quality" who wears gaudy apparel risks no greater sin than that implied by her little excess and the few who may be scandalized by it. But in a person of greatness, who is "the Example and Rule of others," this same display will constitute "a publick approbation of Vice, a Seminary of crimes, and a Lawful Authorizing sin." This demonstrates "what a strange difference the various conditions of men create in actions which outwardly appear the same." But there is no moral excuse to be drawn from this necessity: "For if it be necessary that they live in the World, to comply with their engagement therein, there is yet a greater necessity they should not be corrupted by it. No necessity, no Engagement can oblige us to fill our heads with lyes, nor to live in a continual illusion; and no body ought to be so wretched as to think, that falsity and error ought to be the allotment of his state and condition." "Of Grandeur" II, p. 121, s. 34; p. 110, s. 13; "Of Conversation, p. 161, s. 29.

are charged with the education of the powerful to keep "firmly in mind" his theory of self-love's mimicry of charity,

so that, if they should be unable to inspire in them the sense of charity they would like to develop, they will try at least to shape their self-love and to teach them that most of the routes they take to satisfy it are quite wrong, inappropriate, and contrary to their true interests and that they could very easily take different routes that would lead them without effort to honor and glory and afford them the affection, esteem, and admiration of the world. By such means they would not succeed, to be sure, in rendering their pupils useful to themselves, but at least they would render them useful to others and also help them enter a path closer, at any rate, to the road to heaven than that on which they are engaged, as they would have to do little more than change their ends and their intentions to become as pleasing to God for their truly Christian virtue as they would be to men for the luster of the human *honnêteté* that would have been imparted to them.[73]

It is worth drawing attention once again to the fact that Nicole in describing these mechanisms believes them to be wholly vicious in origin. In arguing that these beneficial social effects could all be produced by self-love, Nicole meant to draw attention to, not away from, the fact that, from the ultimate standard of divine judgment, most human action was wholly uncharitable and therefore depraved, regardless of its potential beneficial effects. But by comprehensively extending the concept of sinfulness so far beyond human comprehension and differentiation, the modern Augustinians such as Nicole may have left an opportunity for those like Mandeville who could make use of their contempt for this world for more worldly purposes. For if self-interest, through self-conscious mimicry of charity, was capable of bringing about *all* the positive social consequences of social charity, why should we not leave charity to God? He is, after all, the only one who will recognize it when he sees it.

BERNARD MANDEVILLE

Let me tell you something. People will always gamble. So now you see — the government's — huh? — the lottery? — And I'll tell you, by the turn of the century, the government, you watch ... the government will be running, not only gambling: gambling; prostitution; drugs — why? Because that's where the money is. That's where the money is ... Sore throat: chicken soup. (David Mamet, *Lansky*)

Private vices, Bernard Mandeville famously argued, create public benefits. At first glance this is such an arresting invocation of the Machiavellian

[73] CSL ch. II, p. 383.

problem of dirty hands that it is surprising so little attention has been paid to the resemblance.[74] Mandeville's innovation is fundamentally a commercialization of Machiavelli's dirty hands dilemma. Yet here the heroic justification of the Machiavellian hero is rendered by Mandeville into an anti-heroic justification as prosaic as bread and butter.

But even though ordinary private vices are indispensable to the creation of public benefits, they are not by themselves sufficient: only the right combinations of private vices will do, and this requires, inevitably, deliberate shaping by a political agency. Following the tradition of political thought derived from the Romans and given its modern extension by Machiavelli and Hobbes, Mandeville adopts the premise that it is the very essence of government, because it bears responsibility for the human beings in its charge, to try to maximize what it understands to be the public benefit. But he draws from this a significant new implication: that if extremism in the pursuit of the public benefit is no vice, then (given that industries driven by private vice are fertile producers of the public benefit) it follows that to become the managers and panderers of these industries is for their practitioners no vice at all.

MANDEVILLE'S PHILOSOPHICAL ANTHROPOLOGY

Whether, as has sometimes been claimed, Bernard Mandeville was himself a strict moralist, a sort of secular inheritor of the seventeenth-century Jansenist moral outlook, is not a question we should undertake to explore here.[75] Certainly his contemporaries took him to be precisely the opposite, an apologist for the worst kind of moral laxity. What is clear is that the strict Augustinian moralism of the Jansenists provided Mandeville with a platform from which to assault the cherished platitudes of his age. Laying one of the key foundations of the emerging commercialist ideology – albeit

---

[74] It is abruptly mentioned, and then just as abruptly dropped, in the most influential study spanning the whole literature of pre-Smithian capitalist writings, Albert Hirschmann's *The Passions and the Interests* (Princeton University Press, 1977). (Hirschmann's account does not follow up on this particular suggestion, but its many other virtues have made it an indispensable guide to pursuing the interpretation of parts of that literature that forms the next two chapters.)

[75] On this question, see further Hector Monro, *The Ambivalence of Bernard Mandeville* (Clarendon Press, 1975), a study which (as its title suggests) arrives at no firm conclusion about whether or not to characterize Mandeville as a genuine moralist, but which nevertheless contains several useful suggestions about Mandeville's thought. Philip Pinkus, in "Mandeville's Paradox," in Irwin Primer, ed., *Mandeville Studies* (Martinus Nijhoff, 1975), makes the unusual move of treating Mandeville's orthodoxy seriously, with interesting results. Henry W. Spiegel, in "Adam Smith's Heavenly City," *History of Political Economy* 8 (1976): 478–493, takes the opposite view.

in the ambiguous and satirical form appropriate to his "paradox" – Mandeville was stepping through a door the Jansenists had unwittingly opened. The Jansenists would have been thoroughly scandalized to see it put to such a use, and even the more conventional moral thinkers of Mandeville's age did not at first quite know how to cope with this immoralist assault firmly grounded in the most rigid Augustinian moralism.

Mandeville's infamous *Fable of the Bees* began life in 1705 as a piece of doggerel, one of several he had written on moral themes, entitled "The Grumbling Hive: or Knaves Turn'd Honest." For almost a decade, the poem went largely unnoticed, but in 1714 a volume entitled *The Fable of the Bees* (volume one, as it was to turn out), was published anonymously, containing the poem and an extensive commentary on practically every line from the piece. By 1723 it had drawn so much criticism that the Grand Jury of Middlesex censured the book as a public nuisance, and the most prominent moral philosophers of the day weighed in to attack its thesis. In 1728 there followed a second part of the *Fable*, also published anonymously, consisting of a dialogue between a proponent of the original *Fable* and a critical but open-minded representative of decent society.[76]

Mandeville's central metaphor was carefully chosen: since antiquity, the beehive had served as a symbol of how self-seeking animal nature could yet be harnessed to produce cooperative, mutually beneficial effects.[77] Humanity's fundamentally animal nature served as a central premise of Mandeville's theory, and in the *Fable*'s introduction he signals his indebtedness to the two great modern political philosophers who had focused on humanity's animal nature, Machiavelli and Hobbes. Mandeville practically quotes from the crucial Chapter 15 of *The Prince*: "One of the greatest Reasons why so few People understand themselves, is, that most Writers are always teaching Men what they should be, and hardly ever trouble their Heads with telling them what they really are."[78] And when Mandeville comes to spell out his realism, it has a distinctly Hobbesian flavor: he believes "meer man, in the State of Nature" to be "a compound of various Passions, that all of them, as they are provoked and come uppermost, govern him by turns, whether he will or no . . ."[79]

[76] On the publication history of the *Fable*, see the account in F. B. Kaye's "Introduction" to his edition of the *Fable*.
[77] Cicero, *De Officiis*, ed. and trans. Walter Miller, Loeb Classical Library (Harvard University Press, 1913), 1.157, p. 160; Thomas Hobbes, *Leviathan*, ed. Richard Tuck (Cambridge University Press, 1991), ch. 17, pp. 119–120.
[78] Bernard Mandeville, *Fable of the Bees* vol. 1 (hereafter *FB*1), ed. F. B. Kaye, (Oxford University Press, 1924), Introduction, p. 39.
[79] Ibid., pp. 39–40.

Mandeville's indebtedness to both Machiavelli and Hobbes is shown further by the philosophical anthropology Mandeville lays bare in his opening essay, "An Enquiry Into the Origin of Moral Virtue." Mandeville bases his account of early human beings on the assumption of the priority of self-love among them. Prior to the establishment of society, these "untaught animals" look solely after their own selfish pleasures without regard for others.[80] Mandeville's account of pride and related vices is drawn straight from the Jansenist moral psychology:[81] pride, Mandeville asserts, is "so inseparable from [man's] very Essence (however cunningly soever some may learn to hide or disguise it) that without it the Compound he is made of would want one of the chiefest Ingredients"; it is "so riveted in our natures, that there is no profession, nor no set of men, but what would lord it, and tyrannize over all the rest if they could."[82]

But, Mandeville tells us, following Nicole almost word for word, these radically self-oriented creatures in the state of nature soon encountered a difficulty: others were equally self-oriented, and therefore equally unlikely to be disposed to aid them in achieving their own hearts' desires. As a consequence, it became necessary to contrive a strategy to make people believe it to be "more beneficial for every Body to conquer than indulge his Appetites, and much better to mind the Publick than what seemed his private interest," and this according to Mandeville was the original aim of all government.[83] Thus we find in Mandeville an important advance from Nicole's theory: whereas Nicole envisions the useful features of pride and related vices as arising due to individual moral failings, Mandeville sees it as a *social* solution to a fundamentally social problem. In order to achieve

---

[80] *FB* I, Enquiry Concerning Virtue (hereafter Enquiry/Virtue), p. 41.

[81] Mandeville defines pride as "that Natural Faculty by which every Mortal that has any Understanding over values and imagines better Things of himself than any impartial Judge, thoroughly acquainted with all his Qualities and Circumstances, could allow him" (*FB* I, Remark M, p. 124).

[82] *FB* I, Enquiry/Virtue, pp. 44–45; Bernard Mandeville, *Free Thoughts on Religion, The Church, and National Religion*, intro. Stephen H. Good (Scholars' Facsimiles and Reprints, 1981), ch. 10, p. 306. It may exist in a variety of forms, moderate or excessive. When indulged moderately, our self-liking and desire of applause and approval often "stirs us up to good actions," and our relative control over its force will make us endeavor to ensure that it is "kept out of sight, or is so well disguis'd as not to appear in its own Colours." When excessive, we are unable to control and conceal it, and it is this part of self-liking alone that "gives Offence to others, renders us odious, and is call'd Pride." But this last is regrettably the more common application, and exercises over us an extraordinary power. For those who have developed a taste for it (and everyone does to some extent), Pride "doubles our Happiness in Prosperity, and buoys us up against the Frowns of Adverse Fortune"; it is "the Mother of Hopes, and the End as well as the Foundation of our best Wishes," our "strongest Armour against Despair." Bernard Mandeville, *An Enquiry into the Origin of Honour, and the Usefulness of Christianity in War*, intro. M. M. Goldsmith (Cass Reprint, 1971) (hereafter *Enquiry/Honour*), 1st Dialogue, pp. 3, 6–7; *FB* II, 3rd Dialogue, p. 136.

[83] *FB* I, Enquiry/Virtue, p. 42.

social cooperation, Mandeville argues, it was necessary for these early leaders to contrive an "imaginary" reward that could serve as a "general Equivalent for the trouble of Self-denial," and what was hit upon was flattery, taking advantage of the natural human love of praise derived from self-love.[84] So men were gradually taught to view honor as the greatest good and shame as the greatest evil. Indeed, the very difficulty of overcoming our selfish passions was enlisted as an argument to prove "how glorious the Conquest of them was on the one hand, and how scandalous on the other not to attempt it."[85]

Moreover, the creation of this order of values was, as Mandeville repeatedly insists, a deliberate political act. Throughout his works Mandeville draws attention to the guiding action of "Moralists" and "Politicians" in the creation of human values (as we will explore in greater detail below). By the terms "Moralists" and "Politicians," Mandeville refers quite broadly to the whole class of people who through a study of human nature "have endeavour'd to civilize Men, and render them more and more tractable, either for the Ease of Gouvernors and Magistrates, or else for the Temporal Happiness of Society in general."[86] Moralists and politicians, discovering that quarrelsome men could be restrained better by their fear of shame than even by the fear of God, resolved to augment this fear in such men "by an artful Education."[87] These politicians introduced an imaginary distinction between two classes of human beings. Some human beings, they told their fellow men, were of the low-minded and intemperate class, "always hunting after immediate Enjoyment, . . . wholly incapable of Self-denial, and without regard to the good of others," with "no higher Aim than their private Advantage."[88] In contrast to this lower and more selfish class of people, the politicians extolled the worth of a few "lofty high-spirited Creatures, . . . free from sordid Selfishness," who, "making a continual War with themselves to promote the Peace of others, aim'd at no less than the Publick Welfare and the Conquest of their own Passion."[89] The boldest of these men strove to be worthy of their own pride, and even the less resolute had at least enough pride to attempt to conceal their selfish impulses.[90]

The politician thus created this imaginary reward of pride, and a corresponding imaginary illness of shame, for the purpose of domesticating his fellow creatures. This imaginary illness is not necessarily a fatal disease: for the same politician who introduces it has a treatment to prescribe for it.

---

[84] Ibid., p. 43.   [85] Ibid.   [86] *Enquiry/Honour*, 1st Dialogue, pp. 40–41.   [87] Ibid., p. 40.
[88] *FB* 1, Enquiry/Virtue, p. 43.   [89] Ibid., p. 44.   [90] Ibid., pp. 44–45.

By "a dextrous Management of our selves, a stifling of our Appetites, and hiding the real Sentiments of our Hearts before others," we are able to avoid those causes that provoke a troublesome sense of shame. These actions will treat shame's negative effects, though they will not cure it, and this is by design, because of the manifest social utility that shame serves.[91] Thus it was this "skilful Management of wary Politicians" that was the motive force which first led man to undertake "crossing his Appetites and subduing his dearest Inclinations."[92] By these means "Savage Man was broke"; and thus were "the first Rudiments of Morality, broach'd by skilful Politicians, to render Man useful to each other as well as tractable."[93] Since the promotion of public-spiritedness is in the interest of all, even of the very worst men, so that the labor and self-denial of others might make things easier for ourselves, we quickly came to agree to call by the name of vice every self-gratifying action that held out the least prospect of injury or diminished capacity for service to others; and to call virtue every action by which man intended to benefit others or conquer his passions.[94] And thus there is a very plain explanation for the origin of the moral virtues: they are simply "the Political Offspring which Flattery begot upon Pride."

However, this politically produced beneficence does not, on Mandeville's account, reflect an underlying psychological reality of charitable dispositions. Despite universal agreement with the proposition that "the good of the whole society, or the majority of it, ought to be preferr'd to the advantages of private persons," a person will usually find upon examination "that he loves himself better than he does all the rest of mankind."[95] Indeed, Mandeville observes that we are taught this habit of self-preferment from the very beginning of our lives, since "the first thing our nurses bid us is to take care of our selves."[96] It is for this reason, Mandeville argues, that human beings began to develop from the very earliest of their interactions after the Flattery Revolution a capacity for concealing their fundamental selfishness from one another. For once the establishment of a higher class of ascetic human beings had been accomplished, those who lacked the mettle to deny themselves pleasures did not wish also to deny themselves the benefits of being (incorrectly) honored by association with it. So concealing their faults and parroting the same moral views as their fellows, and industriously

[91] *FB* I, Remark C, p. 68.
[92] *FB* I, Enquiry/Virtue, pp. 51–52. It is a process that continues even to this day, as "Sagacious Moralists" continue to "draw Men like Angels, in hopes that the Pride at least of Some will put 'em upon copying after the beautiful Originals which they are represented to be."
[93] Ibid., pp. 46–47.   [94] Ibid., p. 48.
[95] *Free Thoughts*, pp. 283–284.   [96] Ibid. p. 284.

"hiding their own Imperfections as well as they could," they proceeded to "cry up Self-denial and Publick-spiritedness as much as any."[97]

Mandeville sees the practice of hypocrisy as the fundamental glue that holds human society together.[98] But the establishment of these practices of hypocrisy also had an additional political usefulness for its creators, for it made the task of the politicians and moralists in shaping the new ethic immeasurably easier by creating an alternative to resistance among those who might potentially lose out under the new code of honor.[99] Hypocrisy, Mandeville asserts, is "utterly necessary" to human existence: it was "impossible we could be sociable Creatures" without it, for "if by Art and prudent Dissimulation" we had not learned to "hide and stifle" our ideas of our own superiority over others, "all Civil Commerce would be lost."[100]

---

[97] *FB* 1, Enquiry/Virtue, p. 45.

[98] Mandeville distinguishes between what he calls the "Malicious" and the "Fashionable" forms of hypocrisy. The malicious hypocrites are those who "pretend to a great Deal of Religion, when they know their Pretensions to be false; who take Pains to appear Pious and Devout, in order to be Villains, and in Hopes that they shall be trusted to get an Opportunity of deceiving those, who believe them to be sincere." The fashionable hypocrites, by contrast, counterfeit their exterior out of a desire to imitate, as for example those who put on a show of devotion, not from religious belief but from a desire to be "in the fashion." The first class of hypocrites, the "malicious," are dangerous, especially in positions of political authority, because the more men must deliberately keep up a front of false virtue or religion, "the less fit they are to judge others." This is because "hypocrites are under greater temptation to be cruel, than other sinners; because they are always in hopes that we shall judge (as many are fools enough to do) of the holiness and purity of their hearts from the hatred and strong aversion they outwardly express against vice, which must make them unmercifully severe against the least frailties of others." The second class of "fashionable" hypocrites, by contrast, should hardly be called hypocrites at all, "when they set out with no ill design, and by their fair appearance, deceive themselves more, ten to one, than they can do others of any tolerable experience." Such is our human capacity for human self-deception that they can imagine themselves to be performing a Christian duty while indulging the most uncharitable of impulses. For these reasons, Mandeville argues, while the malicious hypocrites are "the worst of men," the fashionable hypocrites are in fact "rather beneficial to Society, and can only be injurious to themselves." *Enquiry/Honour*, pp. 200–202; *Free Thoughts* ch. 10, p. 314; ch. 2, p. 36.

[99] *FB* 1, Enquiry/Virtue, p. 46.

[100] *FB* 1, p. 348. Though hypocrisy is necessary to human society, it is nonetheless not without its dangers. The human being "as a Member of a Society and a taught Animal" develops a peculiar set of dangerous qualities: "As soon as his Pride has room to play, and Envy, Avarice, and Ambition begin to catch hold of him, he is rous'd from his natural Innocence and Stupidity. As his Knowledge increases, his Desires are enlarg'd, and consequently his Wants and Appetites are multiply'd; Hence it must follow, that he will be often cross'd in the Pursuit of them, and meet with abundance more disappointment to stir up his Anger in this than his former Condition, and Man would in a little time become the most hurtful and noxious Creature in the World, if let alone, whenever he could over-power his Adversary, if he had no Mischief to fear but from the Person that anger'd him. The first Care therefore of all Governments is by severe Punishments to curb his Anger when it does hurt, and so by increasing his Fears prevent the Mischief it might produce … The only useful Passion then that Man is possess'd of toward the Peace and Quiet of a Society, is his Fear, and the more you work upon it the more orderly and governable he'll be; for how useful soever Anger may be to a Man, as he is a single Creature by himself, yet the Society has no manner of occasion for it" (*FB* 1, Remark R, pp. 205–207).

As a consequence not only selfishness but concealment of it become part of the necessary training in what it means to be human: we are taught not only to take care of ourselves, but also "insensibly to be Hypocrites from [the] Cradle."[101]

More generally, Mandeville never claims that the beneficial effects of pride should alter our judgments of those who do evil themselves: on the contrary, he holds that "men are not to be judg'd by the Consequences that may succeed their Actions, but [by] the Facts themselves, and the Motives which it shall appear they acted from."[102] This can be somewhat obscured by the fact that, as his quasi-Augustinian moral psychology would suggest, it is difficult to know from what motive our conduct proceeds in any particular case. But for Mandeville this opacity does not make intention any less crucial in evaluating the true moral facts of a situation. There is, he maintains, "a vast difference between not committing an immorality from a principle of pride and prudence, and the avoiding of sine for the love of God."[103]

Instead, Mandeville's moral psychology further refines the project, begun in Augustine and advanced by Nicole, of separating the moral significance of the intentions behind human action from the effects or consequences which that action tends to produce. In doing so, Mandeville establishes the psychological preconditions necessary to sustain his extension of the Machiavellian idea into the commercial realm and consequently to the everyday actions of citizens and consumers.

THE POWER OF PRIVATE VICES

Thus, according to Mandeville, those qualities that genuinely count as moral vices are the same qualities that help to fuel the commercial economy with all its beneficial effects. This was outrageous stuff when Mandeville pronounced it: so much so that practically every moral theorist for a generation felt obliged to offer some sort of refutation of Mandeville's scandalous doctrine. Yet, according to Mandeville, there is nothing in this

---

[101] *FB* 1, pp. 348–349. From the point of view of our moral evaluation of the agents in question, this strategy of hypocritical concealment does not necessarily make much difference. Mandeville insists that he does not mean to claim that it makes no difference what motive our conduct proceeds from. On the contrary, "there is a vast difference between not committing an immorality from a principle of pride and prudence, and the avoiding of sine for the love of God." But it is also true that the strategy of hypocritical concealment, particularly from ourselves, serves to obscure the matter of moral judgment of human action significantly. Our ability to be mistaken on this score is extensive and profound. *Free Thoughts* ch. 1, p. 11.
[102] *FB* 1, Remark G, p. 87.   [103] *Enquiry/Honour*, 1st Dialogue, p. 12.

"paradoxical" dynamic that should really surprise us. It is just an inelimin-able fact of human existence, he rather startlingly concludes, that "the worldly interest of the society often interferes with the eternal welfare of every particular Member of it."[104]

> Vast numbers throng'd the fruitful Hive;
> Yet those vast Numbers made 'em thrive;
> Millions endeavouring to supply
> Each other's Lust and Vanity . . .
> These were call'd Knaves, but bar the Name,
> The grave Industrious were the same;
> All Trades and Places knew some Cheat,
> No Calling was without Deceit.[105]

In making his case that private vices constitute public benefits, Mandeville relies particularly on a variety of vices he associates with the commercial sphere. One such vice was dishonesty: for, according to Mandeville, commercial transactions depend by their very nature upon deceit. "What all sellers endeavour with the utmost care to conceal from the buyers," he observes, is the very "intrinsical value and prime cost of things," which would be the most useful information in negotiating a just exchange.[106] Buyers and sellers outwit one another by "innumerable Artifices" which "the fairest of *Dealers*" approve; no tradesman, for example, will disclose "the Defects of his Goods" and every tradesman has at least occasionally "industriously conceal'd them, to the detriment of the Buyer."[107] These are just the facts of business:

Few men can be persuaded that they get too much by those they sell to, how Extraordinary soever their Gains are, when at the same time there is hardly a Profit so inconsiderable, but they'll grudge it to those they buy from; for this Reason the Smallness of the Seller's Advantage being the greatest persuasive to the Buyer, Tradesmen are generally forc'd to tell Lies in their own Defence, and invent a thousand improbable Stories, rather than discover what they really get by their Commodities.[108]

---

[104] *Free Thoughts* ch. 1, p. 12.   [105] *FB* 1, pp. 18–20.
[106] *Free Thoughts* ch. 10, p. 292.   [107] *FB* 1, Remark B, p. 61.
[108] *FB* 1, Remark D, pp. 80–81. For Mandeville, there is no kind of business that does not engage with passions fueled by human desires, and because of this there is none that will not depend at some point or other upon the baldest deception for its efficient operation. "How gay and merry does every Face appear at a well-ordered Ball, and what a solemn Sadness is observ'd at the Masquerade of a Funeral!" Mandeville points out. Yet these appearances are frequently nothing more than appearances: for "the Undertaker is as much pleas'd with his Gains as the Dancing-Master . . . and the Mirth of the one is as much forced as the Gravity of the other is affected" (*FB* 1, p. 349).

But according to Mandeville the most important vice for motivating socially beneficial behaviors is pride. The peculiar importance of pride in Mandeville's scheme is the unique power it has to motivate a taste for luxury. We owe our greatest public benefits, Mandeville believes, precisely to pride and the fashions it gives rise to, "this Emulation and continual striving to out-do one another . . ."[109]

> Thus Vice nurs'd Ingenuity,
> Which join'd with Time and Industry,
> Had carry'd Life's Conveniencies,
> It's real Pleasures, Comforts, Ease,
> To such a Height, the very Poor
> Liv'd better than the Rich before
> And nothing could be added more.[110]

The scope of our modern necessities has broadened, Mandeville observes, "so that many things which were once look'd upon as the Invention of Luxury, are now allow'd even to those that are so miserably poor as to become the Objects of publick Charity, nay counted so necessary, that we think no Human Creature ought to want them."[111] Luxury cannot be defined as anything beyond the immediate necessities of subsistence, Mandeville argues, for then everything in the world, except perhaps water, would properly be called a luxury.[112] But if we once depart from this restricted definition of luxury, Mandeville maintains, "then there is no Luxury at all; for if the wants of Men are innumerable, then what ought to supply them has no bounds."[113] A simple shopkeeper

must have two Dishes of Meat every Day, and something extraordinary for *Sundays*. His Wife must have a Damask Bed against her Lying-in, and two or three Rooms very well furnished: The following Summer she must have a House, or at least very good Lodgings in the Country ... [This means the shopkeeper] must have a Horse; his Footman must have another [and in time a coach] ... [Eventually he hopes] he shall be worth at least a thousand a Year for his eldest Son to inherit, and two or three thousand Pounds for each of his other Children to begin the World with; and when such Men of Circumstances pray for their daily Bread, and mean nothing more extravagant by it, they are counted pretty modest

---

[109] *FB* 1, Remark M, p. 130. This basic fact of luxury is beyond political control, Mandeville claims. There is only one way to render a nation generally frugal, he tells us, and that is through necessity: "let the best Politician do what he can," a populous and wealthy nation will "in spite of his Teeth" be lavish when circumstances permit. *FB* 1, Remark Q, p. 183.
[110] *FB* 1, p. 26.   [111] *FB* 1, Remark P, p. 169.   [112] *FB* 1, Remark L, p. 108.   [113] Ibid., p. 107.

People. Call this Pride, Luxury, or what you please, it is nothing but what ought to be in the Capital of a flourishing Nation."[114]

Thus pride, a great sin, fuels luxury, a sinful practice: yet it is certain, Mandeville argues, that "we are possess'd of no other Quality so beneficial to Society, and so necessary to render it wealthy and flourishing."[115] For in a way Mandeville's signature claim is that it is precisely pride and pride's consequences "that sets the Poor to Work, adds Spurs to Industry, and encourages the skilful Artificer to search after further Improvements."[116]

> The Root of Evil, Avarice,
> That damn'd ill natur'd baneful Vice,
> Was Slave to Prodigality,
> That noble sin; whilst Luxury,
> Employ'd a Million of the Poor,
> And odious Pride a Million more;
> Envy it self, and Vanity,
> Were Ministers of Industry ...[117]

This belief that the taste for luxuries leads to consistently expanding production reveals the ultimate logic behind Mandeville's contention that vices and evils are inexorably connected to the creation of large-scale economic benefits. To understand this, we must first observe Mandeville's intriguing tendency to connect the idea of "evil" directly with the concept of "want." When we say that we "want" something, we may mean either that we desire it or that we lack it (or both). For Mandeville, this is a deep connection: the very concept of "evil" refers properly to "every Defect, every Want" of human existence.[118]

---

[114] *FB* I, Remark Y, pp. 247–248. Obviously such a view is in tension with the traditional asceticism associated with Christianity (at least as formally advanced in traditions drawing upon the moral psychology of St. Augustine). But fortunately the realities of the situation are something to which the actual practices of the contemporary Church have become nicely adapted, Mandeville suggests. Contemporary Christian ministers assure their parishioners that "to indulge themselves in all earthly Pleasures and Sensualities, that are not clashing with the Laws of the Country, of the Fashion of the Age they Live in," so long as such enjoyment is moderate, "is no moral wrong"; and that "Nothing ought to be deem'd Luxury, that is suitable to a Person's Rank and Quality, which he can purchase without hurting his Estate, or injuring his Neighbour." Here as elsewhere religion yields, as it must, to the demands of politics, and never the reverse: "the Politician must have his Business done: Necessity is pleaded, and Religion ever made to give Way to the Urgency of Affairs"; and the Christian clergy have become willing accomplices in this subordination. *Enquiry/Honour*, 2nd Dialogue, pp. 104–105; 4th Dialogue, p. 212.
[115] *FB* I, Remark M, p. 124. [116] Ibid., p. 130. [117] *FB* I, p. 25.
[118] This is especially intriguing because Augustine's theology pioneered the view that evil was a kind of absence or defect of goodness, rather than a positive force in its own right. See further Herbert

From this connection follows Mandeville's intriguing understanding of the relationship between "evil" and the production of public benefits. For Mandeville, our perceived "wants" (which the taste for luxury helps to generate) tend to motivate "all those mutual Services which the individual Members of a Society pay to each other"; and consequently "the greater [the] Variety" of wants, "the larger [the] Number of Individuals [who] might find their private Interest in labouring for the good of others, and united together, compose one Body."[119] He continues:

Is there a Trade or Handicraft but what supplies us with something we wanted? This Want certainly, before it was suply'd, was an Evil, which that Trade or Handicraft was to remedy, and without which it could never have been thought of. Is there an Art or Science that was not invented to mend some Defect? Had this latter not existed, there could have been no occasion for the former to remove it . . . The many hands that are employ'd to supply our natural Wants, that are really such, as Hunger, Thirst, and Nakedness, are inconsiderable to the vast Numbers that are all innocently gratifying the Depravity of our corrupt Nature; I mean the Industrious, who get a Livelihood by their honest Labour, to which the Vain and Voluptuous must be beholden for all their Tools and Implements of Ease and Luxury.[120]

Want, and whatever creates want, is the engine ultimately driving industry and invention. Human beings, Mandeville believes, have always thrived most when most deprived. Not that deprivation is good: in fact it is the very definition of "evil" for Mandeville. Yet at the same time, it is this evil and nothing else that provides humanity's strongest and most reliable motivation for action. Without such evils, Mandeville claims,

as you need not fear great Vices, so you must not expect any considerable Virtues. Man never exerts himself but when he is rous'd by his Desires: While they lie dormant, and there is nothing to raise them, his Excellence and Abilities will be for ever undiscover'd, and the lumpish Machine, without the Influence of his Passions, may be justly compar'd to a huge Wind-mill without a breath of Air. Would you render a Society of Men strong and powerful, you must touch their passions. Divide the Land tho' there be never so much to spare, and their Possessions will make them Covetous: Rouse them, 'tho but in Jest, from their Idleness with Praises, and Pride will set them to work in earnest . . .[121]

Mandeville's premise here, drawn in part from his distinctive philosophical anthropology, is the claim that human beings are "naturally

A. Deane, *The Political and Social Ideas of St. Augustine* (Columbia University Press, 1963), as well as the related treatments by Hannah Arendt in *Love and Saint Augustine* (University of Chicago Press, 1996) and *Eichmann in Jerusalem* (Penguin, 1963).
[119] *FB* 1, Vindication, pp. 402–403.   [120] Ibid.   [121] *FB* 1, Remark Q, p. 184.

selfish, unruly, and head-strong creatures." What makes them sociable is not any mutual benevolence or generosity toward other human beings: it is rather their mutual dependence on one another.[122] Moreover, what motivates this mutual assistance is "the gains or profit accruing to industry for services . . . which in a well-order'd society enables every body, who in some thing or other will be serviceable to the publick, to purchase the assistance of others in other instances."[123]

This frequently concealed, yet utterly dominating, pursuit of our economic self-interest is what enables the commercial market to produce its great public benefits, Mandeville claims. He is ready to grant that money is "the Root of all Evil," that "as an accessary Cause it has done more Mischief in the World than any other one thing besides,"[124] but at the same time he insists that money is of all things the most "absolutely necessary to the Order, Oeconomy, and the very Existence of the Civil Society."[125] And the reason for this is simply that society's foundation is, first, "the Variety of our Wants," and, second, the network of "reciprocal Services" which results.[126]

It is precisely because of our indifference to one another's desires and the intensity of our own selfish predispositions that money has this special importance. No matter how well supplied your neighbor may be with a certain good, no matter how great your need for that particular good is, your only reliable claim on his gift is your possession of "a Consideration which he likes better."[127] For no one, Mandeville insists, "who is at Peace, and has no Contention with any of the Society, will do any thing for a Lawyer; and a Physician can purchase nothing of a Man, whose whole Family is in perfect health."[128] Here again Mandeville draws our attention relentlessly to the fact that, in a world of interdependence, our ability to subsist at one another's hands depends almost entirely on the extensiveness of one another's satisfiable desires. The invention of money aids greatly in answering this dilemma, not merely as a simplifying medium of exchange but as an additional object of covetousness and desire ("by being an acceptable Reward for all the Services Men can do to one another").[129]

> Now mind the glorious Hive and see
> How Honesty and Trade agree.
> The Shew is gone, it thins apace;
> And looks with quite another Face.

---

[122] *Free Thoughts*, On reciprocal duties, p. 283. [123] Ibid. [124] *FB* II, 6th Dialogue, pp. 348–349.
[125] Ibid., pp. 349, 350. [126] Ibid., p. 349; *FB* I, Remark R, p. 221.
[127] *FB* II, 6th Dialogue, p. 349. [128] Ibid. [129] Ibid.

> For 'twas not only that They went,
> By whom vast Sums were Yearly spent;
> But Multitudes that liv'd on them,
> Were daily forc'd to do the same.[130]

This may be a familiar set of thoughts: not only are these ideas repeated throughout Mandeville's writings in one form or another, but they have also been widely adopted by the subsequent tradition of modern political economy. But what may not be so immediately obvious, and is of special interest for our purposes here, is what Mandeville sees as being the unique contribution of these vices to the social process. It is not primarily their constructive, productive energy that in these instances advances the social good, but rather their destructive, consumptive impulses.[131] For as long as these vicious people "continue to wear and otherwise destroy what the Industrious are daily employ'd about to make, fetch, and procure," Mandeville believes, they are "in spight of their Teeth oblig'd to help maintain the Poor and publick Charges."[132] In a world in which we care so little about the well-being of those strangers among us, the destructive and consumptive impulses of scoundrels create precisely the social glue that holds us together – by creating a *need* for one another's labor. Vice, not virtue, is the only reliable producer of interdependence among strangers.

What is often missed about Mandeville's argument is its core motivation. It is because "the Labour of Millions" depends on the activities of the vicious that it is so vital to maintain and even cultivate their vices.[133] In the midst of our moralizing, Mandeville warns, we may fail to recognize our mutual dependence upon them.

It is the sensual Courtier that sets no Limit to his Luxury; the Fickle Strumpet that invents new Fashion every Week; the haughty Dutchess that in Equipage, Entertainments, and all her Behaviour would imitate a Princess; the profuse Rake and lavish heir, that scatter about their Money without Wit or Judgment, buy everything they see, and either destroy or give it away the next Day, the Covetous and perjur'd Villain that squeez'd an immense Treasure from the Tears and proper Food of a full grown Leviathan; or in other words, such is the calamitous Condition of Human Affairs that we stand in need of the Plagues

---

[130] *FB* 1, p. 32.
[131] One of the few writers to draw attention to this aspect of Mandeville's thought is Terence Hutchison in *Before Adam Smith* (Blackwell, 1988), in particular at p. 121.
[132] *FB* 1, Remark G, p. 86.
[133] This point has not been much remarked on in Mandeville scholarship. It should qualify and further complicate some of the distinctions made in Dickey, "Pride, Hypocrisy and Civility," about who precisely Mandeville's paradox is supposed to apply to at given stages of his argument. See further Dickey's article, pp. 406–413.

and Monsters I named to have all the Variety of Labour perform'd, which the skill of Men is capable of inventing in order to procure an honest Livelihood to the vast Multitudes of working poor, that are required to make a large Society: And it is folly to imagine that Great and Wealthy Nations can subsist, and be at once Powerful and Polite without.[134]

This then becomes perhaps the principal task for the government to aim at. "The great Art . . . to make a Nation happy and what we call flourishing," he claims, "consists in giving every Body an Opportunity of being employ'd."[135] Mandeville supports the cultivation of luxurious appetites even when they are vicious, not so much because of the *conveniences* of life that a taste for luxury produces, but rather because of the vastly expanded opportunities for employing human *labor* that such tastes make possible. It is principally to accomplish this end of employing as many people as possible that Mandeville urges the government to make its "first care be to promote as great a variety of Manufactures, Arts, and Handicrafts as Human Wit can invent."[136]

There is, it should be noted, a darker side to Mandeville's concern for motivating labor, an aspect that emerges in Mandeville's discussion of the public policies necessary to provide an adequate manual work force. Much labor is required to keep human beings supplied even with the bare necessities of life, and vastly more labor is required to supply their taste for luxuries and comforts. Consequently societies like those of commercial Europe which allow many of their members to live in idle luxury must of necessity also require "great Multitudes of People" to do the reverse, and "by use and patience inure their Bodies to work for others and themselves besides."[137]

This need for persons accustomed to delivering hard work in exchange for the bare necessities leads Mandeville to his famous opposition to charity schools.[138] Society requires unpleasant labor, reasons Mandeville, and consequently it also requires a large group of people willing to perform such tasks. Mandeville conceives of this group as a distinct class, a "Breed," whom the legislature will "cultivate . . . and provide against their Scarcity as he would prevent the Scarcity of Provision itself."[139] This requires what is tantamount to coercion, for "no Man would be poor and fatigue himself for a Livelihood if he could help it."[140] But here we are aided once again by

[134] *FB* 1, Essay on Charity-Schools. [135] *FB* 1, Remark Q, p. 197. [136] Ibid.
[137] *FB* 1, Essay on Charity-Schools.
[138] This concern of Mandeville's is treated extensively by Monro in *The Ambivalence of Bernard Mandeville*, ch. 4.
[139] *FB* 1, Essay on Charity-Schools, p. 287. [140] Ibid.

that fundamental dependence of human beings upon what is necessary for subsistence: the absolute necessity of food and shelter "makes them submit to any thing that can be bore with," and "the greatest Hardships are look'd upon as solid Pleasures, when they keep a Man from Starving."[141] Labor follows after "want," the conjunction of desire and need: for "if no body did Want no body would work."[142]

If the public requires their work, it follows that the government must procure for the public the necessary precondition of their work: their want. But the government must be careful to cultivate one kind of want and not another: it is their *need* that must be increased, while the range of their desires (unlike those of the consuming classes) must be kept under strict control.[143] Thus the government must contrive to keep this class of people "Ignorant as well as Poor," for "knowledge both enlarges and multiplies our Desires, and the fewer things a Man wishes for, the more easily his Necessities may be supply'd." If their want is sharp but limited, one can keep them "happy . . . and easy under the meanest Circumstances"; but the more they know of what lies beyond their work and subsistence, the less fit they will be "to go through the Fatigues and Hardships of it with Chearfulness and Content."[144] Nevertheless this policy, Mandeville insists, benefits the poor as much as the rich: for "among the labouring People, those will ever be the least wretched as to themselves, as well as the most useful to the Publick, that being meanly born and bred, submit to the Station they are in with Chearfulness."[145]

Thus Mandeville's attitude toward the laboring masses is complex. On the one hand, his entire theory in a sense is geared to confronting the problem that, under increasing commercial sophistication, the *need* of human beings for one another – and thus their self-interested motivation to provide for one another's subsistence – is undergoing rapid and unyielding decay. The cultivation of vice is ultimately the cultivation of vicious desire, that is, of vicious commercial *demand* – because that is the only natural force within human nature which might be sufficiently powerful to counter the speed of that decay. At the same time, we begin to grasp what a bleak picture of human existence really underlies Mandeville's perspective when we observe the depths of bare subsistence for which he is prepared to settle in this bargain. Far from aspiring to a utopian equality for his

---

[141] Ibid.   [142] Ibid.
[143] On the distinction between the consumption of the rich and that of the poor in Mandeville's thought, see further W. A. Speck, "Mandeville and the Eutopia Seated in the Brain," in Primer, *Mandeville Studies*, pp. 70–71.
[144] *FB* I, Essay on Charity-Schools, pp. 287–288.   [145] *FB* II, 6th Dialogue, p. 351.

citizens, in Mandeville's world one is lucky to get even the bare equality at which Hobbes aimed, that of mere mutual survival.

But on Mandeville's account such brutal realism about labor may be necessary given the premises of his own moral psychology. For a related economic consequence of Mandeville's contention that everyone values themselves "above their worth," he observes, is that everyone will predictably "over-rate his Labour."[146] This fact might appear to present a profound obstacle to rational economic coordination. But Mandeville believes that a systematic management of human vices can help to overcome this problem as well. The solution, Mandeville explains, lies in the fact that money "will always be the Standard, which the worth of every Thing will be weigh'd by," so long as due care to supervise its use is taken "by the Legislature."[147] Thus, in a world of boundless self-esteem, what is needed to limit the attendant irrationality is to make money the measure of all things. Everyone must eat and drink: this fact is "the Cement of civil Society."[148] And because our subsistence needs are universal and abject, creatures of pride can yet become sociable: for "let Men set what high Value they please upon themselves, that Labour, which most People are capable of doing, will ever be the cheapest," just as in other areas exchange value attends on what is scarce, not what is beneficial.[149]

Prior social theorists – perhaps most notably Hobbes – had held that those brutal pride-driven impulses of natural man conventionally called "evil" were the greatest obstacle to human social cooperation and economic flourishing. Mandeville's theory provides an alternative account that locates the ultimate origin of human sociability in evil itself. For ultimately, Mandeville observes, it is "what we call Evil in this World, Moral as well as Natural," that is "the grand Principle that makes us sociable Creatures," and when once "Evil ceases, the Society must be spoiled, if not totally dissolved."[150]

Hobbes's predecessors, most notably Aristotle, had tended to assert the natural sociability of human beings. Hobbes in contrast had declared that human beings were naturally ill-suited to society and could only be made social by the force of reason and artifice. Mandeville shows us a third option. Human beings are naturally sociable, he grants, but then goes on to assert that this sociability naturally exists only in the aggregate, when large numbers are "joyn'd together and artfully managed."[151] By themselves, human beings are not necessarily built for society, but just as

---

[146] Ibid., pp. 349–350.   [147] Ibid., p. 350.   [148] Ibid.   [149] Ibid.
[150] *FB* I, p. 369; cf. p. 325.   [151] *FB* II, 4th Dialogue, p. 188.

every Grape contains a small Quantity of Juice, and when great Heaps of them are squeez'd together, they yield a Liquor, which by skillful Management may be made into Wine: But if we consider, how necessary Fermentation is to the Vinosity of the Liquor, I mean, how essential it is to being Wine; it will be evident to us, that without great Impropriety of Speech, it cannot be said, that in every Grape there is Wine.[152]

Politics is the science of this process of fermentation, according to Mandeville. Its success depends upon the presence of both virtue and vice among its citizens: society requires both the magnanimity and self-sacrifice of its noble class, on the one hand, and at the same time the pride and hypocrisy of all its citizens, on the other, to bring about society's well-being. There is no particular human being in which vice must absolutely be cultivated – there is room for both heroes and scoundrels among a society's citizens – but both virtue and vice must absolutely be present *in the aggregate* if society is to endure for long. This has been the truth about society from its earliest moments: but it is especially true amidst the new realities of the emerging commercial world. For, as we will see, Mandeville argues that, as modern life increases in complexity, a flourishing society can be maintained only by means of deliberate political management of increasing delicacy and subtlety.

THE POLITICAL MANAGEMENT OF PRIVATE VICE

> This was the State's Craft, that maintain'd
> The Whole of which each Part complain'd:
> This, as in Musick Harmony,
> Made Jarrings in the main agree;
> Parties directly opposite,
> Assist each other, as 'twere for Spight;
> And Temp'rance with Sobriety,
> Serve Drunkenness and Gluttony.[153]

For Mandeville, then, private vices are a necessary component of the process of creating public benefits. But this is not a process that occurs by accident: on the contrary, Mandeville makes clear that his subtitle refers to the *deliberate* conversion of private vices to public benefits "by the

---

[152] Ibid. [153] *FB* 1, p. 24.

dextrous Management of a skilful Politician."[154] In Mandeville's vision of politics, the politician's business is "to promote, and, if he can, reward all good and useful Actions on the one hand; and on the other, to punish, or at least discourage, every thing that is destructive or hurtful to Society."[155] The incentives and regulations necessary to govern any large number of people may be unimaginably numerous, but they will all aim at the same end, "the curbing, restraining, and disappointing the inordinate Passions, and hurtful Frailties of Man."[156] Politicians lack the power to "contradict the Passions, or deny the Existence of them," but they have great power to "guide Men in the Indulgence of them, as they please" (having once made the devil's bargain of acknowledging those same passions to be "just and natural").[157]

> Thus every Part was full of Vice,
> Yet the whole Mass a Paradise ...
> Such were the Blessings of that State;
> Their Crimes conspir'd to make them Great:
> And Virtue, who from Politicks
> Had learn'd a Thousand Cunning Tricks,
> Was, by their happy Influence,
> Made Friends with Vice: And ever since,
> The worst of all the Multitude
> Did something for the Common Good.[158]

Among these manipulations, the most conspicuously successful has been the politician's "happy Contrivance of playing our Passions against one another."[159] To understand this, we need to consider in greater detail the mechanics of Mandeville's political manipulation of ordinary vices.

---

[154] Bernard Mandeville, *A Letter to Dion*, intro. Jacob Viner (Augustan Reprint Society Publication 41, 1953), pp. 36–37. By this phrase "dextrous management," which recurs throughout his writings, Mandeville seems to have in mind such activities as the raising of public money by licensing the importation of superfluities despite the vices they encourage, or taxing or totally prohibiting certain goods while lowering duties on others in such a way as to "turn and divert the Course of Trade which way they please ..." Similarly, he justifies the practice of plea bargaining in capital cases by pointing out that "all Law-givers," because of their responsibility for the public welfare, must be willing "to submit to any Inconveniency, any Evil, to prevent a much greater, if it is impossible to avoid that greater evil at a cheaper rate," again identifying this as an instance of using "skilful Management" to convert private vices to public benefits. *Letter to Dion*, pp. 42–43, 45; *FB* I, Remark L.

[155] *FB* II, 6th Dialogue. Few scholars have devoted significant attention to the important issue of the political guidance of vice in Mandeville's theory. The exception to this inattention is M. M. Goldsmith, *Private Vices, Public Benefits* (Cambridge University Press, 1985), which provides much the best account of political action and especially the political guidance of vice in Mandeville.

[156] *FB* II, 6th Dialogue, pp. 320–321.   [157] *Enquiry/Honour*, p. 28.

[158] *FB* I, p. 24.   [159] *FB* I, Remark N, p. 145.

Mandeville's observation in "The Grumbling Hive" that virtue sometimes "made friends with vice" drew upon a rather old idea, but with a
significant twist: the claim that vices and virtues were neighbors has a
long history in the rhetorical tradition, but they had never been described
as "friends."[160] Mandeville's elaboration on this point shows clearly that
his paradox is not just about private vices and public benefits being
connected in some accidental sense, but about the ordinary commercial
procurer of public benefits being profoundly implicated in the vicious
processes that underlie them.

> It may be said, that Virtue is made friends with Vice, when industrious good
> People ... get a Livelihood by something that chiefly depends on, or is very much
> influence'd by the Vices of others, without being themselves guilty of, or accessary
> to them, any otherwise than by way of Trade, as a Druggist may be to Poisoning or
> a Sword-Cutler to Blood-shed. Thus the Merchant, that sends Corn or Cloth into
> Foreign Parts to purchase Wines and Brandies, encourages the Growth or
> Manufactury of his own Country; he is a Benefactor to Navigation, increases
> the Customs, and is in many ways beneficial to the Publick; yet it is not to be
> denied but that his greatest Dependence is *Lavishness* and *Drunkenness* ... The
> same may be said ... of Mercers, Upholsterers, Tailors, and many others, that
> would be starv'd in half a Year's time, if *Pride* and *Luxury* were at once to be
> banished from the nation.[161]

Thus, for Mandeville part of the political management of private vices
requires an understanding of the way particular vices must be properly
combined in order to produce beneficial results. Take, for example, the
useful ways in which the vices of the greedy person and the spendthrift
may be combined to good effect politically. Greed, Mandeville tells us,
"notwithstanding it is the occasion of so many evils, is yet very necessary to
the Society, to glean and gather what has been dropt and scattered by the
contrary Vice [Prodigality]."[162] Without the avarice of some, "spendthrifts
would soon want Materials; and if none would lay up and get faster than
they spend, very few could spend faster than they get."[163] These two vices
may "appear very opposite, yet they often assist each other."[164] For by
serving as an enabler of prodigality, the greedy man allows his opposite
the spendthrift to return to the realm of public consumption what wealth
had been removed from it, thus becoming "a Blessing to the whole
Society."[165]

---

[160] On this subject see especially Quentin Skinner, *Reason and Rhetoric in the Philosophy of Hobbes*,
     ch. 4 (Cambridge University Press, 1996).
[161] *FB* I, Remark F, p. 85.   [162] *FB* I, Remark I, pp. 24–25.   [163] Ibid., p. 101.
[164] Ibid.   [165] *FB* I, Remark K, p. 103.

Thus avarice and prodigality, though perhaps each undesirable on its own, become in society like "two contrary Poisons in Physick, of which it is certain that the noxious Qualities being by mutual Mischief corrected in both, they may assist each other, and often make a good Medicine between them."[166] Some moralizing types might prefer "frugality" as a mean between the extremes of avarice and prodigality, but anyone arguing this "shews himself a better Man than he is a Politician," Mandeville believes.[167] Frugality is

a mean starving Virtue that is only fit for small Societies of good peaceable Men, who are contented to be poor so they may be easy; but in a large stirring Nation you may soon have enough of it. 'Tis an idle dreaming Virtue that employs no Hands, and therefore very useless in a trading Country, where there are vast Numbers that one way or other must all be set to Work. Prodigality has a thousand Inventions to keep People from sitting still, that Frugality would never think of; and as this must consume a prodigious Wealth, so Avarice again knows innumerable Tricks to rake it together, which Frugality would scorn to make use of.[168]

Through the flattery of pride – and its converse, the dread of shame – these politicians set out to manipulate the emotions of human beings along paths that are morally vicious in order to turn their weaknesses to good public purposes. "Whoever would civilize Men, and establish them into a Body Politick," Mandeville asserts, "must be thoroughly acquainted with all the Passions and Appetites, Strengths and Weaknesses of their Frame, and understand how to turn their greatest Frailties to the Advantage of the Publick."[169] In a sense, the central purpose of the *Fable*, Mandeville finally asserts, is not to criticize the faults of any of society's members, but rather to praise the effective political *guidance* of vice. If he has shown "the Vileness of the Ingredients that all together compose the wholesome Mixture of a well-order'd Society," Mandeville elaborates, it was only "in order to extol

---

[166] Ibid., p. 106.   [167] Ibid., p. 104.
[168] Ibid., pp. 104–105. Mandeville is willing to acknowledge that the cultivation of private vices might be unnecessary "where People are contented to be poor and hardy"; but if they wish to "enjoy their Ease and the Comforts of the World, and be at once an opulent, potent, and flourishing, as well as a Warlike Nation, it is utterly impossible." An increase in desire (in the form of commercial demand) is the inevitable effect of, as well as the cause of, this augmentation of national greatness: for the larger and greater the society, "the more extensive they have rendred the Variety of their Desires, and the more operose the Gratification of them is become among them by Custom." This reflects, according to Mandeville, the relentless march of the progress of human nature: "while Man advances in Knowledge, and his Manners are polish'd, we must expect to see at the same time his Desires enlarg'd, his Appetites refin'd, and his Vices increas'd." *FB* I, Remark X, p. 245, Remark Q, pp. 183–185; *FB* II, 6th Dialogue, p. 350.
[169] *FB* I, Remark R, p. 208.

the wonderful Power of Political Wisdom by the help of which so beautiful a Machine is rais'd from the most contemptible Branches."[170]

Mandeville offered his contemporaries an especially shocking and controversial example of what he had in mind in his notorious argument for publicly managed brothels, *A Modest Defence of Publick Stews*.[171] In that work, Mandeville acknowledges that the disadvantages of prostitution are numerous: it harms the public health, discourages thrift and industry by distraction, increases infanticide, forestalls new marriages and destroys existing ones. But he argues that practically none of these effects are the necessary results of prostitution *per se*, but instead follow only from the lack of good management necessitated by its private, illegal status.[172]

Mandeville's solution is to get government into the prostitution business. By regulating – even running – the trade, the state "will not only prevent most of the mischievous Effects of this Vice, but even lessen the Quantity of Whoring in general, and reduce it to the narrowest Bounds which it can possibly be contain'd in."[173] To his contemporaries' objection that making prostitution public constituted an unacceptable compromise with evil, Mandeville replied that to suppose we can do otherwise is wishful thinking. Sexual passion "is too strong to be opposed by open Force": the most we may hope is that it may be possible to discover "an Expedient to divert it by Policy, and prevent the mischief tho' we can't prevent the Crime."[174] Once these facts are accepted, however, a new range of possibilities for political action presents itself. For he points out that

tho' the Laws can't prevent Whoring, they may yet regulate it; the *Quid* is not in their power, but the *Quomodo* is. A man must Eat, but he may be directed how to Eat. The strongest Curb can't stop an unruly Horse, but the weakest will serve to turn him: And the smallest Stream is not to be obstructed, tho' we can change the Course of the greatest River.[175]

The reason some types of state action cannot curb vice, Mandeville (following the Augustinian moral psychology) asserts, is that what actually constitutes wrongdoing is evil *intention*, which is utterly beyond the scope of state control. Intentions, even if not brought to fruition in action, are themselves fully constitutive of sin: and intentions can neither be observed

---

[170]　*FB* 1, Preface, p. 6.

[171]　On Mandeville's argument for public prostitution, see further Monro, *The Ambivalence of Bernard Mandeville*, ch. 4. It is striking how closely Mandeville's argument for public prostitution tracks contemporary arguments for the legalization of drugs.

[172]　Bernard Mandeville, *A Modest Defence of Publick Stews*, reprint of 1st edition, intro. Richard I. Cooke (Augustan Reprint Society Publication 162, 1973), p. 6.

[173]　Ibid., pp. 11–12.　　[174]　Ibid., p. 57.　　[175]　Ibid., pp. 60–61.

nor forcibly corrected. Not only can the legislature not prevent the sin of fornication (which consists in the intention to gratify rather than the gratification itself), it is even likely to "increase rather than lessen the Desires" by attaching penalties to the execution. One might object that the execution of a sinful desire constitutes a wrong *in addition* to the intention, but this is to play directly into Mandeville's hand. For

> since the Sin of the Intention is entirely out of the *Legislature's* Power, the utmost they can do, with regard to this Sin, is to prevent its being aggravated by actual commission. But the *Publick Stews*, as we have already prov'd, will prevent as much as possible this actual Commission. Therefore the *Publick Stews* will prevent as much as possible this SIN.[176]

Not all evils are within the effective influence of state action, Mandeville wants to claim. Fornication is prohibited by Scripture, but so is "the Eating of Blackpuddings," and the former ought to be of no greater concern to the government than the latter.[177]

Thus Mandeville's theory implies that there is a certain sphere of human action, specifically that characterized by the ethical problem of excessive desires, in which moral evils cannot be effectively reduced by means of state policy. There is instead a distinct area in which governments can and ought to act, but this space is demarcated less by principle than by efficacy. Among the concerns that fall within this sphere of useful state action, perhaps the most important is the government's customary role in the administration of justice, in particular the task of attempting to secure "every one's property and the publick peace, and to prevent any thing being transacted against the interest of the nation or country under their care."[178] In this sphere, the government's particular concern is the prevention of harm, and therefore it will measure out its punishments in proportion to the visible harm to society or its members caused by the actions they sanction.[179] It is of course quite otherwise with moral wrongs more generally, where the harm is to God, and which bear no proportion to the degree of the harm to others but make each offender equally liable to damnation.[180]

It is perhaps not surprising, given the fact that Mandeville sees the cultivation of vice as a necessary task of the political trade, that he believes politics itself to be invariably the scene of considerable vice. It would of course be a "great Blesing to a Nation to have all its public offices filled with

---

[176] Ibid., pp. 70–71.   [177] Ibid., p. 70.   [178] *Free Thoughts* ch. 1, pp. 14–15.
[179] Ibid., p. 15.   [180] Ibid.

capable and virtuous men," Mandeville allows, and adds caustically "look out for such as fast as you can."[181] But such good men are necessarily scarce in politics.[182] Public leadership is "an ungrateful task, when well-perform'd," and "honest men generally fare the worst at it."[183] Yet it remains necessary to society to have effective faculties of political judgment and action. Good men are scarce, but in the meantime "the Places can't stand open, the offices must be served by such as you can get."[184]

So since good men cannot be guaranteed, the best solution is to ensure that bad men behave like good men. This can be done by ensuring that government is "so wisely contriv'd, that every Man of midling Capacity and Reputation may be fit for any of the highest Posts."[185] Like James Madison half a century later, Mandeville asserts that the best constitution of a state will be that "which provides against the worst contingencies, that is armed against knavery, treachery, deceit, and all the wicked wiles of human cunning, and preserves it self firm, and remains unshaken, though most men should prove knaves."[186] The trustworthiness of ministers in positions of responsibility may frequently be ascribed to their virtue and honesty, but more often it is wholly a byproduct of the regulations dictated by the form of government they serve under. In private life "one good Man may take another's Word," but it is not so on the larger scale: a nation "ought never to trust to any Honesty, but what is built upon Necessity; for unhappy is the People, and their Constitution will ever be precarious, whose Welfare must depend upon the Virtues and Consciences of Ministers and Politicians."[187]

*

[181] *FB* II, 6th Dialogue, p. 212.
[182] Mandeville's explanation for this is that those who hate "noise and insincerity" and who have no particular "irregular passion to gratify" will necessarily find court life distinctly disagreeable. And because court intrigues are a "perpetual warfare," men who are concerned with preserving their own moral innocence will strive to avoid a scene where invariably "men are oblig'd to cut their trenches crooked, or be unavoidably expos'd to all the artillery of their enemies' hatred" (*Free Thoughts*, pp. 381–382, 384).
[183] Ibid., p. 382–383.   [184] *FB* II, 6th Dialogue, p. 323.
[185] Ibid., pp. 322–323.   [186] *Free Thoughts* ch. II, p. 332.
[187] *FB* I, Remark Q, p. 190 (referring to the Dutch). In particular, this is to be accomplished by the deterrent power established by the existence of two different institutions of political rule independent from the ordinary executive functions of government: the legislature on the one hand, and the laws themselves on the other. The existence of a legislature is a deterrent to the abuse of power: for "when parliaments are sitting, all the busy part of the year ministers have no great opportunities of doing any considerable damage to the nation, and seldom will attempt it." And the laws themselves, Mandeville asserts in addition, can be "curbs which the boldest as well as the craftiest stand in awe of, and a better security for the people than all the virtues ministers can be possess'd of." The same effect may be produced by checks internal to the executive agency itself. It is the division of labor and authority itself, and not the precise distribution of it, which according to Mandeville produces the needed effect. *Free Thoughts*, p. 384.

At its heart, then, Mandeville's "private vices, public benefits" paradox draws not only on Augustine's moral psychology, but also on the insight (originating with Augustine but fully developed by Nicole) that what Augustine had identified as vices could be made use of in providing for the welfare of society and the needs of its citizens. Augustine of course had thought this was a characteristic feature of the operation of divine providence in the world: and Mandeville, while not explicitly endorsing the underlying theology, also retains the implicit view that some sort of providence indirectly makes use of evil means for good ends. This process is hard for observers to follow, Mandeville acknowledges, not merely because of their moral prejudices but also because of how complex the operation of cause and effect is in social phenomena. Few people are able to understand such complex causal linkages, he tells us, "but those who can enlarge their View, and will give themselves Leisure of gazing on the Prospect of concatenated Events, may, in a hundred places, see *Good* spring up and pullulate from *Evil*, as naturally as Chickens do from Eggs."[188]

It is at this juncture that Mandeville turns to tackle the central problem head on: does he assert that politics requires doing "*Evil that Good may come of it*"? Presented with an opportunity to deny that this is his argument, he chooses instead tacitly to acknowledge that it is. At the same time, however, he tries to redescribe this assertion as being merely the claim that "*of two Evils we ought to chuse the least.*" By introducing this distinction, Mandeville implies that, for ordinary citizens, there is indeed something like a moral dilemma here, that doing evil in some form is inevitable.[189] For if the needs of society cannot be met without private people exhibiting the requisite vices, how can such people *rightly* refrain from the exercise of the actions those vices demand?

In the private case, Mandeville merely raises this worry without fully resolving it: indeed, its unresolved character is at the heart of his continual assertion that his theory constitutes a kind of moral "paradox." But while Mandeville means to leave this question ambiguous with respect to the actions of the private citizen, there is no ambiguity about this claim with respect to the actions of government. Should a private citizen do evil in order to promote the good of society, "this evil Action may possibly answer the Goodness of the Intention," Mandeville asserts. Such wrongdoing will

---

[188] *FB* 1, Remark G, p. 91. This is of course only to say that these vices are necessary, not that they ought to be maximized: Mandeville insists that it is laughable to interpret his doctrine as implying that "the more Mischief Men did, the more they acted for the Publick Welfare." *Letter to Dion*, p. 54.
[189] *Publick Stews*, p. 67.

be "universally condemn'd," and "justly" so, but not on the grounds that doing evil that good may come of it is wrong in itself. Rather, the private citizen is to be criticized for such actions because it constitutes an "unwarrantable Presumption" to perform "a certain Evil, for the Prospect of an uncertain good."[190]

When such an evil is charged to the account of the *legislature*, however, things stand in a very different light.

For they, and they only, are trusted with the Welfare of the *Society*. This Publick Welfare is, or ought to be, the whole End and Scope of their Actions; and they are fully impower'd to do whatever they judge conducive to that End. If their Intentions come up to this, they are certainly in their Consciences acquitted: But as to the World, their Actions, that is, their Laws, are judg'd good or bad, just or unjust, according as they actually prove beneficial or detrimental to the *Society* in general.[191]

Not only is it incorrect to criticize a government for committing evil that good may come of it, but such an accusation is on Mandeville's account entirely incoherent. Any public action which "taking in all its Consequences, really produces a greater Quantity of good . . . must, and ought to be term'd a good Act: altho' the bare Act, consider'd in itself, without the Consequent Good, should be in the highest Degree wicked and unjust."[192]

As an example, Mandeville offers that of a quarantine ship sunk by a storm in the harbor, where the infected survivors, swimming back to shore, are upon landing shot to death on the government's orders. By itself, Mandeville acknowledges, this is "no less than a downright unchristian and inhuman Murther"; but, he adds, "since the Health and Society of the Nation is secured by this severe Precaution, it is no Wonder, if we allow the Action to be not only justifiable, but in the strictest Sense of Morality Just."[193] As another example, Mandeville elsewhere considers the practice of plea bargaining with witnesses who turn state's evidence against their fellow criminals. Permitting such a practice would be "an unpardonable Folly, nay a wicked Action in any Legislature . . . if what is design'd by such extraordinary Conduct, to wit, the Decrease of Thefts and Villanies, might be obtain'd by any other Method."[194] The conclusion to be drawn is that "the only Reason that can be given, why Enacting this is neither Wickedness nor Folly, is Necessity, and the Publick Benefit, which is expected from it."[195]

---

[190] Ibid.   [191] Ibid., pp. 67–68.   [192] Ibid., p. 68.   [193] Ibid., pp. 68–69.
[194] *Letter to Dion*, p. 45.   [195] Ibid., p. 4.

Mandeville ridicules the idea that "either Christianity or Morality could possibly object against a *Scheme*, which is entirely calculated for the Welfare and Happiness of Mankind."[196] For Mandeville, it is unthinkable to suppose that "a Law may be unjust and wicked, tho' it evidently promotes the Publick Good: as if the right enjoyment of this Life was inconsistent with our Happiness in the next."[197] Instead he argues that not only is it true that "no sinful Laws can be beneficial," but that as a direct logical consequence (so he seems to suggest) "no beneficial Laws can be sinful."[198]

It therefore appears that Mandeville's commercialization of the Machiavellian idea, investing ordinary citizens with the ethical excuses previously reserved for the heroic leader, requires, when all is said and done, a return to the more traditional Machiavellian model. For if politicians come to believe, as Mandeville claims, that the nature of political responsibility is such that no evil can be done, provided that good comes of it, then it will inevitably be a feature of political agency that the moral purity of those who exercise power will be at constant risk. Even more so will this be the case in a Mandevillean polity, where one of the certainties of public life is that it will require the cultivation of private vice by deliberate policy in order to procure those public benefits on which each member of the society depends.

Mandeville believes his account of the beneficial features of well-managed private vice is so obvious as to be indisputable: yet he acknowledges that if so it is a truth that is very hard for others to swallow (as the intense focus on refuting Mandeville among eighteenth-century moralists bears out). Despite the obvious implications of facts they do accept, society remains unaccountably resistant to drawing the obvious conclusion that public benefits depend upon the cultivation of private vices. People are willing to acknowledge that hunger is necessary to ensure the species' self-preservation, and that lust is necessary to ensure its continual propagation, but few are willing to concede, "tho' it be equally demonstrable, that in the Civil Society the Avarice of Some and the Profuseness of Others, together with the Pride and Envy of most Individuals, are absolutely necessary to raise them to a great and powerful and ... polite Nation."[199] Yet despite these beneficial effects of pride, the vice itself remains "generally detested."[200] Many people will acknowledge that "among the sinful Nations of the Times, Pride and Luxury are the great Promoters of

---

[196] *Publick Stews*, p. 66. [197] Ibid., p. 67. [198] Ibid., p. 69.
[199] *Letter to Dion*, p. 20. [200] *FB* 1, Remark M, p. 124.

Trade," but these same people "refuse to own the Necessity that in a more virtuous Age, (such a one as should be free from Pride) Trade would in a great Measure decay."²⁰¹ Of course this failure to acknowledge the truth in Mandeville's theory is on his account itself a vice – the vice of hypocrisy – that may well be the most important vice of all in ensuring the proper functioning of society.

It may be for this reason that, when Mandeville closes his analogy of the beehive with an imaginary "curing" of the society of all its vices, it is the vice of hypocrisy more than any other whose absence precipitates the decline of the beehive's public fortunes. The bees, Mandeville tells us, though beneficiaries of all these public vices, could not refrain from hypocritically denouncing them, and each, "tho' conscious of his own [vice] / In others [would] *barb'rously bear none* ..." At last the gods grew angry at the hypocrisy of the bees ("always to rail at what they lov'd"), and Jove resolved to rid the hive instantly of all forms of fraud. Through this device Mandeville pictures to us the dire implications of the vice-less utopia for which his opponents profess to yearn. We see that the changes that follow – yielding not merely pietistic but also economic consequences of the greatest severity – all begin from the moment that "The Mask Hypocrisy's flung down / From the great Statesman to the Clown ..."²⁰²

> The very Moment it departs
> And Honesty fills all their Hearts;
> There shews 'em, like th' Instructive Tree,
> Those Crimes which they're ashamed to see;
> Which now in Silence they confess,
> By blushing at their Ugliness.²⁰³

And thus when Mandeville turns at the conclusion of the poem to offer what he bills as "THE MORAL," it turns out to be the hypocrisy of denying vice's beneficial features at which he principally aims:

> Then Leave Complaints: Fools only strive
> To make a Great an Honest Hive
> T'enjoy the World's Conveniencies,
> Be fam'd in War, yet live in Ease,
> Without great Vices, is a vain
> EUTOPIA seated in the Brain ....
> Fraud, Luxury, and Pride must live,
> While we the Benefits receive ...²⁰⁴

²⁰¹ Ibid. ²⁰² *FB* 1, p. 28. ²⁰³ Ibid., pp. 26–27. ²⁰⁴ Ibid., pp. 36–37.

Thus on Mandeville's theory, modern commercial society, which has now become the indispensable mechanism for supplying human need in all its forms, depends abjectly for its continued existence upon the practice of both vice generally and hypocrisy specifically, not just by its individual members but by society as a whole. The commercial society cannot bear to look at itself; it is like the fallen couple of Eden ashamed to be seen in its naked ambition. To persevere, it needs a strategy to keep its true nature hidden from itself, to render its viciousness, to its own critical eye, invisible. And so it is to the most successful strategy of rendering these features of commercial life invisible, Adam Smith's revisionist moral philosophy and groundbreaking political economy, that we turn in our final chapter.

CHAPTER 6

How dirty hands become invisible:
Adam Smith's solution

> *I came to a phrase that I'd heard before, a strange, upsetting, sort of ugly phrase: ... "the fetishism of commodities." I wanted to understand that weird-sounding phrase, but I could tell that, to understand it, your whole life would probably have to change ...*
>
> *People say about everything that it has a certain value. This is worth that. This coat, this sweater, this cup of coffee ... as if that coat, suddenly appearing on the earth, contained somewhere inside itself an amount of value, like an inner soul ... But what really determines the value of a coat? The coat's price comes from its history, the history of all the people who were involved in making it and selling it and all the particular relationships they had. And if we buy the coat, we, too, form relationships with all of those people, and yet we hide those relationships from our own awareness by pretending we live in a world where coats have no history but just fall down from heaven with prices marked inside. "I like this coat," we say, "it's not expensive," as if that were a fact about the <u>coat</u> and not the end of a story about all the people who made it and sold it ... The cup of coffee contains the history of the peasants who picked the beans, how some of them fainted in the heat of the sun, some were beaten, some were kicked ...*
>
> *For two days I could see the fetishism of commodities everywhere around me. It was a strange feeling. Then on the third day, I lost it, it was gone, I couldn't see it anymore ...* Wallace Shawn, *The Fever*

In Wallace Shawn's short drama *The Fever*, the protagonist finds himself suddenly gifted for two days with the ability to perceive "the fetishism of commodities" in the world around him. But after this brief period of insight, he says, "I lost it, it was gone, I couldn't see it anymore ..." The claim – or at least the hope – of philosophy and critical theory is that human beings can achieve just this sort of insight into our everyday values and practices: to see *through* the taken for granted, to see reality around us as if it was altogether new. The purpose of our endeavor here as well has been to try to jar our accustomed patterns of apprehension a bit in order to see the moral world anew, and in the process to introduce a greater degree of moral ambiguity into our perception of familiar institutions.

But this kind of altered perception is hard to achieve, and, as the example of Shawn's protagonist warns, even harder to maintain. This is true of the modern theory of the state; and, as we will see, it is perhaps even more true of Adam Smith's commercial market. For it is not Nicole's picture of the commercial market, nor Mandeville's, that we have inherited as the reflexive justification for our economic actions. That we have adopted a different and more relaxed attitude toward the market is more than any other factor due to the influential apologetic work produced by Adam Smith, not only in his foundational contribution to economics, but also, if less obviously, in his moral theory. In what follows, we will turn first to see how Smith shaped that moral theory in response to Mandeville's economic problem of dirty hands, before turning in the second part of the chapter to see how Smith's revised moral theory was able to undergird his own economic solution to this apparent set of dilemmas.

SMITH'S CRITIQUE OF MANDEVILLE

When Adam Smith, at the conclusion of the second edition of his *Theory of Moral Sentiments* and at the conclusion of his career, turned his attention to evaluating alternative systems of moral philosophy, he reserved a prominent if ignominious position for Bernard Mandeville in his analysis. Mandeville stands at center stage in Smith's chapter "On licentious systems" of moral theory, in which Smith's assault on Mandeville's *Fable* is unsparingly critical. Yet, at the end of his critique of Mandeville, Smith acknowledges that the Dutch author's system "could never have imposed upon so great a number of persons, nor have occasioned so great an alarm among those who are the friends of better principles, had it not in some respects bordered upon the truth"[1] and had even "a considerable mixture of truth" in it.[2] Smith himself does not tell us in what respect he takes Mandeville's system to border upon the truth. But, by considering the various claims Smith stakes in the rest of the work, we can deduce an answer that is on its face rather surprising. What Smith took to be, at its heart, factually credible was the inner structure of the very "private vices, public benefits" argument we have been considering in Chapter 5.

---

[1] Adam Smith, *Theory of Moral Sentiments* (hereafter *TMS*), ed. D. D. Raphael and A. L. Macfie (Liberty Fund, 1984), VII.ii.4.14, p. 313.
[2] Ibid., p. 314.

In other words, despite his vociferous criticism of Mandeville on a variety of separate isues, Smith nevertheless accepted as fundamentally sound Mandeville's account of the tendency of what he took to be vices to produce social utility. We will return to this issue in a moment.

Where Mandeville stepped wrong, according to Smith, was in his account of what vice actually *was*. Smith tells us that Mandeville's account of morality tends to eradicate the very basis of the distinction between virtue and vice, and is for that reason "wholly pernicious."[3] But when Smith's objections to Mandeville are given a closer inspection, it becomes clear that the brunt of his dissent was directed, not against the structure of Mandeville's core paradox, but rather against the Augustinianism of his moral theory. The flaw of Mandeville's system, Smith claimed, was that Mandeville believed whatever actions were taken "from a sense of propriety, from a regard to what is commendable and praise-worthy" to be done "from a love of praise and commendation, or as he calls it from vanity."[4] Mandeville's account renders self-interest so strong, according to Smith, that benevolence is impossible and every apparent altruism is the cause for the deepest suspicion: for apparently benevolent moral agents instead truly act "from the same selfish motives as at all other times."[5] So, Smith tells us, "all public spirit, . . . all preference of public to private interest, is, according to [Mandeville] a mere cheat and imposition upon mankind"; and virtue, he quotes Mandeville as saying, is thus "the mere offspring of flattery begot upon pride."[6] As we have seen, this is more or less a fair characterization of Mandeville's point of view.

When Smith turns to evaluate this argument, he wastes no time in identifying the central issue at stake between him and Mandeville: it is a normative, and not a factual, disagreement about the force of self-love in human action.

Whether the most generous and public-spirited actions may not, in some sense, be regarded as proceeding from self-love, I shall not at present examine. The decision of this question is not, I apprehend, of any importance towards establishing the reality of virtue, since *self-love may frequently be a virtuous motive of action.* I shall only endeavour to show that the desire of doing what is honourable and noble, of

[3] *TMS* VII.ii.4.6, p. 308.
[4] *TMS* VII.ii.4.7, p. 308. In what follows I have been much helped by the interpretation of this dispute offered in E. J. Hundert, *The Enlightenment's Fable* (Cambridge University Press, 1994), ch. 5.
[5] *TMS* VII.ii.4.7, p. 308. Vanity being the strongest passion, Mandevillean man is willing to forego some present interests for the pleasure and advantage that derive from the good opinion of others: indeed he may in doing so flatter himself with the belief that he is "entirely disinterested."
[6] Ibid., p. 309.

rendering ourselves the proper objects of esteem and approbation, cannot with any propriety be called vanity.[7]

Smith thus chooses deliberately to set aside those questions about the ubiquity of self-oriented motivation that had provided such fertile ground for so many of Mandeville's most prominent eighteenth-century critics.[8] In doing so, Smith implicitly isolates their core disagreement: namely, their widely varying estimation of the *moral* worth of self-love, which as we have seen both Mandeville and the Jansenists had unhesitatingly identified with vanity and pride, in the evaluation of human action.[9]

It quickly becomes apparent just how far Smith is willing to go in the rehabilitation of pride against the old Augustinian moral psychology.[10] To begin with, Smith argues that the love of what is estimable, even in ourselves, cannot properly be called vicious. He has in mind here first the love of virtue, "the noblest and the best passion in human nature"; but "second" he puts "the love of true glory, a passion inferior no doubt to the former, *but which in dignity appears to come immediately after it.*"[11] The term "vanity," Smith says, he would reserve for a more egregious category of cases: those in which one desires praise for qualities that are not praiseworthy, or desires greater praise than the qualities deserve, or desires praise for (praiseworthy) qualities which the agent himself does not possess. Vanity in particular should refer, not to all self-oriented action, but rather

---

[7] *TMS* VII.ii.4.8, p. 309; emphasis added. In fact Smith did possess a view on the question he sets aside about the centrality of self-love in explaining the motivation of human action. Earlier in the *Theory of Moral Sentiments*, he had argued that those writers who deduce everything from the premise of self-love attribute sympathy to a refinement of self-love: a human being, conscious of his dependence upon others, rejoices when others share his passions and grieves when they do not share them, because these coincidences of passion signal the availability of their assistance in his preferred causes. But Smith objects that this is phenomenologically all wrong: both the pleasure and the pain of sympathy "are always felt so instantaneously, and upon such frivolous occasions, that it seems self-evident that neither of them can be derived from any such self-interested consideration." *TMS*, I.i.2.1, pp. 13–14. With respect to Smith's distinction between self-love and self-interest, see also Athol Fitzgibbons, *Adam Smith's System of Liberty, Wealth, and Virtue* (Clarendon Press, 1995), pp. 137–139.

[8] For a helpful treatment of the questions Smith here sets aside, see Charles L. Griswold, Jr., *Adam Smith and the Virtues of Enlightenment* (Cambridge University Press, 1999).

[9] See Bert Kerkhof, "A Fatal Attraction?: Smith's 'Theory of Moral Sentiments' and Mandeville's 'Fable,'" *History of Political Thought* 16 (1995): 217–233, which addresses in a similar vein some of these connections between the two moral theories.

[10] Despite the prominence of Augustinianism in Hundert's account, his treatment of Smith does not touch on this aspect of Smith's thought. At a higher level of abstraction, my argument here runs parallel to Albert Hirschmann's characterization of Smith's project in *The Passions and the Interests* (Princeton University Press, 1977), as that of abandoning the Augustinian project of repressing the passions in favor of a strategy of legitimating the pursuit of interests while simultaneously erasing the distinction between passions and interests. (See particularly pp. 14–15, and 107–108.)

[11] *TMS* VII.ii.4.8, p. 309; emphasis added.

to excessive attention to the "frivolous ornaments of dress and equipage," or to ordinary behavior and good manners; to the desire for "noisy expressions and acclamations" of one's virtue where the "silent sentiments of esteem and approbation" are more appropriate.[12] These indeed are the symptoms of vanity, "the passion of the lowest and the least of mankind"; but it is "altogether different" from the love of virtue and of true glory, which are "the noblest and the greatest" of the passions.[13]

To be sure, all these kinds of behavior have something in common, namely that they "aim at acquiring esteem and approbation"; but they differ in that the love of virtue and the love of true glory have a "just, reasonable, and equitable" claim on our esteem and approbation, while what Smith calls vanity obviously does not.[14] There is nevertheless, according to Smith, a real affinity between "the desire of becoming what is honourable and estimable, and the desire of honour and esteem, between the love of virtue and the love of true glory": and together these share something else in common with mere vanity, namely, "some reference to the sentiments of others."[15] Even a man properly indifferent to the general opinion of mankind can take delight in what others *should* think of him, and such a man thereby "applauds and admires himself by sympathy with" what others' sentiments *ought* to be with respect to his own virtue.[16] Only his own impartial judgment justifies this response, but if he is genuinely impartial then this endeavor to "think himself worthy" of others' admiration becomes, Smith tells us, a "great and exalted motive of his conduct." Indeed, Smith goes so far as to say that such a man can be said to act from "the most sublime and godlike motive which human nature is even capable of conceiving."[17]

PRIDE AND IMPARTIALITY

Adam Smith, then, was intent to argue that what the Augustinian tradition had called the worst vice, pride, was hardly a vice at all, and certainly lacked the grandeur that had come to be attributed to it.[18] Smith's book is filled

---

[12] Ibid., pp. 309–310.   [13] Ibid., p. 310.

[14] *TMS* VII.ii.4.9, p. 310. Though of course it is we ourselves who, assessing the situation with philosophical impartiality, will ultimately have to be the judge of what claims on our esteem are "just, reasonable, and equitable."

[15] *TMS* VII.ii.4.10, p. 310.   [16] *TMS* III.2.5, p. 116; VII.ii.4.10, p. 311.   [17] *TMS* VII.ii.4.10, p. 311.

[18] Central to Smith's moral theory generally was the claim that the virtue or vice of any action ultimately depends upon "the sentiment of affection of the heart" from which it proceeds. These sentiments, Smith goes on to explain, must be distinguished into the causes or motives of action, on the one hand, and on the other the "end which it proposes or the effect which it tends to produce."

with comments that bring this point to light once one is primed to look for it. "The principle of self-estimation may be too high, and it may likewise be too low," Smith observes: we tend to favor high self-estimation in ourselves over its contrary, because the pleasure thus derived is greater, while in others we are much more offended by their pride than by their excessive deference (when we are its object).[19] In fact, in almost all cases, Smith asserts, it is better to err on the side of being a little too proud,[20] a sentiment as foreign to the Augustinian moral psychology as one can get.

Once we have begun to see Smith's criticism of Mandeville as involving centrally a rehabilitation of pride against the attacks of the Augustinian tradition, it becomes easier to spot the vital role this rehabilitation plays in his larger moral theory. The chief instance of this is to be found in Smith's familiar device of the impartial spectator, so influential in the development of both Kantian moral theory and neutralist liberalism, which viewed from this angle begins to take on a new significance.[21] For of course the whole point of the impartial spectator device is that it hinges knowledge of moral worth on rightly judged moral *self-approval.*[22]

We can observe this first in the fact that, for Smith, the proper moral evaluation located in the device of the impartial spectator finds its origin, phenomenologically, in the desire for glory. Smith describes the chain of events thus: "from admiring other people we come to wish to be admired ourselves ... [And] we cannot always be satisfied merely with being admired, unless we can at the same time persuade ourselves that we are in some degree really worthy of admiration."[23] Thus Smith brings in the device of the impartial spectator as a means of providing such proper moral

This in turn yields the structure of Smith's moral philosophy: in the suitableness or unsuitableness of the motive consists the "propriety or impropriety, the decency or ungracefulness" of the action; while in the "beneficial or hurtful nature of the effects which the affection aims at, or tends to produce, consists the merit or demerit of the action, the qualities by which it is entitled to reward, or is deserving of punishment." By thus separating intentions from effects as two separate objects of moral evaluation, Smith's moral theory provided the best possible framework for defusing moral criticism based on motives alone, as had been the case in the Augustinian tradition. *TMS* 1.i.3.5–7, p. 18.

[19] *TMS* VI.iii.22, pp. 246–247.   [20] *TMS* VI.iii.52, pp. 261–262.

[21] See the excellent account of Smith's connection to Kantian moral theory in Samuel Fleishacker, "Philosophy in Moral Practice: Kant and Adam Smith," *Kant-Studien* 82 (1991): 249–269; on the larger trend, see also J. B. Schneewind, *The Invention of Autonomy* (Cambridge University Press, 1997).

[22] It is this emphasis on *self*-approval that constitutes the truly original aspect of Smith's impartial spectator device. Previous writers in Enlightenment moral philosophy had employed the device of the impartial spectator, but Smith is the first to invoke it as a judgment of conscience about *one's own* actions, rather than about the actions of other people. See further Samuel Fleishacker, *On Adam Smith's Wealth of Nations* (Princeton University Press, 2004) and Hiroshi Mizuta, "Moral Philosophy and Civil Society," in Andrew Skinner and T. Wilson, eds., *Essays on Adam Smith* (Oxford University Press, 1975), pp. 114–131.

[23] *TMS* VII.iv.24, p. 336.

self-approval. "We either approve or disapprove of our own conduct, according as we feel that, when we place ourselves in the situation of another man, and view it, as it were, with his eyes and from his station, we either can or cannot entirely enter into and sympathize with the sentiments and motives which influenced it," Smith explains.[24]

This way of viewing moral judgment depends fundamentally on our beliefs and concerns about the judgments of others, in a way that historically had troubled a variety of moral thinkers (Rousseau perhaps the most deeply). On Smith's account, the origin of our moral judgments bears analogy with the regard that a pre-social man might have for the question of his personal appearance. Absent an awareness of the opinions of others regarding his personal beauty, he perhaps would never trouble himself about it. But bring him into contact with his fellow creatures, and he will quickly become greatly concerned with the matter, frequently checking the mirror to see if he looks presentable. Similarly, in the state of nature man follows his passions blindly; but in society, witnessing their effects on other people, he soon wishes to make his moral behavior presentable, and thus must acquire a kind of moral mirror. This is the function of the impartial spectator, and thus of properly executed moral judgment: "anxious to know how far we deserve [others'] censure or applause, ... we begin, upon this account, to examine our own passions and conduct, and to consider how these must appear to them, by considering how they would appear to us if in their situation."[25] Thus the mechanism of the impartial spectator:

I divide myself, as it were, into two persons; and ... I, the examiner, and judge, represent a different character from that other I, the person whose conduct is examined into and judged of ... That the judge should, in every respect, be the same with the person judged of, is as impossible, as that the cause should, in every respect, be the same with the effect.[26]

And so it comes to be that, although proper moral judgment may originate in our desire to merit the praise of others, we find its highest form in our own well-judged self-approval of our actions. Though the mistaken judgments of others with regard to our own worthiness may naturally be upsetting, the impartial spectator within our hearts constitutes a "much higher tribunal" to which the sentence of the censorious world can be appealed.[27] The virtuous person thus desires "not only praise, but

[24] *TMS* III.i.2, pp. 109–110.   [25] *TMS* III.5, p. 112.
[26] *TMS* III.i.6, p. 113.   [27] *TMS* III.ii.32, p. 130.

praiseworthiness; or to be that thing which, though it should be praised by nobody, is, however, the natural and proper object of praise."[28] He will not be satisfied with unearned praise, but where it is justified the love of fame and glory "even for its own sake, and independent of any advantage which he can derive from it, is not unworthy even of a wise man."[29] Even when others fail to acknowledge his virtue, his own self-approbation is "alone sufficient, and he is contented with it."[30] Such self-approbation, Smith goes on to insist, is virtually the sum and substance of morality: it is "if not the only, [then] at least the principal object about which he can or ought to be anxious." Pressing the point even further, Smith goes on to claim that "the love of it [proper self-approbation] is the love of virtue."[31]

Thus Smith's moral theory attempts to rehabilitate self-love; yet there are significant problems with self-love as a moral motivation, as Smith is prepared to acknowledge. To begin with, self-love may be difficult to distinguish from its less desirable relatives among moral phenomena. The person who desires to act in a praiseworthy manner "may likewise desire the praise which is due to it, and sometimes, perhaps, more than is due to it"; in such a case, the two principles are "blended together" such that "how far his conduct may have been influenced by the one, and how far by the other, may frequently be unknown even to himself."[32] Here Smith notes that this resemblance of self-love to related moral phenomena is the reason why "some splenetic philosophers" (the context makes clear that he means Mandeville) have attributed to the love of praise every action done merely out of a desire of achieving praiseworthiness.[33]

In addition, Smith admits that the prominence of self-love in our moral psychology, though unproblematic in its own right, nevertheless causes us to be naturally predisposed *against* impartiality; and this effect of self-love, moreover, is itself the cause of the general indifference of human beings to one another's welfare. We are frequently so blinded by self-love (or in Smith's psychology by the strength of our passions) that our judgment is greatly impaired by this natural inclination against impartiality.[34] Men are naturally sympathetic, according to Smith, and yet remarkably they can

feel so little for another, with whom they have not particular connexion, in comparison of what they feel for themselves; the misery of one, who is merely their fellow-creature, is of so little importance to them in comparison even of a small conveniency of their own; they have it so much in their power to hurt him, and may have so many temptations to do so, that if this principle did not stand up

[28] *TMS* III.ii.1, p. 114. [29] *TMS* III.2.8, p. 117. [30] Ibid. [31] Ibid.
[32] *TMS* III.ii.26, p. 126. [33] *TMS* III.ii.27, p. 127. [34] *TMS* III.iv.2, p. 157.

within them in his defence, and overawe them into a respect for his innocence, they would, like wild beasts, be at all times ready to fly upon him; and a man would enter an assembly of men as he enters a den of lions.[35]

In a famous comparison, Smith goes on to ask us to suppose that "the great empire of China, with all its myriads of inhabitants, was suddenly swallowed up by an earthquake"; what man in Europe, Smith wonders, having expressed his great regret and thoughtfully considered the import of the event, would nevertheless fail to return to his own life with little disturbed tranquillity?

> If he was to lose his little finger to-morrow, he would not sleep to-night; but, provided he never saw them, he will snore with the most profound security over the ruin of a hundred millions of his brethren, and the destruction of that immense multitude seems plainly an object less interesting to him, than this paltry misfortune of his own.[36]

This effect of our self-love, then, is at the root of one of the most important pillars of Smith's economic theory: his awareness of the drastic lack of practical claims which human beings have on one another's benevolence.

Such is the extent of our self-absorption, which Smith has no interest in denying. He acknowledges that "this self-deceit, this fatal weakness of mankind, is the source of half the disorders of human life."[37] But Smith argues that there are two factors Mandeville failed to recognize which mitigate the negative features of excessive self-love. First, Smith feels, the ideal of impartiality offers a normative standard to curb this excess and relieve the problems it creates; and second, the Mandevillian structure of the world means that even these selfish inclinations need not produce radically anti-social effects, but rather can serve as the foundation, even the fuel, of a providential economy.

Genuine impartiality, Smith argues, can thus serve both as a corrective to excessive self-love and as a mechanism by which we can overcome the blinding of our own self-interestedness. In practice, the tool which is most useful for this purpose is the general code of morality, established in our minds as useful rules of thumb by constant reflection on the praiseworthiness or blameworthiness of others' actions.[38] We resolve always to behave with the nobility we have seen our benefactors exhibit, or never to be so boorish or cruel as that man who has offended

[35] *TMS* II.i.3.4, p. 86.   [36] *TMS* III.iii.4, pp. 136–137.   [37] *TMS* III.iv.6, p. 158.
[38] *TMS* III.iv.7–8, p. 159. On this see further Griswold, *Adam Smith*, ch. 5.

us.[39] And these general rules, when internalized with the proper rever-
ence, "are of great use in correcting the misrepresentations of self-love
concerning what is fit and proper to be done in our particular situation."[40] For Smith, this passion for proper self-approbation is
ultimately what makes human beings capable of being truly sociable.
The desire merely for the approbation of others, without the added
desire for authentic and impartial self-approbation, could only have
made man "wish to *appear* to be fit for society"; it could only have
produced "the affectation of virtue" and "the concealment of vice."
Only the desire to be genuinely worthy of his own self-approbation
could render him "anxious to be really fit" for society, and to fill him
"with the real love of virtue, and the real abhorrence of vice."[41]

Smith does not however rely on our moral aspiration for genuine
impartiality alone to counter all the negative effects of self-love. For, as
we will see in greater detail in the following section, without drawing
attention to the resemblances between his theory and Mandeville's,
Smith nevertheless constructs a social and political theory that enlists the
energies of self-love in providing for those public needs and benefits which
he claims benevolence alone could never hope to supply. In this way too the
potentially anti-social effects of self-love are in Smith's theory not merely
countered but coopted and redirected as a tool for producing benefits that
are no part of their real intention.

Notice, then, where Smith's maneuvering has taken us. Self-love is no
longer the root of all evil; it no longer bears any *necessary* relation to vice at
all. It would be impossible, of course, to deny that it frequently has
pernicious effects; but this is simply because passion has distorted our
proper judgment, creating a kind of optical illusion.[42] And we happen to
have on hand a very apt corrective lens, in the device of the impartial
spectator. Impartiality will do; anything more ambitious, such as the
criterion of charity espoused by the Augustinians, has become dispensable.
And so, once the proper corrections have been made, it becomes possible
for self-love, or more precisely self-approval or self-esteem, to take its place
as the indispensable precondition of correct moral judgment. We desire,
and ought to desire, to judge ourselves praiseworthy: this, the "monster

---

[39] *TMS* III.iv.7–8, 11, pp. 159–160. Smith is careful to point out that the rules of morality are established
as inductions from our natural approval or disapproval of certain classes of actions, and never from
an original desire to deduce what a particular rule should be.

[40] *TMS* III.iv.12, pp. 160–161.   [41] *TMS* III.2.7, p. 117; emphasis added.

[42] *TMS* III.iii.2, pp. 134–135.

within our breast" for the Augustinians, has become for Adam Smith the very basis of morality.

Mandeville's moral theory, seen against this backdrop, is simply too hard-edged to suit Smith's taste: its "great fallacy," he argues, is "to represent every passion as wholly vicious, which is so in any degree and in any direction."[43] If a taste for the finer things in life is to be regarded as luxurious even in those who can afford them, Smith acknowledges, then of course "luxury, sensuality, and ostentation are public benefits," since without such a taste "the arts of refinement could never find encouragement, and must languish for want of employment."[44] But this judgment is too stringent. Mandeville treats as "gross luxury and sensuality" any case in which "our reserve with regard to pleasure falls short of the most ascetic abstinence"; anything is luxurious that exceeds what is absolutely necessary for subsistence; even the pleasures of a lawful marriage bed are unchaste sensuality, "so that there is vice even in the use of a clean shirt."[45]

Smith correctly identifies the origin of this view as residing in "some popular ascetic doctrines which had been current before his time"; he seems curiously to think that the doctrines in question were those that placed virtue in "the entire extirpation and annihilation of all our passions."[46] But having accepted these doctrines,

it was easy for Dr. Mandeville to prove, first, that this entire conquest never actually took place among men; and secondly, that, if it was to take place universally, it would be pernicious to society, by putting an end to all industry and commerce, and in a manner to the whole business of human life. By the first of these propositions he seemed to prove that there was no real virtue, and that what

---

[43] *TMS* VII.ii.4.12, p. 312.   [44] Ibid., p. 313.

[45] *TMS* VII.ii.4.11, p. 312. Really of course Mandeville says that there *is* no such thing as luxury properly understood. See ch. 5, pp. 212–213.

[46] *TMS* VII.ii.4.12, p. 313. It is unclear whether Smith had the Augustinians in mind or not. It sounds more like the traditional criticisms of the Stoics, although not precisely like Smith's own more mixed review of Stoic doctrine elsewhere in the *Theory of Moral Sentiments*. It would be odd if Smith were conflating the positions of the Stoics and the Augustinians, since the two camps were sharply at odds and indeed the alleged pride of the Stoics was in fact typically the central issue at stake. One suggestion – which I owe to comments on this manuscript by Christopher Brooke – is that Smith may be deliberately describing Jansenist moral theory in Stoic terms to create a striking parallel between two moral systems generally regarded as antagonistic – drawing attention to the extreme distinction both theories drew between rare virtue and all-too-common vice. On this see further William J. Bouwsma, "The Two Faces of Humanism: Stoicism and Augustinianism in Renaissance Thought," in Heiko A. Oberman and Thomas A. Brady, Jr., eds., *Itinerarium Italicum: the Profile of the Italian Renaissance in the Mirror of its European Transformation* (E. J. Brill, 1975), pp. 3–60, as well as Christopher Brooke, "Rousseau's Political Philosophy: Stoic and Augustinian origins," in Patrick Riley, ed., *The Cambridge Companion to Rousseau* (Cambridge University Press, 2001), pp. 94–123.

pretended to be such, was a mere cheat and imposition upon mankind; and by the second, that private vices were public benefits, since without them no society could prosper or flourish.[47]

In other words, if self-love and pride understood in the Augustinian sense were truly vices, Smith concedes, then Mandeville's paradox would hold. The factual claim that such behaviors as Mandeville criticizes are necessary to generate utility and well-being in a commercial society is taken on board almost completely intact.[48] What is instead required is a new strategy for evaluating these behaviors normatively: not perhaps to try to represent them as positive goods, but at least to understand them as relatively harmless in the larger scheme of things, certainly not the center of the moral universe as they had been for the Augustinians and for Mandeville. Pride or vanity may be base, to be sure, but it is much too base to be morally epic. It rises below vice;[49] it is to be winked at. And thus the dirty hands of Machiavelli's thought, commercialized by Nicole and Mandeville, have been made ready to be rendered by Adam Smith invisible.[50]

THE INVISIBLE HAND

Thus Adam Smith's moral theory attempted to defuse Mandeville's paradox of "private vices, public benefits" by challenging the Augustinian moral psychology that provided its underpinnings, and replacing it with one far less critical of self-love and pride (and the luxurious desires to which they gave rise).[51] We will now turn to see how this substitution of moral psychologies, far from being an abstruse maneuver internal to Enlightenment moral

---

[47] *TMS* VII.ii.4.12, p. 313.

[48] The fact that Smith accepted the general structure of the private vices, public benefits paradox does not mean that he accepted each of Mandeville's applications of it. For example, see the important distinction drawn by Donald Winch in his *Riches and Poverty* (Cambridge University Press, 1996), esp. at p. 77, between Mandeville and Smith on the relative value of prodigality (which Mandeville sees as a crucial generator of economic activity, while Smith views it as at least sometimes a serious obstacle to the productive economic behavior of saving and capital accumulation).

[49] I borrow this phrase from Mel Brooks, who defended his (at the time controversial) film *The Producers* by asserting, "It rises below vulgarity."

[50] One of the very few studies to explicitly connect Machiavelli's thought with the emergence of Smith's defense of capitalism – though quite briefly – is Hirschmann, *The Passions and the Interests*, pp. 33 and following.

[51] In this respect, my argument can be seen as an extension of Hirschmann's assertion in *The Passions and the Interests* that Smith "blunted the edge of Mandeville's shocking paradox by substituting for 'passion' and 'vice' such bland terms as 'advantage' or 'interest.'" I claim that, at an even greater level of abstraction, Smith's purpose was to "blunt the edge" of the Mandevillean paradox by substituting, not just specific terms, but a substantially different evaluation of the same moral phenomena.

From dirty hands to the invisible hand

philosophy, in fact carried profound implications for the political theory of the emerging commercial age.[52]

The broad outline of Smith's argument in the *Wealth of Nations* will be familiar to many contemporary readers, but parts of that argument may take on a new significance in the light of the themes we have been considering. Let us begin by recalling that, on Smith's theory, a nation is supplied with the "necessaries and conveniences of life" according to the skill and judgment with which it is able to engage its labor to produce goods in proportion to the number of those who are to consume them. "Civilized and thriving nations," Smith argues, have so contrived matters that

> though a great number of people do not labour at all, many of whom consume the produce of ten times, frequently of a hundred times more labour than the greater part of those who work; yet the produce of the whole labour of the society is so great, that all are often abundantly supplied, and a workman, even of the lowest and poorest order, if he is frugal and industrious, may enjoy a greater share of the necessaries and conveniences of life than it is possible for any savage to acquire.[53]

Much of this is attributable to increases in productivity brought on by technological advances, increasing the usefulness of capital stock. But it has also followed from the more efficient and extensive uses of human labor which the increasing sophistication of the division of labor as well as the accumulation of capital stock has occasioned.[54] So these two forces, capital and labor, must be carefully directed by some force in order to produce the necessaries and conveniences of life.

Nevertheless, Smith's account does not suppose that human beings devised the division of labor and the accumulation of stock in all their complexity for the purpose of acquiring this opulence. Instead, it arose as a

[52] In so arguing, I complicate Hirschmann's influential claim in *The Passions and the Interests* that Smith's moral theory is properly situated within the development of a tradition trying to eradicate the harmful effects of the glory-centered culture of the European aristocracy. My argument is that Hirschmann is correct that Smith's theory is designed to *domesticate* glory, but that an important part of this conception involves a rehabilitation of a subtler form of self-glory in the form of pride.
[53] *An Inquiry into the Nature and Causes of the Wealth of Nations* (hereafter *WN*), ed. R. H. Campbell, 2 vols. (Liberty Fund, 1994), Introduction, s. 4, p. 10. The argument here, which recurs several times in Smith, will be familiar from Locke's rendition of it in his *Second Treatise*, in *Two Treatises of Government*, ed. Peter Laslett (Cambridge University Press, 1960), ch. 5.
[54] Smith observes that the proportion of those who are "employed in useful labour" to those not so employed "is everywhere in proportion to the quantity of capital stock which is employed in setting them to work, and to the particular way in which it is so employed" (*WN*, Introduction, s. 6, p. 11). On the relation between Smith's theory of the division of labor and the argument about the division of labor in Plato's *Republic* (discussed in Chapter 1), see the very useful account in Gloria Vivenza, *Adam Smith and the Classics* (Oxford University Press, 2001), ch. 4.

natural result of the propensity of human nature "to truck, barter, and exchange," and as the unintended consequence of the commercial and productive diversification that took place.[55] The emergence of these unintended yet favorable consequences over time is a key innovation of Smith's theory, captured most famously by Smith's metaphor of the "invisible hand" of the unfettered market.[56] In describing this mechanism in the *Wealth of Nations*, Smith details a theory of micro-economic motivations that follows the reasoning of Mandeville's paradox almost exactly:

> As every individual, therefore, endeavours as much as he can both to employ his capital in the support of domestick industry, and so to direct that industry that its produce may be of the greatest value; every individual necessarily labours to render the annual revenue of the society as great as he can. He generally, indeed, neither intends to promote the publick interest, nor knows how much he is promoting it. By preferring the support of domestick to that of foreign industry, he intends only his own security; and by directing that industry in such a manner as its produce may be of the greatest value, he intends only his own gain, and he is in this, as in many other cases, led by an invisible hand to promote an end which was no part of his intention.[57]

So, as in Mandeville's paradox, for Smith public economic flourishing is brought about by the individual pursuit of selfish and even (mildly) vicious interests and purposes. Nevertheless, according to Smith there is nothing too morally worrying about the fact that the intentions of his economic man are so distant from any sign of virtue (at least from the point of view of the public benefit and perhaps even with regard to our evaluation of the moral agent himself). For "by pursuing his own interest he frequently promotes that of the society more effectually than when he really intends to promote it."[58] Indeed, according to Smith, those who affect "to trade for the publick good" typically do little to promote that good, and so fortunately this hypocritical affectation is "not very common among merchants."[59]

The notion of the invisible hand does not imply, for Smith any more than for Mandeville, that self-interest is the sole means by which socially beneficial outcomes can be achieved. Society will of course flourish where mutual assistance "is reciprocally afforded from love, from gratitude, from friendship, and esteem";[60] and Smith finds these acts of (genuine) fellow feeling far more likely to occur than Mandeville would have. But because of

---

[55] *WN* I.ii.1, p. 25.
[56] For the story of the development of this concept told in rich detail, see Michael Rosen, *On Voluntary Servitude: False Consciousness and the Theory of Ideology* (Harvard University Press, 1996).
[57] *WN* IV.ii.9, p. 456.   [58] Ibid.   [59] Ibid.   [60] *TMS* II.ii.3.1, p. 85.

the invisible hand, Smith thinks, even in the absence of such "generous and disinterested motives" among society's members, society will nevertheless persist, if somewhat "less happy and agreeable" than it might have been.[61] In such a case, cooperation will subsist, not as it would among friends, but rather as it might among merchants, "from a sense of its utility, without any mutual love and affection; and though no man in it should owe any obligation or be bound in gratitude to any other."[62] The advantage of this more reliable and efficient style of providence is that it does not require widespread virtue: indeed, it really asks for nothing more from human beings than what Smith unsentimentally describes as a "mercenary exchange of good offices."[63] Under the division of labor human beings in society have become profoundly interdependent, needing one another's help, vulnerable to one another's harms.[64] Thus it is from this quality of mutual interdependence that both the division of labor and its necessary consequence, inequality (both of station and of talent), arise.[65]

Interdependence both motivates and reinforces the market system's reliance on such non-virtuous (though not, on Smith's moral psychology, necessarily vicious) micro-economic motives as self-interest and need. In civilized society, Smith observes, a given human being "stands at all times in need of the co-operation and assistance of great multitudes, while his whole life is scarce sufficient to gain the friendship of a few persons."[66] Thus if the invisible hand is to perform the *providential* function that Smith has implicitly assigned to it, it is necessary for it to rely on these less than fully virtuous motives to aid in its work. No longer is scarcity the central concern of economic thinking, though of course it will never entirely recede from view. Rather, the profound and enduring new problem of modern commercial societies is productive and distributive coordination – grounded in the fact that our mutual interdependence as human beings is so great, and yet our practical claims on one another's benevolence are so small.

Charity alone is simply not sufficient to provide for human needs. Instead, Smith argues, a man must interest others' "self-love in his favour, and shew them that it is for their own advantage to do for him what he requires of them."[67] This implicit bargain is the foundation of all human society, Smith claims: "Give me that which I want, and you shall have this which you want."[68] It is in this fashion that we obtain most of the necessaries of life. Thus Smith's celebrated remark: "It is not from the

---

[61] *TMS* II.ii.3.2, p. 86.   [62] Ibid.   [63] Ibid.   [64] *TMS* II.ii.3.1, p. 85.
[65] *WN* I.ii.4, p. 29.   [66] *WN* I.ii.2, p. 26.   [67] Ibid.   [68] Ibid.

benevolence of the butcher, the brewer, or the baker, that we expect our dinner, but from their regard to their own interest. We address ourselves, not to their humanity but to their self-love, and never talk to them of our own necessities but of their advantages."[69]

This is perhaps not the most heartwarming account of human moral motivation, but Smith prefers the reliable motives of interest and need to the more unreliable promptings of charity and benevolence. For whatever moral costs human beings may have incurred by means of this bargain, Smith wants to maintain, they have gained far more by means of the vast increases in humanity's productive power which the more sophisticated division of labor has brought about. This is not to say that Smith overlooks the moral and political difficulties inherent in the system he is describing. But he holds that these dangers should not dissuade us when they are weighed against the numerous beneficial effects of the division of labor. By its means "the most dissimilar geniuses are of use to one another; the different produces of their respective talents [are brought] as it were, into a common stock, where every man may purchase whatever part of the produce of other men's talents he has occasion for."[70] By its means the most critical needs of humanity find a reliable mechanism for their fulfillment which, as Smith observes, we would in vain expect to be met by human virtue.

Smith does not of course rely on the market to meet all the needs of human society; he assigns several critical providential functions to the work of government, including national defense, domestic justice and law enforcement, and a potentially extensive set of public works projects (perhaps encompassing transportation, education, and other societal needs which individual members of the commercial market are ill-motivated to provide).[71] Yet in a sense, and in a similar fashion to Mandeville, it is not just private economic benefits but also those public goods that can be acquired only through collective political action which Smith relies upon his invisible hand to produce. The additional factor needed to motivate the production of these latter, public goods is the peculiar human affection for efficiency and systematic beauty. As in commercial transactions, so also in political life: when most people work "for the improvement of any part of the public police," it is typically not because of "pure sympathy with the

[69] *WN* I.ii.2, pp. 26–27.   [70] *WN* I.ii.5, p. 30.
[71] *WN* IV.ix.51, pp. 687–688. On this see further Pierre Force, *Self-Interest Before Adam Smith* (Cambridge University Press, 2003), ch. 6; Fleischacker, *On Adam Smith's Wealth of Nations*, esp. ch. 11; and Jerry Evensky, *Adam Smith's Moral Philosophy* (Cambridge University Press, 2005), ch. 9.

happiness of those who are to reap the benefit of it."[72] Rather, one can engage our interest more surely by describing "a great system of public police which procures these advantages," because we believe "the perfection of police, the extension of trade, and manufactures" to be in themselves "noble and magnificent objects" which it pleases us merely to think upon.[73] This prioritization of abstract beauty over concrete benefits is characteristic of human nature, according to Smith, for "we sometimes seem to value the means more than the end, and to be eager to promote the happiness of our fellow-creatures, rather from a view to perfect and improve a certain beautiful and orderly system, than from any immediate sense of feeling what they either suffer or enjoy."[74] Feelings of humanity and a sense of public responsibility are far from being necessarily linked.

THE ENGINE OF PRODUCTION

When we turn to examine Smith's "invisible hand" mechanism more closely, it turns out to be driven (at least in considerable part) precisely by the forces of pride and emulation which Mandeville had highlighted and which the Augustinians had condemned.

Naturally, it is not pride and vanity alone that drive commercial life; on Smith's theory, many other factors also play a crucial part in motivating economic productivity. Some of these factors reflect human qualities that are either morally praiseworthy or at least harmless. In describing the course of economic change in Europe, Smith distinguishes between the contributions of "two different orders of people" who have effected this "revolution of the greatest importance to the publick happiness."[75] One such order, the "great proprietors," helped to drive the economic revolution out of pure folly, from the "sole motive" of trying "to gratify the most childish vanity."[76] But there was another order, of "merchants and artificers," Smith tells us, whose actions were "much less ridiculous," notwithstanding the fact that they too acted "merely from a view to their own interest, and in pursuit of their own pedlar principle of turning a penny wherever a penny was to be got," without "the least intention to serve the publick."[77] On Smith's view, these industrious merchants and artisans, and not just the consuming classes, contributed substantially to that revolution in commerce and manufacture which "gradually intro-duced order and good government, and with them, the liberty and security

---

[72] *TMS* IV.i.11, p. 185.   [73] Ibid., pp. 185–186.   [74] Ibid., p. 185.
[75] *WN* III.iv.17, p. 422.   [76] Ibid.   [77] Ibid.

of individuals, among the inhabitants of the country."[78] Thus Smith is very far from arguing that the vicious forms of self-interest that drive commercial consumption are the only forces that contribute to the production of the public benefit in the economic sphere.

Nevertheless, none of the factors capable of fueling economic production, Smith is at various points forced to acknowledge, is more potent than Mandeville's favorite vices of luxury, pride, and self-absorption. Like Nicole, Smith believes that these vices tap into one of the truly infinite qualities in the human being: his imagination and his capacity for desire.[79] The limits of luxurious consumption, on Smith's account, are set only by the horizon of the human imagination – a distant horizon indeed because its boundaries are set by the most intoxicating of human loves, the love of ourselves. Therefore Smith believes that the principal reason we pursue riches is in order to gain the esteem of other men and to emulate those whom we esteem.[80] If we were to observe the pleasures derived from riches and power more objectively, we would be able to see them as "consisting of springs the most nice and delicate," requiring constant attention and ready, "in spite of all our care . . . every moment to overwhelm the person that dwells in them."[81]

Thus Smith is forced to confess that something very like the (mild) vice he had labeled as vanity is perhaps the principal reason why we as human beings devote so much of our lives to material pursuits, to making "parade

---

[78] *WN* IV.4, p. 412.

[79] On Smith's connection to the Augustinian moral psychology as well as his departures from it, see further Force, *Self-Interest Before Adam Smith*.

[80] *TMS* I.iii.2.1, pp. 50–51. Furthermore, what really impresses us about the luxuries of the rich and powerful has very little to do with the genuine satisfactions or pleasures they provide, and much more to do with the "order, the regular and harmonious movement of the system, the machine or oeconomy by which it is produced." We admire "how every thing is adapted to promote their ease, to prevent their wants, to gratify their wishes, and to amuse and entertain their most frivolous desires," but it is really the fact of the abstract beauty of this system of accommodation, rather than the particular accommodations themselves, that appeals to our imagination "as something grand and beautiful and noble" and makes it appear "well worth all the toil and anxiety which we are so apt to bestow upon it." If we were to observe the pleasures derived from riches and power more objectively in themselves, apart from the aesthetic qualities of the system of their provision, we would be able to see them as "consisting of springs the most nice and delicate," requiring constant attention and ready, "in spite of all our care . . . every moment to overwhelm the person that dwells in them." They are able to protect their possessor "from none of the severer inclemencies of the season"; they "keep off the summer shower, not the winter storm, but leave him always as much, and sometimes more exposed than before, to anxiety, to fear, and to sorrow; to diseases, to danger, and to death" (*TMS* IV.i.8–9, p. 183).

[81] It is significant that in this respect pride is *contrasted* with self-interest in the usual sense: the wealthy pursue these ends because they are vain rather than because they are attentive to their real interests. On this point see further Stephen Holmes, "The Secret History of Self-Interest," in *Passions and Constraints* (Univerity of Chicago Press, 1995), pp. 44–45.

of our riches, and conceal[ing] our poverty."[82] It would be truly foolish for us to devote so much effort to the acquisition of material goods if we sought only to meet our natural necessities, food, clothing, shelter, and family, which "the wages of the meanest labourer can supply."[83] But this is not our true purpose in these activities, Smith believes. Instead, we expend most of our efforts on "conveniencies, which may be regarded as superfluities," and in order occasionally to "give something even to vanity and distinction."[84] Indeed, Smith follows Mandeville in arguing that the distinction between luxury and necessity cannot be drawn at the point of bare subsistence, and goes on to follow Rousseau in judging that true need is as much a socially created as a natural phenomenon. Thus Smith urges that we define "necessities" to include, "not only the commodities which are indispensably necessary for the support of life, but whatever the custom of the country renders it indecent for creditable people, even of the lowest order, to be without . . ."[85] For instance, Smith observes that a linen shirt is "strictly speaking, not a necessary of life," nor is a pair of leather shoes; but since an ordinary laborer might "be ashamed to appear in publick without" them, they count as necessaries of life more broadly conceived.[86] This definition has the effect, remarkably progressive in its application, of indexing the distinction between necessity and luxury directly to the forces driving the expansion of commercial demand.[87]

It is thus not really the fear of poverty's discomforts, but rather of the stain it places upon our vanity, that transforms human labor into true industriousness. We wish "to be observed, to be attended to, to be taken notice of with sympathy, complacency, and approbation," and not so much to find pleasure for its own sake: "it is the vanity, not the ease, or the pleasure, which interests us."[88] Yet at the same time

vanity is always founded upon the belief of our being the object of attention and approbation. The rich man glories in his riches, because he feels that they naturally draw upon him the attention of the world, and that mankind are disposed to go along with him in all those agreeable emotions with which the advantages of his situation so readily inspire him. At the thought of this, his heart seems to swell and dilate itself within him, and he is fonder of his wealth, upon this account, than for all the other advantages it procures him . . . It is this, which, notwithstanding the restraint it imposes, notwithstanding the loss of liberty with which it is attended,

---

[82] *TMS* I.iii.2.1, p. 50.   [83] Ibid.   [84] Ibid.   [85] *WN* v.ii.k.3, pp. 869–870.   [86] Ibid., p. 870.

[87] Smith's move on this point is followed by contemporary economist Amartya Sen, who has defined poverty as the inability to appear in public without shame. Among several articulations of this idea, see Sen's article "Poor, Relatively Speaking," *Oxford Economic Papers* 35 (1983): 153–169.

[88] *TMS* I.iii.2.1, p. 50.

renders greatness the object of envy, and compensates, in the opinion of mankind, all that toil, all that anxiety, all those mortifications which must be undergone in the pursuit of it; and what is of yet more consequence, all that leisure, all that ease, all that careless security, which are forfeited for ever by the acquisition.[89]

But while Smith contends that this admiration for the rich is necessary to order society, he simultaneously acknowledges that our worship of wealth is "the great and most universal cause of the corruption of our moral sentiments."[90] It teaches us, in particular, to dishonor wisdom and virtue, and instead unjustly to give their due honor to such cheap and contingent phenomena as ownership and conspicuous consumption. Yet this corruption is a useful corruption: for a rich man's expenditures upon luxuries that flatter his own self-love will be boundless, "because he frequently has no bounds to his vanity, or to his affection for his own person";[91] and so the labor and expenditure that his vanity can motivate are also boundless. Thus, we are deceived as to both the moral and practical worth of these aspirations, but nevertheless "it is well that nature imposes upon us in this manner. It is this deception which rouses and keeps in continual motion the industry of mankind. It is this which first prompted them to cultivate the ground, to build houses, to found cities and commonwealths, and to invent and improve all the sciences and arts, which ennoble and embellish human life."[92]

Thus the revisions of Smith's ethical theory, including particularly his rejection of the Augustinian moral psychology, turn out to make possible a profound set of changes in the moral evaluation of economic action as well. For from the perspective at which we have now arrived, the engine that drives all this improvement is nothing more than the growth in scope of the very human desires that Augustinian moral psychology had condemned, only now denoted by the new and more insistent nomenclature of *demand*. Smith's familiar argument here is that supply naturally suits itself to demand; it is in the interest of producers that supply should not exceed demand, and in everyone else's interest that it should not fall short of it, because prices vary from the natural price to someone's detriment when either of these two imbalances occur.[93] The more the effectual demand, the more the employment of labor, land and stock. So according to Smith one of the causes to which we must attribute the great advances in production

---

[89] *TMS* I.iii.2.1, pp. 50–51.
[90] *TMS* I.iii.3.1, p. 61. The most important explication of this theme is to be found in Griswold, *Adam Smith*, ch. 7.
[91] *WN* III.iv.16, p. 422.   [92] *TMS* IV.i.10, p. 183.   [93] *WN* I.vii.12, pp. 74–75.

and social improvement is the great expansion of effectual demand, driven, as we have seen, in the first place by human pride and the desire of emulating others.

In the *Wealth of Nations*, Smith has little to say directly on the moral status of these changes, but he is quick to allay fears that they will bear adverse consequences from a strictly economic point of view. Though expansion of desire may initially

> sometimes raise the price of goods, [it] never fails to lower it in the long run. It encourages production, and thereby increases the competition of producers, who, in order to undersell one another, have recourse to new divisions of labour and new improvements of art, which might never otherwise have been thought of. The miserable effects of which the [East India] company complained, were the cheapness of consumption and the encouragement given to production, precisely the two effects which it is the great business of political oeconomy to promote.[94]

Thus Smith has shown that the very augmentation of human desire that was anathema to the Augustinian tradition is precisely the engine that produces cheaper consumption and increased production, the two great ends of "the great business of political economy."

As we have seen, this increase in desire has its foundation in a kind of moral folly and deception, that of self-love and emulation, which the Augustinians did not hesitate to call by the name of pride. But Smith's moral psychology has much reduced the opprobrium that might attach itself to that accusation. Instead, the more harmless variety of pride that we encounter in Smith's moral theory is now capable of being enlisted against its will in the noblest sort of work: feeding the hungry, sheltering the homeless, clothing the naked. It is capable of this precisely and only because of the limitlessness of its desires and the finiteness of its actual condition: that is, because of its folly. Smith asks us to picture for ourselves "the proud and unfeeling landlord [who] views his extensive fields, and without a thought for the wants of his brethren, in imagination consumes himself the whole harvest that grows upon them."[95] But all this self-love is "to no purpose": for

> the homely and vulgar proverb, that the eye is larger than the belly, never was more fully verified than with regard to him. The capacity of his stomach bears no proportion to the immensity of his desires, and will receive no more than that of

---

[94] *WN* v.i.e.26, p. 748. On demand and natural price in Smith's thought, see further S. Hollander, "The Role of Utility and Demand in *The Wealth of Nations*," in Skinner and Wilson, *Essays on Adam Smith*, pp. 313–323.
[95] *TMS* IV.i.10, p. 184.

the meanest peasant. The rest he is obliged to distribute among those, who prepare, in the nicest manner, that little which he makes use of, among those who fit up the palace in which this little is to be consumed, among those who provide and keep in order all the different baubles and trinkets, which are employed in the oeconomy of greatness; all of whom thus derive from his luxury and caprice, that share of the necessaries of life, which they would in vain have expected from his humanity or his justice.[96]

The possibilities of human production are too vast, providence is too generous, Smith believes, for self-love not to fall victim to its own excesses and become the author of a wholly unintended benevolence. "The produce of the soil maintains at all times nearly that number of inhabitants which it is capable of maintaining. The rich only select from the heap what is most precious and agreeable. They consume little more than the poor ..."[97] Thus not only does Smith deny that pride and self-love in the broader senses are truly vices, he also claims that there is really nothing very evil about so many human beings finding themselves helplessly dependent on the self-love of others.[98]

Throughout Smith's work he is remarkably at ease with the fact of inequality among human beings. This condition is part and parcel of the very nature of commercial society, and Smith makes no apology for its sometimes ruthless inequities:

The division of opulence is not according to the work. The opulence of the merchant is greater than that of all his clerks, tho' he works less; and they again have six times more than an equal number of artisans, who are more employed. The artisan who works at his ease within doors has far more than the poor labourer who trudges up and down without intermission. Thus he who, as it were, bears the burthen of society has the fewest advantages.[99]

But given Smith's premises it is reasonable for him to remain relatively unconcerned about economic inequality, and we are now in a position to

---

[96] Ibid.

[97] Ibid. This points out that it is not the self-interest of everyone in a society, however situated, but rather that of rich *consumers*, which is necessary to make this aspect of the invisible hand mechanism work. These are the particular hands that Smith needs to keep invisible and clean, and this fact limits (though it does not obviate) the extent to which Smith's theory is a thorough democratization of dirty hands, in the sense in which I have used that term.

[98] The fact that the argument in the *Wealth of Nations* is seen to have this purpose of moral justification puts me at odds with Vivienne Brown's characterization of that work as a "basically amoral discourse." Vivienne Brown, *Adam Smith's Discourse* (Routledge, 1994), p. 218.

[99] Adam Smith, *Lectures on Jurisprudence*, ed. D. D. Raphael and R. L. Meek (Liberty Fund, 1995), s. 210–213, pp. 489–490.

see the reason. Smith is able to be so comfortable about inequality because of his confidence that

> when Providence divided the earth among a few lordly masters, it neither forgot nor abandoned those who seemed to have been left out in the partition. These last too enjoy their share of all that it produces. In what constitutes the real happiness of human life, they are in no respect inferior to those who would seem so much above them. In ease of body and peace of mind, all the different ranks of life are nearly upon a level, and the beggar, who suns himself by the side of the highway, possesses that security which kings are fighting for.[100]

Not only is pride no real vice, but economic inequality is no real calamity.

We can now see that, if pride and vanity in the firmer Augustinian or even Mandevillean sense were still real vices, Smith would be doing nothing more than adopting wholesale the private vices, public benefits argument. The pride and vanity of the rich are the principal motivating factors in economic life: full of "selfishness and rapacity," they seek "only their own conveniency," and "the sole end which they propose from the labours of all the thousands whom they employ ... [is] the gratification of their own vain and insatiable desires." Nevertheless, they find themselves compelled to "divide with the poor the produce of all their improvements," being led by "an invisible hand to make nearly the same distribution of the necessaries of life, which would have been made, had the earth been divided into equal portions among all its inhabitants, and thus without intending it, without knowing it, advance the interest of the society, and afford means to the multiplication of the species."[101]

THE HAND THAT RULES

Much recent scholarship on Smith's moral and political theory has noted that the invisible hand metaphor has tended to be misrepresented by contemporary conservatives and libertarians as promoting an anachronistically systematic version of *laissez faire* industrial capitalism.[102] Their criticisms have been well founded, in part: it is certainly easy to read too much into the invisible hand metaphor, and an uncritical attribution to Smith of excessively libertarian views is certainly a very real danger for those approaching Smith's texts with twenty-first-century eyes. But there is one

---

[100] *TMS* IV.i.10, p. 185.   [101] Ibid., pp. 184–185.

[102] Among the most important commentaries on the subject, see Fleischacker, *On Adam Smith's Wealth of Nations*, esp. ch. 11, and Emma Rothschild, *Economic Sentiments* (Harvard University Press, 2001), esp. ch. 5.

significant respect in which Smith's use of the invisible hand metaphor captures something not only deliberate but also pervasive in his social and political theory. For at the heart of Smith's philosophy is a systematic substitution – not everywhere, but in crucial areas – of the agency of individual economic choice in place of the guiding action of government policy.

Throughout his writings, and especially in the *Wealth of Nations*, Smith exhibits a profound skepticism about both the capability and the trustworthiness of state agency with respect to certain critical social functions. In particular, it is a large subsection of what we have been calling providential functions that Smith is disinclined to trust to government hands. In part this results from a general disdain for what he designates as "that insidious and crafty animal, vulgarly called a statesman or politician . . ."[103] But primarily it is not the moral untrustworthiness of the politician, but rather his (understandable) lack of practical competence to undertake the task of providential guidance, that makes Smith disinclined to commit such matters to his care. In attempting to provide such guidance, Smith predicts, the politician will find himself "exposed to innumerable delusions," for indeed "no human wisdom or knowledge could ever be sufficient" for the task such a statesman sets himself: "the duty of super-intending the industry of private people, and of directing it towards the employments most suitable to the interest of the society."[104]

Instead, Smith urges that each *individual* "can, in his local situation, judge much better than any statesman or lawgiver can do for him" how most effectively and productively to employ his capital.[105] Smith elaborates:

Every system which endeavours, either by extraordinary encouragements, to draw towards a particular species of industry a greater share of the capital of the society than what would naturally go to it; or by extraordinary restraints, to force from a particular species of industry some share of the capital which would otherwise be employed in it; is in reality subversive of the great purpose which it means to promote. It retards, instead of accelerating, the progress of the society towards real wealth and greatness; and diminishes, instead of increasing, the real value of the annual produce of its land and labour.[106]

For example, Smith thinks that for a government to attempt to give a home monopoly in any market to any domestic industry by means of tax duties

---

[103] *WN* IV.ii.39, p. 468. On Smith's skepticism about both the moral and cognitive vices of politicians, see the very helpful account of Samuel Fleishacker, *On Adam Smith's Wealth of Nations*, ch. 11.
[104] *WN* IV.ix.51, p. 687.   [105] *WN* IV.ii.10, p. 456.   [106] *WN* IV.ix.50, p. 687.

or other legislation "must, in almost all cases, be either a useless or a hurtful regulation."[107] Similarly, laws that prohibit manufacturers from also acting as retailers, or that require farmers to act as their own wholesalers, are examples of government actions Smith sees as both "evident violations of natural liberty, and therefore unjust," and also "as impolitick as they were unjust" (appealing to the persistent categories of expedience and moral rightness).[108] Instead, Smith claims, it is in the interest of society that the law in commercial matters should instead "always . . . trust people with the care of their own interest, as in their local situations they must generally be able to judge better of it than the legislator can do."[109]

Smith goes on to warn that there is not only danger of providential inefficiency, but real political danger as well, from those who would assume the burdens of ambitious social guidance. Thus:

> The statesman, who should attempt to direct private people in what manner they ought to employ their capitals, would not only load himself with a most unnecessary attention, but assume an authority which could safely be trusted, not only to no single person, but to no council or senate whatever, and which would nowhere be so dangerous as in the hands of a man who had folly and presumption enough to fancy himself fit to exercise it.[110]

In the *Theory of Moral Sentiments*, Smith had already inveighed against the pretensions of political guidance in the face of the complexity of fragmented modern forms of social agency. Such a person, Smith warns,

> seems to imagine that he can arrange the different members of a great society with as much ease as the hand arranges the different pieces upon a chess-board. He does not consider that the pieces upon the chess-board have no other principle of motion besides that which the hand impresses upon them; but that, in the great chess-board of human society, every single piece has a principle of motion of its own, altogether different from that which the legislature might chuse to impress upon it. If those two principles coincide and act in the same direction, the game of human society will go on easily and harmoniously and is very likely to be happy and successful. If they are opposite or different, the game will go on miserably, and the society must be at all times in the highest degree of disorder.[111]

The wise man of policy, by contrast,

---

[107] *WN* IV.ii.11, p. 456.
[108] *WN* IV.v.b.16, p. 531. It should be noted that Smith's employment of the term "justice," however, has a much more specialized meaning in the context of his other writings than that which might be straightforwardly inferred from its echoing of the ancient rhetorical paradigm.
[109] Ibid., pp. 530–531.   [110] *WN* IV.ii.10, p. 456.   [111] *TMS* VI.ii.2.17, p. 234.

though he should consider some of [the features of the current order] as in some measure abusive, he will content himself with moderating, what he often cannot annihilate without great violence. When he cannot conquer the rooted prejudices of the people by reason and persuasion, he will not attempt to subdue them by force ... He will accommodate, as well as he can, his public arrangements to the confirmed habits and prejudices of the people; and will remedy as well as he can, the inconveniencies which may flow from the want of those regulations which the people are averse to submit to. When he cannot establish the right, he will not disdain to ameliorate the wrong; but like Solon, when he cannot establish the best system of laws, he will endeavour to establish the best that the people can bear."[112]

So in preference to excessive political guidance, Smith prefers instead what he calls "the obvious and simple system of natural liberty." In such a system, Smith argues in one of his most familiar remarks, "every man, as long as he does not violate the laws of justice, is left perfectly free to pursue his own interest in his own way, and to bring both his industry and capital into competition with those of any other man, or order of men."[113] Because of the natural dynamics of the market, Smith argues, we can expect in economic conditions of "perfect liberty" – and only in conditions of "perfect liberty" – that the various "advantages and disadvantages of the different employments of labour and stock" will necessarily "be either perfectly equal or continually tending to equality."[114] It is therefore generally in the interest of society, Smith urges, that the law in commercial matters should instead "always trust people with the care of their own interest, as in their local situations they must generally be able to judge better of it than the legislator can do."[115]

Thus Smith has taken a crucial step forward in the process of both commercializing and domesticating the problem of dirty hands. As we saw in Chapter 5, for Nicole and for Mandeville, the proud and self-absorbed impulses of human beings were capable of motivating and fueling the socially beneficial actions that secured temporal well-being, but those same vicious impulses required political guidance and direction if they were to fulfill rather than thwart those providential purposes. Smith, by contrast, conceives of those same motives (though less dramatically condemned) as being capable of both fueling *and* guiding the production of social benefits,

---

[112] *TMS* VI.ii.2.16, p. 233.
[113] *WN* IV.ix.51, p. 687. See further Smith's description of "perfect liberty" as consisting in the freedom of every man "both to chuse what occupation he thought proper, and to change it as often as he thought proper," wherein "every man's interest would prompt him to seek the advantageous, and shun the disadvantageous employment" (*WN* I.x.i, p. 116).
[114] *WN* I.10.I, p. 116.   [115] *WN* IV.v.b.16, p. 531.

through the mechanisms of supply and demand and the invisible hand of the unfettered market.

In light of the argument advanced thus far in this book, there are now sufficient reasons for supposing that this is no accident. For the device of the invisible hand constitutes the culmination of an evolving set of modern strategies for evading the problem of dirty hands, and thus also of our collective moral responsibility for the consequences of those social choices represented by the state as well as the commercial market. It is to a consideration of this question that we will now turn in the conclusion.

Conclusion

"Dirt's a funny thing," the Boss said. "Come to think of it, there ain't a thing but dirt on this green God's globe except what's under water, and that's dirt too. It's dirt makes the grass grow. A diamond ain't a thing in the world but a piece of dirt that got awful hot. And God-a-Mighty picked up a handful of dirt and blew on it and made you and me and George Washington and mankind blessed in faculty and apprehension. It all depends on what you do with the dirt . . ."
Robert Penn Warren, *All the King's Men*

The history of philosophical reflection about dirty hands in public life is necessarily also the story of conflicts and tensions among large systems of values. The idea of value conflict and the plurality of values has been a major theme in contemporary moral philosophy and political theory, but the history of the concepts involved has yet to receive anything like a systematic examination. The preceding chapters have sought to trace the development over time of one of the most prominent problems connected to value pluralism: the question of the distinctive moral dilemmas associated with political action. The historical account that has emerged suggests that the problem of dirty hands – far from being resolvable by means of an appeal to the intrinsic logic of consequentialist or deontological theories – points instead toward an underlying framework of far older and more intractable value conflicts that help create the problem's peculiar tensions.

It is obviously impossible to study the history of value pluralism from the point of view of what various thinkers had to say about the subject directly, just as it is impossible to study the history of liberalism from what its progenitors had to say about it. Value pluralism, like liberalism, is a category of our own contemporary devising, used to label something important to us that emerged in such a way that those who participated in its formation were scarcely aware of it.

This is no reason for supposing that the history of value pluralism cannot be studied, any more than it is for supposing that we should abandon our attempt to understand the origins of liberalism. But to study it will require an interpretive approach to the history of ideas that is rigorous yet flexible, one capable of tracing the diverse themes its subject matter implies through a variety of historical contexts. The ideas that constitute value pluralism will not be constant over time, because part of their story involves substantial change in the conceptual categories within which these issues were treated. Consequently, we may have to introduce our own terminology at times to mark these transformations, because the family resemblances *we* perceive among the ideas we study may not always be obvious and unmistakable to the authors who helped to shape them (though we will of course have cause for concern if we believe they would be wholly unrecognizable to them).[1] But if we accord the proper importance to these observable similarities among ideas and doggedly pursue their underlying causes, we should be able to make some headway toward an archaeology of value pluralism: an understanding of how and why the value conflicts we intuit in moral life came to take the particular shape they hold for us today.

As we saw in Chapter 1, central to the emergence in Western culture of the value conflict at the center of the problem of dirty hands were two tensions that emerged in antiquity: one between philosophy and politics in classical culture itself; the other between classical political values and the very different values of the Christian religion. Within ancient philosophy we find the theoretical grounding for dirty hands – encapsulated in Plato's theory of the special moral permissions accorded to the *Republic*'s guards. We find there also an emerging tension between the philosophical justification for those permissions and the practical exercise of them – captured in Plato and other ancient thinkers' general preference for the life of contemplation and retreat over that of action and political responsibility. Cicero's moral theory sought to resolve these tensions with an ethic of citizen responsibility: one that grounded moral permissions to contravene conventional moral standards in responsibility for the community's welfare. In doing so, his account helped to provoke the second key tension of the period, between Roman political culture and the emerging moral commitments of the Christian religion. For the early Christians, with their theologically shaped hostility to idolatry and their historically shaped hostility to empire and wealth, could not countenance Roman assertions

---

[1] See further Richard Rorty, J. B. Schneewind, and Quentin Skinner's "Introduction" to *Philosophy in History: Essays on the Historiography of Philosophy* (Cambridge University Press, 1984).

that political welfare should override the rules of morality or trump the distinctive claims of their humble, pacifist ethic. They consequently defined their moral theory in uncompromising opposition to the priorities of Roman politics and culture.

It was in response to these tensions within and between ancient and early Christian thought that Augustine developed his unique and influential solution to the problem of dirty hands. As we saw in Chapter 2, Augustine (drawing eclectically on the ethics of Plato and Cicero as well as his early Christian predecessors) went further than any previous moral thinker in interiorizing the locus of ethical activity, and consequently also in severing any necessary connection between the morality of intention and the morality of consequence. This move was made possible partly by Augustine's turn toward inwardness in both the autobiographical and the theological dimensions of his thought; but it depended also, as we have seen, on his lesser-known theory of the inclination of pride and vice to imitate the outward behaviors and effects of charity and virtue. This reconceptualization of ethics enabled Augustine to forge an ingenious synthesis of the classical and early Christian value systems, employing a metaphorical relationship between earthly political loyalties and the higher moral loyalties of Christians to create a limited but sufficient justification for political action, grounded on an ethic of responsibility arising from love for one's fellow creatures. But Augustine's ethical revisions also laid the foundation for many of the innovations that later theories of dirty hands would employ to argue for the special status of the representative and providential roles of political leaders, in two principal ways. First, Augustine's theory awarded such leaders moral permission to do *for others* what it would not be morally permissible for them to do for themselves (as seen most famously in Augustine's rationale for just war). And, second, it greatly expanded the moral permissions that could be awarded to secular and even sinful instruments of divine will, by theorizing that God's employment of imperfect means was a central part of God's plan to *provide* for his creatures' needs in their earthly existence.

Augustine's solution was a fragile and ultimately unsatisfactory one. Yet it may be that some part of the hope it embodies continues to occupy and haunt our modern souls, even the souls of those who have abandoned Augustine's theistic worldview. We cling, in some form or another, to Augustine's synthesis of Christian transcendence and Roman responsibility because this synthesis points toward possibilities for our own world that we are unwilling simply to abandon. Indeed, one intriguing way of understanding the dirty hands problem is as a theological problem confronted by its mortal heirs. In one sense, the dirty hands problem is our human glimpse, in our own sphere of action, of an ongoing divide in the moral world (as we understand it) between the order of providence and the order of redemption. The providential order seeks the happiness and well-being of creation and all its creatures; the redemptive order focuses instead on cultivating the compassion, peacefulness, and authenticity of the agents it summons to do its work. Part of what holds the Western soul together is the belief, or at least the hope, that these providential and redemptive orders (however understood) are working together (however mysteriously) toward the same end. Yet in conditions of modernity it is not enough for this to remain merely a hope. For, as time goes on, we find ourselves more and more the executors of providence, will we or no – without lessening our need to find our place in the redemptive order as well. Thus, in a way, it is not at all that these conflicts are new; it is that they are new to us. For if on earth God's work must now more and more be our own, then the famously troubling paradox of theodicy will become not just God's problem, but ours as well.

In Chapter 3, we saw how Renaissance thinkers such as Machiavelli and Thomas More charted the dissolution of Augustine's carefully constructed synthesis of classical and Christian views of political ethics. Like Augustine, Machiavelli and More continued to view pride as the chief evil (according to the Christian scheme of virtue); but, pressing further than Augustine, they launched a modern trend of seeing pride as being socially disruptive in a systematic way (a trend which in different ways Nicole, Mandeville, and Smith would over time contribute to reversing). Machiavelli's new political ethic sharply undermined the truce between classical and Christian moralities, arguing that the aristocratic virtues nurtured by ancient politics must stand in for – and compensate for – the weakness of the modern (Christianized) populace at large. For Machiavelli, this weakness constituted a moral corruption on the part of the citizens that is the major factor that creates the need for his new political ethic. But in Machiavelli's approach to the problem the city is to be redeemed, not primarily by a democratic conversion to political virtue, but rather by the heroic assumption of the country's moral burden by an aristocratic leader who rises to meet the demands of a different, more responsible brand of virtue.

More's *Utopia* accepts (though on quite different grounds) Machiavelli's diagnosis that the moral dilemmas of political leaders find their origin in the moral character of the people those leaders serve. Yet, unlike Machiavelli, More (as we explored in Chapter 3) urged that, because of the democratic origins of the dirty hands dilemma, *only* a democratic solution will ultimately serve to relieve political leaders of their moral burdens. Only if it is possible to eliminate the snares and pitfalls of pride as a *systematic* feature of human interaction, More asserts, can political leaders ever hope to act morally in public life, and thus avoid the taint of dirty hands in fulfilling their political responsibilities. As such, *Utopia* is the first text among the great works of political theory to identify an intimate connection between the ethical quandaries of political leadership and the character of the social order.

This leads us to Hobbes and his solution to the problem of dirty hands: namely, an offer of virtually limitless moral justification for the actions of the modern sovereign state. As Chapter 4 showed, Hobbes's account of religion accepted and radicalized Augustine's interior-focused ethic. By arguing that in conditions of necessity (such as the state of nature) all that matters morally (to God) is intention, Hobbes was able to separate even more firmly than Augustine had the ethics of intention from the decisively *political* questions of outward consequence. In doing so, Hobbes crafted a solution to the dirty hands problem that draws on an ingenious combination of aristocratic and democratic responses to the problem. First, from the premise of natural equality in the state of nature, Hobbes afforded his natural Hobbesian man precisely the same set of moral exemptions that Machiavelli had offered to his prince – and for approximately the same reasons. Having done so, Hobbes then allows the sovereign to *import* these permissions from the state of nature to the context of civil society, on condition that there he alone (with the obedient help of his subjects) be allowed to exercise their extensive moral permissions. In doing so, Hobbes implicitly appealed to the idea that, in some form at least, life in civil society remains precariously balanced always at the edge of the state of nature, and that the rights appropriate to that state, with all their extravagant moral claims, remain somehow in force, by means of the sovereign's authority, in all the business of the state.

But as the account in Chapter 4 also suggested, Hobbes's moral argument here is based on some fancy conceptual footwork that when viewed as an answer to the problem of dirty hands has some decidedly unsettling implications. This is fairly easy to see if one holds all the pieces of Hobbes's argument about moral responsibility together at once (as we are not necessarily accustomed to doing). First, Hobbes argued, the sovereign has special permission to contravene ordinary moral rules, because his actions as a representative are properly his *subjects'* actions and not really his own. The subjects, on the other hand, *also* have a special permission to contravene ordinary moral rules (as they understand them) whenever the sovereign commands them to do so, and they possess this permission because their actions when they obey the sovereign are not properly considered *their* actions but rather the actions of the sovereign.

Hence we have a kind of shell game of moral responsibility.[2] The state acts for me, not itself, and that clears the state of moral guilt; yet it is the state that acts, and not me, and that clears me. And after all that shuffling, does anyone remember which shell we left the moral responsibility under? But perhaps that is the point. And if so that is troubling: because it suggests that there may be a fundamental moral instability at the heart of Hobbes's theory of the artificial and representative state; and of course a version of Hobbes's theory is still at the heart of our *own* dominant conception of the state.

Another equally pervasive (if less obvious) modern solution to the problem of dirty hands is to be found (as Part III shows) in the institution of the commercial market. In contemporary political theory, it is typical to treat states and markets as conceptual opposites: and indeed our partisan divisions in contemporary Western politics largely revolve around this posited opposition. But the line of thought pursued in the book's final chapters draws our attention to several ways in which there are important similarities between states and markets, similarities that begin to emerge most clearly when we consider both as kinds of responses, and indeed as proposed solutions, to the problem of dirty hands.

We can begin by noting at a very general level two important similarities between states and markets from a moral point of view. First, states and markets both bear *responsibility* for the public welfare. We rely on states to make sure that people are cared for, employed, fed, rewarded. But we rely on markets to make sure of the same thing (though we are by and large willing to tolerate an even greater degree of sloppiness on the part of markets in their performance of these functions). This is the understanding of markets that ultimately explains Adam Smith's celebrated rhetoric of the "invisible hand": for just as Hobbes's state was a "Mortall God," so Adam Smith's market is, in its own way, a *providential* mechanism.

---

[2] The shell game referred to here takes place at the level of *overall* responsibility for the actions of the state. There may of course be further sub-games of the same type operating *within* the state itself: for example, the separation of powers within the United States government may serve some of the same functions of moral apologetic for those who hold power within it.

But states and markets share another similarity, which is that they are not only *responsible*, but also, though perhaps not as obviously, *representative*. That is, both states and markets are mechanisms by means of which actions are taken on our behalf which are not, or at least are not with any phenomenological directness, *our* actions; they are rather institutions within which things are done *for* us, sometimes for our reasons or purposes, but never or rarely *by* us, through our agency or by our choice. Rather, in a fashion that resembles the element of Hobbes's state theory we have examined, markets like states are institutions in which moral agency is curiously fragmented, and in which not only is collective action difficult to organize, but also collective as well as individual responsibility is hard to assess.

As Chapter 5 showed, Nicole's moral theory accepted and dramatically expanded Augustine's imitation dynamic, arguing on this basis that the motivation of pride (and its related vices) could in fact explain any and every benefit apparently produced by virtue and charity. By adapting Nicole's argument, his successor Mandeville was able to further radicalize the force of Augustine's interiorized ethic, extending its potential implications in an even more far-reaching direction. From Machiavelli and Hobbes's position that evils done to benefit the public were not really evils, it is still quite some distance to the proposition Mandeville defends: that doing evil is permissible (on grounds of necessity) if one benefits the public, even if in doing so one *intends* only to benefit one's self. Yet Nicole and Mandeville share a way of framing the problem that leaves the underlying Machiavellism of government *guidance* of necessary vice up-front and obvious: theirs remains a more or less transparent economic Machiavellism.

What is needed to transform Nicole and Mandeville's paradoxical reformulation of the dirty hands problem into its own apparent solution is Adam Smith's moral and political theory. For Smith couples the neo-Augustinian idea of unintended consequences with an anti-Augustinian redefinition of what *counts* as moral. Smith in a way constitutes the ultimate fulfillment of the modern trend toward diversifying dirty hands. By putting the power to provide public benefits (through what might otherwise count as vicious means) into the hands of ordinary citizens and consumers, Smith offers what can be seen as at last a fully inclusive solution to the dirty hands problem. In much the same way as Hobbes, Smith employs a partial version of the Augustinian moral psychology to fragment and obscure our account of the moral agency of the public at large – with the effect of eliding from view the dirty-handed dimensions implicit in everyday commercial activity. With Smith's help, consumers and producers can both go about their business in the marketplace without worrying whether their pursuit of their ordinary self-interest puts them at risk of moral corruption. Smith's theory thus employs the notion of the invisible hand to make the need for (Machiavellian) government management of economic activity and its associated vices disappear – and to make the collective moral agency of actors in the economic sphere increasingly difficult even to glimpse out of the corner of our critical eye.

Some readers may fairly ask what if anything is wrong with Smith's revision of the neo-Augustinian moral theory. To raise this question is to confront the oddity of how central the concept of *pride* has been to much of the preceding story. The category of pride has not been a central one in contemporary thinking about politics and ethics (though as we have seen in past centuries it was profoundly influential). When the concept of pride is discussed in political theory today, it is usually as a historical artifact, a residual feature of the thought of Augustine or Rousseau that needs to be acknowledged but not taken seriously. This estrangement might lead some to question the continuing relevance of Smith's revisionist moral psychology. Perhaps like Smith we too no longer think of pride as being humanity's dominant moral evil; and if so, how can this story about the moral criticism of pride by Augustine (and his successors Nicole and Mandeville) inform our understanding of dilemmas of inescapable wrongdoing in modern life?

There are at least two responses to this question. First, even those who do not believe pride to be a significant evil in its own right may find something worthy of serious consideration in the *structure* of the arguments we have studied. By a kind of analogical reasoning, the structure of the private vices, public benefits argument (for example) might well have something to teach even those who have abandoned Nicole and Mandeville's view of which vices are relevant to moral life. And, second, even if we come to believe that the phenomenon of pride to which they point is not *intrinsically* worthy of moral blame, it is still plausible that pride (or something quite like it) remains inseparably connected to certain vices (such as cruelty, greed, and hypocrisy) whose importance to political life has never been questioned. It is equally plausible that pride (or something quite like it) remains intransigently hostile to certain other values – most notably equality – that continue to lie at the heart of our shared moral aspirations.[3]

---

[3] For a fascinating exploration along related lines in contemporary philosophy and social science (though not one framed specifically in terms of pride), see Geoffrey Brennan and Philip Pettit, *The Economy of Esteem* (Oxford University Press, 2004).

So if, for example, we should define poverty as an inability to appear and participate in public life without shame (as Smith argues and as Amartya Sen among our contemporaries endorses), then there is cause for moral concern in the solution at which Smith ultimately arrives: that of linking production to ever-expanding commercial desire. For by fueling expanded consumption and therefore expanded demand, we run the risk that the scope of experienced shame will continually be redefined and extended, to the enduring detriment of the poorest among us. Such thoughts are unfamiliar to us, at least as concerns in the field of political ethics. But if this is so, perhaps that itself is cause for concern: perhaps we need to ask ourselves whether the forms of life that dominate our society today, with all the great public benefits they have brought, feel comfortable to us only because they have come to rest on the soft cushion of Adam Smith's redefinition of our ordinary private vices.

The solutions to the dirty hands problem we have traced in this book are not of course the *only* important or influential solutions that have been offered over time. On the contrary, there are a variety of other well-known responses to the problem. One of the most enduring of such solutions we explored briefly in both Chapter 1 and Chapter 3: the ancient impulse, somewhat wistfully revisited by More's Hythloday in *Utopia*, that the solution to the problem of dirty hands is simply to withdraw from public life. Another solution, unfortunately all too familiar from the twentieth century, invokes a once-for-all resolution of the problem: it claims that the evils done in the name of the present revolution or crusade will bring about a world in which no evils are necessary, and thereby an end to evils altogether. Far too many evils have been committed in the name of such solutions, and they have generated in the process far too little evidence that the end of all evils is just around the bend.

What is distinctive about the three main solutions to the problem of dirty hands traced in this book is their *familiarity* to us as unproblematic aspects of our contemporary ways of life – coupled with their general *unfamiliarity* as ways of resolving worries about political and collective ethics. As we have seen, the conceptual strategies of the interiorized ethic, the sovereign state, and the commercial market are characterized more than anything else by their evasive character: their tendency to conceal from the people at large the extent and moral seriousness of the value conflicts created by the requirements of public responsibility.

Since Plato, philosophy has struggled to make sense of the moral implications of the fragmentation of agency occasioned by the division of labor. Since work is action, any division of labor is also necessarily, at least in part, a division of *moral* labor: and by its very nature this division offers an opportunity to insulate individuals and groups from moral responsibility. This insulation can have both an external and an internal dimension. Externally, the division of labor insulates from moral responsibility by claiming that the deeds in question are in some way not one's own – either because one does not perform them, or because one does not perform them for one's own sake. Internally, we find the familiar multi-directional insulation from responsibility associated with modern bureaucratic structures.[4] The production of actions and outcomes is a complex process in which attribution of responsibility is always difficult. There are a variety of roles in such processes – for example, those of advisers, legislators, and executives – whose responsibility for the results of their deeds varies in complexity, but is rarely direct or straightforward. In contemporary politics this has given rise to the (now regrettably familiar) concept of *deniability*, whereby political leaders avoid making decisions directly so as to avoid the moral consequences (or at least the public evaluative consequences) of having made them. Such folly is the logical policy extension of the dynamic whose development this book has traced.

Consequently, if we want to understand what truly drives the dirty hands problem – and where the moral responsibility for its troubles truly lies – we must focus sharply on those institutions that function most effectively to conceal any suggestion of democratic and commercial dirty hands. Such a focus will enable us to distinguish correctly those cases that qualify for our concern, our endorsement, our condemnation, and our forgiveness.

The idea that fragmented agency and representative relationships modify the moral responsibility of those involved is not without a basis in moral reasoning; indeed, there are versions of fragmented agency that are worthy of serious consideration as a moral excuse in appropriate circumstances. But it is crucial to this kind of argument's having any genuine and proper claim on our moral sympathies that two conditions should apply. First, necessary evils must be linked in some way with goods that are not only in themselves fully justified but also justified to a degree that compensates for the evils they are linked with. And, second, this linkage itself must be something which the agents involved cannot reasonably be considered to be at liberty to sever.

---

[4] See Dennis Thompson, *Political Ethics and Public Office* (Harvard University Press, 1987), ch. 2.

Together, these two requirements point toward the shared flaw in the distinctive modern solutions to the problem of dirty hands. Perhaps a collectivity is not fully responsible for the *means* required to achieve its utility; but it must be responsible, at least in part, for what *constitutes* its own utility. Collectively, the members of a democratic state or the actors in a commercial market cannot ask for excuse for what they do out of necessity – necessity, that is, in pursuit of utility specified by the general will or the aggregate demand – when it is their own will and their own demands that constitute the public utility they seek.

All of us, but especially those of us in systems where political power is available to us in even a limited way, have a responsibility for the outcomes of political and social life, as well as for the means chosen to attain them. As a consequence, there are, more frequently than we realize, democratic and commercial forms of dirty hands in public life. Yet the quintessential modern public institutions, the state and the commercial market, tend to obscure these relationships of responsibility. More than this, as this book has tried to show, often it is precisely the evasive character of the modern institutions of state and market with respect to democratic accountability which more than any other factor creates the wrenching dilemmas of individual agency which we associate with the problem of dirty hands.

Perhaps such dilemmas are unavoidable at the limits. But they are worsened by institutions whose tendency is to create an illusory sense that those who benefit from the processes that create public utilities can escape implication in the actions that constitute the necessary means to achieve those same utilities. So it is vital to appreciate that the reality of dirty hands in public life need not preclude us from insisting on moral accountability, in particular at the democratic level. For until such time as the public's democratic and economic agency is exercised collectively and clearly – and that time may never come, and perhaps never should – it remains our responsibility to call into question the variety of moral excuses offered for their public conduct by both statespersons and citizens, and to compel them, as far as possible, to stand alone and answer for themselves.

Index

Luban, David 14 n. 38
Lucian 128 n. 72, 137
luck, moral 95, 95 n. 109. *See also* fortune.
lust 73, 74, 79, 211, 229
    domination and 75 n. 18, 87, 95, 100. *See also*
        Christianity; desire; ethics; love.
Luther, Martin 93–94, 94 n. 102, 147–148
luxury 36, 77, 83, 124, 144, 149, 185, 189,
        201, 212 n. 109, 212–213, 213 n. 114,
        222, 223 n. 168, 230, 242, 242 n. 45,
        243, 244, 249 n. 80, 249–258. *See also*
        desire; economy; need; pride;
        rich/wealthy.
Lynn, Jonathan 154

Macbeth, Lady 2
Machiavelli, Niccolo 13 n. 36, 18, 22, 83,
        106, 107, 126, 133, 152, 154, 155,
        158–159, 186, 188, 203, 204, 205–206, 210,
        229, 243, 243 n. 50, 262, 263, 265, 266
    ambition in 106, 117, 118
    Discourses on Livy 106, 107, 109, 110, 115, 116,
        118, 119–120, 124
    economics and 265
    ethics and 186
    History of Florence 116
    Machiavellism 24
    modes, ordinary vs. extraordinary 121–122
    political instability 119–120
    The Prince 106, 107, 109, 117–118, 119, 121, 122,
        123, 159, 205
    problem of dirty hands, diagnosis of 122
    problem of dirty hands, solution to 115–125
    state of nature and 205
    virtù/new virtue ethic 105, 108–125, 262
MacIntyre, Alasdair 10 n. 28, 10 n. 26, 18 n. 44
MacQueen, D. J. 75 n. 18
Madison, James 226
Mamet, David 203
Mandeville, Bernard 21, 24, 185–231, 233–235,
        234 n. 5, 235 n. 9, 239, 240, 241, 242 n. 45,
        242–243, 243 n. 51, 243 n. 48, 245, 247,
        248, 249, 250, 254, 257, 262, 265, 266
    education and 207
    "Enquiry Concerning Virtue" 206 n. 80
    *An Enquiry into the Origin of Honour, and
        the Usefulness of Christianity in War*
        206 n. 82
    "An Enquiry Into the Origin of Moral Virtue"
        206
    "Essay on Charity-Schools" 217, 217 n. 134
    Fable of the Bees 204, 205–231
    "flattery revolution" 208
    *Free Thoughts on Religion, The Church, and
        National Religion* 206 n. 82

"The Grumbling Hive" 185, 204, 205, 222
    happiness and 207
    A Letter to Dion 221 n. 154
    manipulation 221, 223
    A Modest Defence of Publick Stews 224 n. 172,
        224–225
    philosophical anthropology of 204, 214
    political management of vice 208, 219–231
    politicians and moralists 207–210, 212 n. 109,
        213 n. 114, 221–231
    "private vices, public benefits" and 24, 227
    prostitution 203, 224 n. 171, 224–225
    public and 206
Mansfield, Harvey 109 n. 5
market 16, 20, 21, 24, 25, 185–231, 233–258,
        264–267, 269. *See also* economy.
Markus, R. A. 75 n. 18, 78 n. 38, 81 n. 43, 84 n. 62,
        98 n. 125
Martin, Rex 84 n. 62
Martinich, A. P. 156 n. 3, 160 n. 16
martyrdom 61, 78 n. 35, 168. *See also* Christianity.
Meinecke, Friedrich 21 n. 49
mercy 14, 111, 112, 113, 115, 122, 196, 197. *See also*
        cruelty; virtue.
metaphor 70, 71, 72, 84, 105, 112, 205, 261
Mill, John Stuart 5, 10
    Utilitarianism: justice and 5
    moral rightness and 5. *See also* utilitarianism.
Mizuta, Hiroshi 237 n. 22
Mohammed 196
money 38, 68, 83, 133, 141, 142, 144,
        148, 190, 203, 215, 216, 219.
        See also economy.
Monro, Hector 204 n. 75, 217 n. 138,
        224 n. 171
moral dilemma 1, 2, 4, 12, 13, 15, 40, 54, 95, 125,
        133, 152, 163, 168, 181, 185, 227, 259, 262,
        266, 269
    apparent 3, 5, 8, 12
    metaphor of 2
    possibility of 3
    residual, moral 4, 5. *See also* dirty hands; ethics;
        value pluralism.
moral rightness 21, 47–58, 136, 137, 144,
        152, 256. *See also* ethics; *honestas*/
        honorableness.
Morality, ordinary/traditional 69, 106, 108, 111,
        113, 114, 115, 117, 120, 208, 240–241
    rules of 241 n. 39, 263–264. *See also* ethics.
More, Thomas 22, 23, 106–107, 125–153, 154, 186,
        188, 194, 262–263, 267
    Confutation of Tyndale's Answer 147, 147 n. 116
    Dialogue of Comfort Against Tribulation
        148–149, 149 n. 119
    The Four Last Things 128 n. 72